# WORLD
# RELIGIONS

# Other Books in the Greenhaven Encyclopedia Series

THE GREENHAVEN ENCYCLOPEDIA OF

# WORLD RELIGIONS

by Jeff Hay

Linda Holler, *Consulting Editor*

Christine Nasso, *Publisher*
Elizabeth Des Chenes, *Managing Editor*

**GREENHAVEN PRESS**
*An imprint of Thomson Gale, a part of The Thomson Corporation*

Detroit • New York • San Francisco • New Haven, Conn. • Waterville, Maine • London

*For more information, contact:*
Greenhaven Press
27500 Drake Rd.
Farmington Hills, MI 48331-3535
Or you can visit our Internet site at http://www.gale.com

**LIBRARY OF CONGRESS CATALOGING-IN-PUBLICATION DATA**

World religions / Jeff Hay, Linda Holler.
    p. cm. -- (Greenhaven encyclopedia of)
    Includes bibliographical references and index.
    ISBN-13: 978-0-7377-3217-7 (lib. : alk. paper)
    ISBN-10: 0-7377-3217-2 (lib. : alk. paper)
    1. Religions--Encyclopedias. I. Hay, Jeff. II. Holler, Linda.
    BL80.3.W643 2007
    200.3--dc22
                                       2006034676

Printed in the United States of America
10 9 8 7 6 5 4 3 2 1

# Contents

Contents

*The Greenhaven Encyclopedia of World Religions*

Contents

# Contents

*The Greenhaven Encyclopedia of World Religions*

# Preface

"A friendly study of the world's religions is a sacred duty."

—Mohandas K. Gandhi

The Indian nationalist and spiritual leader Mohandas K. Gandhi, known to millions as Mahatma, or "great soul," was born and lived his life as a Hindu. But like others around the world during the violent twentieth century, he saw a need to move beyond the boundaries of traditional religions in search of the common ground shared by the major faiths. His hope was not to combine the world's religions into a new one, but to find ways to minimize the often deadly conflicts that religious differences tend to inspire. Recognizing common concepts and understanding religious practices besides one's own, Gandhi believed, was an antidote to entrenched prejudice, mistrust, fear, and antagonism between religious and cultural communities and a catalyst for greater tolerance and, ultimately, peace. After all, tolerance and understanding, as Gandhi and many others have pointed out, lie at the heart of the teachings of history's religious teachers and masters, from the Buddha to Jesus of Nazareth to the Prophet Muhammad.

Resolving world conflict is an important reason for studying religion, but it is not the only reason. Religious belief and practice have always been central to the human experience. The hunter-gatherers of prehistoric eras formed religious societies, as their burial practices and other customs indicate. Humankind's first cities—in Iraq, Eypt, and India—grew up as religious centers and temples were their greatest structures. As settled civilizations grew more complex, the world's major religious traditions emerged, mostly in the period from about 800 B.C. (when Hinduism was taking shape) to the first decades of the seventh century A.D. (the era of the founding of Islam). Today most of the world's more than 6 billion people either adhere directly to or live in societies shaped and informed by these great traditions, now many centuries old. In religion, people find solace, hope, meaning, connection with nature, and a sense of community. These religious traditions are living institutions that continue to evolve as human society evolves, and knowledge of them is essential to any understanding of human nature as well as global politics.

Knowledge of religious traditions is also essential to understanding world history. Many of the violent conflicts of recent decades have religious overtones rooted in religious conflict dating back at least to the third millennium B.C. Hindus, Muslims, and Sikhs in the Indian subcontinent clashed violently and repeatedly in the late 1500s, for example, just as they have in recent decades; Christians and Muslims fought each other in the medieval Crusades and have fought each other much more recently in southeastern Europe and the islands of Indonesia in the early twenty-first century. The early twenty-first century conflict in the Middle East is based in part on centuries-old hatreds between Muslims and Jews. Meanwhile, virtually all religious traditions include ultraconservative groups who are fearful of or reject elements of the modern world such as secularism, materialism, and progressive social movements. Among them are the Islamic fundamentalists responsible for numerous terrorist acts around the world in the last twenty-five years. Many of these conflicts have nonreligious motives as well, notably competing claims for territory or economic rivalry, but the emotional rhetoric of conflict is often couched in religious terms, as it has been for thousands of years. In an echo of the Crusades, for example, spokespersons on both sides of the current war on terrorism even speak of a "war of civilizations" between Christianity and Islam.

The "friendly study" of world religions is thus both a personal and a public duty. It is personal because through knowledge one can aspire to achieve greater nearness to God, the goal of most of the major religions. It is public because the study of religions also develops greater understanding of one's fellow human beings, of their beliefs, aspirations, behavior, and ways of life. Ultimately, this understanding is an important step toward a more peaceful world for all.

## Abraham
## (ca. 2000 B.C.–1800 B.C.)

The patriarch of the ancient Hebrews and founding prophet of Judaism, Christianity, and Islam. Little about Abraham can be cited confidently by historians or archaeologists; what is known of him comes primarily from accounts in the Tanakh, the Hebrew Bible. Notions that he might not have been an actual historical figure but was rather a literary composite—an amalgamation of several historical persons for the purposes of telling a simplified story—can be no more than conjecture.

According to the book of Genesis, the first book in the Hebrew Bible, Abraham was called on by God to lead his people, the Hebrews, from the city of Ur in Mesopotamia (modern Iraq) to a land unknown to him. In this new land, west of Mesopotamia, Abraham became the father of a new nation. While on the journey, which he begins at the age of seventy-five, Abraham entered into a covenant, or agreement, with God. As part of this covenant, God promised Abraham that his new nation will be fruitful and his people will be protected. Abraham, for his part, is to sacrifice his first-born son to God as a test of his faith.

Abraham fathered sons by both his wife, Sarah, and a servant named Hagar. Sarah's son, Isaac, was the youth designated for sacrifice. In the biblical account, God mercifully substituted a ram for Isaac when Abraham proved his faithfulness and obedience to God by willingly preparing to slay his own son. Hagar and her son, Ishmael, were banished from the tribe.

Abraham, Sarah, Isaac, and their followers settled in the land of Canaan, roughly the area of present-day Israel, Jordan, and Lebanon. According to Genesis, the patriarch purchased land near Hebron and designated it as a family burial place. To cement his clan's ties to the region and secure the fulfillment of God's promises, Abraham assured Isaac's marriage to a Canaanite woman and Isaac's succession to leadership of the tribe before Abraham's death at the age of 175.

To Jews, Abraham is the founder of Judaism, the first figure to accept the existence of one true God and the first to seal a covenant with God. Traditionally, all Jews likewise are expected to observe the same covenant and seek to match Abraham in his righteousness. He is also credited with establishing such Jewish rites as circumcision (the symbol of the sacrifice called for in the original covenant) and prayers of benediction.

Christians consider Abraham the first of all believers, and in Roman Catholicism he is the model for all the saints. Abraham is cited as the first who put his complete trust in God, demonstrating the Christian concept that faith alone leads to salvation.

In Islam, teachings connected with Abraham draw on more sources than teachings in Judaism or Christianity, as various scholarly religious texts over the centuries have been added to the biblical sources. Abraham figures largely in the

Qur'an, the holy book of Islam, as one of Islam's major prophets. Muslims too consider Abraham the first among all prophets, the "Friend of God," ready to tolerate humiliation and suffering out of his love for God. Muslims also view Abraham as the founder of the first monotheistic faith (worshipping one God), a religion that was later perfected by Muhammad. Muslims also credit Abraham with building the Ka'aba, Islam's holiest shrine, in Mecca with the help of Ishmael (thought to be the founder of an important Arabic line of kings) and with establishing the rituals associated with Muslim pilgrimage to Mecca.

SEE ALSO: Hebrew Bible; Moses; Qur'an

## Abu Bakr
## (ca. 573–634)

The first caliph, or successor to the prophet Muhammad as the leader of Islam. Abu Bakr was a merchant and relation to Muhammad who became one of the Prophet's first converts and a member of the first Islamic community established at Medina in 622. There he became known as the "truthful one" thanks to his loyalty. After Muhammad's death in 632, Abu Bakr, whom the Prophet had designated to lead prayers after his own death, was selected to replace him. His accomplishments were mostly political as opposed to religious, but in them he made substantial contributions to the faith. Under Abu Bakr numerous contentious Arabic tribes agreed to unite, and he assured that captured opponents would be treated with honor and respect in the hope that they would join the new faith. With this example he provided Islam with the concept that unity under Allah should take precedence over political differences, and reinforced the Prophet's insistence that "every Muslim is a brother unto every other Muslim." When he died

in 634 Abu Bakr was buried alongside Muhammad.

SEE ALSO: caliph; companions of the Prophet; Islam

## Acts of the Apostles

The fifth book of the New Testament in the Christian Bible, and one of the most important sources of knowledge of the earliest days of the Christian Church. It was probably written by Luke, one of the authors of the four Gospels contained in the New Testament (although not one of Jesus' original twelve apostles) sometime between 70 and 90 A.D., in Rome. In Acts, as this text is commonly known, Luke touches on what were to be the basic themes of this early, foundational period of Christian history. The book begins with the Pentecost, or the beginnings of the Christian Church, when God's Holy Spirit descends upon the apostles. It describes how early Christians began to break away from their society's Jewish traditions to form an entirely distinct church, and how they tried to spread Christianity to the world, or at least to other parts of the Roman Empire. Acts also emphasizes the preaching and travels of Paul, helping to firmly establish Paul as Christianity's first great teacher and thinker (after Jesus Christ himself).

SEE ALSO: apostles; New Testament; Paul

## Adi Granth

The primary scripture of Sikhism. The title means "original book" or "first book," but the text actually evolved over time, compiled first by Guru Arjan, the fifth Sikh guru, in 1603 and 1604, and appended several times over the remainder of the seventeenth century. When it reached its final, canonical form, the Adi Granth contained more than 6,000 hymns and verses. Over 4,500 of these are attributed to the first ten Sikh gurus, with the heart of the text being those composed by Gum Nanak (1469–1539), the founder of Sikhism. They were written in a language called Sant Bhasha, a poetic form of the Hindi language common in much of northern India. The authors used a script known as Gurmukhi, which is the script of the modern Punjabi language spoken by most Sikhs.

Modern printed editions of the Adi Granth contain some 1,430 pages, each of a standard length. This consistency is carried forward in the organization of the text, with the hymns and verses organized according to author, meter, and form. The verses are intended to be sung, and the main portion of the texts appends the proper musical mode for each verse. At the beginning of the book are three prayers intended to be recited daily at sunrise, sunset, and day's end. The theme of the verses is also consistent: The proper form of worship is meditation on the name of God.

Under the last of the ten Sikh gurus, Guru Gobind Singh (1666–1708), the Adi Granth became itself an object of veneration, as it replaced the series of living gurus. In this context the text is known as Guru Granth Sahib, meaning "guru in book form." The text remains at the center of Sikh devotional life, and copies of the text maintain places of honor in Sikh temples, which are known as gurdwaras, or "houses of the guru [in book form]."

SEE ALSO: Guru Nanak; Sikh gurus; Sikhism

# African religions

Africa is a vast continent of many peoples and many religions. Nevertheless, in sub-Saharan Africa many of the largest groups of peoples are descended from Bantu-speaking migrants who came to dominate the region after 500 B.C. and, in the broadest of terms, their religions may be considered collectively and are distinguished by some common features. They are polytheistic, often featuring a belief in an ultimate divine Creator as well as gods of natural forces or deities considered messengers between this world and the divine realm; these lesser deities are more important in daily life. A number of African religions also believe in the importance of the souls of dead ancestors who are able to intervene in the world, a likely reflection of the importance of kinship in African societies. Likewise, African religions are concerned with the maintenance of social order; rather than abstract ideas about the divine, African religions emphasize earthly relationships and proper behavior. Many rituals and ceremonies are intended to keep various otherworldly beings happy in order to ensure their generosity in this world. Commonly these rites are directed, again, at lesser deities or dead ancestors rather than the creator god, whom many African traditions believe withdrew from any interest in the world following the Creation. Central to these rites, and another feature of many African religions, are rituals of magic and witchcraft.

*West African Practices* Among the major peoples of West Africa are the Yoruba, who number over 10 million and live mostly in the modern nation of Nigeria. Among the Yoruba, the creator god is known as Olodumare. But far more common is devotion to the hundreds of so-called orishas. Although many myths describe the orishas as the children of Olodumare, in practice they have their own separate cults complete with shrines, priests, prayers, and festivals. Among them are Ogun, the god of ironworking (and, in the modern world, mechanics and drivers); Shango, the god of thunder and lightning; and the trickster orisha, Eshu. Orunmila, meanwhile, is the patron of divination, an important part of Yoruba religious practice. Divination is conducted by a figure known as the babalawo, or "father of secrets." It involves the chanting of sacred verses and the reading of the signs apparent through the tossing of various ritual objects such as palm nuts. People consult a babalawo to gain insight into their personal futures, and the ritual often ends with visits to the shrines of appropriate orishas. Orisha cults as well as divination practices have spread to other West African peoples as well. The Fon people of modern-day Benin, for example, refer to the orishas as Vodun and consider them subdeities to a male-female pair of high gods known as Lisa and Mawu. Lisa represents the sun and daily work, while Mawu represents the moon, rest, and fertility. They, and the orishas, are a microcosm of both cosmic and earthly order, and are invoked through divination rituals. Orishas are commonly worshipped using iconic objects sometimes known as fetishes, both in larger ceremonies and within the home. These objects are thought to "contain" divine power and to give their holders or wearers a measure of that power.

The Mende peoples, who live primarily in the coastal areas of central West Africa, present a clear focus on ancestors. Their creator god is known as Ngewo, communication with whom almost always takes places through "near" ancestors, or Kekeni, or "distant" ancestors, known as Ndebla. To facilitate the intermediation of ancestors, Mende funeral rites are very elaborate, and the living continually give offerings at grave sites. A distinct feature of Mende religion is the presence of secret

societies that control specific groups of rituals. Among them are the Poro, the secret society of male initiation and political leadership, and the Sande, which controls female initiation and motherhood. Both teach initiates proper social and sexual behavior, as well as the distinct "powers" of women or men. For boys, initiation ceremonies often include circumcision, as they do elsewhere in Africa. The Mende do not practice female circumcision, however, although some peoples in other parts of the African continent do. Both male and female initiation rituals are thought to be important ways of clearly defining gender and, therefore, of ensuring fertility.

*Divination, Offerings and Numerology* To the south and east, in parts of modern-day Congo and Sudan, live the Azande people. Their creator god is known as Mbori, but few prayers or other rituals are devoted to him, and in a variation from other African practices, little devotion is granted to lesser deities or spirits. Instead, Azande ritual focuses on explanations for earthly behavior and events using witchcraft and magic. Azande witch doctors, or abinza, are consulted for divination purposes and have special training in reading omens or in the health-giving properties of plants, but all people are thought to be capable of gaining access to the divine. In southern Africa, the Zulu peoples refer to the creator god by several names, some of which connote a god of the sky and his "female twin," the earth, which are the source of human life. These deities are thought to control most large natural forces, such as thunder. Mundane aspects of individual life, meanwhile, are the domain of the ancestors in the Zulu world, who are believed to live under the earth. Worship commonly involves the giving of offerings or sacrifices to the ancestors, who will be angry if they are neglected. Divination among the Zulu is commonly conducted by women known as inyanga, who are thought capable of being possessed by the spirits of ancestors. As with the Azande, witchcraft is generally considered the source of danger or bad health, and diviners try to combat it with rituals and herbs.

The Dogon people of Mali have an elaborate system of myth, ritual, and social organization based on a highly esoteric view of the universe; theirs is one of the most distinct of African faiths. Their creator god is known as Amma, who created the universe by mixing his spoken word with the elements. Most Dogon devotion, however is granted to the Nommo, who are described variously as the created universe, the first ancestors, and the guardian spirits. They are most commonly thought of as matched pairs of male and female twins, which in Dogon cosmology imply the balance of Creation. In Dogon myth the original ancestors consisted of four pairs of twins; the number 8 became a sacred number, as did the notion of matched pairs. Dogon villages, for instance, are built in pairs and contain eight storehouses to contain eight varieties of grain. The Dogon high priest, or hogon, is both the intermediary of Amma and the successor of the first man, Lebe. Lebe was thought to have been sacrificed to preserve the order of the world. The hogon's house, which is considered sacred ground, contains eight stones to honor past hogons and eight to honor future ones. At the center of much Dogon ritual is the need to preserve the purity of the hogon in order to maintain the order of the world.

African religion remains dynamic as well as very diverse. The faiths of the peoples of the continent are not fixed but continue to evolve and to overlap. Newer influences such as Islam and Christianity, which are both practiced widely, combined with the challenges of secular modernity, ensure the continued multiplicity of African religion.

SEE ALSO: Afro-Brazilian religions; Afro-Caribbean religions; divination

## Afro-Brazilian religions

Thanks to its ethnic mix of Native American peoples, European settlers, and Africans originally brought to the region as slaves, Brazil has been the center of a number of syncretic religious movements. These religions combine features of many different traditions: African religions, Native American spirit worship, and Roman Catholicism. Most of these began to take shape in a formal sense in the nineteenth century with the emancipation of Brazil's slaves, and they have continued to grow in appeal. Today millions of people belong to Afro-Brazilian religions, whose popularity is expanding to countries beyond Brazil.

One of the largest of the Afro-Brazilian cults is Macumba, which is practiced mostly in Rio de Janeiro and other big cities. At its heart is the belief in ancestral spirits rather than gods. These spirits are thought to be able to possess believers; the Macumba were the original founders of the faith or those who are otherwise advanced enough to be possessed. Macumba ceremonies often involve communication between these spirits and the mediums who conduct the rites. Ceremonies usually take place outdoors, and might involve animal sacrifices and the giving of offerings. A vivid example of Macumba syncretism is the worship of Roman Catholic saints, who are given African names. One of the most revered of the Macumba saints is Jemanja, the Virgin Mary. The word *Macumba*, meanwhile, is often used as a blanket name for all Afro-Brazilian religions. Brazilians also tend to view religions as not mutually exclusive; devout Roman Catholics, for example, might from time to time engage in Macumba or other rites, while even nonbelievers might take part in festivals or other events.

*Spirit Possession* Another important Afro-Brazilian cult is Candomble, centered in Bahia state in the northern coastal regions of the country. Candomble is thought to be the earliest Afro-Brazilian faith, and most of its adherents are women. It also involves possession by the spirits of ancestors, and its rites remain similar to those of traditional African religions. Although they generally involve singing, dancing, and the appearance of spirit mediums, rites vary depending on which location in Africa its original adherents came from or which religions their ancestors practiced. There are even Candomble sects based in African Islam. Unlike Macumba, Candomble beliefs feature the worship of gods, notably Shango, the thunder god of the Yoruba people of West Africa.

Umbanda is a third major Afro-Brazilian religion, with hundreds of thousands of small congregations. Born in the late nineteenth century, its appeal is primarily in the big cities, and its followers come from a spectrum of social groups, including the educated middle classes. Umbanda features a focus on contact with a spirit world whose ancestor spirits possess various powers depending on their origins. Some spirits are derived from those of great Native American leaders, while others are derived from respected elders during the days of Afro-Brazilian slavery. Prominent among the spirits are the orixas, no doubt variations of the orishas found in West Africa. These might be either the spirits of African gods such as

Shango, of Roman Catholic saints such as Mary, or even of Jesus. Umbanda rites, which take place in ritual houses, involve music and the giving of offerings. Leaders of these rites are known as "saint fathers" or "saint mothers," thought capable of communing with the spirits. Aside from the general emphasis on spirits, believers often undertake Umbanda rites to solve specific problems such as joblessness, trouble with the police, or illness. An unusual influence on Umbanda was the French spiritualist Alan Kardec (1804–1869), who was thought to have pioneered ways to understand and communicate with the spirit world, and who believed that human life could be improved by such means. Modern rites have expanded, furthermore, to include versions of Hindu or Buddhist practices such as Tantricism. Umbanda numbers many prominent Brazilians among its adherents, and it has spread to other South American countries, notably Argentina and Uruguay.

SEE ALSO: African religions; Afro-Caribbean religions; new religious movements, Western

# Afro-Caribbean religions

The various faiths or cults that emerged in the islands and coastal areas of the Caribbean Sea over the last three hundred years. They are the product of several cultural influences and religious traditions, including the Roman Catholicism of European settlers and colonists, various African beliefs and practices maintained by slaves and their descendants, and elements of Native American religions.

Santeria, or the "way of the saints," is a faith that originated among slaves in Cuba but has spread to other islands and, especially in recent years with the suppression of religion in Cuba, to the United States.

Its believers are not solely people of African descent; adherents include many Caucasians and people of mixed race or ethnicity. Santeria combines many elements of Roman Catholic Christianity with certain African beliefs. The Santeria tradition features faith in a single, omnipresent God, but much more prominent is its worship of various spirits. The common pattern is to view these spirits as both Roman Catholic saints and as orishas, the ancestral spirits of the Yoruba peoples of West Africa. The Yoruban war and thunder god Shango, for example, is associated with Saint Barbara, the Catholic saint and patron of gunfire; Jemanja, the Virgin Mary, is another common focus of devotion. Each of these spirits has its own distinct characteristics, and devotion to them is expressed in specific ways. Shopana, the smallpox orisha associated with Saint Lazarus, likes to eat corn and uses crutches. Shango wears red and white beads. Rituals devoted to these figures might include giving the appropriate offerings and the "baptism" and "feeding" of the spirits in the form of iconic sacred stones. Drumming is often thought of as the "voice" of the spirits, while believers might also sing or chant, often in a Yoruba language. Believers also might practice animal sacrifice, which is thought to aid in the possession of the believer by the spirit. Once you attain possession by a spirit you are considered a santero, one who is capable of using the spirit's power. On a more mundane level, believers in Santeria might call on their patron spirits, using various divination methods, to aid them in their daily lives.

**Obeah and Voudou** Obeah, a separate Afro-Caribbean faith, arose among the slave populations of Jamaica and is very much a product of the slave experience. Its founders were the Akan people of West Africa, and it retains far more African than European or Christian features. Obeah is fundamentally a form of witchcraft in its belief that bad forces can affect human behavior and destiny. In Obeah, each person possesses a "duppy," a spirit or soul, that is vulnerable at various times of his or her life, notably during times of sickness or weakness and at the time of death. An obeahman (sometimes in fact a woman) is thought to have the ability to take possession of one's duppy and force it to work for him. These obeahmen are also considered to have special knowledge about such matters as health and medicine. Since African belief in witchcraft was driven underground by slave owners and overseers, Obeah arose as a way to use witchcraft to explain the conditions of slavery, to try to live a healthy life under harsh conditions, and sometimes to challenge the slave owners themselves. The more positive Jamaican counterpart to Obeah is Myalism, which is much more clearly influenced by Christianity and came to feature such rites as baptism. Myalists also hold a strong belief in the power of good, and work to combat the more evil aspects of Obeah by seeking converts and rooting out Obeah medicines and ritual objects. Like Santeria, Obeah and its Myalist counterpart have spread from Jamaica to other islands.

Voudou, or voodoo, which originated in Haiti in the 1700s, is the largest of the Afro-Caribbean religions. Some 80 percent of the population of Haiti professes it, and Haitian migrants have taken it to other islands as well as to the North American mainland. Like other Afro-Caribbean faiths it is syncretic, combining aspects of Roman Catholicism, particularly the French version practiced by Haiti's colonizers, and various African religions; studies suggest that as many as 115 distinct African ethnicities were transported as slaves to Haiti. The word *voudou* is derived from a word for god or spirit in the Fon language of the people of Benin.

Adherents to Voudou believe in one supreme God as well as in Jesus and the Holy Spirit. Most regular worship, however, is directed at spirits known as loa. The loa might be Catholic saints, the spirits of ancestors, or African gods, and each has distinct properties. Believers usually give most of their devotion to a single loa, who is thought capable of providing protection, good health, and other benefits. The loa are capricious and unpredictable, however, and need frequent propitiation. Many Haitians divide the loa into two groups. One, the Rada, are loa who are benign, wise, and generous. The other, the Petro loa, are meaner and more violent. Among the Rada loa are Guede, associated with the process of birth and death; Legba, who protects entrances; and Erzulie, a female loa. An important Petro loa is Mait' Calfour, the master of the crossroads and a manifestation of the forces of slick manipulation.

Rituals in Voudou commonly involve the gathering of devotees of a particular loa at a temple or some other meeting place. There, under the guidance of a male or female priest, the devotees engage in prayer, drumming, dancing and singing, the giving of offerings (usually of food) and, sometimes, animal sacrifice. It is possible during these ceremonies for believers to become possessed by their loa. In this state, perceptible because the believer has entered a trance, the devotee, or the loa through him, might give advice, cure disease, or perform other feats. When the loa possess their devotees they are said to "ride" him or her, and to encourage this, patterns of symbols associated with that loa are drawn on the floor of temples, a process similar to the use of mandalas in Tibetan Buddhism. Far less common in Voudou, although much more sensationalized, is the appearance of so-called zombies. These are either the souls of dead persons used in magic or actual bodies that have been raised from the dead but which appear to have no soul or being. All people, meanwhile, are said to possess "zombies" and dangerous sorcerers, known as bocor, are able to draw them out in a manner similar to the "duppies" of Obeah. They are more commonly an aspect of Voudou folklore than of everyday belief or ritual.

SEE ALSO: African religions; Afro-Caribbean religions; divination

## agape

A Greek word for love. In Christianity, agape is used to refer to the love of God or of Jesus Christ, or alternatively the love a believer feels for his fellow Christians. The New Testament of the Christian Bible, written in Greek, used this word in that regard and therefore avoids the connotations of sexual or romantic love contained in the Greek word *eros*. In the modern world agape is generally accepted to mean simply "Christian love."

## agnosticism

The school of thought claiming that human beings cannot know anything about God or other aspects of religious belief that lie outside the realm of their observation or experience. Popularly, agnostics are often those who remain in a state of doubt about the existence of God or the gods. The term is derived from a Greek root word meaning "unknowable." It was first used by Thomas Huxley, a nineteenth-century English philosopher who rejected both theism and atheism on the grounds that the Christian doctrine was unprovable in a modern scientific or rationalist sense, and that only science and reason could allow people to understand worldly or human affairs. From some standpoints, agnosticism does not necessarily repudiate religious faith, although Huxley's work largely rejected most aspects of Christian belief. From others, agnosticism is simply impossible: To doubt God is to deny him altogether. Since Huxley's day agnostics have generally been taken to be those opposed to conventional Christian doctrine. In other religious traditions, such as Hinduism, the question is largely irrelevant since it is not up to human beings to either prove or disprove God's existence.

SEE ALSO: atheism; pantheism; theism

## ahimsa

A Sanskrit word meaning "not-harming," although it is usually translated in modern times as "nonviolence." It is a central idea in many Indian religions, notably Buddhism and Jainism, where it is taken to mean not doing harm to any living creature by thought or by deed. Both Buddhists and Jains place it first among their lists of precepts. The Indian king Ashoka, who reigned in the third century B.C., converted from Hinduism to Buddhism and pledged to rule according to the principles of ahimsa and instill it as an ideal among Indians. In the twentieth century two religious and political leaders, the Hindu Mahatma Gandhi in India and the Christian Martin Luther King Jr. in the United States, used nonviolent methods of protest to help bring about social reform. King was influenced by Gandhi, who was said to have been himself influenced in this regard by a Jain, Srimad Rajcandra (1867–

*To followers of Zoroastrianism, Ahura Mazda, seen in this relief sculpture at the ruins of Persepolis in Takht-i Jamshid, Iran, is thought to be all powerful and the only god deserving of absolute worship.* © CHARLES AND JOSETTE LENARS/CORBIS

1901), who taught that good conduct can be an active and practical form of ahimsa.

SEE ALSO: Buddhism; Gandhi, Mohandas K; Jainism

## Ahura Mazda

The "Wise Lord" of Zoroastrianism. Ahura Mazda was spoken of by Zoroaster (seventh and sixth centuries B.C.) as the supreme god of ancient Iranian religion; Zoroaster claimed that of all gods, only Ahura Mazda, the Creator, was entirely good and deserving of absolute worship. Later believers, including the Persian emperors who were to control territories stretching from Iran to Greece in the sixth and fifth centuries B.C., revered Ahura Mazda as the guardian of kings and protector of all.

According to Zoroaster, who claimed to have personal visions of Ahura Mazda, the god created not only the world and universe but two groups of spirits. The first, the Amesha Spentas, were embodiments of Ahura Mazda's divine nature and helped to transmit that divine nature to humankind. The second, the Yazatas, were themselves worthy of worship and had manifestations and functions rather like the angels of Judaism or Christianity. Later Zoroastrian thinkers refined and clarified these notions, arguing that Ahura Mazda, or Ohrmazd as he was also known, created not only these benign "angels" but an evil spirit known as Ahriman. While Ohrmazd was the source of all light, goodness, truth, and order, Ahriman opposed him, representing lies, darkness, evil, and chaos. The history of the world is characterized by the struggle between this god and the "devil" (Ahriman), whose actions lay outside of Ohrmazd's control. Over the centuries, remaining Zoroastrians, notably the Parsis of India, came to see Ahura Mazda as the sole, omnipotent deity with Ahriman not a spirit but a representation of the evil and dark sides of humanity.

SEE ALSO: Avesta; Parsis; Zoroastrianism

# Ali
## (ca. 600–661)

The fourth Islamic caliph, or successor to the prophet Muhammad. Ali is considered the first legitimate caliph by Shia Muslims because he was, as Muhammad's cousin and son-in-law, a direct relative of the Prophet and because they assert that he and his familial descendants were directly chosen by Muhammad to be successors.

As a boy, Ali was in Muhammad's care even before the Prophet heard the call from Allah in 610. Ali became one of the first converts to Islam. He served for a time as one of Muhammad's scribes as well as an officer in early battles among tribes in and around Mecca. He is credited with cleansing the Ka'aba in Mecca of its earlier idols after Muhammad accepted the city's surrender. Meanwhile, Ali married Fatima, one of Muhammad's four daughters, and the couple had two daughters of their own as well as two sons, Hassan and Hussein.

After Muhammad's death in 632, controversy arose over whether the Prophet had named Ali as his successor or whether he had not named anyone. In the event, Abu Bakr was chosen as caliph before Ali had any opportunity to stake his claim. Abu Bakr was followed by two others, Omar and Uthman. Ali, meanwhile, retreated to help assemble the Qur'an and take part in religious debates.

After Uthman was killed in 656, Ali found himself named caliph. He tried to govern according to Islamic tenets of justice and equality but was unable to control opposing factions. He faced two major rebellions. The first, supported by wealthy Meccan leaders who wanted him to avenge Uthman's murder, was put down. The second was led by Mu'awiya, the governor of Syria and a relative of Uthman. Ali was unable to control Mu'awiya, which weakened his authority in his own domains. Ali was assassinated while engaged in prayers in the town of Kufa in Iraq. He was buried in the Iraqi city of Najaf, which remains an important pilgrimage site for Shia Muslims.

All Muslims, not only the Shia, revere Ali. Not only was he a caliph and relative of the Prophet, he is also credited with assembling much of the canon of Islamic scripture. This includes not only the Qur'an itself but also a number of other sermons and commentaries.

SEE ALSO: caliph; Fatima; Shia (Shiite) Islam

## Allah

The Arabic name of God, and therefore the familiar term for the God of Muslims, although Arabic Christians use the same term in their own worship. For Muslims, Allah is all-powerful; there is no other God nor multiple forms of God (as in the Christian Trinity). Allah is the Creator who has already determined people's destinies, and he will one day place judgment on all humankind. He is also merciful and ever-present. All individuals are expected to submit to the will of Allah.

Affirmation of Allah is a constant part of Islamic worship. The assertion "There is no God but Allah and Muhammad is his prophet" is one of the Five Pillars of Islam, the core of the faith, and daily prayers also invoke Allah's name. The name also commonly appears in ordinary conversations in such forms as "if Allah wills."

The Qur'an and Hadith, the holy books of Islam, contain ninety-nine "names" of Allah, which some believers recite as a form of meditation. These names are mostly poetic images or metaphors, including "the one and only," "the sublime," "the omnipresent," and "the constant forgiver." Sufi Muslims seek to achieve union with Allah through various mystical rites and ceremonies.

SEE ALSO: Islam; Qur'an; Sufism

## Amaterasu

The Shinto sun goddess and the central deity of the Shinto religion. Her full name is Amaterasu-o-Mikami, which means "heavenly-shining deity." According to classical Shinto myths, Amaterasu is the daughter of the two parent *kami* (or gods) of Shintoism, Izanagi and Izanami. Amaterasu was born from the eye of Izanagi and, after he retired, she replaced him as the chief of all deities and lord of heaven. Her godly descendants subjugated the earth (or more precisely, the Japanese islands) and established that the heavenly *kami* would remain superior to earthly ones.

Amaterasu is also considered the founder of the Japanese imperial line, as during the process of subjugating the earth, her legendary descendant, Jimmu Tenno, became the first emperor in approximately 660 B.C. Her status as the great imperial ancestor has ensured that Amaterasu has continued to play an important role in Shinto ceremonies connected to politics and the state. In this regard she is thought to have great power over such matters as governance and the harvest. Amaterasu is worshipped at thousands of shrines across Japan, but the most important of these is the inner shrine at Ise.

SEE ALSO: Ise shrines; Izanagi and Izanami; *kami* Shinto

## Amhitabha

One of the chief Buddhas of the Mahayana form of Buddhism, particularly within the Pure Land sect. Amhitabha, whose name means "infinite light," was originally the focus of devotion for Indian Mahayanists in the first few centuries A.D. He was later the center of cults in China and Japan as well.

Believers think that Amhitabha became a bodhisattva, an enlightened soul on the path to becoming a Buddha, during the course of one of his earlier human lives.

At that point he pledged that, once he reached full Buddha-hood, he would reign over a Pure Land nobler than all others and that those who revered him would be reborn in this Pure Land, which some scholars describe as an abstract "Buddha-realm." Amhitabha went on to reach full enlightenment, and took his place in the Pure Land. Believers were urged to meditate on him and his achievements, focusing all the while on rebirth in the Pure Land. Adding appeal to Amhitabha's teachings is his status, particularly in China and Japan, as one of the compassionate Buddhas. He is known as Amida in Japan, and in an earlier, Tibetan version, as Amitayus.

SEE ALSO: bodhisattva; Mahayana Buddhism; Pure Land Buddhism

## Analects

The accepted collection of the sayings of the Chinese sage Confucius. In Chinese the text is known as *Lun Yu*, or *Selected Sayings*. The text's precise origins are obscure, and many scholars suspect that much of its material did not come from Confucius himself. Nevertheless, the *Analects* are accepted as an authoritative source on Confucius's thinking and remain one of the so-called Four Books in classical Chinese thought. The *Analects* are presented in the form of brief question-and-answer dialogues between Confucius and his students, and are generally held to have been compiled by his students although, again, there is little certainty over where or when this occurred. The compilation was likely made long after Confucius's death, probably in the middle of the fourth century B.C., by which time there were a number of different Confucian schools. In any case, the *Analects* was already a highly revered collection by the time of the Han dynasty (206 B.C. –A.D. 220), when Confu-

cianism became a kind of state cult. Thanks to the influence of Confucianism not only in China but throughout East Asia, the *Analects* has been one of the most influential texts in human history.

The uncertainty over the precise origins and authorship of the material in the *Analects* is not entirely inappropriate given Confucius's conception of himself as a transmitter of wisdom and values rather than a creator. He saw his role as revitalizing and refining long-standing traditions, particularly with regard to governance and leadership. One of the common themes that runs through the *Analects*, indeed, is an attempt to define the proper characteristics of leaders. They should be humane and wise, and should govern according to virtue and righteousness rather than through greed or the thirst for power, which are signs of small men. The *Analects* also make plain the basic Confucian notion that nobility is derived from virtue and behavior rather than birth.

On a broader level, social relations should be characterized by what the *Analects* term *li*, which here means observance of various kinds of ritual: ceremonial, political, and religious. *Li* provide the basis for human interaction, and allows individuals to demonstrate their understanding of their rights and obligations and their respect for tradition. Religious rituals, meanwhile, help to create positive relationships with the spirits, although as was his custom, Confucius had little to say directly about the spirit world or other matters of religious faith beyond their meaning for society. The importance of *li* is at the heart of the following selection from Book 12 of the *Analects*, translated by Arthur Whaley:

Yen Hui [a student] asked about Goodness. The Master [Confucius] said, he who can submit to ritual is Good. If [a ruler] could for one day "himself submit to ritual," everyone under Heaven would respond to his Goodness. For Goodness is something that must have its source in the ruler himself; it cannot be got from others.

Yen Hui said, I beg to ask for the more detailed items of this [submission to ritual]. The Master said, To look at nothing in defiance of ritual, to listen to nothing in defiance of ritual, to speak of nothing in defiance of ritual, never to stir hand or foot in defiance of ritual. Yen Hui said, I know that I am not clever; but this is a saying that, with your permission, I will try to put into practice.

## ancestor worship

A common theme in Chinese religious and cultural traditions that actually predates the emergence or arrival of any classical religion in China. It can also be found in numerous other religious traditions around the world. Ancestor worship refers to the veneration of one's ancestors in forms of and using rituals similar to those one would use toward any gods or spirits. It is based on the belief that the dead, somehow and somewhere, live on and that living people can communicate with them. Believers also think that the spirits of ancestors can intervene in earthly affairs.

In China, ancestor worship appears to go back to the time of the Shang dynasty, which governed in the second millennium B.C. There the chief deity, Shangdi, was held to live in a spirit world but was too distant, too aloof, to be approached or prayed to directly. Living people therefore prayed to the souls of their dead ancestors, also inhabitants of this spirit world, in hopes that their ancestors could intercede on their behalf with Shangdi. Documents and records of the era, notably in-scriptions on so-called oracle bones, show that kings were buried with weapons and other implements needed for their afterlives, and that kings believed they could communicate with their dead predecessors while still on earth. They did so by reading the oracle bones and by means of various rituals such as complicated funeral and mourning practices and the placing of devotions on grave sites. These rituals, which continued long after the disappearance of the Shang kings, also came to be practiced widely by ordinary Chinese people.

Ancestor worship in China, as well as in parts of Asia highly influenced by China, has had a secular and social impact as well, and forms of it appear in Confucian social philosophy. It is considered highly important to maintain good relations with one's elders as well as one's children, and various rites are practiced in order to maintain the continuity of the family. The feeling of reverence toward family relations is known as filial piety.

SEE ALSO: African religions; Confucianism; filial piety

## ancient Greece and Rome, religions of

The religions of ancient Greece and Rome were closely connected, a legacy of the widespread influence of Greek civilization in the Mediterranean world and the Middle East in roughly the thousand years stretching from 500 B.C. to A.D. 500. Greek religion, particularly, began to take shape with the rise to popularity of the epic poems of Homer, the *Iliad* and the *Odyssey*, around the eighth century B.C. It was a highly flexible form of religion, consisting primarily of numerous local cults dedicated to particular gods. Greek religion had no specific founder, no orthodox body of doctrine, and no central texts. Instead, the Greeks based their belief and practice on the need to maintain good relations with their various gods. They did this through sacrificial and other rituals as well as through public festivals, which were often unique to particular Greek city-states.

Myths such as those expressed by Homer provided the Greek view of the origins of the universe and of the natures of the gods, and in so doing helped to establish a distinct pantheon of deities. Like many other Indo-European peoples, the Greeks believed that the universe had been created out of a formless void innumerable eons earlier. In the process, gods connected to important natural forces emerged and were engaged in constant conflict. Out of this chaos, the earth and sky gods ultimately produced Zeus, the ruler of the heavenly realm known as Olympus. Zeus presided over an Olympian court that included a number of other important deities who were loosely subordinate to him, but who more accurately simply represented different natural forces or aspects of life. Among the most popular was Zeus's son Apollo, the god of wisdom, justice, and agriculture connected with the sun. Other important Greek deities included Hera, the queen of the gods, wife of Zeus, and patron of marriage and women, and Poseidon, the god of the sea and earthquakes, frequently shown holding a forked staff called a trident. Eros and Aphrodite were the god and goddess of erotic love; Aphrodite, the more popular of the two as a subject of Greek (and later European) art, was likely adapted from Astarte or Ishtar, the fertility goddess of the ancient Near East. Ares was the Greek god of war and in many myths a consort of Aphrodite.

*Local and Cultic Deities* Gods and goddesses also served as the patrons of Greek city-states. The goddess Athena was the patron of the largest of these, Athens, and numerous temples to her were constructed on the city's acropolis, most notably the Parthenon of the fifth century B.C. In other aspects Athena was a goddess of war and the crafts, and the daughter of Zeus. Lesser deities often became the focus of popular cults. Demeter, the goddess of grain, was widely worshipped by women; her cult did not permit the involvement of men. Cult rituals involved feasting and sacrifice in the autumn season of planting intended to ensure rich harvests. Another popular cult was that of Dionysius, the god of wine, whose celebrants were also mostly women, although men too took part. Dionysian festivals took place during spring, and involved feasting, music, dance, and sometimes intoxication. The Dionysius cult allowed devotees to temporarily ignore social and moral boundaries, but Greek morality also understood that such forces could easily grow dangerous.

Rites dedicated to these deities took place in a number of different places. Large temples employing more or less professional priests were the sites of rituals dedicated to state deities such as Athena. But smaller temples abounded, often outside the limits of towns, and the Greeks believed the gods could be celebrated even in the open air. Large-scale festivals might involve processions and sacrifices of animals associated with particular deities; bulls were sacrificed to Zeus or Dionysius, for instance, and cows to Hera. Other festival events included sporting contests, plays, and feasts. Even outside of ritual events, Greeks frequently took advantage of divination. For example, the famous oracle of Delphi, often a woman, was thought to be a medium of Apollo and was frequently consulted on important matters of state.

Believers commonly used oracles for insight into their daily lives as well.

The Greeks believed that the gods intervened actively in daily life when they so chose. Like humans, however, the gods could be unpredictable. They might be open and generous, or angry, jealous, or forbidding. Consequently believers were careful to appease their deities, and they thanked them for every good thing that happened to them. Bad events, meanwhile, might be blamed on human beings neglecting or insulting their gods although, alternatively, the gods might simply not be paying attention, preferring peace and quiet and their own affairs at Olympus. In times of anger toward humans, the gods might send vengeful subdeities known as Furies, while in more generous moods, they might also send inspiration through other goddesses known as Muses. Ultimately what governed life was fortune, which was personified in a goddess of that name.

*A Dark Afterlife* In keeping with their relatively dark view of humanity's existence, the Greeks believed that the afterlife was for most people an unhappy place. Ordinary humans were taken to Hades, a dark underworld realm, by the messenger Hermes. There the dead remained in a vague state of limbo unless revived by blood or wine. Very few people, only those considered valued sons or daughters-in-law of the gods and therefore worthy of a kind of immortality, entered the heavenly realm known as Elysium. Only one human being, the hero Heracles (Hercules), who was in truth the son of Zeus and a mortal woman, was able to join the gods in Olympus.

*Rome's Dynamic Religious Life* Roman religion was constantly changing, and the result of many influences. The original Romans were, like the Greeks, descended from Indo-European migrants. Stories and myths suggest that they established the city of Rome in the eighth or seventh century B.C., and archaelogical evidence indicates that these early Romans worshipped a pantheon of nature gods who had to be propitiated through prayer and sacrifice. As the Roman Republic emerged in the fifth century B.C., numerous well-defined gods emerged. These included Jupiter, the sky god and chief of all the deities, and the war god Mars, who was also the protector of agriculture and animals. Other important early dieties included Diana, the patron of mothers; Janus, the god of doors and gateways who might also have been the god of all beginnings (the month of January is named for him); and Vesta, the goddess of the hearth and home. Vesta was extremely popular and worshipped with few changes for the entire period of the Roman Republic and Empire, which lasted nearly a thousand years. Households commonly maintained shrines dedicated to her, and her main temple at the Roman Forum was tended by special priestesses known as Vestal Virgins.

As Roman territorial possessions expanded beginning in the sixth century B.C., the Romans encountered numerous other peoples and often adopted their gods or forms of worship. From the Etruscans the Romans took over the cults of Juno, the goddess of the moon and women and the female counterpart to Jupiter, and Minerva, a goddess of wisdom, war, and handicrafts. As the Romans encountered the Greeks, Greek gods were adapted or incorporated into the Roman pantheon. Jupiter became associated with Zeus, Juno with Hera, Mars with Ares, and Minerva with Athena. Aphrodite, the Greek goddess of erotic love, came to be known in Rome as Venus, while Dionysius, the Greek god of wine, was Bacchus in Rome. Meanwhile, the Romans adopted Apollo as an important deity of their own, and he went on to become the patron god of some of Rome's emperors. The great Roman epic poem, Virgil's *Aeneid*, was derived from the earlier works of Homer and continued its themes of capricious gods, human courage, and unpredictable divine intervention.

*Sacrifice and Saturnalia* Roman religious rituals in major temples were conducted by a hierarchy of priests, the highest of whom were state officials known as pontifices. They included sacrifices, the reading of omens such as the flights of flocks of birds, and the care of sacred objects. An important purpose of these larger rites was to determine whether the gods approved of a particular course of action. Priests also performed divination, sometimes by "reading" the internal organs of the animals used in sacrifices. Rome also maintained a thick schedule of festivals that generally had religious components. These included the springtime Latin Festival devoted to Jupiter, which featured the ritual sacrifice of a white heifer, and the December festival known as Saturnalia, a seven-day period of freedom from work, feasting, and gift giving dedicated to Saturn, the god of agriculture. At the household level, meanwhile, Romans revered not so much the gods of the state cults but either local deities or the guardian spirits of dead ancestors.

In the late first century B.C., Rome changed from a republic, governed by elected representatives, to an empire, governed by a single, unchallenged leader. The first emperor, Caesar Augustus, claimed Apollo as his patron deity and urged Roman citizens to grant him religious reverence as well as earthly respect. This resulted in an emperor cult, which dominated much of the period of the Roman Empire. Emperors were declared to be divine only after their deaths, although their status was not precisely equal to the gods since they were the objects simply of reverence, not of prayer or sacrifice. The model for this sort of emperor worship had been set by the Greek conqueror Alexander the Great, who in the fourth century B.C. had taken over many of the lands later conquered by the Roman Empire. Alexander had demanded to be treated as a god because of the great gifts he had provided for his subjects. The custom was adapted to Rome fairly easily, and emperors came to be seen as divine protectors of the people and the embodiment of such Roman qualities as courage, intelligence, and adaptibility.

The Roman habit of reverence for dead ancestors probably also influenced the rise of emperor worship, but Romans had no set ideas about the nature of the afterlife. Folktales and other sources indicate that they believed in the ghosts or spirits of the dead, who might be capable of returning to interfere with earthly events. Burial practices also suggest that the Romans were concerned about an afterlife, since elaborate tombs were constructed in order to ensure peace for the dead soul. Some Romans, especially well-educated, sophisticated people aware of Greek ideas, adopted the Greek conceptions of a blessed afterworld known as Elysium and a dark underworld known as Hades.

The Roman Empire collapsed both from within, through internal corruption and misgovernment, and from without, through invasion, in the third through fifth centuries. Many Romans, meanwhile, had already begun to turn to the personal religious experiences offered by the many

Near Eastern mystery cults, some of which were dedicated to Roman gods. In the same era, the new Christian religion was also expanding rapidly, and was adopted as the official religion of Rome in the late fourth century.

SEE ALSO: ancient Near East, religions of; Christmas; Manichaeism

## ancient Near East, religions of

The ancient Near East was the site of some of the world's earliest urban civilizations. These included Sumer (ca. 2800–2350 B.C.), the first Babylonian Empire (ca. 1800–1600 B.C.), Assyria (ca. 1300–650 B.C.), New Babylon (ca. 600–537 B.C.) in Mesopotamia (modern Iraq) and the long-standing, rich civilization of ancient Egypt. A region of many peoples and of both inward and outward migration, the Near East was also the home of such distinct civilizations as the Hittites and the Canaanites. Its richness and diversity gave rise to many religious traditions, including the mystery religions that may well have had an influence on Judaism and Christianity.

Mesopotamian religions were polytheistic, their gods generally representing natural and social forces. Mesopotamian gods were unpredictable and could be both generous and selfish, benign and evil. In Sumer, dating back to the third millennium B.C., major deities included Enlil, the god of water, and Ninhursag, the goddess of the earth. Both were central to the maintenance of life in Mesopotamia, which relied on the waters of the Tigris and Euphrates rivers, and in particular the annual flooding of the rivers, to replenish the fields. Indeed, a Sumerian word for these floodplains, in southern Iraq, was *eden*, which may well have been the model of the biblical Garden of Eden. Other important Sumerian gods were Utu, the god

of the Sun, and Sin, the god of the moon. Presiding over them all was the great lord, Anu, and perhaps most popular of all was Inanna, the goddess of fertility. Versions of these gods were to appear in later Mesopotamian civilizations, although sometimes under new names. Inanna, for example, came to be more commonly known as Ishtar.

Sumer was also the source of the world's first writing. With this advancement, priests and scribes could record rites, make established calendars of religious festivals, and tell and retell myths. The greatest of the Sumerian myths is the *Epic of Gilgamesh*, the story of a legendary king, Gilgamesh, and his search for eternal life. A common theme of the story is the relationship between people and the gods. Gilgamesh faces down the temptations of Inanna but finds that humans cannot attain immortality. His last adventure takes him to the underworld realm of Utnapishtim, as the only survivor of a great flood that devastated the Near East sometime in the third millennium B.C. There Gilgamesh discovers a plant able to confer immortality, only to lose it, since eternal life is only available to the gods.

*A Great Flood* Mesopotamian deities were worshipped in vivid ways, and appeasing them was central to the maintenance of society. Indeed, the greatest responsibility of emperors was to ensure that the gods were kept happy. The area's cities were full of temples, including the great stepped pyramids known as ziggurats whose ruins still stand in such cities as Ur and Ninevah. The earliest of these was likely the massive ziggurat dedicated to Inanna, constructed in the city of Uruk around 3200 B.C. Religious rituals were generally designed to allow humans to care for the gods. Temples contained statues in which the gods were thought to dwell, and those statues were richly dressed and fed daily. The temples themselves were considered the palaces of the gods, and often their statues were put to rest nightly at their highest spot. The festival year was full of holidays dedicated to the gods, many of which reflected stages in the cycle of agriculture such as planting, the harvest, or the new moon. Many people also maintained shrines in their houses for specific patron deities. There statues of those gods were given the same sort of special care as in the larger temples.

Ancient Egypt remains one of the longest-lasting civilizations in world history, dating from roughly 3100 B.C. to its incorporation into the Roman Empire in the first century B.C. At its heart was the Nile River, which flowed hundreds of miles northward from its origins in central Africa to the Mediterranean Sea, and whose vast floodplain gave the region great agricultural richness. As in Mesopotamia, Egyptian religious traditions were based at first on the need to appease the gods in order to ensure the growth of crops, but as Egyptian culture developed, a complex body of stories, rituals, and beliefs emerged. The highest of all gods was Re, the sun god, who was also known as Amon. Others included the sky god, Horus, and the god of wisdom, Thoth. Gods were often associated with animals. Horus, for instance, was generally depicted as a falcon and Thoth with the head of an ibis, a storklike bird.

*Isis and Osiris in Egypt* The most popular Egyptian gods were Isis and Osiris. Isis was associated with fertility and may have been an Egyptian version of Ishtar. Osiris, her husband and brother, was the god of the Nile and the greatest exemplar of moral standards. The most well known re-

ligious story in ancient Egypt tells how Isis and Osiris ruled over all the gods until Seth, their brother, killed Osiris in a jealous fit, scattering parts of his body across the land. Isis, heartbroken but loyal, retrieved all of the parts and gave him a proper burial. At this, the gods restored Osiris to life but only as the lord of the underworld.

As lord of the underworld, Osiris was thought to have the power to grant a kind of immortality to human beings, although they would remain in the underworld. After a human death, Osiris performed a ceremony in which he weighed the person's heart against a feather, which symbolized justice. Those whose hearts outweighed the feather were thought to be burdened with guilt and sin, and in some stories were then thrown into the mouth of a crocodile. Those with light, unburdened hearts were granted immortality. The story reinforced the Egyptian belief in the importance of universal order and righteousness, a concept called ma'at.

*Mummies, Pyramids, and Monotheism* Egyptian civilization was full of preparation for the afterlife. Pharoahs, the emperors of Egypt, were themselves considered gods who were guaranteed immortality, and provision for their afterlife was especially elaborate. Their bodies were preserved with advanced techniques of mummification and buried within sealed tombs surrounded by rich goods and often wives and servants. Egypt's pyramids were among these tombs; the tomb of the relatively minor pharaoh Tutenkhamen, unearthed in the 1920s full of gold objects and treasures of other kinds, indicates how rich these tombs could be. Eventually the Egyptians came to believe that immortality was available to all, not just to pharoahs. One of the most famous Egyptian religious texts, the *Book of the Dead*, describes the Osiris ceremony as well as the necessary rituals to be carried out before burial.

Egyptian religion also was characterized by cults dedicated to daily worship of particular deities. As in Mesopotamia, cult worship centered around the tending of an icon thought to "contain" a specific god. Priests would waken it, purify it, feed and clothe it, and offer prayers and services before returning it to its sacred shrine. On festival days, these icons might be taken out in public, where people could ask it questions. Answers were provided by priestly mediums known as oracles. Believers might also be granted answers or even greater divine girls while asleep, and so would spend nights sleeping in a temple compound to be near their god. Ancient Egyptian cities such as Memphis and Thebes were full of such temple compounds.

Scholars estimate that the Egyptians regularly worshipped more than two thousand gods. A further sign of its religious diversity, however, was adherence to monotheism, the belief that only a single god reigns over all creation. During the fourteenth century B.C., the pharaoh Akhenaten declared Aten, a variant of the sun god Re, to be the sole, supreme deity. Aten's cult, under the patronage of the pharaoh, grew rapidly and resulted in the construction of a new temple city known as Amarna, where Aten was worshipped in the form of a single disk with rays radiating outward. The cult, however, did not outlast the pharaoh's death in 1362 B.C.

### Hittite Religious Practices

The Hittites were related to the Indo-European tribes whose branches ultimately migrated to both India and western Europe as well as the Near East. They settled in modern-day Turkey around 1800 B.C., where they established a powerful empire that lasted until approximately 1200 B.C.. Over these centuries they both traded with and fought Egypt and the Mesopotamian empires, and their skill in ironworking and invention of the war chariot transformed the ancient world. Hittite religious beliefs were a mix of Indo-European beliefs and others adopted from their Near Eastern neighbors. Hittite gods included a weather god known as Tarhun, whose qualities included the granting of kingship and success on the battlefield. Hittite artwork often depicted Tarhun holding both a bolt of lightning and an axe. Tarhun's wife, Arinitti, was the goddess of the sun. The Hittite pantheon also included a war god known as Wurunkatti and Shaushka, a goddess of both love and war. As elsewhere, these gods were thought to inhabit temple statues, and it was the responsibility of priests to provide them with daily care and nourishment or risk endangering earthly life.

Hittite kingdoms were also characterized by national religious cults, of which kings and queens were high priests. Rituals in these state cults included the invocation of the gods to provide successful harvests or battles as well as the confession and expiation of sins. There is some evidence that these rituals involved human sacrifice. Festivals also took place to commemorate the changing of the seasons. Many of these included huge feasts presided over by kings and queens. Hittite burial ceremonies, meanwhile, included cremation as well as burial.

### The Land of Canaan

The Canaanites, or people of Canaan, dominated the eastern shore of the Mediterranean from approximately 2000 B.C. to the establishment of ancient Israel in the tenth century B.C. Closely related to the Canaanites were the

Phoenicians, whose communities stretched along the coastline and who were great traders, sailors, and explorers. The influence of both stretched far beyond the end of the independent Canaanite kingdoms, and as Semitic-speaking peoples they were related to both the Hebrews and the Arabs.

Canaanite gods were often adapted from Mesopotamian ones. At the top of their pantheon was the great god El, the bull, often also depicted as a wise old man. El was thought to be the father of all but one of the gods and goddesses, and some scholars think that he was the god chosen by Abraham to be the only god of the Hebrews in around 2000 B.C. The one god not viewed as a son of El was Ba'al, the widely worshipped Canaanite fertility god, described as the lord of the earth and the lord of the rain, and as such, central to the maintenance of life. Canaanite myths describe him as in constant combat with the forces of death. His name, meanwhile, became a common synonym for "god"; there were various local Ba'als in Canaan, as well as cults dedicated to them, by the time Israel was established.

Other important Canaanite deities included Asherah, the wife of El and a mother goddess, and Astarte, goddess of love and war. Astarte, adapted from the Mesopotamian Ishtar, was perhaps even more widely worshipped than Ba'al, with cults dedicated to her among the Egyptians and Hittites as well as in Canaan. The Hebrew Bible refers to her as Ashtoreth and the Greeks later adapted her in their pantheon as Aphrodite. Many temples and cults arose around the worship of Astarte, where ceremonies included feasting, dancing, and the presence of sacred temple prostitutes as symbols of fertility. Many people also maintained icons of Astarte in their homes, where she received great care, affection, and reverence.

*Mystery Cults* By the first century B.C. the ancient Near East featured more religious ferment than ever before. To the gods and practices of earlier times were added those of the Greeks and Romans, and the region also witnessed the rise of the two great religions of Judaism and Zoroastrianism. One result, especially among ordinary people seeking religious experience outside of those sanctioned by the region's various states, was the so-called mystery religions. These were secret cults generally dedicated to both a particular deity and to the expression of inner religious feeling. Believers generally had to take an oath of secrecy to enter one of the cults, and baptism was often used to symbolize entrance into a mystery community. Rites involved purification, such as abstention from meat, wine, and sexual activity. Festivals were commonly held according to changes in the agricultural or celestial calendar. One of the most important was the celebration of the winter solstice on December 24 and 25. The period was regarded as the time of rebirth of both gods and of life itself, since the days began to grow longer. Many of the mystery cults also promised eternal life to devotees.

The mystery cults, which often were focused on particular locations or groups of people practicing a specific profession or craft, were generally dedicated to gods, or versions of gods, which already existed in the region. Among the largest were the cults dedicated to Isis, to Astarte, to the Greek Dionysius, and to the Roman Demeter and Jupiter. Also important were cults devoted to a great mother deity known as Magna Mater and to Mithras, the Zoroastrian god of light. Mithras was particularly important in the first few centuries A.D.,

Saint Jerome and the Angel. *In Christian theology, angels will be both warriors and messengers during the predicted apocalypse to come.*

when his cult was one of the chief competitors to Christianity in the ancient Near East.

SEE ALSO: ancient Greece and Rome, religions of; Hebrew Bible, Zoroastrianism

## angels

Intermediaries between God and humanity. Angels, whose name is derived from a Greek word meaning "messenger," appear in Judaism, Christianity, and Islam, although not all traditions, especially in Judaism, fully accept them.

In early Judaism, believers held that there was literally a ladder between heaven and earth. Angels, they thought, traveled up and down on this ladder. After the Babylonian Exile, and perhaps under the influence of Iranian Zorastrianism, Jewish angels began to be described as having wings to take them back and forth. A number of angels appear in the Hebrew Bible, including Gabriel, Michael, Raphael, and Uriel. Gabriel and Michael rank at the top of a complex angel hierarchy and are known as archangels. Angelic acts include taking prayers to God and accompanying believers on holy days. Some stories of angels, meanwhile, discuss the fallen angels who remained on earth to marry humans.

Christians also took up the notion of fallen angels, as well as much of the rest of

Jewish angelology. Fallen angels refuse to accept, or having accepted it originally, reject the love and redemption of God. Being willful, these fallen angels, notably Satan, are thought capable of causing much trouble among humans and, according to some interpretations, are the source of all evil. In Christianity angels generally are not considered to play direct roles in believers' lives, as much of their intermediary function has been taken over by Jesus Christ. They are thought to play important parts, however, in the apocalypse, the predicted cosmic cataclysm in which God will destroy evil ruling powers and raise the righteous to a heavenly kingdom. According to Christian theology, at the apocalypse angels will be not only messengers but militants fighting on God's behalf.

In Islam, the most important angel is Jibril (Gabriel), the angel of revelation who initially brought Allah's message to Muhammad. The Qur'an also mentions an angel of death (but leaves him unnamed) and an angel named Israfil who will announce the day of Allah's judgment.

SEE ALSO: apocalypse; Jibril

# Anglican (Episcopalian) Church

The main form of Christianity practiced in Great Britain as well as in the many parts of the world that were once within the British Empire. Anglicanism is Protestant, but of all the Protestant churches it remains closest to the Roman Catholic Church in its rituals and practices.

The Anglican variant arose when England's King Henry VIII rejected papal leadership of England's churches in the 1520s. He wanted to name himself the head of the church in England so that he could grant himself an annulment, ending his first marriage to a Spanish noblewoman who had not borne him a son. When the pope refused the annulment, Henry pushed ahead with his plan to separate the churches. In this he was supported by some English leaders who sympathized with the Protestant Reformation then under way on the European continent. Although Henry was by no means a committed church reformer, the momentum of the split increased when, in the 1530s, the English government nationalized the nation's monasteries and made their lands available to the wealthy and powerful. England remained split by religious differences for 150 years among Anglicans, remaining Catholics loyal to the church of Rome, and stricter Protestant reformers known as Puritans. Except for the decade of the 1650s, when there was a Puritan interlude, Anglicanism has remained the state church of England since Henry's day. The titular head of the church remains the English monarch, although the functional leadership is in the hands of the archbishop of Canterbury.

The central liturgy of the Anglican Church is the Book of Common Prayer, initially introduced by Henry's first archbishop of Canterbury, Thomas Cranmer, in 1533 but only achieving its final form in 1688. The liturgy of the Book of Common Prayer was intended to be a compromise between Roman Catholicism and Protestantism, and Anglicanism in general reflects this compromise. Anglican churches maintain some of the formality of Roman Catholic worship including, on occasion, the use of Latin in services. But Anglicans reject the authority of the papacy, or the ability of any church official to grant salvation, and Anglican priests are allowed to marry and have children. The global Anglican community maintains its connections through the so-called Anglican communion, uniting bishops from as far afield as South Africa, Canada, and Australia. In the United States, meanwhile, Anglicanism is known as Episcopalianism.

SEE ALSO: Luther, Martin; Reformation; Roman Catholicism

## animism

A term with several different spiritual or religious meanings. Most broadly, animism is the belief that the natural world is animated by various unseen spirits, which themselves may or may not be manifestations of a larger divine spirit that is all-powerful and all-pervasive. Of the major world religions, Shinto most clearly contains elements of this understanding of animism.

In a related sense, the term is used to describe, in general, the religions practiced by small, tribal groups. This meaning can be misleading as the religions of these groups are not always based around "nature" or "animal" spirits nor do they necessarily hold that the world is "animated" by divine forces.

Finally, animism is used by some European scholars of religion to describe the basis of all religions. By this they mean the belief, common to virtually all peoples at all times, in spiritual beings that can aid or hurt individual human beings. To these scholars, notably the nineteenth-century British writer Edward Burnett Taylor, animism is the minimum religion, involving spirits ranging from ghosts and dream-beings to omnipotent gods. According to this school of thought all subsequent religious systems, including highly developed religions such as Christianity or Hinduism, evolved from the basic "animistic" sense.

SEE ALSO: philosophy of religion; Shinto

## anti-Semitism

Anti-Jewish prejudice. The word *Semitic* applies broadly to the languages belonging to the Semitic family, including Hebrew and Arabic, but according to Western custom "anti-Semitic" refers specifically to anti-Jewish acts or sentiment among cultures coming mostly from the European Christian tradition. The term was first used by the German author Wilhelm Marr in an 1873 book. Anti-Semitism also occurs among some Muslim groups. It is often based as much on cultural differences as religious ones. Official anti-Semitism, the placing of legal restrictions on Jewish affairs, has had devastating effects but is historically relatively rare. Much more common has been a sort of cultural anti-Semitism, in which Jews are targeted for being different, for refusing to fit in, or for stubbornly holding onto minority customs.

European anti-Semitism first arose on a large scale when Christianity became a major religion in the Roman Empire in the third and fourth centuries. Some early Christians blamed the Jews for the death of Jesus of Nazareth, a charge that has been the basis for Christian anti-Semitism ever since. During the European Middle Ages, such events as the Crusades helped to make anti-Semitism a fundamental characteristic of European Christian culture, and in the same centuries European Jews faced such official oppressions as confinement to ghettos and restrictions on the sorts of jobs they could do.

Jews remained Europe's only major minority group, and thus were easy targets for scapegoating. Despite the lifting of legal restrictions in western Europe in the 1800s, Jews found themselves the targets of blame for such problems as economic recessions and even wars. Anti-Semitism was particularly vivid in the culturally and politically charged climate of the late 1800s and early 1900s. Then, such documents as the forged *Protocols of the Elders of Zion* appeared. This false but widely believed pamphlet, which claimed that Jewish elders were planning a global campaign of terrorism in order to establish a Jewish world state, had inflammatory and divisive effects. Anti-Semitism reached its notorious extreme in the Holocaust of World War II, when Germany's Nazi regime under dictator Adolf Hitler murdered some 6 million Jews in mass shooting operations or extermination camps, considering them a racial and cultural threat rather than a religious entity. Many Jews responded by arguing that they would never truly be allowed to fit into the mainstream of European life and that only with their own nation could Jews and Judaism survive. One result was the founding of the modern State of Israel in 1947, a secular state that today is home to approximately 37 percent of the world's 13.3 million Jews.

Muslims are enjoined to consider Jews one of the Peoples of the Book who should be respected as long as they accept a somewhat subordinated status in Muslim-dominated states. The status is a recognition among Muslims that Judaism plays an important part in their own religious traditions. Only when Jews appear to be threatening Islam or Muslims is a more active form of anti-Semitism called for, according to Muslims who oppose the actions of modern Israel. This opposition, however, is based not so much on religion as on interpretations of political events.

SEE ALSO: Holocaust; Judaism; Peoples of the Book

## apocalypse

The period of wars, disasters, and other forms of chaos that is to precede the judgment of God upon humankind at the end of time, according to some religious interpretations. The term comes from a Greek word meaning "revelation," and was used originally to refer to things of a future time that remained unknown; both the Jewish and Christian traditions contain bodies of "apocalyptic" literature (such as the New Testament book of Revelation) that do not necessarily predict any so-called end times. In recent decades, however, the term has been understood to mean catastrophic events, or even the end of the world.

SEE ALSO: millennialism; Revelation

## Apocrypha

In general, the books of sacred literature not included in the biblical collections of the Jews or Christians. Apocrypha is a Greek word meaning "hidden things." A consideration of the Apocrypha remains worthwhile to show that the collections of biblical texts by Jews and by different groups of Christians was a historical process involving controversy and dispute.

In the Jewish tradition, the Apocrypha include a large number and wide variety of texts that rabbis and teachers came to consider "falsely inscribed," meaning that their authorship and provenance could not be accepted as legitimate or authoritative or that had been attributed to authors who did not actually write them. The scholarly term for this category is pseudoepigrapha. Among this material are apocalyptic texts such as the books of Esdras, prophetic works attributed to Judith and Tobit, a Life of Adam and Eve, and a text written in Greek known as the Wisdom of Solomon.

In Roman Catholic and Eastern Orthodox Christianity, the Apocrypha refers to texts that Christians accept as scripture but which are not part of the Hebrew Bible (Old Testament) as accepted by Jews. One source of these texts was the translation of the Hebrew Bible from Hebrew into Greek, a work of Jewish scholarship known as the Septuagint. The Septuagint included many of the Jewish Apocrypha that were later translated into the Latin Bible, the fourth century Vulgate, which was to remain authoritative in Roman Catholicism for centuries. The specific texts considered canonic for Catholics and Eastern Orthodox Christians vary, but neither of their versions of the Old Testament completely matches the Hebrew Bible. When Protestantism arose in the sixteenth century, its officials used the Hebrew Bible of the Jews, making the additions used elsewhere in Christianity "apocryphal" for Protestants.

The Christian New Testament also has a number of Apocrypha, the legacy of the early years of the faith when no centralized authority had arisen to establish textual canons or set official doctrine. Some of these are alternative Gospels, different from the four included in the New Testament. These include the Gospel of Thomas or the Gnostic Gospel. Others are alternative Epistles or apocalyptical descriptions. Most of these texts were rejected at early church councils on pseudoepigraphic grounds or because they supported heresies that church officials condemned. A variation on the notion of the Apocrypha in the New Testament were those texts acknowledged to have been "added later." These include Paul's alleged Epistle to the Hebrews, the letter written to Jesus' brother James, the book of Revelation, and fragments of the Gospels of Mark, Luke, and John. Roman Catholics accept all these additions as authoritative, while Orthodox and Protestant Christians accept most of them.

See Also: Hebrew Bible; New Testament; Septuagint

## apostles

Most commonly, the twelve followers of Jesus of Nazareth. The term also refers to important teachers in the early Christian Church (such as Paul) or, even more broadly, as an official of the Roman Catholic or Eastern Orthodox churches. The word *apostles* is derived from a Greek word meaning "one who is sent out."

The twelve original apostles were, according to the Gospels, Peter, James, John (sons of Zebedee), Andrew, Philip, Bartholomew, Matthew, Thomas, James (son of Alphaeus), Thaddeus, Simon, and Judas Iscariot. They had such privileges as being able to remain constantly in Jesus' presence and being the first hearers of his teachings. Very little is known of the lives of most of them, either before their attendance with Jesus or after his death and resurrection.

Peter, the effective leader of the original twelve and the founder of the first Christian Church in Jerusalem, argued that the term "apostle" should mostly be limited to himself and his fellows. Later prominent Christians felt that the term should also be applied to those who established themselves as special authorities or, as in the case of Paul, who had received further missions directly from Christ. The Acts of the Apostles, the fifth book of the New Testament of the Bible, provides the main account of the "apostolic age" that followed the death and resurrection of Jesus.

See Also: Acts of the Apostles; Christianity; Jesus of Nazareth

## Apostles' Creed

The most important statement of faith in the Roman Catholic and Anglican churches and a central portion of the liturgy of both. It is common in other Protestant churches as well but the Eastern Orthodox Church does not recognize it officially. The Apostles' Creed was derived from early statements of Christian converts within the Roman Empire seeking to prove their commitment to church officials, although tradition credits it to the twelve original apostles themselves. Its final form, which was probably reached in the late sixth or early seventh centuries, was made the official statement of faith in the Roman Catholic Church by Pope Innocent III (r. 1198–1216). A standard English translation of the Apostles' Creed is:

> I believe in God, the Father Almighty, creator of heaven and earth.
> I believe in Jesus Christ, his only Son, our Lord.
> He was conceived by the power of the Holy Spirit and born of the Virgin Mary.
> He suffered under Pontius Pilate, was crucified, died, and was buried.
> He descended to the dead.
> On the third day he rose again.
> He ascended into heaven, and is seated at the right hand of the Father.
> He will come again to judge the living and the dead.
> I believe in the Holy Spirit, the holy Catholic Church, the communion of saints, the
> forgiveness of sins, the resurrection of the body, and the life everlasting. Amen.

## Al-Aqsa Mosque

The third holiest site of Islam after mosques in Mecca and Medina. Literally "the farthest mosque," Al-Aqsa mosque was built in Jerusalem in the seventh century by al-Walid, the Islamic ruler of Syria, whose domains included Jerusalem. It was built near the site of the second Temple of the Jews, which had been mostly destroyed by the Romans in the first century. The former esplanade of the second Temple serves as the mosque's largest open space.

Al-Aqsa Mosque achieved its revered status in the twelfth century when it was determined that the site was the one mentioned in the Qur'an as the "distant mosque" to which Muhammad had once made a night journey from the Grand Mosque of Mecca. Many Muslims believe that the Prophet led other prophets in discussion there before finally ascending to heaven. Since the mosque proper had not been built in Muhammad's lifetime, it was the site itself that was determined to be sacred. Known as the Temple Mount, the site had been long considered "the noble sanctuary" by Muslims.

In recent years Al-Aqsa Mosque and the nearby Dome of the Rock have served as focal points for Muslims in the modern State of Israel. Its current administration is in the hands of the Jordanian government's Ministry for Religious Endowments.

SEE ALSO: Jerusalem; Mecca; Muhammad

## Aramaic

An ancient Semitic language usually written using the Hebrew alphabet, and the spoken language of Jesus of Nazareth and his apostles. It was apparently widespread in the ancient world, as Aramaic inscriptions dating back to 700 B.C. have been found as far away from the Near East as Afghanistan and Turkmenistan. It was commonly employed in Jewish teachings, and was the original language in which the Talmud was written. The entire Hebrew Bible was also translated into Aramaic prior to the first century A.D. Few people speak Aramaic today.

SEE ALSO: Hebrew Bible; New Testament; Septuagint; Talmud

## Aranyakas

A collection of early sacred Hindu texts appearing around the middle of the first millennium B.C. The Aranyakas, which is Sanskrit for "books of the forest," are connected to the larger collection of scriptures known as Brahmanas, which are mostly commentary in some form on the earlier Vedas. In particular, the Aranyakas are connected to the Rig Veda and the Yajur Veda. Their focus is on the description and nature of rites to be carried out by those devoting their lives to meditation and speculation by leaving the world and going into "the forest." At the time the texts were composed these rites were intended to be secret, understandable only to ascetics and their gurus.

SEE ALSO: Brahmanas; Vedas

## arhat

A Buddhist who has achieved nearly the highest level of awareness and enlightenment, and is therefore a kind of Buddhist saint. The term is most common in Theravada Buddhism, where the status of arhat is the highest an individual can hope to reach, since a living person cannot realistically hope to become a full Buddha, or enlightened one. According to Theravadans, there can be only one Buddha in each historical cycle, and this cycle's has already appeared in the form of Siddhartha Gautama. Arhats, nevertheless, are thought to have freed themselves from the cycle of rebirth and to have attained special knowledge and powers. These include the ability to understand and hear all sounds, read other people's thoughts, and remember their earlier incarnations. Arhats are also believed to enter nirvana, the Buddhist concept of heaven, at the time of their death.

Mahayana Buddhists also accept the notion of arhats, but they mostly reject it as not being fully true to the teachings of the original Buddha. They find arhats selfish, since their focus is on personal enlightenment. Instead of raising up arhats to an extremely high level of respect, Mahayana Buddhists prefer the bodhisattvas, thought ready to postpone their own enlightenment to help others. The term is also frequently rendered as arhant.

SEE ALSO: bodhisattva; Siddhartha Gautama; Theravada Buddhism

## ark of the covenant

An important religious symbol in ancient Judaism. The ark of the covenant was the chest that contained the two stone tablets on which were inscribed the Ten Commandments during the period of approximately 1100 B.C. to 600 B.C. Thought to be a carved wooden box with a gold overlay, it first appears in biblical stories in the book of Numbers, where it is described as being carried about by Jews during their wanderings in the wilderness following their escape from Egypt and the revelation of God to Moses. As Hebrew tribes battled to take control of the land of Canaan, they occasionally used the ark as a source of inspiration, carrying it onto the battlefield on the belief that it had special powers. After the establishment of the ancient Hebrew kingdom in the tenth century B.C., the ark was installed by King David in the Temple of Jerusalem. There it was maintained in a sacred shrine, or tabernacle, seen only by Jewish high priests on holy days. The ark disappeared following the conquest of Jerusalem, and the destruction of the Temple, by the Babylonians in 587 B.C. Its precise fate is unknown; some claim that it was taken by the Babylonians, others that it remains buried in Jerusalem's Temple Mount. Some Ethiopian Christians maintain that it was taken to a temple in their city of Axum and remains there still.

SEE ALSO: Exodus; Judaism; Temple

## artha

A Sanskrit word meaning "goal" or "advantage." For Hindus, artha is one of the four goals of life, along with kama (pleasure or artistic expression), dharma (duty), and moksha (release). Artha is often understood to imply such matters as the accumulation of wealth or possessions or the establishment of an important position in the world, and such matters are thought to be completely legitimate according to Hindu ethics (provided they do not interfere with dharma or moksha). In the fourth century B.C. Kautilya, a brahmin-caste adviser to an Indian emperor, published the Artha-Shastra, classical India's great text of political philosophy. The Artha-Shastra focused on the attainment and maintenance of political power, recognizing the occasional need for deceit and war but also arguing that it is an emperor's duty to ensure the safety of his subjects.

SEE ALSO: dharma; Hinduism; four stages of life

## Ashkenazim

One of two major groups of European Jews. The Ashkenazim were Jews whose origins were in eastern or central Europe (the term means "German"). The other major group, the Sephardim, were from areas under Muslim control during parts of the Middle Ages, notably Spain. From their original base in the Rhineland, the border area of France and Germany, the Ashkenazim spread to Poland and Russia during the late Middle Ages and in the centuries afterward. Due to their large Jewish populations, Poland and Russia became the center of Ashkenazi culture, complete with their own ceremonies and interpretations of Jewish texts. The group even spoke their own language: Yiddish, a mixture of Hebrew and German with certain Slavic components. Most Jewish immigrants to the United States and other English-speaking countries are descendants of Ashkenazim, and in modern Israel, Ashkenazim maintain a distinct Jewish identity.

SEE ALSO: Judaism; Sephardim

## Ashoka
## (r. 269–232 B.C.)

An Indian emperor of the Mauryan dynasty, which controlled most of northern India from 362 to 184 B.C. Ashoka's conversion from Hinduism to Buddhism, as well as his attempts to instill Buddhist principles within his government, helped to transform Buddhism from one of many Indian sects to the status of a major religion.

Born and raised a member of the Hindu kshatriya, or warrior caste, Ashoka converted to Buddhism following a bloody battle at Kalinga in eastern India, according to tradition. His victory in the battle allowed him to consolidate his kingdom, but it came at the price of thousands of deaths. Regretting this loss of life, Ashoka turned to Buddhist teachings, particularly those emphasizing kindness, generosity, and nonviolence, or ahimsa. As part of his effort to teach by example, Ashoka erected hundreds of stone pillars across India on which Buddhist teachings, as well as parts of his own story, were etched. Some of these pillars still stand. He also enacted such measures as state-supported medical care and complete religious freedom. He did not actively seek Buddhist converts, and was little concerned, in fact, with doctrine or theology. But his reign likely gave validation to those in India who wanted to pursue Buddhism, and the number of Buddhists as well as organizations like orders of monks grew in India during and after his reign. His son Mahinda brought Buddhism to the island of Sri Lanka, according to local tradition, and Mahinda helped turn the island into the first center of Theravada Buddhism.

SEE ALSO: ahimsa; Buddhism; Hinduism

## ashram

A center for religious meditation and study, usually within the Hindu tradition. The term, and indeed the concept, became common in the twentieth century only when Westerners in large numbers grew interested in Hinduism and when various popularized forms of Hinduism emerged. Prior to this time Hindu training generally took place as it always did and still often does, through instruction between a brahmin priest and a small group of students.

Ashrams are usually centered around a particular teacher or guru who represents or preaches a distinct branch of the faith. Mahatma Gandhi, for example, maintained an ashram at Sabarmati in western India where followers tried to live according to his teachings of simplicity and religious toleration. In more recent years some ashrams have become places to gain refuge from a complicated world or to pursue alternative lifestyles. In the late 1970s, for example, a guru known as the Baghwan Sri Rajneesh set up an ashram in central

Oregon known, until it was shut down, for loose sexual guidelines and the fondness of the guru for wealth and possessions. More respectable ashrams of recent years include that maintained by Sathya Sai Baba at Puttaparthi in India's Andhra Pradesh state, which has become a major institution complete with its own university and hospital, and the ashram in Kerala state maintained by Mata Amritanandamayi, the "hugging" guru. Both attract residents and visitors from within Hindu India and from around the world.

SEE ALSO: guru; new religious movements, Western; Sai Baba, Sathya

## atheism

The rejection of the existence of God or the gods and therefore the opposite of theism, belief in the existence of God or the gods. It may also be distinguished from agnosticism, which claims that the existence of any supernatural beings is unknowable. Atheism has a long history in Western thought, and atheists can be found as far back as ancient Greece. It has been grounded in a wide variety of philosophies, from the materialism, or emphasis on the sole reality of the physical world, of ancient Greece to the attempt by Italian political philosopher Niccolo Machiavelli in the sixteenth century to deny the importance of religion or morality in politics. In recent centuries the case for atheism has been made by such figures as the German philosopher Ludwig Feuerbach (1804–1872), who argued that God was nothing more than a projection of the ideals of humanity and reflected nothing real or actual. The German economist Karl Marx (1818–1883) contemporaneously argued that religion was the "opium of the masses," a false set of visions that prevented people from realizing the extent to which they were being economically or socially exploited. The founder of modern psychology, Sigmund Freud (1856–1939) argued that religion amounted to a childlike wish to hold onto a father figure. In the twentieth century many thinkers have rejected God on the grounds that religion questions human reason and human potentialities, while scientific discoveries continue to challenge the traditional Christian conception of the universe.

In other religious traditions, aside from Islam, the question of atheism has less relevance than in Christianity. Judaism is built on attachment to a people and its traditions, not necessarily a set of religious beliefs. In Hinduism, very few would deny the existence of a supernatural reality, and so much of Hindu thought and practice is built around symbol and metaphor and the belief that there is plenty of room for all sorts of approaches to religion. And Buddhism offers at its heart no supernatural being.

SEE ALSO: agnosticism; deism; theism

## atman

A notion in Indian religious philosophy that is understood differently by Hindus, Buddhists, and Sikhs. Most broadly, the atman is the self, the true nature of every person (and of every living creature). It remains constant despite the growth, decay, or other changes experienced by the body and the mind. Sometimes translated into English as "soul," the atman is coexistent with or parallel to Brahman, which is the ultimate divine spirit of the universe. Hindus believe that their ultimate goal of moksha, or release from the wheel of birth and death, constitutes the union of atman with Brahman in the way drops of water in a river ultimately rejoin the larger ocean. More precisely, moksha is

the understanding of this union rather than the union itself, since atman is indivisible from Brahman. Some Hindus think that it is possible for people to deeply grasp their own atman during certain yoga practices or during dreams and thereby get a taste of the divinity within themselves.

Buddhists view the notion of atman negatively since they reject the idea that there is such a thing as an individual soul. They speak instead of "an-atman," or noself. Sikhs, in contrast, emphasize more strongly than even Hindus the individualistic aspects of atman, claiming that believers should look within, to their own atman, to seek union with God because God is present there.

SEE ALSO: Brahman; Hinduism; moksha

## Augustine, Saint
## (354–430)

Christian thinker and writer whose profound influence on Christianity is reflected in his status as one of the fathers of the church. Augustine was born in Hippo in Roman North Africa and, following his education, practiced a Manichean religion. He converted to Christianity in 387 while working in Italy and returned to North Africa shortly thereafter, where he served as bishop of Hippo from 396 to 430. While in that office he preached and wrote prolifically, producing a number of works that are still read widely. These include *The City of God*, in which he argues that the church's holiness was derived from its purposes and not the moral character of its members. In the same text he also claims that, likewise, political leaders serve God's will as long as they act justly. In *On Christian Doctrine* and *On the Trinity*, Augustine focuses on the training of priests and on explaining basic Christian ideas in ways meaningful to nonexperts. His most well-known work

*Aboriginal artwork representing "dreamtime" figures. Australian aboriginal dreamtime mythology links the future, past, and present in the same time and space.* © PENNY TWEEDIE/ CORBIS

is the *Confessions*, a semiautobiographical text in which Augustine explores his own path to conversion and an understanding of the will of God. In this text he emphasizes the notion that God allows people to pursue their free will and go astray, but that an understanding of God's all-pervasive mercy and forgiveness, as well as his power, should inspire a return to a proper path.

Among the other ideas Augustine discussed in these texts and elsewhere, and which became central to Christian debates, was the doctrine of original sin, or the claim that all people are guilty of sin from birth and are therefore in need of God's grace. He also examined the notion of predestination, or the belief that God has, for his own reasons, selected some persons for salvation, leaving others to eternal damnation. Never fully judgmental, however, Augustine could not bring himself to a complete belief in predestination. Augustine's work remains authoritative among Roman Catholics, ranking along with that of Thomas Aquinas as secondary only to the Bible.

SEE ALSO: Roman Catholicism; theology; Thomas Aquinas, Saint

## Australian aboriginal religions

The aboriginal peoples of Australia, migrants from elsewhere in Asia thirty thousand to forty thousand years ago, were until recently among the most isolated peoples on earth. Before the settlement of Australia by Europeans beginning in 1788, very few records indicate any contact between the widely dispersed aboriginals and other peoples. Their religions therefore remained distinct and relatively unchanged over a very long period of time. The vastness of the continent and the fairly small and isolated nature of aboriginal groups contributed to a wide diversity among religions, but most sects share a common worldview as well as certain common practices.

The key concept in aboriginal religion is that of the Dreaming, or Dreamtime. The Dreaming links the past, present, and future as well as the realms of the divine and those of the human and animal. At the beginning of the Dreaming, mythological beings created the world and all things in it in forms that were eternal and unchangeable; therefore, animals, plants, and even rocks and trees are thought to have "souls." As the mythological beings traveled across the earth, they left marks of their presence, such as Ayers Rock in central Australia. The Dreaming beings also created the rules by which human beings were to exist. In the Dreaming, human beings are just as much a part of the natural world as animals or plants, neither outside it nor above it. Humans also share qualities of the beings who created the universe, as well as of animals. Although one can never be truly separated from the Dreamtime, many aboriginal rites are designed to provide clearer insight into the spirit world. One also is thought to gain strength, health, a sense of identity, and peace of mind by following such rites. Dreams while sleeping are also thought to provide insight into the eternal Dreamtime.

The Dreaming beings also serve as individual totems. Many of the beings represent a particular natural phenomenon: an animal, plant, or a heavenly body such as the sun or moon. Aboriginal religion holds that many Dreamtime beings transformed themselves into natural forms such as hills or rocks, or turned into animals or plants once their creative work was done; aboriginal Australia is full of sacred sites where these founder spirits are said to be sleeping. Each person, meanwhile, is thought to be an incarnation of one of these beings, a manifestation of the life force behind each of them. The being's spirit enters the child while it is in its mother's womb, when she walks by the spot where the spirit is sleeping. Since this spiritual force is not finite, however, it can be incarnated into any number of living beings. Once an aboriginal reaches maturity and goes through the proper rites of initiation, he or she is forever after a member of that particular totem's spiritual clan. One becomes a kangaroo man, for instance, if one is initiated into the Dreaming of the kangaroo being. In addition, aboriginal tribes or individuals often feel a particular attachment to an area of land because their Dreaming beings are associated with or "found" in that land. When an aboriginal goes on "walkabout," disappearing into the Australian outback for months and sometimes years, he is commonly seeking reconnection to his totem, and therefore a kind of spiritual restoration, by returning to the land associated with it.

### On Walkabout to Meet Spiritual Ancestors

Initiation into one's totem group is one of the essential aboriginal rituals. It is often considered a symbolic death and rebirth. For boys, initiation might involve a period of isolation away from the tribe, food prohibitions, or physical markings such as circumcision, scarring, or the breaking of a tooth. Initiation for girls might also include the cutting of the hymen as well as seclusion. In a more practical sense these initiation rites also marked entrance into adulthood. Women might now be ready for motherhood, while men who had undergone initiation might be expected to undertake religious or other responsibilities. A kangaroo man, for instance, would perform rituals to ensure that his tribe had enough kangaroo meat to sustain them. These and similar practices are known as "increase rituals." Other important rites include the visiting of sacred sites, body painting or decoration in order to look like a version of one's totem, and the recitation of special stories and songs, often accompanied by dancing. Each of these rites is designed to invoke the spiritual power of the Dreaming beings.

Aboriginal religions tend not to have a priestly caste, since no person is separate from the Dreaming or from his or her totem, and no one can perform religious duties for others. Some tribal groups had special elders, however, who maintained stores of knowledge in such matters as methods to invoke the spirits or who were the keepers of myths and stories. There were also medicine men who were consulted for purposes of healing or for divination or sorcery. These medicine men commonly used a ritual object known as a tjurunga in the language of the Aranda, one of the largest aboriginal groups. The tjurunga was often a flat board with patterns of stones on it. Commonly considered a means by which to communicate with a spirit being, the tjurunga might also be used by a sorceror to kill someone at a distance in a rite known as "pointing the bone." Most other objects used by aboriginals in their daily lives are considered to possess spiritual properties as well, and the creation of them was in and of itself a sacred rite, as are sand and cave paintings and other forms of aboriginal art.

Some aboriginal groups believe in an all-powerful god known as a sky father as well as a pantheon of lesser sky beings. But these beings have little impact on daily life. At the center of aboriginal religious life are individual and clan totems. At the time of death, one's soul, or life force, returns to the original Dreaming being that had granted it.

SEE ALSO: animism; Oceania, religions of

## Avalokitesvara

An important bodhisattva, or enlightened one who refrains from entering nirvana to aid others, in the Mahayana Buddhist tradition. Avalokitesvara is considered the embodiment of compassion, and is depicted in Buddhist stories and artwork as having eleven heads and one thousand arms so that he can see all the sufferings of humankind as well as lend his aid whenever necessary. Indeed, his name is a Sanskrit term for "the one who sees in all directions."

Avalokitesvara receives devotion in a number of forms. In China he is generally worshipped in female form under the name Kuan Yin, the goddess of mercy. In Japan he is known as Kannon. Kannon, who is also sometimes depicted in female form, is thought to have the ability to understand all human suffering and to lead human beings to enlightenment. In both traditions the text known as the Lotus Sutra is central to the worship of Avalokitesvara's various forms.

In Tibet, a four-armed version of Avalokitesvara is frequently worshipped, not least because the Dalai Lama, the spiritual head of Tibetan Buddhism, is considered an incarnation of the bodhisattva. Avalokitesvara even provides a connection between Buddhism and Hinduism, as some early Indian Mahayanists considered him the father of Hindu gods such as Shiva.

SEE ALSO: bodhisattva; Lotus Sutra; Mahayana Buddhism

## avatar

An earthly incarnation of a Hindu god. Usually the concept is associated with the avatars of Vishnu, a god who is thought to have maintained the ability to transform himself into a living creature (complete with the experiences of birth and death) in order to accomplish a specific purpose. According to traditions that emerged by the tenth century, there are ten avatars of Vishnu. The first three are a fish, a turtle, and a boar. The next is a half man, half lion. Vishnu's remaining avatars are human, including Rama and Krishna, who are considered gods in their own right. Another is Siddhartha Gautama, the original Buddha. Vishnu's tenth avatar, Kalkin, has not yet appeared and serves as a sort of messianic figure in Vishnu worship.

The term can also be applied more broadly to imply the perceived presence of god in earthly forms, even inanimate ones. This is true not only within Hindu traditions but in other religions as well. Some Hindus consider such figures as Mahatma Gandhi and Sathya Sai Baba to be avatars. Christians and Muslims might speak of Jesus Christ or Muhammad, respectively, in similar terms.

SEE ALSO: Krishna; Vishnu

## Avesta

The main scripture of Zoroastrianism. Much of it is ascribed to the prophet Zo-roaster, although portions of it likely predate Zoroaster's life and preaching, which took place in Iran of the seventh and sixth centuries B.C. Existing versions of the Avesta are only about one-quarter of the original; the remainder is said to have been destroyed when the Greek king Alexander the Great conquered Iran in the late fourth century B.C. Present editions were compiled from surviving remnants under the Sassanid kings, who ruled Iran before the arrival of Islam in the seventh century A.D.

The Avesta consists of five sections. The *Yasna* provides descriptions of rituals and sacrifices, cholars suspect that much of this section dates back to the Indo-Europeans who settled in Iran long before Zoroaster. The *Gathas*, which are hymns thought to be composed by Zoroaster and are the heart of the Avesta, are embedded in the *Yasna*. The *Visp Rat* is a less important collection of rites dedicated to early high priests, while the *Vendidad* is a compendium of Zoroastrian religious and civil law that also provides the religion's creation story. The final section is a collection of myths in verse form known as the *Yashts*, devoted to spirits and heroes.

The archaic language and poetry of the Avesta are difficult to translate, and the text is mostly employed by Zoroastrian clergy in religious ceremonies. Modern believers, such as India's Parsis, generally employ instead a smaller text known as the Khorda Avesta, or Little Avesta. It contains prayers and hymns useful for daily life.

SEE ALSO: Ahura Mazda; Parsis; Zoroaster

# B

## Babylonian Exile
### (597 B.C.–538 B.C.)

The period of Jewish history following the destruction of the first Temple of Jerusalem and the conquest of the Jewish kingdom of Judah in ancient Palestine. Having lost their kingdom, many Jews were taken as slaves or prisoners to Babylon, a kingdom to the east in Mesopotamia (modern Iraq). Their fate there was mixed. In some cases Jews apparently were free enough to maintain their traditions. Some groups of Jews even maintained the freedom to travel back and forth between Babylon and Palestine, and some Jewish prophets whose teachings later appeared in the Hebrew Bible, notably Ezekiel, promised that one day all the Jews would return to Jerusalem. Practical aspects of the faith developed as well; it may have been during the Babylonian Exile that groups of Jews established synagogues to facilitate the observances of rituals as well as the Sabbath and other holidays.

The Babylonian Exile ended in 538 B.C., when the Persian warlord Cyrus the Great, having conquered Babylon, granted permission to the Jews to return to Palestine. In 516 B.C., the second Temple of Jerusalem was consecrated as returnees tried to rebuild their homeland. Some Jewish families chose to remain in Babylon, however, marking the beginning of the Jewish Diaspora.

SEE ALSO: Diaspora; Judaism; Temple

## Baha'i

A universalist religion that arose out of a Shia Islamic sect in Iran in the 1800s. Its founder was Mirza Hussein Ali Nuri, who, along with his predecessor Mirza Ali Muhammad, was the leader of a sect known as the Babis (*Bab* means "gateway" in Arabic). The Babis, founded by Mirza Ali Muhammad in 1844, was based on the Shia belief that a twelfth imam, a successor to Muhammad, would appear to guide and teach the faithful. This prophet would be known as the Baha'ullah. The sect was suppressed by Iranian authorities, and Mirza Hussein, who claimed to be this Baha'ullah, was jailed. After his release in 1853 he moved to Constantinople, the capital of the Ottoman Empire, where he received the acclaim of the local Babi community, which began to call itself the Baha'i. Despite further oppression by Ottoman authorities, the sect continued to thrive. Mirza Hussein was followed by his son, Abd ol-Baha, who took the faith to western Europe and North America. This new leader accepted an earthbound leadership role, however, and did not claim to be a prophet.

The Baha'i movement remains strong in North America, western Europe, and around the world. It separated from Islamic sectarianism to become truly universal, preaching that all religions are equal and unified. Baha'is believe furthermore in gender equality, the importance of education of both sexes, and actively striving for world peace. Believers are enjoined to pray every day, to stay away from drugs and alcohol, and to practice monogamy. There are few regular rituals aside from an annual 19-day fast followed by commemorative feasting and prayer days on the first day of every month (the Baha'i calendar divides the year into 19 months of 19 days). Services are generally informal and are organized by an administrative structure based first on local, then on national and international elective bodies. There are an estimated 150 national governing bodies involving over 20,000 local communities, with hundreds of thousands of adherents. Baha'i remains strong in Iran, with some 300,000 adherents, although there it has suffered official persecution by Islamist officials since the nation's 1979 revolution.

SEE ALSO: imam; Shia (Shiite) Islam

## baptism

A fundamental Christian rite, or sacrament. In most churches, baptism signifies formal entrance into a Christian community. Although specific forms of the rite differ, virtually all baptisms involve the use of water and of the statement by the officiator, "I baptize you in the name of the Father, and of the Son, and of the Holy Spirit."

Baptism likely developed out of earlier Jewish rites that involved symbolic purification with water (such practices are common in Hinduism as well). According to the biblical Gospels, Jesus of Nazareth was baptized by John the Baptist prior to embarking on his own teachings, and in the Gospel according to Matthew, Jesus urges his followers to turn peoples of all nations into disciples by baptizing them. The early church fathers maintained the ritual in the first few centuries of Christianity, although they differed on whether it meant the lit-

eral rebirth of those baptized or was simply the symbol of conversion. Although most early converts were adults at the time of their baptism, infant baptism became an accepted practice in both Roman Catholicism and Protestantism, although some Protestants argued that infants should not be baptized since they do not make the decision on their own accord to enter into a Christian community. Another controversy that survives is whether baptism should involve full bodily immersion, the pouring of water over the head, or simply the sprinkling or placing of a few drops.

SEE ALSO: sacraments

## bar mitzvah/bat mitzvah

A Jewish ritual associated with coming of age. Jewish boys are considered to become bar mitzvah—that is, to reach religious adulthood—at age thirteen, and they celebrate this initiation on their thirteenth birthday. Jewish tradition holds that Jewish girls reach bat mitzvah, the female counterpart to bar mitzvah, on their twelfth birthday, reflecting the average ages of reaching puberty, but many non-Orthodox Jewish girls choose to celebrate their bat mitzvah on their thirteenth birthday, as boys do. Once they are bar mitzvah, boys are free to wear Jewish religious symbols and partake in public prayers. They are also called on to maintain the Jewish commandments. Girls are likewise considered responsible enough to take part as adults in proper ceremonies once they become bat mitzvah.

For boys, the center of the bar mitzvah ceremony is a public reading from the Torah in Hebrew. The service, usually held on the first Sabbath following the boy's birthday, also includes a formal acknowledgment by the father that his son has reached manhood. A family party usually follows the ceremony. The bat mitzvah ceremony is similar in Reform and Conservative Judaism, but some Orthodox Jews do not celebrate bat mitzvahs.

The custom arose among European Jewish communities during the Middle Ages, and until 1810 Jewish communities held common ceremonies for the confirmation of boys and girls. In 1810, however, Reform Jewish communities began staging separate bar mitzvahs. Other sects followed and some separately added the bat mitzvah.

SEE ALSO: Judaism; Orthodox Judaism; Reform Judaism

## Bhagavad Gita

An important and influential Hindu scripture, and in translation probably the most popular Hindu text of the last century. Written in Sanskrit, the Bhagavad Gita comprises some seven hundred verses in eighteen chapters from the epic Mahabharatha, although scholars believe it was actually composed separately and then added to the larger poem. It probably dates from the first two centuries A.D.

The Bhagavad Gita, commonly called the Gita, is a sort of conversation between the god Krishna and Arjuna, a member of one of the Mahabharatha's warrior clans, just before a great battle at Kurukshetra. To disguise his true identity, Krishna takes the form of Arjuna's charioteer, although he reveals his divinity to Arjuna. Poised on the battlefield, Arjuna rebels against the prospect of killing beloved relatives, friends, and teachers. In a set of teachings and instructions, Krishna convinces Arjuna of the necessity of joining the battle despite his misgivings. The god's wide range of arguments include, most notably, Arjuna's obligation to fulfill the dharma requirements of a member of Hinduism's kshatriya, or warrior caste, and the more philosophical notion that because the soul is eternal, no one who is killed truly disappears, but is reborn in a new body. Krishna also insists that it is not for humans to question the order of the universe or the purpose or will of the gods but to fulfill their earthly purposes and duties.

Krishna's description of Arjuna's dutiful conduct, and of religious conduct in general, can be summarized as taking three right paths to enlightenment. One path is through spiritual knowledge, or jnana yoga, commonly followed by gurus and ascetics. Another is through devotion, or bhakti yoga, generally through popular, daily worship. But the Gita mostly emphasizes the third right path, karma yoga, or right action. Right action is the performance of one's earthly duties with detachment, without concern for rewards or punishments or the self. Just as Arjuna should conduct himself on the field of battle, others should perform right action in their own spheres, and the Gita's central theme is therefore universally applicable. In the third of the Gita's eighteen teachings, Krishna asserts:

As the ignorant act with attachment
to actions, Arjuna,
so wise men should act with detachment
to preserve the world.
No wise man disturbs the understanding
of ignorant men attached to action;
he should inspire them,
performing all actions with discipline.
Actions are all affected
by the qualities of nature;
but deluded by individuality,
the self thinks, "I am the actor."
When he can discriminate
the actions of nature's qualities

and think, "The qualities depend on other qualities," he is detached.

SEE ALSO: Krishna; Mahabharatha; yoga

# bhakti

One of three paths to salvation, or enlightenment, in Hinduism and by far the most common of the three. The bhakti path is the devotional path, in contrast to the path of spiritual knowledge, generally pursued only by gurus or ascetics, and the path of right action, the performance of earthly duties with complete detachment from the self. The term is derived from a Sanskrit root word meaning "to share" and has come to imply not only devotion but sharing, love, and worship as well.

Bhakti can be found as far back in time as the Rig Veda, composed before 1000 B.C. In this Hindu scripture, gods are urged to demonstrate love and forgiveness to their devotees, while devotees sing the praises of the gods. Later texts were filled with examples of bhakti, perhaps most notably the relationship between Krishna and Arjuna in the Bhagavad Gita. During the first millennium A.D., bhakti became the common form of Hindu worship, as many writers and teachers began to emphasize the grace and other benign qualities of the gods rather than karma, or the consequences of action. A major influence in this was likely the Tamil poets of southern India who, beginning in the sixth century, produced a wide range of hymns in their own language devoted to Shiva, Vishnu, and other deities. These vernacular hymns helped to make the gods more accessible and understandable to ordinary Hindus than the often arcane philosophies and obscure Sanskrit of brahmin priests (although bhakti has a philosophical dimension of its own, reflected in the work of, among many others, the eleventh- and twelfth-century thinker Ramanuja). In the physical world, meanwhile, the construction of temples, temple offerings, public ceremonies, and even household shrines became important acts of bhakti expression.

The writing of bhakti poetry continued, with some of its greatest works appearing in the vernacular languages, during the twelfth through sixteenth centuries (and to a lesser degree such literature has been written to the present day). It has generally taken one of two forms. In the first, known as Saguna, poets often depict deities in humanist ways and examine the relationships between gods and people using human relationships as a model. One of the greatest examples of this form is the *Gitagovinda*, written by Jayadeva in the twelfth century. This erotic poem describes the love of Krishna for his beloved Radha, but devotees of Krishna and Vishnu also see it as an allegory of the love between the gods and their worshippers. Other notable Saguna poets include two women, Mahadevi in the twelfth century and Mirabia in the sixteenth century.

The second form of bhakti poetry is Nirguna poetry, which emphasizes the singular nature of the divine, asserting that God is simply a divine force known by many unnecessary names and worshipped in many unnecessary rituals. Among the greatest of these poets was Kabir, who lived from the late fifteenth to early sixteenth century. Kabir and other Nirguna poets urged simple meditation on the name of god. Neither form of poetry excludes the other, since Hindus recognize a diversity of paths toward devotion to, and reunion with, the divine.

SEE ALSO: Bhagavad Gita; Hinduism; puja

# bhikku/bhikkuni

A bhikku is a Buddhist monk. A bhikkuni is a Buddhist nun, the female equivalent of the monk accepted in some Buddhist sects. Monkhood or nunhood is a central tenet in Buddhist practice.

Bhikku likely derived their status in the years following the death of the original Buddha. The first ones bore some similarities to wandering Hindu ascetics who survived on charity, and the first Buddhist orders evolved from groups among the Buddha's original followers, who sought to live with minimal attachment to worldly things. In time, bhikku settled into established orders, called sangha, in dedicated monasteries still maintained by gifts and charity. A few monks, meanwhile, upheld the ideal of virtually complete detachment by going into forests or other isolated areas for solitary meditation.

The bhikku are most closely identified with Theravada Buddhism. Indeed, in Theravada countries such as Sri Lanka and Thailand they are the most visible manifestation of Buddhism, easily identifiable even on city streets by their shaved heads and saffron-colored robes. Believers, meanwhile, "make merit" by presenting monks with food or other offerings. Theravada bhikku can join monasteries after reaching the age of eight, after which they serve as novices for a number of years. While monks, the bhikku pledge to live according to a strict code of conduct that includes celibacy, never handling money, and never eating anything after noon. They are also forbidden from touching women, and in some traditions women are forbidden from handing anything directly to a bhikku; they must put down all items for him to pick up or place them in a begging bowl. Unlike Christian monks, Buddhist bhikku do not make a lifelong commit-

ment to their orders. Indeed, it is common for young men to serve for a year as a bhikku as a sort of rite of passage, and even older men return to monasteries to live as monks in temporary retreat from the world. Theravada bhikku are not formal priests, but they are nevertheless highly respected and often called on to give blessings or recite prayers at important events such as weddings or the openings of new buildings.

Bhikku are less common in Mahayana Buddhism, but they can be found in some sects such as Zen. There, monks likewise do not necessarily make lifetime commitments and agree to live according to strict rules governing work, hierarchy, and meditation.

Bhikkuni, like their male equivalents, emerged in the years following the death of the Buddha, who asserted that women should be as free as men to seek spiritual progress and service in this manner. There are numerous orders of Bhikkuni in both Theravada and Mahayana Buddhism, and their meditative practices and codes of behavior are similar to those of bhikku. These orders generally have lesser status than men's orders have, however, and far fewer women than men ever seek to join them. This is probably partly because, unlike bhikku, the bhikkuni receive little veneration from the lay community and have few public roles such as the invocation of blessings.

SEE ALSO: monasticism; Theravada Buddhism; sangha

# Bible

The holy scriptures of Judaism and Christianity. The word *Bible* is derived from the Greek word *biblia*, or "books"; hence, the Bible is a collection of sacred texts.

***Hebrew Bible, Old Testament*** The Jewish

version of this collection, commonly known as the Hebrew Bible, consists of 39 texts divided into 3 groups. Because some of these texts are combined, Jews number the total at 24 rather than 39. The first of the groups, the Torah, or "law," consists of the 5 books of Genesis, Exodus, Leviticus, Numbers, and Deuteronomy. These 5 books are collectively known as the Pentateuch. The second section, the Nevi'im, or "prophets," comprises the books of Joshua, Judges, 1 and 2 Samuel, 1 and 2 Kings, Isaiah, Jeremiah, Ezekiel, and the 12 prophets (Hosea, Joel, Amos, Obadiah, Jonah, Micah, Nahum, Habakkuk, Zephaniah, Haggai, Zechariah, and Malachi). The third section, the Ketuvim, or "writings," consists of the books of Psalms, Proverbs, Job, Daniel, Ezra, Nehemiah, 1 and 2 Chronicles, and the five "scrolls" (the Song of Solomon, Ruth, Lamentations, Ecclesiastes, and Esther). This canon of sacred texts is sometimes referred to in Judaism as the Tanakh, derived from an acronym of the first letters and syllables of the names of the three sections. Originally written in Hebrew, the Tanakh was well established by the first century B.C., and it was translated into Greek, in a text known as the Septuagint, and Aramaic in the same era.

The Hebrew Bible remains the core of Jewish teachings, which as a whole are also known as Torah. Much subsequent Jewish thought and scholarship, such as that contained in the Talmud, is commentary or elaboration on the Hebrew Bible. The text also provides the early history of the Jews as well as descriptions of their culture, providing the basis for Jewish cultural identity as well. Historically and in the present day, it is common for synagogues to maintain copies of parts of the Hebrew Bible, the "Torah scrolls," in places of honor and reverence.

In Christianity, the Bible consists of two parts. The first is the Hebrew Bible, which is commonly known as the Old Testament in the Christian tradition. Versions of the Old Testament differ among the major branches of Christianity. The Roman Catholic and Eastern Orthodox versions contain numerous books beyond the original 39. Many of these books are the so-called Apocrypha, which Jewish leaders originally left out but which early Christians deemed canonical. Most were part of the Greek translation, the Septuagint. Protestant Christianity views only the 39 texts contained in the original Hebrew Bible as canonical, but arranges them in a different order than they appear in the Hebrew Bible.

*New Testament* The New Testament is the second part of the Bible for Christians. This collection consists of 27 books. The first 4 are the Gospels according to Matthew, Mark, Luke, and John, histories of the life and teachings of Jesus of Nazareth. The Gospels are followed by the Acts of the Apostles, the 14 letters (or Epistles) attributed to Paul, 7 further Epistles, and the book of Revelation. The texts were written in Greek sometime between A.D. 40 and 140 and, aside from 13 of Paul's Epistles, their specific authorship is uncertain according to biblical scholars. The collection was compiled by early Christian leaders who began to consider their own texts just as authoritative as those of the Hebrew Bible. The New Testament reached its current form in the fourth century and was eventually translated into the languages of early Christian communities: Latin, Armenian, Ethiopian, and Coptic (for Egypt). Translations of the entire Bible, both New and Old Testaments, into major European languages were not widely known until the sixteenth century, spurred by the invention of the moveable-type printing press around 1440. The first major English edition of the Bible was the monumental King James Version, published in 1611. Many others have followed.

For Christians, the New Testament provides the "good news" offered by Jesus Christ concerning human redemption and the means to salvation. But the New Testament did not entirely supplant the Old Testament, which Christians reinterpreted in light of New Testament concepts such as the Trinity. Unlike Judaism, the Christian tradition is not built around interpretation and reinterpretation of scripture, although different understandings of it and uses of it have arisen nonetheless. Modern schools of biblical criticism, for instance, urge further research into the authorship of the New Testament books as well as a thorough grasp of the historical context in which it was written. Some Protestants, on the other hand, assert that the Bible is the literal word of God, expressing eternal truths that cannot be "contextualized." In the Roman Catholic and Orthodox traditions, meanwhile, scripture must be mediated by the church itself.

*The Bible's Significance in Islam* The Bible is also a sacred text in Islam, and Muslims consider both Jews and Christians "Peoples of the Book" because of their trust in holy scripture. But Muslims view the Bible as an incomplete or compromised version of God's word, unlike the perfected version contained in the Qur'an. One reason for this has to do with beliefs in the nature of the authorship of the Bible's texts. Most Jews and Christians accept that they were written with divine inspiration but not literally dictated to their authors by God or his agents. This left open the possibility for human mistakes or misinterpretations in the Muslim view. Muslims believe that the Qur'an was the result of God's dictation and is therefore a more perfect revelation than either the Hebrew Bible or the New Testament.

SEE ALSO: Peoples of the Book; Qur'an; Torah

# bodhisattva

In Buddhism, someone who has taken a vow to become a Buddha, a fully enlightened one. The first, and prime example, is Siddhartha Gautama himself, the first (and to some, only) Buddha of the current historical age. He was reincarnated into a number of lives as a bodhisattva before, in his final life, he achieved full enlightenment. Then, upon his death, he entered nirvana. Buddhist texts suggest that once a potential bodhisattva takes his vow, he begins the first of ten spiritual stages that altogether are thought to last thousands of years. Through this path the bodhisattva attempts to gradually achieve "perfection," or the six characteristics of giving, morality, acceptance, strength, meditation, and wisdom.

Although all Buddhists accept the concept, bodhisattvas play a far larger role in Mahayana Buddhism than in its Theravada counterpart. Indeed, in Mahayana Buddhism bodhisattvas receive the sort of devotion that other religions accord their gods, incarnations, and prophets and often bodhisattvas are awarded more attention than the Buddha himself. The most well known of these figures are Maitreya, Amhitabha, and Avalokitesvara (who in one form is Kuan Yin, the Chinese "goddess" of mercy). For Mahayanists such figures represent an improvement on the Theravadan ideal of arhat (one who reaches the highest level of personal freedom from suffering available to humans). Bodhisattvas, by contrast, are considered to have chosen to postpone their own entrance into nirvana to assist others in various ways. They exist and act according to the ideal that compassion is equal to wisdom. Since Buddhist texts do not mention how bodhisattvas postpone their own enlightenment to demonstrate compassion, it is possible that the focus on them in the Mahayana tradition is a relic of earlier or non-Buddhist beliefs in generous gods or spirits who are omnipresent and have great powers to give assistance in individual lives.

SEE ALSO: Buddhism; Mahayana Buddhism; Maitreya

# bohdi

A Sanskrit and Pali word meaning "awakened," which refers to related concepts in Buddhism and Hinduism. Most commonly it refers to the experience of becoming enlightened, as opposed to the ultimate state of enlightenment known as nirvana. Boh-di is achieved when one reaches true mental clarity about the nature of the universe and of human existence. The epitome of bohdi is the example of the original Buddha, who reached this clarity while meditating under a tree; the tree itself has been known since as the bohdi tree. Many Buddhist temples plant a cutting of a similar tree on their grounds to signify the presence of the Buddhist dharma. In Hinduism, meanwhile, bohdi refers to perfect knowledge as derived from the intellect.

SEE ALSO: bodhisattva; Buddhism

# Bon

The pre-Buddhist religion of Tibet, and a strong influence on Tibetan Buddhism. Bon, which is still practiced among small groups on the Tibetan frontiers, is a shamanistic faith centered around such practices as blood sacrifice to propitiate evil spirits and the institution of soothsayers believed capable of reading signs and divining the future. Bon adherents worship a sky god, the embodiment of positive forces, who is manifested in the kingship, as well as a lesser pantheon of gods of the atmosphere, earth, and underworld. The term bon itself probably comes from a ritual chant used by believers.

Tibetan Buddhists still view the Bon atmosphere, earth, and underworld gods as lesser deities among their versions of the Buddhist bodhisattvas. It is also likely that their belief in the Dalai Lama as the reincarnation of earlier lamas is derived from Bon notion of divine kingship. The triumph of Buddhism over Bon during conflicts among Tibet's ruling clans in the eighth and ninth centuries did not prevent some merging of the two religious traditions.

SEE ALSO: Tibetan Buddhism

# Brahma

A major Hindu god. Brahma, characterized as Lord Brahma (the Creator), is considered the first of the three gods that make up the Hindu Trinity, along with Vishnu (the preserver) and Shiva (the destroyer). Brahma is also characterized as the archetypal priest. Most artistic portrayals of Brahma show him as an elderly yet strong bearded man holding a set of prayer beads or, alternatively, as a figure in red with four heads and four arms. The four heads represent the four directions of the compass, while he holds in his four hands a priest's water pot, a bow, a sceptre, and the Vedas (Hindu sacred texts). His main consort is Sarasvati.

Although Brahma figured prominently in early Hindu texts such as the Ramayana and Mahabharatha, and versions of Brahma also appear in Buddhism and Jainism, few Hindus worship Brahma directly today. Shiva and Vishnu appear much more frequently in worship, and Brahma has become a relatively distant deity.

SEE ALSO: Shiva, trimurti; Vishnu

## Brahman

In Hinduism, the Supreme God, the one eternal, omnipresent spirit, the divine essence of the universe. The Sanskrit word *brahman*, meaning "growth" or "expansion," is in the language's neutral gender; Brahma is the masculine form of the word and connotes the Hindu creator god. The use of the neutral form reinforces the notion that Brahman is irreducible; it cannot be reduced to any specific deity or force smaller than itself, although it is this divine force that permeates the universe and all creation.

The term likely came into general usage during the age of the Vedas (ca. 1200–600 B.C.), when priests used it as a sacred chant. The understanding of the term later was enlarged to mean that Brahman was the source of all ritual power and of the gods themselves. One way of characterizing the goal of Hindu belief is to assert that one must achieve the understanding that there is no difference between Brahman, the universal spirit, and atman, the individual "soul." In other words, one must realize the divine within oneself as well as in all creation.

SEE ALSO: atman; Vedas

## Brahmanas

A group of important early Hindu texts, dating from 1000 B.C. to 600 B.C. and possibly even earlier than that in ancient oral traditions. The Brahmanas are commentaries on the Vedas, intended to guide priests in carrying out sacrifices and other

rituals by making the somewhat obscure and vague language of the Vedas more accessible. In this they join the Upanishads and other groups of texts in elaborating central parts of early Hindu belief and practice. Among them are the Aitareya and Kaushitaki, which comment on the Rig Veda, and the Satapatha-Brahmanas, which are attached to the Yajurveda. This last is the best known of the Brahmanas.

SEE ALSO: Puranas, Smriti; Vedas

## brahmin

A member of the highest of the four Hindu castes, or divisions of society. The brahmin caste emerged as an identifiable class during the Vedic period (ca. 1200–600 B.C.) when Hindu belief and practice were becoming somewhat standardized. At that point the brahmins were the priestly caste, responsible for carrying out important rituals and for mastering and carrying forward the spiritual knowledge contained in the Vedas. According to Hindu mythology, the brahmins were created from the head of Brahma, the creator god, while the other three castes were created from lower, or "lesser," parts of Brahma. Not even the second caste, the kshatriya or kingly caste, could rule directly over the brahmins, and early Hindu ethical teachings asserted that to kill a brahmin was one of the gravest of all sins.

Brahmins remain among the elites of Hindu society as their historical priestly status implies that they are closer to moksha, or release from the wheel of existence, than other Hindus. The sense also persists that they are likewise closer to the gods than other Hindus. Relatively few brahmins serve as priests; indeed they can be found in virtually any job or profession. Nevertheless, leadership in ceremonies is reserved for members of this caste and they might set themselves apart by certain caste markings on the forehead or, in men, a sacred thread draped across the right shoulder. The name is also commonly spelled "brahman."

SEE ALSO: caste; Laws of Manu

## Buddha

In Buddhism, a person who has achieved ultimate enlightenment. The term is derived from Sanskrit and Pali words meaning "awakened one." One becomes a Buddha when one is awakened to the true nature of reality; that is, that the world is illusory and full of suffering but that it is possible to transcend that suffering and achieve nirvana.

Buddhist tradition identifies three general uses of the term. The first and most common usage refers to the original awakened one, Siddhartha Gautama, the founder of Buddhism. Gautama Buddha, or the Buddha, as he is known by one of several names, became enlightened as the result of a spiritual search thought to have taken place in the sixth century B.C. He then became a teacher exemplifying one who has followed the path to enlightenment. Some Buddhists describe him as a physician who has diagnosed the cause of humankind's spiritual ills and provided a cure.

The second main use of the term is the one most common in Theravada Buddhism. This school recognizes a rare few people in history in addition to Gautama Buddha who have achieved Buddha-hood. Most human beings cannot hope to achieve the full awakened state, although it is possible to achieve a state of arhat-hood, that of a Buddhist saint.

The Mayahana Buddhist tradition provides the third common usage of the term.

For Mahayanists, many figures have achieved enlightenment. Those Buddhas who compassionately choose not to enter nirvana immediately but instead remain to serve humankind are known as bodhisattvas. Moreover, Mahayanists teach that all beings possess an essential "Buddha-nature" linking them to the possibility of full awakening in this lifetime.

SEE ALSO: bodhisattva; Buddhism; Siddhartha Gautama

## Buddhism

The diverse set of religiuns traditions based on the teachings of the Buddha, Siddhartha Gautama, who lived in the sixth and fifth centuries B.C. Buddhism originated in northern India, and over the course of many centuries spread westward as far as Afghanistan and eastward through eastern Asia, from Mongolia in the north to Indonesia in the south. It remains one of the dominant religions of eastern Asia today, practiced by an estimated 300 million people. Emigration and conversion also contributed to the rise of Buddhism in Western countries in the twentieth century. In contrast to other world religions, Buddhism offers no belief in gods. Instead, its emphasis is on the achievement of enlightenment or awakening, of a true insight into the nature of reality, and on the serenity and wisdom that come with that insight.

*Origins and History* The founder of Buddhism was Siddhartha Gautama, an Indian prince, who according to the Mahayana Buddhist tradition lived from 565 to 486 B.C. (other Buddhist traditions use different dates). Siddhartha gave up a life of luxury to seek the cause of human suffering, a reality that had been hidden from him while growing up, as well as some way to end that suffering. His searches eventu-

*Visitors walk the grounds at the Buddhist Peace Shrine in Kyoto, Japan, where Mahayana Buddhism is the dominant form of the faith.* © RIC ERGENBRIGHT/CORBIS

ally ended in a period of meditation, during which he realized that the cause of suffering was desire, or attachment to worldly things. Since those things, which included power and position as well as material wealth, were only temporary and illusory, too much attachment to them could only lead to suffering. This realization enabled Siddhartha to become an enlightened one, or Buddha, one who had been awakened to the true nature of things. He began to teach his message of awakening to a small group of students, the first Buddhist monks. He urged them to follow a middle path between the extremes of denial and indulgence, to realize what he called the Four Noble Truths, which explained the source of suffering, and to follow the Eightfold Path, by which one could be released from suffering. The ultimate end of

this path was nirvana, an eternal state of being that might be described simply as "the great peace."

Buddhism grew steadily in the centuries following the death, and entrance into nirvana, of the original Buddha. Monks compiled the original Buddhist texts from Siddhartha's teachings and from their own debates and meditations, most importantly the Tripitaka, or "Three Baskets" of wisdom. The new faith remained mostly confined to monks and ascetics, an offshoot of Hinduism, until the Indian king Ashoka (r. 269–232 B.C.) converted to Buddhism in response to his horror over the meaninglessness and destruction of war. Ashoka, seeking to rule according to the principle of ahimsa, or nonviolence, gained many new converts among ordinary Indians and his children helped to spread Buddhism to

Sri Lanka. There it became the dominant faith and Sri Lanka proved an effective base for its spread to Southeast Asia, mostly after the first century A.D. Sri Lankan Buddhists came to believe that their form of Buddhism was closest to that practiced and taught by the original Buddha, while their counterparts in India diverged into several different schools developed around such matters as meditational practices and the organization of monasteries.

Buddhism spread slowly from India to China, often via wandering monks and ascetics, taking firm hold there by the fifth and sixth centuries A.D. In China, Buddhism flourished with the foundation of numerous new schools, and it became integrated with the native traditions of Confucianism and Daoism. From China, Buddhism spread to Korea, Vietnam, and Japan in a process that began around A.D. 700 and continued for centuries. As in China, numerous schools of Buddhism emerged in those areas and merged with local traditions such as Shinto in Japan. Meanwhile, an esoteric form of Buddhism influenced by Tantric Hinduism took hold in Tibet, influencing areas to the west and north of China proper. Back in India, however, Buddhism largely disappeared in the eleventh and twelfth centuries, targeted by Islamic invaders and conquerors.

*Central Beliefs of Buddhism* Following the teachings of the original Buddha, almost all Buddhists believe that the true source of suffering, or dukkha, is attachment or desire and that, as the Four Noble Truths indicate, it is possible to overcome that desire and to reach, or nearly reach, nirvana. The proper Buddhist dhamma, or path, is described by the Eightfold Path, a list of the most beneficial attitudes and approaches toward other beings and to-

ward earthly life and activities. Buddhists are urged to hold all life sacred, to practice kindness, and to avoid those activities that perpetuate ignorance about the true, illusory nature of things. The most effective way to do this is to serve, at least for a time, as a Buddhist monk (bhikku) or nun (bhikkuni). This allows the devotee to direct his or her entire energies to the Buddhist path. Living in or joining monasteries is not absolutely necessary, however, since it is also possible to follow the Eightfold Path in ordinary life.

Like Hindus, Buddhists believe in reincarnation, the rebirth of the individual human soul in new bodies over hundreds of lifetimes. Also like Hindus, Buddhists hope to gain release from this cycle of birth, death, and rebirth. To do so, to reach full nirvana, is to achieve Buddha-hood, a state of full enlightenment. What enables a person to continue on the path toward nirvana, aside from following the Buddhist dhamma in general, is the accumulation of good karma, often by performing good deeds. Likewise, the building up of bad karma might result in one being reborn further away from rather than closer to enlightenment. The various Buddhist traditions differ on exactly what earns good and bad karma—some, for example, reinforce social customs such as the lesser status of women and others reject such customs—but virtually all agree that living an immoral, greedy, or unkind life will simply result in many more rebirths and many more lifetimes of suffering and discontent.

Though Buddhism is a religion with no gods, it offers instead many Buddhas and bodhisattvas as ideals, exemplars, and sources of solace and inspiration. The Buddhist traditions differ on the number of accepted Buddhas and on the possibility of achieving Buddha-hood; at one extreme, some claim that there can only be one true Buddha in each historical era, and that the Buddha of the current era, Siddhartha Gautama, has already appeared. Bodhisattvas, meanwhile, are enlightened souls who, in some Buddhist sects, are thought to have delayed entrance into nirvana in order to assist human souls. These bodhisattvas are often thought of as gods in Chinese, Japanese, and other traditions. In general Buddhists do not believe in an afterlife, although conceptions of heaven and hell are often used metaphorically in Buddhist folklore and literature. The major exception are Pure Land Buddhists, who maintain faith in a "western paradise" presided over by the Buddha Amhitaba, where one can achieve full enlightenment and dwell in nirvana.

*Three Main Branches of Buddhism* The three major branches of Buddhism are Theravada Buddhism, Mahayana Buddhism, and Tibetan, or Tantric, Buddhism. Theravada Buddhism is the predominant form of the faith in Sri Lanka, Myanmar (Burma), Thailand, Laos, and Cambodia. Adherents believe it is the closest of all forms of Buddhism to that practiced by the original Buddha and his first followers. Theravada Buddhists focus on the path to individual enlightenment. For the most devout this requires joining and submitting to a monastic order, or sangha; even many less devout Theravada Buddhists join a sangha for a year or two. Self-discipline and meditation, if pursued diligently and properly, might result in a believer's becoming an arhat, a kind of Buddhist saint. For Theravadins, full enlightenment is considered impossible in one's current lifetime. Arhat-hood, however, is possible for the truly devout. The focus of ordinary believers' religious life is on following a relevant version of the Eightfold Path and on "making merit" through good works and on building up good karma. Ceremonies and festivals are often conflated with those commemorating the changing of the seasons, such as the beginning of the Southeast Asian monsoons. The most important Theravada holiday is Buddha's Day, celebrated on the day of the full moon during the Buddhist month of Visakha (April or May). Then, believers visit monasteries and temples to grant offerings to Buddha images as well as listen to lessons and stories.

Mahayana Buddhists consider Theravada Buddhism the "narrow path" or "lesser vehicle" (to enlightenment). They believe Mahayana Buddhism, which emerged out of the diversity of Buddhist sects in India around the first century B.C., is the alternative "broader path" or "greater vehicle." Mahayana Buddhism is the dominant form of the faith in China, Korea, Japan, and Vietnam. At its heart is the belief in the presence of bodhisattvas, a notion not found in Theravada Buddhism. Bodhisattvas, these benign spirits, are constantly available to help one along the path to enlightenment, or even to provide more mundane benefits such as safety while traveling or success in school or business. Pure Land Buddhism is a Mahayana school, offering the hope of a beneficial afterlife. Zen, or Ch'an as it is known in China, is another important Mahayana sect. It offers to devotees the experience of enlightenment in this lifetime through study, thought, or meditation. Mahayana festivals and ceremonies vary greatly depending on national traditions, Buddhist sects, non-Buddhist influences, and other factors. Some common features include the giving of offerings and prayers to Buddhas and bodhisattvas and festivals devoted to important texts, such as the Lotus and Diamond Sutras.

Tibetan Buddhism differs from its counterparts more in terms of ritual than basic belief. Tibetan Buddhists worship Buddhas and bodhisattvas in vivid and colorful forms, using prayer wheels, mandalas, and other ritual objects. They believe that they hold a spark of the divine within them that might be released through such worship or through meditation. Tibetan Buddhism is also distinct in the level of devotion of most of its adherents, who make religion the central part of their daily lives to an extent that most other Buddhists do not. The head of Tibetan Buddhism, the Dalai Lama, remains perhaps the world's most recognizable Buddhist.

***Buddhism in the Modern World*** Buddhism continues to flourish. The nature of the faith, its emphasis on release from suffering and detachment from material desire, has allowed Buddhists to adapt their faith and practice fairly easily to the modern fast-paced, highly technologized world. In some Buddhist countries practical reforms have taken place within religious institutions, allowing women or laypeople, for instance, to take on larger roles. The major exception is China, whose official atheism has resulted in the repression of official Buddhism within China and in occupied Tibet; the Dalai Lama, for example, lives in exile in India. Even in China, however, Buddhism is too much a part of traditional culture to be fully suppressed. In the West, immigrants have implanted Buddhist traditions of all kinds while many Westerners, perhaps seeking solace from the pressures and dissatisfactions of industrialized society and consumerism, have turned to Buddhism as an alternative to Western faiths. Zen, in particular, has proven extremely popular in the West. Buddhism has even been revived in India, the land of its birth, where Tibetan exiles, converts from Hinduism's lower castes, and others have established large and vibrant communities.

SEE ALSO: Four Noble Truths; Mahayana Buddhism; Siddhartha Gautama; Theravada Buddhism; Tibetan Buddhism; Zen Buddhism

## calendars

Many of the world's major religious traditions have their own calendars. These calendars serve many functions, from the organization of liturgy and ritual to the sequence of festivals and holidays to expressions of beliefs in the nature of time.

*Hinduism* The Hindu calendar dates back to about 1000 B.C. It is a lunar calendar, with each of the 12 lunar months consisting of a full cycle of the phases of the moon. Since the 12 lunar months add up only to 354 days per year, Hindus reconcile the lunar calendar with the solar one of 365 days per year by adding an extra month every 30 months. Religious thinking further divides the 12 months into halves, with each month containing 15 "bright" days and 15 "dark" days. The year, meanwhile, is divided into 6 seasons of 2 months each: spring, hot season, rainy season, autumn, winter, and cold season. Many human activities are coordinated with the cycles of the larger universe through the celebration of festivals defined by the movements of the stars and planets, such as the autumn festival of Divali. Hindus do not pinpoint a moment of Creation, since they commonly view the gods and the cosmos as being timeless.

*Confucianism and Other Chinese Traditions* The Chinese use both the lunar and solar calendars, and by their calculations the two coincide every nineteenth year. The solar calendar is primarily used in reference to seasonal weather, while the lunar calendar is used in daily and festival life.

The largest annual festival is the Chinese New Year. Each new year begins with the second new moon following the winter solstice, in the last 10 days of January or the first 20 days of February. Months are associated with the 5 elements that make up the earth and the universe, according to traditional Chinese thought: water, fire, earth, metal, and wood. Years are generally associated with one of 12 animals that, Chinese mythology indicates, have specific dominant characteristics and influences. The year 2007, for example, is the year of the pig; 2008 is the year of the rat.

*Buddhism* Buddhism maintains no specific calendar system; instead, believers generally have adapted Buddhists events and celebrations into the calendars mostly used locally. Buddhists in China, for instance, use the Chinese calendar system described above. The major exception is that in Theravada Buddhist countries the common dating system begins with the year of the enlightenment of Siddhartha Gautama, the first Buddha in the current historical era. The year 2006 is therefore year 2549 of the Theravadin Buddhist calendar.

*Judaism* Judaism employs the lunar calendar, dividing the year into 12 months known by Babylonian names given them during the Babylonian Exile of the sixth century B.C. Reconciliation with the solar calendar is achieved by adding extra months 7 times every 19 years around the time of February or March. The first month of the Jewish calendar, known as Tishri, takes place in September or Octo-

ber. The festival of Rosh Hashanah includes the celebration of this new year.
Other Jewish holidays are scheduled very
precisely using this calendar; Passover takes
place during 8 days of the month of Nisan
(March or April) and Hanukkah lasts for 8
days beginning on the 25th day of the
month of Kislev (November or December).
It was the Jews who first divided each week
into 7 days; an interesting feature of the
Jewish week is that days are considered to
begin and end at sunset. Pious Jews believe that the Creation took place in 3761
B.C.; therefore, 2007 is the year 5768. In
daily life, however, most Jews use the
Christian, or Gregorian, calendar, substi-
tuting B.C.E. (before the common era) for
B.C. (before Christ) and C.E. (common era)
for A.D. for anno domini (the year of our
Lord).

*Christianity* Christianity currently employs
the Gregorian solar calendar, named for
Pope Gregory XIII, which replaced the so-
called Julian calendar, also solar in construction. In 1582 Gregory realized that
the Julian calendar was 10 days ahead of
the actual solar calendar, so he instituted a
general reform to correct the discrepancy.
Some Eastern Orthodox Christians continue to use the Julian calendar, which,
due to ongoing discrepancies, is now 12
days ahead of the Gregorian. The custom
of designating the years following the birth
of Christ as anno domini, or "year of our
Lord," began in the sixth century. Some
Christians believe that the world was created in 4004 B.C., a notion put forward by
sixteenth-century Irish clergyman and
scholar James Ussher, who drew the conclusion through a study of biblical chro-
nologies and other resources.

The Christian religious calendar of festivals echoes the coming and life of Jesus
Christ. It starts with the pre-Christmas

and Christmas season of Advent, followed
by the Epiphany, which begins on January
6 and lasts for 3 Sundays. Ash Wednesday
introduces the fasting period of Lent,
which is to last roughly 45 days until Holy
Week, the climax of which is Easter Sunday. Easter season itself continues for 40
more days until Pentecost. According to
the principle of organizing the calendar by
Sundays, the remaining Sundays between
Pentecost and Advent are numbered simply "after Pentecost." Christianity recognizes 3 kinds of festival periods: Sundays,
"moveable" feasts such as Easter, whose
dates change every year, and "immoveable"
feasts, the best known of which is Christmas, December 25.

*Islam* The islamic calendar begins with the
hijra, the prophet Muhammad's journey
to exile from Mecca to Medina in A.D. 622,
which is the year A.H. 1 (after hijra). Muslims also use the lunar calendar, dividing
the year into 12 months of 29 or 30 days
each for a total of 354 days. The Islamic
tradition makes no attempt to coordinate
the lunar with the solar calendars, so for
every 100 years of the solar calendar, there
are 103 Muslim years. The year 2007 will
therefore be mostly A.H. 1428 rather than
A.H. 1385. For this reason, also, the timing
of the festivals fixed in the Muslim calendar change greatly when the solar calendar
is used. The fasting month of Ramadan,
for instance, might take place at any point
of the solar year. The month of Muharram, meanwhile, marks the Islamic new
year and is the occasion for celebration
across the Muslim world as well as elaborate commemorations of martyrdom
among Shia Muslims. Many Muslim areas
have made adaptations to the solar calendar for practical purposes, with Turkey using the Gregorian calendar in civil life and

Iran devising a religious calendar based on the solar year.

# caliph

From the Arabic word *khalifa*, meaning "successor," the title of caliph commonly denotes successors to the prophet Muhammad as the head of the Islamic community in both a religious and political sense. The first four caliphs—Abu Bakr, Omar, Uthman, and Ali—are known as the "right-guided" caliphs among most Muslims because they bore close connections to the Prophet himself. All contributed to early ideas about the faith, such as the desire to expand Islam and uphold Islamic law, as well as to its administrative functions. The first four caliphs were followed by those belonging to the Ummayad dynasty (661–750), the Abbasid dynasty (750–1517), and the sultans of the Turkish Ottoman Empire (1517–1924). The Turks, now citizens of a secular state, abolished the title in 1924. In addition to these mainstream figures, others have laid claim to the title of caliph as well, notably the Fatimid rulers of Egypt (909–1171), and the issue of legitimate succession is one of the most bitter conflicts in Islamic history.

Sunni and Shia Muslims have different interpretations of a caliph's legitimacy. Among the Sunni, caliphs are supposed to be members of the Arabian Quraysh tribe to which Muhammad belonged. This is apparently not a firm requirement, as the Ottoman sultans were not related to the tribe. Moreover, the Sunni consider caliphs to be earthly authorities only. For the Shia, caliphs are supposed to be direct lineal descendants of Muhammad, and they view the office as being divinely ordained. The Shia consider the first three "right-guided" caliphs to be illegitimate. Ali, the Prophet's son-in-law, is the first caliph in the Shia tradition.

SEE ALSO: caliphate; Islam; Shia (Shiite) Islam; Sunni Islam

# caliphate

In the broadest sense, the leadership of the global community of Islam. The institution of the caliphate began with the death of Muhammad, the founder of Islam, in 632. The title of caliph was granted to his successors as leaders of the 'umma, the universal Islamic community. The legitimate election of caliphs has been one of the most contentious issues in Islamic history, although the Sunni branch of Islam, to which some 90 percent of believers belong, accepts a fairly straightforward line of caliphs. In this narrower sense the caliphates were the regimes governed by these historical caliphs. Some of these caliphates ruled substantial empires and were leading military, economic, and cultural powers, a reflection of Islam's growth and influence in world history. They also reflect the blurred boundary between religion and political authority in Islam.

The first of these was the Ummayad caliphate. It was established in 661 by Mu'awiyya, a member of the Ummayad clan of the Quraysh tribe, to which Muhammad had belonged. The new caliph transferred the administrative center of Islam from Medina to Damascus in Syria, although the religious centers of the faith remained Medina and, first and foremost, Mecca. The empire itself spread rapidly, and by 732 the Ummayads controlled territories stretching from Spain in the west to the borders of India in the east. Their march into Europe was halted only by the Germanic, Roman Catholic warlord Charles Martel at the historic Battle of Tours in 732. The cultural center of the

Ummayad empire was Spain, where trade, learning, and the arts flourished and the contributions of minority groups, notably Jews, was welcome. But the caliphs ruled brutally elsewhere, forestalling much innovation in Islamic scholarship and inspiring rebellion among non-Arabs such as the Iranians and among splinter Islamic sects. In 750 the last Ummayad caliph was assassinated in Egypt, although relatives continued to reign in Spain for several more centuries.

The Ummayads were replaced by the Abbasids, who were named for al-Abbas, one of Muhammad's uncles and the scion of another important Qurayshi clan. The first Abbasid caliph, al-Saffab, gained his renown for his assassinations of Ummayads. His successor, al-Mansur, founded the city of Baghdad and transferred his capital there. Baghdad soon became one of the world's greatest and richest cities, a center of trade, scholarship, science, and the arts. The most famous of the Abbasid caliphs is Harun al-Rashid (736–809), whose court is the setting for the telling of the *Thousand and One Nights*, one of the great classics of world literature. Other Abbasids encouraged the translation from Greek into Arabic of numerous classical texts, helping give rise to what were then some of the world's greatest advances in medicine and other sciences. Abbasid contact with India, meanwhile, helped introduce into the Middle East and Europe the "Arabic" number system based on the symbols 0–9, which had been devised by Hindu thinkers. The Baghdad enviroment also encouraged and facilitated the work of some of the greatest Islamic thinkers, including al-Tabari, Ibn Sina, and al-Ghazali, giving rise to the complex of works that supported the sunna, the mainstream body of Islamic scholarship and interpretation.

Over time the Abbasid empire splintered, weakened by outside invasions and the rise of centers of power outside of Baghdad. From 909 to 1157 one of its main challengers was the Shia Fatimid dynasty, which had risen to power in Egypt. The Fatimids claimed that their leaders, not the Abbasids, were the legitimate successors of the Prophet. The other major challenge was more strictly political and military in nature. It came from the Turks, warlike groups of former nomads from Central Asia who settled in the Middle East and converted to Islam. The Seljuk Turks slowly took possession of much Abbasid territory and, in 1055, sacked Baghdad. The caliphate, however, was based on proper descent and on leadership of the global Islamic community, not on sheer military might, and the Seljuks were not able to establish a legitimate claim to the caliphate. The Abbasid caliphate survived until 1258 or 1517, depending on the criteria used, although it controlled little of its former empire by either measure. In 1258 the last leader of the main branch of the clan was killed by invading Mongols. A subsidiary branch remained in power in Cairo, Egypt, until 1517.

That year Cairo was overtaken by the Ottoman Turks, whose empire across the Middle East and southeastern Europe had been expanding since the 1300s. It was the Ottoman sultans who next held the status of caliphs in mainstream Islam, especially after their territory grew to incorporate Mecca and Medina, giving them responsibility for the protection of those holy sites. Broad interpretations of the sunna, devised during the Abbasid period, made it possible for most Muslims to accept the sultans even though they were neither Arab nor related in any way to Muhammad's tribe. The political decline of the Ottoman Empire in the 1700s and 1800s corresponded with a decline in the global power of Islam, especially in comparison with the rise of European nations. The institution of the caliphate was abolished in 1924 by Kemal Ataturk, a modernizing leader of Turkey, which by that time had lost its territorial possessions beyond Turkey itself.

Shia Muslims have never accepted this line of caliphs. They hold that all such leaders, who are more properly referred to in the Shia tradition as imams, must be of Muhammad's direct lineage. The first proper caliph, therefore, was Ali, Muhammad's cousin and son-in-law, who ruled from 656 to 661, when he was assassinated by Mu'awiyya, the first Ummayad. The Egyptian Fatimids were also held to be broadly legitimate due to their alleged descent from Fatima, Muhammad's daughter and Ali's wife.

SEE ALSO: caliph; companions of the Prophet; Shia (Shiite) Islam

## Calvinism

A major branch of Protestant Christianity based on the teachings of the French-Swiss reformer John Calvin (1509–1564) and Calvin's successor as head of their Genevan church, Theodore Beza (1519–1605). Calvin's most important writing, the *Institutes of the Christian Religion*, lays out the basis of the Calvinist belief, which is that true Christian belief must be reflected in daily life and behavior, and in the mid-1500s he and Beza established a brief Calvinist theocracy in the city of Geneva. There life was organized by series of strict guidelines on such matters as dress and sexual behavior, and wrongdoers were subject to church-based disciplinary action. Roman Catholicism was completely banned.

Among the central tenets of Calvinism is a belief in the literal truth of the Bible and in the complete sovereignty of God. Also important was the notion of predestination, or the belief that God elects those who are to be saved and those who are to be damned, and there is no action one can take on earth to change that fate. Calvinists believe, however, that righteous living, and even worldly success, are signs that one is a member of the elect. In any case, Calvinists are supposed to act according to the dictates of God's commandments literally and in all phases of daily life.

A variety of Calvinist churches arose and became highly influential. Among them were the Presbyterian and Reformed Churches, each of which became a national church in Scotland and the Netherlands, respectively. Puritanism, another name for the English Congregationalist denomination, is also descended from Calvinism.

SEE ALSO: Luther, Martin; Protestantism; Reformation

## canon

The texts or collections of texts that a religion deems authoritative. Although in some religions, notably Christianity and Islam, these texts are generally considered by believers to come from God, the process of writing or assembling them can also be traced historically. Of the major religions, the central canonical texts are: Vedas, Upanishads, Puranas, and the Bhagavad Gita (Hinduism); Tripitaka (Buddhism); Tanakh and Talmud (Judaism); the Bible, both Old and New Testaments (Christianity); the Qur'an (Islam); the Five Classics and Four Books (Confucianism); and the Dao De Jing (Daoism). In many cases sects within these religions have added other authoritative texts to their canons, such as the Diamond

Sutra and Lotus Sutra in Mahayana Buddhism.

SEE ALSO: Bible; Qur'an; Vedas

# Cao Dai

A major religious sect that emerged in southern Vietnam in 1926. It was a syncretic movement, attempting to bring together many different beliefs in a Vietnam split by different interest groups and suffering outside interference from France, Japan, and the United States.

Cao Dai, short for Dai Day Tam Ky Pho Do, or the Third Revelation of the Great Path, was founded on the belief that all religions are, at bottom, the same. Its teachings tried to unite those of Christianity, Buddhism, Taoism, animism, and Confucianism, the main schools of thought and religion in Vietnam. Cao Dai followers believed that those five faiths had been founded in the past by prophets during the so-called First Revelation. During the Second Revelation, they were altered by human shortcomings and therefore inspired conflict instead of unity. In their period, the period of the Third Revelation, the God who is the source of all belief systems and prophets would once again bring all schools of religious thought into a final unity. The term Cao Dai, meaning "high palace," is how followers referred to God. Teaching in addition that all human beings, as well as all animals and plants, possess a part of the spirit of God and are therefore one, Cao Dai had a great appeal. One reason was that it reinforced traditional Vietnamese beliefs about the everyday presence of the spirit of God and about reincarnation, or the movement of this spirit from body to body through a number of lives and deaths, which was also an aspect of Vietnamese Buddhism.

Cao Dai leaders found themselves deeply involved in Vietnamese politics during the mid-twentieth century. At one point they even maintained their own army, complete with its own bases, helping French colonialists as well as local groups fighting off a Communist takeover of southern Vietnam. This private army was incorporated into that of the new nation of South Vietnam after 1954, but their wealth and power ensured that followers of Cao Dai continued to play an important part in the politics of the nation and in the next phase of the anti-Communist struggle, which lasted from 1959 to 1975 and which included massive American military involvement. After North Vietnamese Communists reunified the country in 1975, many Cao Dai believers went into exile, notably in the United States, where they continue to practice their faith. Cao Dai survives in modern Vietnam as well. Worldwide, believers number about 6 million.

SEE ALSO: new religious movements, Japanese; new religious movements, Western

# Carnival

An important festival period in the Christian calendar for Roman Catholics. Originally Carnival connoted the actual beginning of Lent, a period of fasting (generally in the form of avoiding meat eating) and repentance that lasts for forty days before Easter. In practice Carnival has more often meant a period of festivity before the beginning of Lent, and as such it has some association with pre-Christian customs. Carnival features such celebrations as masked balls, parades, and theatrical productions. Among its prominent themes is that of topsy-turvydom: During Carnival people feel free to do things they could not do at other times, such as assume false identities, and traditional roles, such as gender ones, might be overturned or reversed.

The beginning of Carnival varies according to the customs of different areas. In both southern Germany and New Orleans, Louisiana, in the United States, for instance, Carnival begins on January 6, following the Christmas season, while in France the season is much shorter, beginning on Shrove Tuesday during Holy Week, the week preceding Easter Sunday. In New Orleans, the climax of Carnival is Mardi Gras also beginning on Shrove Tuesday. Mardi Gras means "fat Tuesday" in French, and the name is derived from the custom of using up all the fats in the home before Lent. In recent decades Mardi Gras has taken on an increasingly secular tone in New Orleans as well as in Rio de Janeiro in Brazil, another city famous for its Carnival celebrations.

SEE ALSO: calendars; Easter; Holy Week

## caste

A term referring to the social or class structure of India, where society has been traditionally divided into a hierarchy of groups based broadly on profession. Caste is not a strictly religious concept, but it overlaps with Hindu beliefs. Furthermore, caste has so permeated Indian society that aspects of it are found among other Indian religious groups as well, including Sikhs and Christians. The word *caste* is Portuguese in origin, a relic of the era of European colonialism in India. The most common Indian term for the caste system is *jati*, a Sanskrit word most accurately translated as "race." Another common term for the concept is *varna*, or "color."

Traditionally there have been four castes in India. According to customs and beliefs that first appeared during the Vedic era (ca. 1200–600 B.C.), there are three "twice-born" castes. These are the brahmin, or priestly caste; the kshatriya, or kingly caste; and the vaisya, or merchant caste. They are called twice-born (a figurative term) because members of these castes are believed to have lived through many reincarnations and are therefore closer than others to moksha, or release from the wheel of birth and death, provided they do not accumulate too much bad karma in any particular lifetime. The fourth caste is the sudra, or laboring caste. Finally, Indian society has always contained an "outcaste" group not part of this system. These so-called untouchables (today, Dalits) performed the dirtiest jobs, such as handling dead bodies. The general sense among Hindus is that members of these lower groups are born into them because of an accumulation of bad karma.

Over the centuries hundreds of new *jati* groups emerged, based not only on specific jobs but on areas of origin. Most of these were subdivisions of the fourth caste, the sudra. The first three castes generally looked down on these groups in some instances considered physical contact with them to be ritually polluting. In modern, urban India the sense of these kinds of distinctions has begun to break down, but they remain very powerful in the nation's thousands of rural villages. Meanwhile, as Indian society grew more complex, members of the top three castes began to practice a wider variety of jobs as well. Few brahmins in modern India, for instance, make their livings as priests, although almost all priests are brahmins.

The twentieth century saw many attempts in India to reform the caste system. Mahatma Gandhi, for example, devoted special attention to the untouchables, calling them *harijans*, or "children of God." India's secular government, furthermore, set aside privileges such as university admissions and government jobs for members of lower-caste groups. Nonetheless, caste distinctions remain extremely common in such matters as arranged marriage, where Hindus consider it a part of a parent's duty, or dharma, to ensure that their children marry within the same caste. A child's dharma, likewise, is to accept such a marriage out of loyalty and respect toward his or her parents. In these and similar matters, caste ideas appear among Sikhs and other religious groups as well.

SEE ALSO: brahmin; Hinduism; moksha

## Christian heresies

Christian history offers numerous examples of heresies, which in general are systems of belief that religious authorities claim to be false or which are in opposition to the beliefs and practices of most devotees. Arguments over heresy can be found in almost every major religious tradition, but only in Roman Catholic Christianity did authorities develop institutional methods to identify and discourage them.

The early Christian Church established its orthodoxy in belief, ritual, and hierarchy partly by identifying and rejecting certain heresies. Among them was Arianism, preached by an Alexandrian Christian named Arius in the fourth century. The Arian heresy argued that Jesus Christ was not a divine figure but a "created being," human because he was changeable. Jesus was born, grew up, and died: Only God, Arius argued, was unchangeable. Early Christian leaders rejected Arianism at the Council of Nicaea in 325, asserting that Jesus was of "one substance" with God the Father and therefore divine.

Another important heresy was that preached by the Monophysites, who claimed that Jesus maintained a single nature that was both divine and human, as opposed to the orthodox Christian belief that Jesus had, simultaneously, two separate natures, divine and human. This Monophysite doctrine was rejected at the Council of Chalcedon in 451. In recent years, however, those Christian churches that have maintained Monophysite doctrine, such as the Armenian and Coptic Churches, have established closer relations with Roman Catholic and Eastern Orthodox authorities. Another small branch of Christianity that was originally deemed heretical but continues to survive is Nestorian Christianity, whose followers, including the Chaldean Christians of Iraq, live mainly in the Middle East. The Nestorians, following the teachings of the fifth-century churchman Nestorius, argued that Jesus Christ was a man inspired by God rather than an incarnation of God, that God "presented himself" in the world through the vehicle of a human being. Nestorianism was condemned at both the Council of Ephesus in 431 and at the Council of Chalcedon.

This issue of heresy rose again during the Middle Ages in the Christian world when heresies were again identified in formal terms by church councils and ratified by the pope in Rome. Major medieval heresies included the Cathar movement, which regarded all of physical creation as evil and postponed baptism, a rite that according to orthodox Christian doctrine should be performed early in life, until the believer had reached a level of spiritual "perfection," which was usually right before death. Other major heretical groups were the Waldensians in France, the Lollards or Wycliffites in England, and the Hussites in what is today the Czech Republic. All in various ways presaged the

Protestant Reformation by rejecting the authority of the popes and other institutions of the church. Each of these movements was suppressed by church and even secular authorities. Having determined that mere excommunication was no longer satisfactory, the church adopted stronger methods to root out these challenges. Among them was the Inquisition, the church-sponsored institution assembled in the twelfth and thirteenth centuries in to identify and punish heresy. Investigators of the Inquisition had the power to arrest, try, and condemn accused heretics. The Cathar movement, furthermore, was also a target of the religious wars known as the Crusades, even though it was based in southern France and not the Holy Land.

In the fifteenth century, the pope officially declared witchcraft to be heretical. Witches, who were most often women, were thought to belong to various cults that had made pacts with Satan, or the devil, and rejected Christian teachings. Their meetings were thought to include the desecration of Christian symbols and images, human sacrifice, sexual perversion, and even cannibalism, although almost no real evidence for these practices has ever come to light. In the 1480s the church published a manual known as *Malleus Maleficarum (The Witches' Hammer)* to describe the techniques Inquisitors might use to counter this threat (including torture) as well as the details of witchcraft and its practices. The Inquisition and other authorities used the text to target an estimated 100,000 people between 1500 and 1700, and the fear of witches spilled over into some sects of early Protestantism as well.

Originally the church proclaimed the sixteenth-century Protestant movements of the Reformation as heretical, but over

time religious tolerance prevailed. In the twentieth century, Roman Catholic doctrine was modified to recognize the difference between those who willfully continued to oppose official doctrine and those who were simply raised to believe in other traditions. Most Protestants, meanwhile, believe that it is possible for someone to adhere to their own denomination without considering adherents of other denominations heretics.

SEE ALSO: councils, early Christian Church; councils, Roman Catholic Church; Inquisition

# Christianity

Chronologically, the second of the great Near Eastern monotheistic religions to arise and, today, the largest world religion. One-quarter to one-third of the world's peoples are Christian or reside in areas with a largely Christian heritage. Numerical estimates of Christians, therefore, range from 1.5 billion to over 2 billion. Christianity predominates in Europe or in New World regions settled and colonized by Europeans, including North and South America, Australia, and New Zealand. Christian communities also exist in the Islamic Middle East, in Hindu India, and indeed all over the world, representing some four hundred different denominations of Christianity.

*Origins of Christianity* Christianity originates in the story of the life of Jesus of Nazareth, its founder. Little is known of Jesus' life aside from what appears in the Gospels of the Christian New Testament, although Roman records refer briefly to a man of that name. He was born to a Jewish couple, Mary and Joseph, in approximately four B.C. in Bethlehem, a town then standing inside a province of the Roman Empire known as Judea. At around the age of thirty, Jesus took up a career as a prophet and religious teacher, and he attracted a wide following among people attracted to his messages of love, peace, and forgiveness and his apparent ability to perform miracles. An inner circle of twelve apostles was at the center of this following.

Most of Jesus' early teachings took place in Galilee, but around A.D. 30 he and the apostles made their way southward toward Jerusalem, the administrative capital of Judea as well as the site of the second Temple, the center of the Jewish religion. There Jesus fell afoul of both Roman and Jewish authorities and, betrayed by one of the twelve apostles, he was condemned to death by crucifixion. After his death, according to biblical accounts, he was resurrected and ascended to heaven after instructing his disciples to spread his message of God's love and forgiveness to the world.

The first Christians were members of the so-called Jesus movement, a sect among many of the contentious branches of Judaism in first-century Judea. Their leaders, notably the apostle Peter, believed that Jesus' life had fulfilled the Jewish prophecy that one day God would send a messiah, or savior, to the earth. Mainstream Jews rejected the claim, and over the course of a few decades in the middle of the first century the Jesus movement broke from Judaism to become a distinct faith. In seeking converts these early Christians spoke of Jesus to Jews and gentiles, or non-Jews, alike. Some of the apostles also took literally the command to spread Jesus' word throughout the Roman Empire and even beyond it. Peter, for his part, is thought to have taken Jesus' message to the imperial capital of Rome itself.

The major contributions to Christianity in the decades immediately following Jesus' life were made by Paul of Tarsus (also, Saul of Tarsus), a former Jewish leader who converted to Christianity and was declared an apostle by early Christian leaders even though he never knew Jesus personally. Paul formulated a Christian theology that was distinct from Jewish theology, rejecting, for example, circumcision and other customary Jewish rites. In the process he composed a number of letters, known in the Christian tradition as the Epistles of Paul, in which he tried to describe to early Christian communities not only the nature of belief but also Christian ethics, or ways believers should behave in the world. One of Paul's important assets was his ability to speak Greek, rather than the Aramaic that Jesus spoke, in addition to the Hebrew of Temple-based Judaism and the Pharisees. Greek was the language of the gentiles and the major tongue of the eastern part of the Roman Empire. When the Gospels, Paul's Epistles, and other books of the Christian New Testament were written, mostly after A.D. 50, they were written in Greek. Paul's contributions so substantial that he might be considered Christianity's second founder.

***The Early Christian Church*** Christianity spread fairly rapidly in its early centuries; by the third century Christian communities had been established as far afield as Armenia, Ethiopia, and perhaps even India. But believers were concentrated in the Roman Empire. At first, largely because Christians refused to worship or make sacrifices to Roman or Greek gods, they suffered episodes of persecution. But these episodes may well have inspired early church leaders to even greater cohesion and the development of lasting institutions in order to preserve and expand their faith. Many Romans found Jesus' teachings appealing, most famously the Roman emperor Constantine, who proclaimed the Edict of Milan in 313, which provided for religious freedom throughout the empire but was mainly directed at ending persecution of Christians. Constantine went on to become the first Christian emperor himself. In 397 the emperor Theodosius declared Christianity to be the official religion of Rome.

Meanwhile the early church had developed such institutions as the New Testament canon, a collection of twenty-seven books that was to form Christianity's holy scripture, and a hierarchy of leadership and organization. This hierarchy, modeled on that of the Roman army, had a command consisting of a core of bishops as well as layers of priests and deacons. Their functions were to pronounce on important matters of belief, usually during and after major church councils; provide communication and dogmatic consistency; and maintain religious authority over lay believers. Important early thinkers, notably Augustine, made their contributions to Christian thinking and practice in this early era, and the Christian monastic movement also took shape. Christian monks, adapting a practice common in a number of earlier, Near Eastern faiths, dedicated themselves to particular orders and pledged vows of poverty, chastity, and obedience.

One of the major bishops was the bishop of Rome, who traced his religious lineage back to the apostle Peter. But the bishop of Rome was not the only leader, nor did he preside any longer over Christians in the imperial capital; by the time of Constantine Roman emperors spent most of their time at their eastern capital; the Greek city of Byzantium, which the Romans renamed Constantinople (now Istanbul in Turkey). The western half of the Roman Empire slowly disintegrated in the fourth and fifth centuries, during which time those areas fell under the control of warlike Germanic kings. Over several centuries these kings, and their peoples, converted to Christianity and pledged their allegiance to the bishop of Rome, whom they called "papa," or pope. This allegiance provided the pope with a basis of political and military support. Meanwhile, the eastern, Greek-speaking part of the Roman Empire remained broadly intact, and Constantinople became the greatest Christian city on earth. There leaders built the Church of Hagia Sophia (divine wisdom) in the sixth century, the first great Christian church. In this state, commonly known today as the Byzantine Empire to differentiate it from the Roman Empire proper, emperors thought themselves to be the heads of the institutional Christian Church and the bishops, including the bishop of Rome, to be their subordinates.

Thanks to political, cultural, and doctrinal differences, the first Christian schism, or split, took place slowly between the western and eastern churches. The split was made permanent in 1054, although the two had been different in practice for centuries already. In that year, at a church council in Italy, Pope Leo IX claimed that he, not any earthly ruler or church committee, was the leader of all Christians, citing the lineage of the apostle Peter. The Byzantine representatives rejected this claim, and furthermore refused to pay homage to the pope as western political decorum demanded. Leo responded by excommunicating the eastern church, which responded in kind. The Crusades, which began shortly thereafter, helped to further harden the split. In addition to being an attempt to reclaim Jerusalem and other Christian holy sites from the Muslims who then controlled them, the Crusades amounted to an attempt by the successors of Leo IX to place all Christians, east and west, under his authority. The two separate churches, known commonly today as the Roman Catholic Church and the Eastern Orthodox Church, have remained split despite efforts to heal their differences.

*Medieval and Reformation Christianity* Ironically, the Crusades opened up western Europe to Arab and Greek scholarship, and the church of Rome became thereby invigorated in the twelfth, thirteenth, and fourteenth centuries, even as the Eastern Orthodox Church grew weaker through the decline of Byzantine emperors. These centuries saw the rise of the first universities, designed to train churchmen, as well as an expanded monastic movement and the appearance of important new thinkers such as Thomas Aquinas. Although the pope and his bishops continually vied with political leaders (and periodically, rival popes known as antipopes) for overall authority, and some gave themselves over almost entirely to politics, the acquisition of enormous power, and displays of wealth, the western church was undeniably the dominant institution in virtually all aspects of European life during the thousand-year period between the fall of Rome and the Renaissance of the fifteenth century.

Increasingly, however, some Christians questioned the secular role of the church as well as its elaborate hierarchy and corrupt practices, and these questions gave rise to Christianity's second schism, between Roman Catholicism and Protestantism. In 1517 a discontented German monk named Martin Luther drew up a list of grievances that he believed church officials should address. This famous list, the Ninety-five Theses, or points of dispute, helped to inspire the movement known as the Reformation and the rise of new Protestant sects that opposed many of the secular activities, and some of the theological beliefs, of the Roman Catholic Church. Religious differences provoked a Counter-Reformation and spilled over into politics, and over a century of religious warfare divided Europe into mostly Catholic or mostly Protestant nations.

The era of the Reformation and Counter-Reformation was also the beginning of the era of European exploration and colonialism. European Christians—primarily the Spanish, Portuguese, Dutch, and English—took their faith with them on their travels and implanted it in their settlements, thereby brought both Catholic and Protestant Christianity to North and South America as well as, in new forms, to Asia and Africa. Christian missionaries were also active; Catholic missionaries were an important feature of the sixteenth, seventeenth, and eighteenth centuries and Protestant missionaries played important roles in the nineteenth and twentieth centuries. Christianity indeed continued to spread broadly even as the rise of modern science and rationalism dominated European culture in the 1700s and 1800s. Meanwhile, numerous loosely national churches emerged in nations formally connected to or influenced by the old Byzantine Empire—Russia, Greece, Armenia, Bulgaria, and others—ensuring that Eastern Orthodoxy maintained a vital tradition as well.

*Basic Christian Beliefs* Despite great schisms and the development of Christianity's many sects, Christians the world over maintain the same central beliefs. They believe in one God, who exists as one substance but is revealed as the Trinity of Father, Son, and Holy Spirit. They hold that humanity is guilty of sin, whether the original sin represented by the biblical Fall of Adam and Eve or the "actual" sins they commit in their lifetimes. They believe that salvation and ultimate judgment come from God. Christians believe that God sent Jesus into the world through the immaculate conception of the Virgin Mary (the actual nature of Jesus as both man and the Son of God has been a matter of major historical dispute) to demonstrate God's love and mercy and provide a means of salvation. Jesus, without sin himself, is believed to have redeemed all the sins of humanity by suffering and dying on the cross. His resurrection from the dead and ascent to heaven are symbolic of the same process that is available to the human soul, provided it is open to Jesus Christ's example and maintains sincere faith in his act of redemption. Those who lack this necessary faith in Jesus Christ stay in a state of sinfulness, and, in the belief of many, will be condemned to hell rather than raised to eternal life in heaven following their deaths.

Christian behavior is guided by several sources. First is the teachings of Jesus Christ, who emphasized mercy, forgiveness, and divine love. Christians are encouraged to emulate Christ's example in this regard. The Epistles of Paul provide a wide range of ethical guidelines connected to such matters as politics, marriage, and sexuality. Since the Middle Ages millions of Christians have used the Ten Commandments of the Hebrew Bible as a basic guide while recognizing that, ultimately and as Christ preached, to love God and to love one's neighbor as oneself are "all the law and the commandments."

*Texts and Rituals* The Bible is the canonical Christian text. It contains two sections: the Old Testament, which is a version of the Hebrew Bible, and the New Testament. For Christians the Old Testament represents the first covenant, or agreement, between God and humankind. The New Testament is the covenant of Jesus, telling of the fulfillment of God's promises. It contains four Gospels, which tell of the life and teachings of Jesus as well as stories of the apostles; letters written by Paul and other early Christians; and the apocalyptic book of Revelation. To some Christians the Bible is the literal word of God, and is therefore without error and unquestionable. To others the Bible is a work of literature that remains open to interpretation, or a diverse collection of stories, lessons, and other material, some of which is intended literally but which contains other elements that should be accepted allegorically or metaphorically. The New Testament was originally written in Greek, the main language of the eastern part of the Roman Empire. In the fifth century a definitive Latin version of the entire Bible appeared, and most translations of it into English, Spanish, or other modern languages are products of the last five hundred years. Roman Catholics add to the Bible the traditions and teachings of their church as essential doctrine subject to the ultimate authority of scripture.

Most Christian worship takes place among communities of believers, although solitary prayer and devotion is also quite common, especially among monks and nuns. Formal worship is often described as liturgy, a variation of a Greek word meaning "work of the people." Specific liturgical services vary according to Christian denominations, but they often contain a statement of faith such as the Nicene Creed, the singing of hymns, group prayers, and the performance of sacraments such as the Eucharist (or Holy Communion). A lesson or sermon by an ordained clergyman is also a common aspect of services. In the second century it became common to celebrate services on the "Lord's day," Sunday. Christians wanted to distinguish their Sabbath day from that of the Jews, which lasts from sundown on Friday to sundown on Saturday, as well as commemorate the day of the week on which Christ was resurrected. Christianity also maintains an elaborate liturgical calendar of holy days and feast days, of which the most famous are Christmas, which celebrates the birth of Christ, and Easter, which celebrates his resurrection. Roman Catholic and Eastern Orthodox Christians also observe holy days connected to saints, although these vary greatly and are often dependent on locality.

*Christianity in the Modern World* Christianity continues to evolve. Major features of recent Christian history include its survival and resurgence in the former Communist, and officially atheist, states of the Soviet Union, Bulgaria, and other Eastern bloc countries as well as the loosening of many of the stricter aspects of Roman Catholic theology, notably because of the Vatican II councils of the 1960s. The ecumenical movement, meanwhile, has sought to build bridges among the many contentious Christian denominations, with some success. "Mainstream" Protestant denominations such as Lutheranism and Anglicanism/Episcopalianism have come to reflect many of the social changes of the twentieth century, with the appearance of such innovations as female clergy. Even the Catholic tradition has produced liberation theology and other liberal or even radical movements, though with less success. In reaction, perhaps, to perceived re-

forms of the church, growing numbers of Christians, both Protestant and Catholic, have sought out more conservative and even fundamentalist readings of the faith, and movements such as evangelicalism are among the fastest-growing in the Christian world.

SEE ALSO: Eastern Orthodox Christianity; Jesus of Nazareth; New Testament; Paul; Protestantism; Roman Catholicism

# Christian Science

A recent branch of Christianity founded by the American Mary Baker Eddy in Boston in 1879. Its major ideas were first proposed in her book, *Science and Health with Key to the Scriptures*, which proved popular first among American Protestants and then around the world.

Christian Scientists believe that the power of prayer can cure all sins and heal the sick, since all matter is created by God and under his constant influence. According to Christian Scientists, Jesus Christ demonstrated the power of prayer through his healing miracles as well as his own triumph over death. The more one develops a true grasp of how Christ did this, the more one understands the "mind of Christ," the more power one has over the material world. Some Christian Scientists take the extreme position of rejecting all scientifically based medical care, although the church's teachings on this are by no means absolute. Believers are free to visit dentists and optometrists and, for some procedures, doctors. Christian Science sanatoria and health care workers also exist to help believers navigate these matters.

The Christian Science Reading Room is an essential institution of the church, designed to assist believers in their efforts to conduct regular prayer and devotions as well as to practice outreach to the larger community. There are no Sunday services but rather weekly meetings on Wednesday evenings. There is also no established hierarchy of priests or ministers, although there are church officers who can be either women or men. Some three thousand Christian Science congregations exist around the world, with a total membership of between 1.5 and 2 million. The church publishes the *Christian Science Monitor*, a well-regarded international daily newspaper.

SEE ALSO: new religious movements, Western; Protestantism

## Christmas

The Christian holiday that celebrates the birth of Jesus Christ. It takes place each year on December 25. The holiday became a regular part of the Christian year in the Roman Empire in the fourth century, when church leaders in the eastern portion of the empire selected December 25 as the date of Christ's birth. The date was likely selected to coincide with various Roman celebrations around the time of the winter solstice. December 25 was also the birth date of Mithra, a god connected to the Near Eastern mystery religions also popular in the Eastern Roman Empire.

Outside of the specifically religious ceremonies of the Christmas season, which mark not only the birth of Christ but the Epiphany, when the infant Jesus was visited by three magi, or "wise men," Christmas is also a popular secular holiday. Elements of its celebration in this regard can be linked to the Roman holiday of Saturnalia, held on December 17, when people exchanged gifts, and to winter celebrations held by the Germanic and Celtic tribes of pre-Christian Europe. These involved such features as Yule logs, decoration with greenery, bright lights, and community festivals involving food and good cheer.

SEE ALSO: calendars; Jesus of Nazareth; Easter

## Chuang-tzu
### (ca. 370 B.C.–286 B.C.)

Along with Lao-tzu, Chuang-tzu is regarded as the founder of philosophical Daoism and the author of the central Daoist text that bears his name, the *Chuang-tzu*. Scholars suspect that he actually wrote only the first seven of the book's thirty-three chapters, the rest having been written by his students. Chuang-tzu's importance lies in not only his contributions to Daoism as such but in the way that they challenged the Confucian ideas growing more and more influential during his lifetime. In this, Chuang-tzu might be considered, within the context of classical Chinese culture, a counterbalance to the excesses of Confucian schools.

In the *Chuang-tzu*, the sage argues that everything is unified, that everything is the Dao. In often paradoxical formulations, he notes that the Dao cannot be spoken of or known, since things that are spoken of or known are not the Dao. The proper approach to human life is to accept the course of nature and not bind oneself to circumstances, material possessions, ambition, or other worldly attachments. The Confucian effort to reform society, the sage argued, was ultimately pointless. It was better, he wrote, to simply embrace the world's contradictions and to develop meditational processes intended to "fast the mind." The following is Burton Watson's translation of one of the more well known of Chuang-tzu's teachings, a vivid example of his use of paradox:

Once Chuang Chou dreamt he was a

butterfly, a butterfly flitting and fluttering around, happy with himself and doing as he pleased. He didn't know he was Chuang Chou. Suddenly he woke up and there he was, solid and unmistakable Chuang Chou. But he didn't know if he was Chuang Chou who had dreamt he was a butterfly or a butterfly dreaming of Chuang Chou. Between Chuang Chou and a butterfly there must be some distinction! This is called the Transformation of Things.

SEE ALSO: Daoism; Lao-tzu

# church

A term used in Christianity that may denote a specific community of worshippers, the building in which worship takes place, a Christian branch or denominational organization, or the worldwide body of Christians throughout history. Thus its meaning depends on the context in which it is used. The word comes from the Greek *ekklesia*, which was used in the New Testament in all of these ways.

For most ordinary Christians, their church is primarily the local religious community they belong to and the administration of its worship services and other activities. The common pattern for church buildings, or at least for the "sanctuaries" where services are held, is the placement of an altar or lectern at the front for the uses of those who conduct services. This altar or lectern faces rows of pews for congregants. Beyond this basic pattern church structures vary greatly. One very noticeable set of differences is that Roman Catholic and Eastern Orthodox churches are commonly decorated with statues, stained glass windows, and other features. They may also contain separate chapels devoted to a particular saint or for small-scale rites. Protestant churches, by contrast, generally disdain decorations. In all traditions church buildings are used for purposes beyond regular worship services, such as weddings, funerals, education, and even secular community gatherings. This is true for even Christianity's greatest churches, such as Istanbul's Hagia Sophia (now an Islamic mosque), St. Peter's Basilica in Rome, and St. Paul's Cathedral in London.

If in another sense the church is the entire Christian community, there have been many challenges to the unity of that community over the centuries, most importantly the first schism, which split the Western Roman and Eastern Orthodox branches of Christianity, and the second schism, during which Protestant denominations split from Roman Catholicism. Each of these three branches of Chrstianity has considered itself either the one true church or at least a part of the true church. To reinforce the sense that, despite schisms and further splits, there is a true church unity, many point to the Nicene Creed, which cites common belief in "one holy, catholic, and apostolic church." Most Christians are baptized into the church, a sacrament satisfying the creed's descriptive *holy*. The word *catholic*, meaning universal, is taken in the creed to mean the universal church. *Apostolic* implies the original Christian communities and their ministries set up by Jesus Christ's apostles, of which the various earthly churches are seen to be continuations. Finally, the word *church* is used as shorthand to refer to Christian institutions. This is seen most commonly in Roman Catholicism, where the papacy and other aspects of its institutional hierarchy are simply referred to as "the church."

SEE ALSO: Christianity; Protestantism; Roman Catholicism

## circumcision

A common ancient Near Eastern custom that became associated with both Judaism and Islam. In Judaism, circumcision is a symbol of the covenant between God and the Hebrew patriarch Abraham, or entrance into the community of Jews. During a ceremony known as a bris, held when newborn males are eight days old (or later if delayed for reasons of health), an expert and observant Jew known as a mohel removes the foreskin of the penis with a sharp knife. The bris is concluded with a small celebration.

In Islam, boys are circumcised as both a rite of passage into manhood and as a sign of entrance into the Islamic community. The ritual generally takes place when boys are seven or eight years old; uncircumcised converts to the faith undergo the ritual upon their conversion at any later age. As in Judaism, the ritual is an occasion for celebration. It is not, however, prescribed by the Qur'an or other Islamic texts.

Relatively few Islamic communities, and no Jewish ones, practice female circumcision, or excision of the clitoris. The Islamic communites that do, located mostly in East Africa, consider it a customary part of their religious observance, although it is likely that the practice predated the arrival of Islam and was a means of customary social control rather than an act of religious significance.

SEE ALSO: bar mitzvah, bat mitzvah; Judaism; Islam

## companions of the Prophet

A term used to refer to the original Islamic community, when all members had personal contact with the prophet Muhammad. More broadly it might also mean early Muslims who actually saw Muhammad. It is from the observations, memories, and teachings of these companions that the Hadith, Islamic narrative texts concerned with the sayings and life of Muhammad, was compiled.

In mainstream Islam there are four categories of companions, although different traditions offer varying opinions about their exact membership. The sahaba include the first four caliphs—Omar, Abu Bakr, Uthman, and Ali—as well as six others to whom the Prophet promised membership in paradise. The sahaba is highly revered among Sunni Muslims but rejected by the Shia. The second category, the muhajirun, include the Meccans who accompanied Muhammad to Medina. The third category, the Ansar, are people of Medina who adopted the Prophet's teachings, and the fourth, the badriyun, were those who fought alongside the Prophet at the battle of Badr in 624, Muhammad's first military victory.

SEE ALSO: Fatima; Hadith; Muhammad; Qur'an

## Confucianism

A philosophy that dominated Chinese civilization and other regions influenced by China such as Korea, Japan, and Vietnam, for over two thousand years. Confucianism differs from other religious traditions in that it has little to do with gods, spirits, or the afterlife. In fact Confucianism is arguably a social philosophy more than a world religion, a philosophy of human roles and relationships and a vision of earthly harmony. Nevertheless, Confucianism shares with other religious traditions an emphasis on ritual, reverence for great founders and teachers, and adherence to basic principles as laid out in a canon of important texts.

*During the Chinese Cultural Revolution of 1965–1975, many of the icons, relics, and writings of Confucius were destroyed.* HULTON ARCHIVE/GETTY IMAGES

***Origins and History*** Confucian philosophy is traced back to the teachings of K'ung Ch'iu, or Master K'ung, or in the Latinized form, Confucius (ca. 551–479 B.C.). Because the sources of information about Confucius were written after his lifetime, much of what is known about the man is considered legendary. Born into the poor family of a minor aristocrat in the state of Lu, Confucius was trained intensively in Chinese classical culture and, after failing to secure a post as an adviser to an important nobleman, he became a teacher. During his lifetime, and indeed for centuries after, China was politically and socially unstable; Confucius wanted to find ways to resolve upheaval and restore harmony and peace. He attracted a number of students, including a core of disciples who are thought to have written down many of his teachings. Although few politicians

were attracted by Confucius's ideas at first, his disciples and their descendants continued to build on a developing Confucian tradition. Important later thinkers included Mencius (ca. 371–ca. 289 B.C.) and Hsun-tzu (ca. 298–230 B.C.).

Central authority was finally restored to China in the late third century B.C. by the authoritarian warlord Qin Shi Huangdi. The short-lived Qin dynasty was followed by the Han dynasty (206 B.C.–A.D. 220), during which time Confucianism became the official state philosophy, credited in important ways with both the long duration and relative stability of the dynasty. Confucian thinking was reflected in such Han practices as keeping the imperial court separate from administration, with the latter being managed by educated elites rather than hereditary nobles. It also appeared in the emphasis on ritual in defining relationships and in terms of legal conduct. Furthermore, the Five Classics associated with Confucianism were placed at the center of Chinese education at all levels. By A.D. 58 Chinese leaders had the Five Classics made permanent by inscribing them on stone tablets. They also required all state schools to make sacrifices and conduct other rituals in honor of Confucius himself.

After the fall of the Han dynasty, China underwent several centuries of disunity, and along with this lack of central authority and administration came a lessening of official Confucian influence. Among ordinary Chinese people as well as many elites, Daoism and Buddhism grew in appeal and, after China was reunified by the Sui dynasty in A.D. 581, the far more powerful Tang dynasty (618–907) gave most of its patronage to Buddhism. Although its influence had never entirely disappeared, Confucianism only reemerged as the official state philosophy of China during the Song dynasty (960–1127). Then Confucianism was integrated into a new school of thought known as neo-Confucianism. Important neo-Confucians such as Chu Hsi (1130–1200) helped to make Confucianism meaningful to individuals in search of spiritual fulfillment as well as to larger entities like families and states. They also helped to restore its place at the center of China's administrative and educational systems. Imperial officials, the Confucian scholar-officials, were selected by passing an elaborate system of examinations in the Confucian classics (with another collection known as the Four Books added to the Five Classics) and in other elements of Chinese traditional culture.

### Confucian Officials and Heavenly Dynasties

The Confucian scholar-officials came to be seen as arbiters and guardians of China's values and traditions and exercised considerable authority at all social levels, since the Chinese educational system was based on preparation for the exams but only a rare few passed them all. The officials continued to be China's governing elite, subordinate only to the emperors, through the Ming dynasty (1368–1644), when both the modern version of the Great Wall of China and the Forbidden City in China's capital of Beijing were constructed as symbols of cosmic and earthly order. During the Qing dynasty (1644–1911), these officials remained important but had to contend with China's imperial Manchu elites as the greatest exemplars of Confucian ideals.

Confucianism began to wane in the 1800s, as China came under the influence of Western science, technology, commerce, and imperialism. Confucian elites and Confucian educational systems were disbanded following the deposing of the last Qing emperor in 1911. When Mao Tse-tung's Communists established the People's Republic of China in 1949, they repudiated Confucian traditions, and during the so-called Cultural Revolution of 1965–1975 Communist "red guards" destroyed many ancient texts, icons, temples, and other relics of Confucianism. Confucian scholarship never disappeared, however, in South Korea, Japan, Taiwan, Hong Kong, and Singapore, and has even undergone a revival in recent decades.

### Basic Confucian Beliefs

Confucius is revered as a great man and great teacher. He did not write down his teachings, although his students later supposedly did in creating the collection known as the *Analects*. Furthermore, many later scholars and leaders attributed to him ideas that appear nowhere in his teachings. Nevertheless the general outline of basic Confucian beliefs is fairly easily extracted from the *Analects*. He was interested in the establishment of earthly order, and professed little interest in the gods or the afterlife, although he apparently believed in traditional Chinese versions of those religious concepts. Indeed, Confucius saw himself not as a creator of new ideas but simply as the transmitter of ancient traditions. He believed that earthly order could be established through education, the encouragement of a sense of strong integrity among individuals, and the proper understanding of human relationships. In this it would mirror the moral order of the heavens, which Confucius referred to using the word *t'ian*. Chinese emperors in particular could only rule effectively if they possessed the mandate of heaven, and it was an emperor's responsibility to mediate between heaven and earth.

Confucian ethics emphasized three notions in particular. One was *ren*, an ethic of personal behavior that some later Confucians would refer to as the "gentleman's code" and others as simply a humane outlook. Those who were motivated by righteousness, rather than by the greed for money or power or by selfishness, demonstrated the qualities of *ren*. So did those who acted according to benevolence and kindness. Confucius believed that rulers and other leaders in particular should cultivate *ren*, since men could only influence others by proper behavior. Likewise, rulers who lacked *ren* would lose the confidence of their subjects and risk a breakdown of order. On a broader level, *ren* meant to simply act in accordance with the Golden Rule, which is given in a section of the *Analects* as "Do not unto others what you would not have them do to you."

Confucius also placed great importance in *li*, the proper performance of rituals. Rituals should be performed sincerely and in good faith, with humility, as if the spirits and dead ancestors themselves were present. By performing them in the right ways, people show that they understand their social roles and the obligations that come with those roles. They also show the necessary respect for tradition and authority that the continuance of earthly harmony demands. By demonstrating respect one earns in turn the respect of others.

The third notion that was of central importance to Confucius was an ancient one: filial piety. For Confucius the family was the most important social entity, more important than the state. States themselves could only be orderly if the families within them were, and it was important to understand that social harmony had to be established in this way, from the bottom up rather than from the top down (by establishing state offices and a wide-ranging bureacracy, for instance). Filial piety demanded that children be respectful to their parents, obey their instructions, care for them in their old age, and faithfully perform the proper rites after their deaths.

*Relationships and Obligations* Confucius's explanation of the Five Relationships elaborated upon the notion of filial piety. He recognized reciprocal obligations in the relationships between father and son, ruler and subject, husband and wife, elder and younger brother, and friend and friend. The basic relationship, and the model for all others, was between father and son. Just as a son should show proper filial piety toward his father, the father is obligated to train his son in morality and in a way to earn a living. If a father fails to do this, then he has neglected his obligations not only to his son but also to his entire family and society at large. Reciprocity in the Five Relationships is not the same thing as equality, however. Confucius was careful to define obligations in terms of superiors and subordinates: In each relationship, the superior person (parent, male, ruler, or older person) had the obligation of benevolence and the subordinate person (child, female, subject, or younger person) had the obligation of obedience. One result was a relatively low social status for women, who in the Confucian system must remain subordinate to their fathers, husbands, and sons. Throughout, Confucianism places emphasis on the welfare of the group rather than the individual, and the maintenance of social hierarchies.

Another idea basic to Confucianism is the importance of education. Nearly all Confucian thinkers emphasized education in some form. Some claimed that it refined human beings who were born good; others claimed it was necessary to turn people away from what was essentially an evil or lazy nature. For these and other reasons, education lay at the center of Confucianism's search for social harmony, because only through education could people gain respect for traditions and a full understanding of both relationships and rituals. Confucius himself believed that education should be practical in nature, that even abstract ideas could be put to use in the family and society.

On a popular level, the Confucian system of ethics affected people's view of the afterlife, even though Confucius himself was not terribly concerned with such matters. It was common for ordinary people to believe that the rites of filial piety were necessary to ensure a peaceful afterlife among previously departed ancestors. One customary belief was that male children were necessary so that they could perform those rites both at funerals and afterward.

*Texts and Rituals* Confucianism's emphasis on education inspired the collection of a distinct canon of texts, which together make up the so-called Confucian classics. The Five Books were largely in use by the time Confucius himself appeared, and he was apparently educated in them, although their content was later reordered. These included the Classic of History, the Classic of Poetry, the Record of Rites, the Spring and Autumn Annals, and the Book of Changes. The neo-Confucians added the Four Books to this corpus: the Doctrine of the Mean, the Great Learning, the major text authored by Mencius, and the *Analects* of Confucius. They also placed the Four Books above the Five Classics in importance. Would-be Confucian officials who passed the full slate of examinations were expected to master all of these texts, even to the point of being able to repeat them verbatim.

Rituals related to Confucianism are varied, and they often overlap with those linked to Buddhism or Daoism. Many Chinese temples, for example, commonly contain images of the Buddha or of bodhisattvas as well as Confucius. Some temples are dedicated to Confucius alone, and their symmetrical construction is meant to mirror the order of the universe. Rites often include the burning of incense, the giving of offerings of food or money, and prayers or supplications. Of China's many religious festivals, one with particular relevance to Confucianism is Qingming, the Clear and Bright Festival, held two weeks after the spring equinox. During Qingming people come together as extended families and renew their ties to dead ancestors. Rites specifically devoted to Confucius include devotional festivals held twice a year, at the spring and autumn equinoxes. These are conducted by bureaucratic officials rather than priests or monks, and Confucius is revered as a man, not a god or spirit. Confucius's birthday, September 28, is also a holiday, celebrated in some places, such as Taiwan, as a day to honor teachers in general.

*Confucianism in the Modern World* Confucian ethics and ideas remain strong in Taiwan, Hong Kong, Singapore, South Korea, Japan, and in areas around the world where populations of Chinese immigrants are concentrated. In Taiwan, for instance, there are still institutes of education based on the Confucian classics. Even in China itself the Communist government has reduced economic and other restraints since the 1980s and once again Confucian ideals are beginning to reassert themselves. Confucianism's emphasis on the search for social harmony, on respect for the past and for tradition, and on the performance of proper social rituals appears to be simply too central to Chinese civilization to fade away according to changing historical circumstances.

SEE ALSO: *Analects*; Confucian scholar-officials; Confucius; Five Classics; Four Books; neo-Confucianism

## Confucian scholar-officials

The class of bureaucrats, educated in Confucian philosophy, that helped to bring continuity and stability to China to a degree unknown in other major cultural traditions. These officials first appeared as a class during the Han dynasty (206 B.C. –A.D. 220) and continued to play a central role in China until the collapse of the Qing dynasty in 1911.

In their most basic sense the Confucian scholar-officials were government workers, fulfilling various posts of state. But they were also embodiments of Confucian teachings themselves. They were trained to view social harmony as the highest ideal, to respect tradition and ritual, and to seek to fulfill the Confucian gentleman's code of honor, duty, and leadership by example. Since they were educated in Confucian traditions (as well as other aspects of Chinese classical culture) they were also personifications of those traditions.

During the Song dynasty (960–1127), after China had well absorbed Buddhist traditions that had threatened the status of Confucian scholar-officials, state Confucianism was reinvigorated with the rise of so-called neo-Confucianism. Confucian officials reasserted their role as the chief advisers to the "sons of Heaven," or emperors, and expanded earlier educational systems built on Confucian principles, claiming that these systems should be the basis of the state and of Chinese society. Potential members of the bureaucracy had to pass an increasingly difficult series of exams, forms of which had existed earlier but which now became elaborate. Provided they passed through the highest level of national exams, officials might be eligible for the highest positions in the state as well as other honors: the right to wear the "robes of office" and have their names inscribed on stones for all eternity, for example. This imperial bureaucracy was recognized as a political, social, and cultural elite.

Confucian scholar-officials did not always live up to the ideals set for them, and some were prone to corruption or other abuses. Their status was also challenged by other elite groups in China, such as landowning warlords or court eunuchs. But these figures, historically known as mandarins in the West, continued to provide China with cultural continuity for centuries, their very presence a reminder of Confucian ideals. Even after the fall of the Qing dynasty, in fact, Confucian examinations continued to take place in Taiwan into the twentieth century.

SEE ALSO: Confucianism; *li*; neo-Confucianism

## Confucius
### (ca. 551 B.C.–479 B.C.)

Founder of Confucianism and the central figure in classical Chinese philosophy. Confucius, whose Chinese name is K'ung Ch'iu, or Master K'ung, ranks as one of the most important thinkers in world history with a profound influence not only in China but throughout East and Southeast Asia.

Because accounts of Confucius's life were written long after his death, scholars regard what is known about him to be largely legendary. Confucius was born in Lu state in the Shantung province of

China. His family were apparently aristocrats, but ranked fairly low in the aristocratic hierarchy and were poverty-stricken when his father died when Confucius was three years old. Confucius received a traditional education for young men of his class, which was based on the so-called six arts: calligraphy, arithmetic, archery, charioteering, music, and ritual. At the age of twenty he took a job as a keeper of grain stores, a government position. He eventually rose to become the prime minister of Lu and an adviser to the local ruler. After four years in the position he quit, disgruntled because the ruler rejected his policy advice. Confucius spent the next thirteen years wandering from one state to another, seeking another position as adviser to a ruler. Along the way he attracted a group of students curious about his political and social teachings. He eventually returned to Lu in his later years, never again holding official office but teaching until his death at age seventy-two. Confucius did not write down his teachings (at least, none have been discovered). Knowledge of his ideas is best preserved in the *Analects* of Confucius, a text supposedly written by his students and compiled after his death. Traditional accounts suggest that his followers numbered three thousand at the time of his death.

Confucius lived during an era of political turmoil when China suffered from ineffective leadership, constant warfare and conflict among local rulers, and hardship among ordinary people. He was likely influenced by these conditions, as his thought focuses on the establishment of social harmony on earth. Confucius did not see himself as an original thinker necessarily. Rather he was a transmitter and clarifier of traditions and, as such, he wanted to revive what he saw as the wisdom and codes of values of traditional Chinese culture. To personify these traditions and give them the authority of antiquity, Confucius idealized an earlier leader, the Duke of Zhou, who died in 1094 B.C. The Duke's way, he argued, was the only way, and leaders would do well to model themselves after him. The Duke of Zhou achieved nobility because of his character, not through inheritance or the sheer exercise of power. He had also consolidated the practice of and demonstrated the importance of ritual, which Confucius refers to using the word *li*. *Li* was not only the body of rituals themselves—social, political, familial, and otherwise—but the spirit in which those rituals were performed, with reverence, humility, and respect. If leaders followed the Duke of Zhou's example, peace might be restored and ordinary people might be content.

Confucius believed that the purpose of education was to train noblemen, or "gentlemen" as they often are referred to in histories, and these gentlemen were expected to play active roles in the affairs of the world. Even though the fundamental purpose of knowledge was self-awareness, this self-awareness included knowledge of one's place in society and the obligations that came with that place. Indeed, a common Confucian premise was the usefulness of knowledge. In a statement still learned by schoolchildren throughout eastern Asia, quoted in T.R. Reid's *Confucious Lives Next Door*,

> Confucius said: Isn't it a pleasure when you can make practical use of the things you have studied? Isn't it a pleasure to have an old friend visit from afar? Isn't it the sure sign of a gentleman that he does not take offense when others fail to recognize his ability?

Confucius was not particularly concerned with spiritual matters or with any conception of an afterlife, but neither was he an atheist or agnostic. He often referred to *t'ian*, the traditional Chinese conception of heaven, as a positive force in human affairs. Confucius also reinforced the importance of religious rituals dedicated to departed ancestors; filial piety was one of the ideas central to his thought.

SEE ALSO: *Analects*; Confucianism; Five Books

## Congregationalism

A form of Puritan Protestantism that arose in England in the late 1500s and early 1600s. Believers took especially seriously the German reformer Martin Luther's idea of the "priesthood of all believers," which underlies two of the key features of Congregationalist churches, the independence of each congregation from any larger organization and the election of Congregationalist officials from within their own communities. Originally, Congregationalist theology was mostly Calvinist in its orientation, like other churches within the English Puritan movement. The Congregationalist Oliver Cromwell led the anti-Royalist forces in the English civil war and succeeded in governing England from 1650 to 1658, but in the end the strictness and austerity of his radical Puritanism proved unpopular and the Anglican king, Charles II, was restored to the throne in 1660.

Congregationalism has been particularly influential in the United States. The Pilgrims who settled early Massachusetts were Congregationalists who sought complete freedom from the Anglican Church. Other Puritan groups in colonial America were also Congregationalist, and the movement was at the center of the religious revival known as the first Great Awakening in the mid-1700s. In 1913 a national con-

vention of Congregationalist leaders formally broke from Calvinist theology (which many congregations had already rejected in favor of more liberal theologies like that of Unitarianism). As a rule, modern Congrationalists, most of whom are connected to the United Church of Christ, founded in 1961, continue to practice a simple, straightforward Christianity based on faith and a personal relationship with God.

SEE ALSO: Calvinism; Great Awakenings; Protestantism

## Conservative Judaism

A relatively modern movement within Judaism most common in North America, where it is the largest of the three main forms of Judaism, along with Orthodox Judaism and Reform Judaism. Its teachings and practices occupy a sort of middle ground between those of the other two forms.

Conservative Judaism was founded in the early 1800s by German rabbis who termed it "historical Judaism." These rabbis disapproved of the tendency among Reform Jews to reject certain central, traditional dogma such as dietary laws or faith in a coming messiah. They found Orthodox Jews to be too hidebound, however, too committed to beliefs and ways of life not necessarily relevant to a world beginning to undergo rapid economic, social, and political changes. The movement placed its authority in historical scholarship, believing that deep and thorough historical research would provide a solid grounding for Jewish beliefs and practices such as dietary restrictions. Members found such methods preferable to the tendency among the Orthodox to simply follow customs like these unquestioningly and the tendency among Reform Jews to reject them outright

Conservative Judaism crossed the Atlantic to the United States along with Jewish immigrants in the second half of the nineteenth century, and a group of rabbis formed the Jewish Theological Seminary of America in 1886. The seminary acquired great prominence in Jewish scholarship, helping to bring about other institutions, notably the United Synagogue of America (1913), an organization of national Conservative congregations. Conservative Jews do not hesitate to take on modern issues about which traditional Jewish teachings have little to say, such as the ordination of women as rabbis, divorce, and modes of conversion. Their typical approach is to consider such issues in the light of Jewish history and tradition as well as the context of the modern world. Among the compromises Conservative Judaism has reached is to assert the equality of women, and therefore the ability of women to become rabbis, but to maintain the notion of matrilineality, that one's "Jewishness" is passed down through the mother's line, an idea rejected by Reform Jews. The Reconstructionist movement in Judaism began as an offshoot of Conservatism in 1922.

SEE ALSO: Orthodox Judaism; Reconstructionist Judaism; Reform Judaism

# Constantine
## (ca. 288–337)

Sole emperor of the Western Roman Empire from 312 to 337, and the first emperor to accept Christianity, both officially and personally. By the time of his reign Christianity had grown to be a major religion in the Roman Empire, particularly in the eastern, Greek-speaking half, and Constantine's wife was herself an adherent of this relatively new faith. The moment of Constantine's conversion, as well as the

depth of his commitment, is disputed. According to the Roman historian Eusebius, at the Battle of Milvian Bridge in 312, Constantine saw a vision of a cross and the words "by this sign thou shalt conquer" in the heavens; tradition holds that he converted to Christianity and won the battle. Other accounts claim, to the contrary, that he only fully accepted Christianity on his deathbed. It is certain that in 313 he promulgated the Edict of Milan, ensuring religious freedom throughout the empire and guaranteeing that Christians would no longer face official persecution. In the event, his conversion gave added impetus to the spread of Christianity, and the city named after him, Constantinople (previously Byzantium, now Istanbul), was one of the most important cities of the Christian world until it was conquered by Islamic Turks in 1453.

SEE ALSO: ancient Greece and Rome, religions of; Christianity; Eastern Orthodox Christianity

# Coptic Christianity

An ancient form of Christianity that still thrives in Egypt. Coptic Christianity remains distinct from the three main branches of Christianity worldwide: Roman Catholicism, Protestantism, and Eastern Orthodoxy.

In the early centuries of Christianity, Eygpt was part of the Greek-speaking world, a center of scholarship, and a natural target for Christian evangelizers. According to tradition, the church there was started in the first century by Mark, the author of one of the New Testament Gospels. As the institutional church developed, the bishop of Alexandria, who presided over Christianity in one of the Mediterranean world's great cultural centers, was nearly as important as the bishop of Rome.

The Egyptian church became distinct as the result of the Council of Chalcedon in 451. There Eastern bishops led by Dioscurus of Alexandria declared their belief in a doctrine known as monophysism, one of several historical interpretations of the divinity of Jesus Christ. The Monophysites asserted that Jesus Christ had a single nature that was indistinguishably both human and divine. Orthodox Catholic doctrine asserts that Jesus Christ was of two natures, fully human and fully divine, united in one divine person. The council ultimately issued a decree endorsing the duality interpretation as official doctrine of the Christian faith, and banished Dioscurus, but the Eastern bishops refused to accept the decree.

After Arabs conquered Egypt in the seventh century, bringing with them Islam and the Arabic language, the split became effectively permanent. Egyptian Christians were free to maintain their beliefs under Islam, but they stopped speaking Greek in favor of Coptic, a language whose roots go back to ancient Egypt, and church leaders ended their official contact with the leaders of the other churches. In other doctrinal matters as well as rituals, Coptic Christianity is similar to Eastern Orthodoxy.

In the modern world, Coptic Christianity maintains an independent institutional presence, with its own patriarch based in Alexandria and a number of other educational and administrative bodies based mostly in Cairo. There is also an important Coptic Church in Jerusalem, and members of the church have taken their faith to Australia, Great Britain, and the United States as well. Services are primarily conducted in Arabic, the common language of modern Egyptians, with liturgical texts in both Arabic and Coptic. The church, moreover, remains the center of the communion of other ancient Christian denominations in Ethiopia, Sudan, Armenia, and Syria whose traditions are also distinct from those of the three main branches of Christianity.

SEE ALSO: Christian heresies; Eastern Orthodox Christianity

## councils, Buddhist

According to most Buddhist traditions, early Buddhist leaders in India held three major councils. The first took place at Rajagha in northern India around 480 B.C., only a few years after the death of the original Buddha. There Buddhist disciples organized the original Buddha's teachings into a set of repetitive oral chants. These form the Tripitaka, or "three baskets" of knowledge passed down by the Buddha, although some Buddhists think that only two of the baskets were decided upon here.

The second Buddhist council was at Vaisali in northern India in around 350 B.C. There Buddhist leaders settled on a collection of classic teachings that went beyond the Tripitaka, but they also argued over whether the Buddha's original teaching might be too difficult or severe for most monks. Attendees also discussed such practical matters as whether monks should handle money.

The third Buddhist council was held at Pataliputra in 250 B.C. It was the most important of the three, reflected in the fact that at the time Pataliputra was the political center of India, the capital of Ashoka and other emperors. The third council likely began the split that was later to become the division of Buddhism into the Theravada and Mahayana paths. Attendees hotly disputed the respective roles and expectations of "elders" (or monks) and the "great assembly" (or laypeople.)

See Also: Ashoka; Mahayana Buddhism; Theravada Buddhism

## councils, early Christian Church

Meetings of high church officials designed to establish authoritative Christian doctrine, resolve doctrinal disputes, and make laws governing church administration in Christianity's earliest centuries. Church traditions deem these meetings ecumenical councils, since their purpose was to establish doctrine for the entire church, for all Christians. This ecumenism was ideal rather than real, however, as one result of some council's decisions was the splitting off of independent churches that rejected council authority, such as the Egyptian Coptic Church.

The councils were usually convened by order of an emperor or later the pope. They drew hundreds of bishops and other delegates from across the Christian world, and were conducted in several sessions sometimes spread over months. Seven councils are considered most authoritative in establishing the official beliefs and practices of what were to emerge as the Roman Catholic and Eastern Orthodox branches of Christianity.

The first was the Council of Nicaea in 325. There delegates determined the date of Easter and the authority of the bishops, rejected Arianism (a heresy that declared that Jesus was created by God but was not himself God), and drafted the Nicene Creed. The second council, at the then Roman imperial capital at Constantinople in 381, established the Nicene Creed as the basic statement of Christian belief. It also condemned other heresies, as did the third council, the Council of Ephesus in 431. In 451, at the Council of Chalcedon, the Monophysites split from the church over the issue of whether Jesus Christ had a singular nature or dual natures. At the fifth council in 553, also in Constantinople, the bishops formally rejected the Nestorian heresy, which implied that Jesus might be two beings, one human and one divine. This council also marks the beginning of the split between the Western (Roman Catholic) and Eastern (Orthodox) churches when the pope and bishop of Rome, Vigilius, hesitated to accept the council's decisions (this split, or schism, would not become formal until 1054). In 680 a third Constantinople council was convened by emperor Constantine IV, who still clung to the title of Roman emperor despite the loss of Western possessions much earlier. The main issue of this sixth ecumenical council was, again, the nature of Jesus Christ. The council declared that he had two distinct natures, as God performing miracles and other divine acts, and as man carrying on the activities of daily earthly life, each nature exercising free will and both mystically united in one divine person. The seventh early church council was held in Nicaea in 787. Its purpose was to settle the so-called iconoclastic controversy, over whether the presence or worship of religious icons—images of Jesus, the Virgin Mary, angels, saints, and others—was idolatry. Veneration of icons had been abolished in 754 but was restored by the seventh council.

See Also: Christian heresies; Eastern Orthodox Christianity; Nicene Creed; Roman Catholic Christianity

## councils, Roman Catholic Church

Even after the Great Schism of 1054 split the Christian Church into Eastern Orthodox and Roman Catholic communities, the Roman Catholic hierarchy continued to convene major councils to discuss and decide doctrinal and administrative issues.

These are known, like early Christian councils, as ecumenical councils both because they were designed to bring together different interests and because the councils claimed authority over all Christians, whether or not they were represented at the council.

There were fifteen councils between the eleventh and nineteenth centuries. Among them was the Council of Clermont, convened by Pope Urban II in 1095. At Clermont, Urban issued his famous "call to crusade," urging western European warrior nobles to journey to the Holy Land to reclaim it from Muslim leaders. The five Lateran Councils, so-called because they took place at the Lateran Palace in Rome, examined important administrative and doctrinal issues. For example, the First Lateran Council in 1123 dealt with the Investiture Controversy over whether the popes, their subordinates, or political leaders had the right to choose, or "invest," the bishops who presided over the churches in a particular area. At the Third Lateran Council, in 1179, church leaders condemned various heresies, established how popes must be elected by the College of Cardinals, and declared that popes must be at least thirty years old. The largest of the Lateran Councils was the fourth in 1215, attended both by hundreds of church officials and by royal representatives. A major concern of the Fourth Lateran Council was the attempt to revive the crusading movement, then waning, and reestablish Roman Catholic control of the Holy Land.

The Council of Constance, another major meeting, took place from 1414 to 1418. There church leaders tried to reconcile the schism of the 1300s, when for a time popes resided in Avignon in France rather than in Rome and were thought to be mere political pawns. Earlier attempts to address this problem had given rise to the election of new popes by rival factions, until at one point there were three men who claimed to be the descendant of Saint Peter and head of the Western Church. The Council of Constance solved this schism by first establishing the supremacy of church councils over popes and then encouraging all three rival popes to step down in favor of a new compromise pope.

The last ecumenical council prior to the modern era was the Council of Trent, which met in three sessions from 1545 to 1563. Its major purpose was to address the challenge represented by the Protestant reform movement; thus the Council of Trent is associated with the Catholic Counter-Reformation and the revitalization of the church. At Trent church leaders affirmed the doctrine that Christian belief and practice derived not only from scripture but also from Roman Catholic tradition. They also condemned most Protestant churches and fine-tuned doctrinal matters on the nature of the Eucharist and the fixing of seven official sacraments.

SEE ALSO: councils, early Christian Church; Crusades: Vatican Councils

## Counter-Reformation

The response by the Roman Catholic hierarchy to the challenge of the Protestant Reformation. Occurring mainly from the 1540s into the early 1600s, the Catholic Counter-Reformation had the effect of reforming and streamlining the Catholic Church, both theologically and administratively.

Church authorities were slow to react to Protestant reformers at first, not considering them much of a threat. But Protestantism expanded so rapidly in the 1520s and 1530s that Pope Paul III (r. 1534–1549) was compelled to call the Council of Trent to address it. The council met in three sessions between 1545 and 1563. Their decrees were largely responses to the ideas of Martin Luther and other Protestant reformers. They agreed with Luther's notion that faith alone was the basis of salvation but asserted that good works, (or "acts" such as confession) were necessary as well, because they demonstrate faith. Delegates also agreed with Luther that the Bible was the primary source of religious authority, but unlike Luther they recognized Roman Catholic teachings and the pronouncements of the popes as authoritative. The church also tried to curtail certain practices Protestants viewed as corruption and clerical abuses of power such as luxurious living, the worldly orientations of priests and popes, and even excessive meddling in politics.

Among the institutional reforms of the Counter-Reformation was the founding of a Roman Inquisition to root out what the Catholics considered heresy, and along with it a much more ruthless Spanish and Portuguese Inquisition. More power was also given to the new, militant Jesuit order of monks, who were very active as educators and missionaries, both within Europe and in far-flung colonial and trading outposts established by Catholic powers during the age of exploration. In 1559 the church also created an Index of Forbidden Books to control the flow of ideas: Believers were forbidden from reading any of the books on the list on pain of excommunication. These efforts helped to stem the spread of Protestantism, especially in central and eastern Europe.

SEE ALSO: councils, Roman Catholic Church; Reformation, Protestantism

## covenant

An agreement or arrangement or, in some cases, a promise of God. The term is commonly used in the Hebrew Bible to refer to the original agreement between God and the Hebrew prophet Abraham (ca. 2000–1800 B.C.) as well as later adjustments to that agreement. This original covenant became a binding contract and helped in the formation of not only Judaism but Christianity and, to a lesser degree, Islam as well. The covenant was reaffirmed during the time of Moses (ca. 1250 B.C.), after which point the Jews considered themselves entirely a people of the covenant. The Ten Commandments were the heart and great symbol of this reaffirmed covenant, and Jews were exhorted to follow not only the commandments but other Jewish laws as part of upholding the agreement. Covenants were a common practice among Near Eastern kings, used not only in religious but also political and personal matters, so it was not surprising that the Hebrew king Josiah further refined the covenant of Moses in 621 B.C. In 587 B.C. the prophet Jeremiah predicted a new covenant. His prophecy was picked up by early Christians, who came to believe the new covenant was fulfilled in the life and resurrection of Jesus of Nazareth.

SEE ALSO: Abraham; Exodus; New Testament

## crucifixion

The method by which Jesus of Nazareth, the founder of Christianity, was executed. Crucifixion was a common means of punishment and execution by the time of Jesus, used by diverse peoples, among them Persians, Greeks, Jews, and Romans, as far back as the sixth century B.C. It was commonly an "insulting" form of punishment and execution for political rebels, religious

Christ Crucified. *As far back as the sixth century* B.C. *crucifixion was used by the Persians, Greeks, Jews, and Romans as both punishment and execution.*

agitators, and slaves, as opposed to the more "honorable" forms of execution granted to, for example, defeated soldiers. In a famous incident around 70 B.C., tens of thousands of rebellious slaves, led by Spartacus, were crucified by Roman authorities.

Commonly people condemned to crucifixion were either lashed to or nailed to the crossbeam of a cross; if nailed the nails passed through the wrists. This step might have been preceded by a whipping and procession in which the condemned was forced to drag his crossbeam through the streets. The crossbeam was then attached horizontally, 8 to 10 feet (2.5 to 3m) aboveground, to a vertical post and the condemned's feet were tied or nailed to the post. The only support for his body might be a small board at the midriff. Crucifixions also served as public spectacles: The condemned's name and crime were often posted on a signboard above his head and the public was free to hurl insults or even objects. Those crucified might die (although many apparently survived) through exposure, heart failure, or even suffocation, the last particularly when supporting bones were smashed at some point during the event.

The Roman emperor Constantine, the first Christian emperor, abolished the practice within the Empire in A.D. 337, three centuries after the crucifixion of Jesus.

SEE ALSO: Christianity; Constantine; Jesus of Nazareth

## Crusades

The series of military campaigns by Christian warriors from western Europe to take possession of Christian holy places in Palestine, the Holy Land of the Middle East, taking place between 1095 and 1294. Motivated by the desire for political power as well as greater religious authority, Pope Urban II called for the Crusades to begin in 1095. He hoped that the Holy Land could be thereby brought under his authority, and that the Western Roman branch of Christianity could be reunited with the Eastern Orthodox branch. Citing alleged (and mostly false) Islamic atrocities against Christian pilgrims, Urban inspired tens of thousands of land-hungry knights to "take up the cross" (the meaning of *crusade*) and free the holy places from Muslims. He promised the European armies both military glory and the expiation of sins.

The First Crusade, from 1096 to 1099, was the most successful, as Christian nobles and their armies both seized Jerusalem and established a string of crusader kingdoms in the Middle East. Later Crusades were less successful; the fourth, in 1294, wreaked great havoc on the Eastern Orthodox capital of Constantinople rather than on any Muslim-held territory. After an early period of disunity, meanwhile, Turkish, Kurdish, and Arab Muslims united under a series of warlords, most importantly Saladin (1138–1193), and steadily forced the crusaders to retreat. The last crusader kingdom was abandoned in 1294.

The idea of crusading did not completely die out, however. Subsequent Crusades were mounted against Christian heretics as well as against Muslim territories in other parts of Europe, notably Spain. Meanwhile, Roman Catholic Christianity took on a militant aspect that could be seen in such developments as the Inquisition, the aggressive acts of Christian explorers during Europe's age of exploration (ca. 1420–1650), and the reaction to the Protestant Reformation of the 1500s.

SEE ALSO: papacy; Roman Catholicism

## cults

In general, movements that stand outside mainstream religion and that adopt non-traditional beliefs or worship practices. Historically, numerous cults have been spawned within established religious traditions, often localized and devoted to particular gods. The pattern is repeated in the Hindu tradition, although in recent times it has been more common to refer to Hinduism's many sects rather than to its cults. Likewise, movements out of the Christian mainstream, such as the Society of Friends, or Quakers, are also commonly referred to as sects rather than cults. In recent years the term has acquired a negative connotation with the rise of isolated groups viewed as strange or dangerous, often with charismatic leaders or associated with sensational or violent incidents.

SEE ALSO: new religious movements, Western

## Dalai Lama

The head of Tibetan Buddhism as well as the Tibetan head of state. Dalai Lamas have held this dual role since the time of the fifth Dalai Lama in the seventeenth century. Each successive Dalai Lama is held to be the reincarnation of his predecessors as well as an avatar of the bodhisattva Avalokitesvara. While the title of lama is applied to any Tibetan religious teacher, the superlative term *dalai* is a Western derivation of a Tibeto-Mongolian phrase meaning "ocean of wisdom." The office of Dalai Lama is not hereditary; upon the death of a Dalai Lama, other high lamas search for a new reincarnation, who might be found anywhere and who shows signs of being a reincarnation of earlier lamas.

The current Dalai Lama, Tenzin Gyatso, is the fourteenth. Ever since Tibet was overtaken by China in the 1950s, he has claimed Dharamsala in India as his base and refuge. The Dalai Lama has maintained his political as well as religious leadership role as the head of the so-called Tibetan diaspora. He has also achieved global recognition for his advocacy of compassion and nonviolence, and he has done a great deal to popularize Buddhism in the West, both in general forms and in its more specific Tibetan variation. The Dalai Lama is the author as well as the subject of many books; for his work he was awarded the Nobel Peace Prize in 1989.

SEE ALSO: Avalokitesvara; lama; Tibetan Buddhism

## Dao De Jing

Classic text of Chinese philosophy and, along with the *Chuang-tzu*, the central text of Daoism. The Dao De Jing, often translated as the Book of the Way, was originally attributed to Lao-tzu, the legendary founder of Daoism, but modern scholars consider it the compilation of the teachings of a number of sources dating between the sixth and third centuries B.C. Parts of the text are critical of Confucianism, an indication that it did not become familiarly known before the fourth century B.C. Another of its Chinese names is the Classic of Five Thousand Signs, because it is composed of five thousand Chinese epigrams, or characters. After the Bible and the Bhagavad Gita, it is the third most translated book in history, with more than eighty different translations into English alone over the last century.

As a complement to the paradoxical lessons of the *Chuang-tzu*, the Dao De Jing formulates philosophical Daoism in a somewhat more systematic although still poetical way. It describes the Dao as "the Way," the underlying essence of the universe that sustains nature and all life. According to Daoism, the Dao operates, or rather simply exists, passively. Human beings should seek to align themselves with the Dao if they seek peace of mind. The best way to do this is through the practice of wu-wei, or not doing, which is understood as taking no action that is not natural. Fully understood and acted upon, wu-wei will allow one to have full knowledge of oneself and the world, which is the only true power, or De.

One common reading of the Dao De Jing suggests its concern with political power as well as individual well-being. This reading is unsurprising, since the text became known during the centuries when China was unstable politically and dangerous for many ordinary people. Like Confucian thought, the Dao De Jing suggests ways for order and harmony to be restored. But unlike Confucianism, the Dao De Jing rejects expending excessive energy in the performance of rituals or in proper education. Instead, rulers are urged to live in accord with the Dao, and when they do, their examples of tranquility will inspire the people to seek it themselves, and end the conflicts, disagreements, and selfish seeking after power that the text cautions against. As translated by Victor H. Mair, one passage of the Dao De Jing reads simply:

> Rule the state with uprightness,
> Deploy your troops with craft,
> Gain all under heaven with noninterference.
>
> How do I know this is actually so?
> Now,
> The more taboos under heaven,
> the poorer the people;
> The more clever devices people have,
> the more confused the state and ruling house;
> The more knowledge people have,
> the more strange things spring up;
> The more legal affairs are given prominence,
> the more numerous bandits and thieves.
>
> For this reason,
> The sage has a saying:
> "I take no action,
> yet the people transform themselves;
> I am fond of stillness,

> yet the people correct themselves;
> I do not interfere in affairs,
> yet the people enrich themselves;
> I desire not to desire,
> yet the people of themselves become as simple as unhewn logs."

SEE ALSO: Chuang-tzu; Daoism; Lao-tzu

# Daoism

A religious and philosophical school that has been central to the culture and traditions of China for more than two thousand years, and which has influenced other East Asian societies and Westerners as well. Daoism is in many ways the counterpart to Confucianism; in contrast to Confucianism's focus on human effort and earthly order, Daoism emphasizes living according to the rhythms of nature and of the cosmos. Daoism has been the major form of popular religion in China, and has likely been an important influence on Chinese Buddhism as well. Relatively few people are Daoists exclusively, but millions of people practice elements of Daoism as part of Chinese and East Asian popular religion.

*Origins and History* Daoism, like Confucianism, was a product of the political and social instability of China during the middle of the first millennium B.C. although many of the elements of religious Daoism appeared much earlier in Chinese history. It was founded, according to tradition, by a mysterious teacher named Lao-tzu who was thought to have lived during the sixth century B.C. and who wrote Daoism's original text, the Dao De Jing. The purpose of the Dao De Jing was to provide potential rulers, sage-kings as some Daoists put it, with a style of rulership based on wu-wei, the principle of not doing, or perhaps more accurately, doing in such a way that one's actions are unobtrusive or even invisible. The second major Daoist text, the *Chuang-tzu*, named after its author, who lived from roughly 370–286 B.C., extended those views to ordinary people's lives. In so doing, it provided a philosophy of life based on attempts to live in concord with the essential force of nature, or the Dao, and therefore was a contrast with Confucianism's emphasis on earthly effort and hard work.

By the time of the Han dynasty (206 B.C.–A.D. 220), Daoist ideas and the Daoist texts were respected by many governmental and other elites. Lao-tzu himself was revered as a deity and a number of new texts appeared, notably the Book of the Great Peace and the Book of the Yellow Court. The latter was linked to a major Daoist sect known as the Yellow Turbans, which attracted hundreds of thousands of followers and became very powerful in northern China in the second century A.D. Another important sect was the Wu Dou Mi Dao, or the Five Pecks of Rice Way because of the annual tribute of rice that adepts were to pay to the organization. The founder of the movement, Zhang Daoling, claimed to have received revelations from Lao-tzu and was seen as a "celestial master" holding special powers. Believers, like most Daoists at this time, were interested in finding ways to cure illness and even gain immortality using rites, confessions, and alchemy, or the devising of potions, powders, and elixirs. They also became involved in politics and helped to bring about the end of the Han dynasty. The movement continued to thrive, and faith in the line of celestial masters, each of which is thought to be a reincarnation of Zhang Daoling, continues in modern Taiwan. Meanwhile, in the centuries of instability following the Han dynasty, Daoism continued to expand as China's primary popular religion, characterized by such notions as the balance represented by the yin-yang symbol and the understanding and manipulation of the five elements: metal, wood, water, fire, and earth. Many Daoist sects during these years were millennialist, as was Zhang Daoling's movement, promising a future age of peace. Daoists also commonly established monasteries for adherents wishing to devote lifetimes to the pursuit of the Dao.

During the Tang dynasty (618–907), Daoism received great official recognition and patronage, as many emperors claimed to be descended from Lao-tzu. The major feature of the era, however, is the increasing integration of Daoism with Confucianism and Buddhism. Scholars began to conflate the Dao ("the Way") with the Buddhist notion of dhamma ("the path") and the concept of wu-wei with the Buddhist state of nirvana. It is also likely that Daoism helped to inspire the Zen school of Buddhism. Leaders argued that the Dao De Jing should be included among the texts used for the examinations preparing Confucian scholar-officials. This process of syncretism continued during the Song dynasty (960–1127); Daoism was an important feature of the neo-Confucian philosophy that prevailed during the era. The Song dynasty also saw the founding of the Quanzhen sect of Daoism by a twelfth-century sage named Wang Zhongfu. Quanzhen emphasizes perfection of the flow of energy through the body, or qigong, and remains an important Daoist sect today.

***Central Beliefs of Daoism*** At the heart of Daoism is the perceived need to understand the Dao, the "way" of nature and of the universe. Even though the Dao is ultimately passive, in that it does not "act" in human terms, it is the source of everything and accomplishes everything. As both of the original Daoist texts make clear, it is often easiest to describe the Dao using metaphors, allegories, and paradoxes. A common one is that the Dao is similar to the empty space inside a pot; without this empty space, a pot would not be a pot and could no longer fulfill a pot's purpose.

Human beings should attempt to live simply, adjusting their behavior to the workings of the Dao. Daoists believe that this will result in a more harmonious and happier life, since ambition and activity have only led to chaos and instability. Both rulers and ordinary people should practice not doing, or wu-wei. Those rulers govern best who govern least, and in ways that are unobtrusive. Ordinary people will be happiest in small, self-sufficient communities with little need or desire to interact with their neighbors. Although Daoism emphasizes introspection and meditation as a means to self-knowledge, it also argues that the purpose, or result, of self-knowledge is unself-conscious "doing" in ways that accord with the Dao. As one Daoist statement claims, one who understands the Dao would "rather go fishing than talk about it." Such an understanding is the true source of De, or power.

Scholars trace two overlapping strands of Daoism: philosophical Daoism (daojia) and religious Daoism (daojiao). Philosophical Daoism is the tradition of ideas that dates back to Lao-tzu and which many scholars and sages have explored since. It centers on understanding the nature of the Dao as well as people's relationship to the Dao, emphasizing not only wu-wei but such notions as detachment and flexibility. Daoist philosophers often even "philosophize" in Daoist ways; rather than serious, earnest discussions of ideas they use riddles, paradoxes, open-ended questions, and other forms of intellectual "play," realizing that in Daoism no answer is ever complete. Among the many schools of philosophical Daoism was the so-called neo-Daoist Seven Sages of the Bamboo Grove of the third century A.D. This group of thinkers and poets took Daoist irreverence to an extreme by ridiculing Confucians and other "serious" thinkers, promoting individuality and eccentricity over prescribed Confucian social roles, and gathering to eat, drink wine, and enjoy other worldly pursuits. Other neo-Daoist sects, however, respected Confucius's ideas about social harmony.

Religious Daoism generally refers to Daoism's many sects, to Daoist rituals, and to the links between Daoism and Chinese folk religion, Buddhism, and other religious traditions. Religious Daoists believe in various deities or gods, such as Zhang Daoling's celestial masters, as well as the presence of spirits or ghosts, sometimes ancestral ones. Religious Daoists might also seek ways to gain immortality by manipulating natural forces or products through alchemy, or failing that, by releasing the spiritual energies that lie within the body. An important school, the Inner Deity Hygiene School, holds that the deities who control the body can be activated in positive ways through exercise, proper diet, breathing in ways that optimize the flow of $qi$, or energy, and even sexual techniques involving focusing the power of sexual release inwardly rather than outwardly. Other schools emphasize, instead, moral behavior and the search for the sacred territories where the immortals, who are often characterized as seven figures called Pa-hsien, live.

**Daoism in the Modern World** Organized Daoist movements, both religious and philosophical, have been oppressed by China's current Communist government. During the Chinese Cultural Revolution (1965–1975), for example, many Daoist monasteries, monuments, and texts were damaged or destroyed. In the last twenty years, however, with increased cultural openness, some of these have been restored and Daoists have been granted greater freedoms. The faith continued to thrive throughout this period in Taiwan, which houses the sixty-third celestial master, Chang En-pu. Since the 1960s Taiwan has seen a great resurgence in Daoism, with the construction of many new temples and the appearance of new schools of priests conducting rites ranging from ancient liturgies to exorcism. Many Daoist activities and festivals are held in other places with large Chinese populations, such as Hong Kong, Singapore, and Malaysia. Meanwhile, elements of Daoism have seeped into the global popular culture of the world in such forms as martial arts, feng shui, the yin-yang symbol, and other aspects of new religious movements.

SEE ALSO: Chuang-tzu; Dao De Jing; Lao-tzu; Pa-hsien

## darshan

Most commonly understood as the "viewing" of a deity, a guru, or a sacred object in Hinduism and thus an elemental form of connection to the divine for ordinary believers. Darshan requires physical nearness to the object or person, whose very presence is thought to confer spiritual benefits. Usually darshan occurs in temples or in shrines in private homes. The processions that accompany many Hindu festivals also provide occasions for darshan when images of gods are paraded through the streets. Some gurus hold mass meetings where they grant regular darshan to

devotees. Hindus believe the process is reciprocal: If believers grant the objects of their darshan reverence and respect, they receive blessings in return.

SEE ALSO: guru; Hinduism; puja

## David
### (– ca. 962 B.C.)

Second king of ancient Israel and a revered figure among Jews, Christians, and Muslims. According to the Hebrew Bible, David was selected as successor to Saul around 1000 B.C. and went on to add new lands to Israel as well as unite various contentious Hebrew groups. He established the city of Jerusalem as his capital, began the construction of the first Temple there, and proclaimed that the God of Jerusalem was to be known as Yahweh, supplanting all other names. He and his successors were to rule as regents of Yahweh, sitting at his right hand. David is also credited with writing a number of the Psalms contained in the Hebrew Bible, a sign of his artistic talent as well as his devotion.

The political unity of Israel did not last, and the kingdom split following the reign of David's son Solomon. But David's legacy remained strong as the ideal king who was also devoted to God. His royal line of succession, known in the Bible as the house of David, became a symbol of the connection between God and his people in the Hebrew tradition. A Hebrew term meaning "anointed one" was later translated into "messiah," the promised redeemer who Jews believed would one day return. Christians believe that Jesus of Nazareth was of the house of David and therefore the promised messiah. For Muslims, David was one of the prophets who preceded Muhammad.

SEE ALSO: Hebrew Bible; messiah; Temple

*Found between 1947 and 1956 in the city of Qumran, the Dead Sea Scrolls describe daily life in the region, and include alternate versions of books from the Hebrew Bible.* © WEST SEMITIC RESEARCH/DEAD SEA SCROLLS FOUNDATION/CORBIS

## Dead Sea Scrolls

The name given to a collection of some 850 manuscripts found between 1947 and 1956 in caves near the Dead Sea, mostly near the ancient village of Qumran. Dated from between about 150 B.C. and 68 A.D., the manuscripts provide hitherto unknown clues to the lives and beliefs of religious communities existing in the region, with significance for both Jewish and Christian history.

Archaeologists and scholars place most of the texts in one of three categories. Some are alternate versions of books from the Hebrew Bible, others are texts known previously in Christian translations made much later, while others are descriptions of some of the communities living in the region. Many experts attribute the texts to a group known as the Essenes, but evidence is by no means conclusive, and many of the manuscripts themselves are only fragmentary. The texts may also be the record of one or more communities seeking refuge in the Qumran region from either Jewish or Roman authorities in Jerusalem. Most of the texts are written in two dialects of Hebrew, but a further if tentative link between the Dead Sea Scrolls and early Christian communities is the fact that some of the manuscripts were written in Greek, the language of the New Testament.

SEE ALSO: ancient Near East, religions of; Essenes; Septuagint

# deism

An approach to religion emerging in Europe in the seventeenth century among certain thinkers who attempted to reconcile Christian traditions with other religions and with their own culture's new emphasis on rationalism and science. Deistic ideas were common in the eighteenth century, drawing adherents such as Enlightenment philosopher Voltaire as well as many educated elites, including the first three U.S. presidents.

Deists came to favor reason over revelation as a source of religious understanding, and they rejected as superstition much of the dogma and practices of the Roman Catholic Church. They were also uncomfortable with what they perceived as the unreflective spiritual "enthusiasm" of many Protestant churches. Their preference was for a kind of calm reasoning and for tolerance. They argued that all religions, not only Protestant and Catholic Christianity but those around the world, shared a common set of moral principles that could be understood and described using reason. Differences in theology and ritual were trivial by comparison.

Deists believed that the world was a rational mechanism that God had created, but they did not believe that God continually guided the day-to-day affairs of individuals or the world; instead, he retreated into his properly transcendent role once the Creation was complete. The world was then left to operate according to its own natural laws: God, the Deists asserted, was like a great clock maker. Human beings,

using their powers of reason, could not only understand but even improve upon God's Creation.

SEE ALSO: agnosticism; atheism; theism

# dhamma

In general, the Buddhist path to understanding as well as, in a larger sense, the true order of the universe. Dhamma is the Pali-language transliteration of the Sanskrit word dharma, used commonly in Hinduism. The concept of dhamma or dharma bears similarities in both religions, namely the sense that one's dhamma, or place along the path, is affected by karma, the consequence of action, and that dhamma in some sense reflects the order of the cosmos. But there are also fundamental differences that make the terms not synonymous.

In Buddhism the dhamma is the universal truth first revealed by the original Buddha as well as the teachings of the Buddha. For most Buddhists, it is furthermore the steps taken to practice and gain a full understanding of that truth in pursuit of the ultimate goal of nirvana. By following the dhamma, believers grow beyond the common ignorance of the true nature of the universe and open themselves up to the possibility of enlightenment.

SEE ALSO: Buddhism; dharma; Eightfold Path

# Dhammapada

A key Buddhist text. The Dhammapada, or Way of Truth, is a collection of 423 Buddhist teachings, generally from gurus to students written in verse form. It is contained in the *Sutta Pitaka* (Basket of Discourses), one of the "three baskets" of wisdom that make up Buddhism's main ancient scripture, the Tripitaka. Containing mostly ethical teachings, the Dhammapada is widely used in both Theravada and Mahayana Buddhism; in Theravadin Sri Lanka, many monks try to memorize it in its entirety for the purpose of recitation. Many of its lessons are attributed to the original Buddha himself, which partly explains its authority and popularity. Scholars suspect, however, that it was compiled from both strictly Buddhist sources and a larger tradition of popular Indian religious literature. Parts of the text indeed sound like folk wisdom. In *Buddhist Teachings*, translated by Edward Conze, the first seven verses of one of the Dhammapada's teachings on morality state:

1. If you want honour, wealth, or, after death, a blissful life among the gods,
Then take good care that you observe the precepts of a moral life!

2.–3. The prudent man will lead a moral life
When he considers it has four rewards:
A sense of virtue gives him peace,
His body is not over-taxed,
At night he sleeps a happy sleep,
And when he wakes he wakes with joy.
A holy man, endowed with vision,
He thrives and prospers in this world.

4. How excellent a moral life pursued till death!
How excellent a well-established faith!
And wisdom is for men a treasure which brings merit,
And which the thieves find very hard to steal.

5. The man of wisdom who did good,
The man of morals who gave gifts,
In this world and the next one too,
They will advance to happiness.

6.–7. His moral habits planted firm, his senses well protected,

In eating temperate, and to vigilance inclined,
The monk who feels no weariness, and struggles day and night,
His progress is assured, and he will win Nirvana soon.

SEE ALSO: Buddhism; dharma

## dharma

One of the most important concepts in Hinduism. Dharma is a Sanskrit word meaning "that which is established." It is employed to refer to the order of the universe, to the forms of law and custom that reinforce that order, and even to religion in general. For many individual Hindus the term connotes the duties that they must perform as members of families, castes, or religious sects as well as the impulse to lead a religious life. With regard to the former, dharma is a code of ethics, but by maintaining this code of ethics one also, and without any necessarily direct intention or volition, leads a religious life and helps to sustain universal order. Hindu sacred texts include collections of Dharma Sutras and, later, Dharma Shastras that lay out some of these ethical codes and indicate their connection to universal order. The most well known and important of the Dharma Shastras is the Laws of Manu.

In other contexts, dharma is the third stage of life (for upper-caste men) described in the Laws of Manu. At this stage one begins to leave behind one's worldly obligations and turns to ritual activity and religious devotion. Using the Pali spelling dhamma, dharma is also a central concept in Buddhism, with related meaning.

SEE ALSO: caste; dhamma; Laws of Manu

## Diamond Sutra

A major text in Mahayana Buddhism. It was composed around A.D. 300 and is one of a number of short Buddhist "perfection of wisdom" texts. Its full Sanskrit title is translated as "The Diamond Cutter Perfection of Wisdom Sutra," implying that with its message one could cut through ignorance like a diamond could cut through objects. Its lessons take the form of a dialogue between the original Buddha and a student. The common theme of these lessons is that the world and universe are illusions, that such apparently real phenomena as the stars and clouds emerge and disappear just like the objects in a dream. Rather than fully explaining the lessons, however, the Diamond Sutra simply presents them, leaving the reader to ponder or meditate upon them. Because of this method, the Diamond Sutra is thought by some scholars to presage the Zen form of Buddhism.

SEE ALSO: Lotus Sutra; Mahayana Buddhism; Zen Buddhism

# Diaspora

From a Greek word meaning dispersal, a cultural term for the communities of Jews living away from Israel. The term also has historical meaning, referring to the period between A.D. 70, when the second Jewish Temple in Jerusalem was destroyed, to 1948, when the modern State of Israel was established. During this long interval the Jewish religion had no geographical focal point and Jewish communities, literally dispersed from North Africa across Europe and the Middle East to as far as India and China, kept the faith alive with a focus on local religion and on passing down traditions from rabbis to students. The historical Diaspora has ended, and modern Israel maintains a "law of return" allowing any Diaspora Jew to return to Israel and attain citizenship. Most Jews, however, remain part of the cultural Diaspora—there are

more Jews living in the United States, for example, than in Israel. Some Jews are concerned that with the spread of secularization and phenomena such as intermarriage, many in the Diaspora are losing their Jewish identity.

The term is also used in a more generic sense to apply to any community, religious or otherwise, whose members identify with a particular region but who have spread throughout the world. There exist, therefore, a Hindu diaspora, a Sikh diaspora, and others. Religions with no particular geographical emphasis and which claim global jurisdiction, such as Christianity and Islam, cannot maintain diasporas.

SEE ALSO: Exodus; Jerusalem; Judaism

# Divali

The Hindu festival of light. Celebrated over four or five days in October or November every year (the specific number of days and the time depend on the lunar calendar), Divali is the most important of all annual festivals in Hinduism. It is celebrated throughout northern India, even among Sikhs, as well as in southern India, where it is known as Dipavali.

The word dipavali, of which divali is a shortened version, means a "row of lamps." One of the features of the festival is the lighting of small oil lamps and setting them in temples and homes as well as floating them in rivers or other waterways. Hindus are also urged to keep light in their hearts, and the occasion is one for the giving of gifts and feasts. The fourth day of Divali is the Hindu new year, a time for breaking out new clothes, new diaries, and new account books. The central deity of Divali is Lakshmi, the goddess of wealth. Consequently, merchants and businessmen are especially conscientious in their Divali observances. Regional differences abound, however; in Bengal Divali is an occasion to worship Kali, and in north-central India celebrations focus on Rama, Sita, Hanuman, and other figures from the Ramayana.

SEE ALSO: calendars; Holi; Lakshmi

## divination

The practice of trying to read natural, psychological, or heavenly signs in order to understand events or predict the future. Divination has been practiced in all cultures and performed in innumerable ways. Among the better-known forms are the rolling of dice, which is a modern version of many ancient ways to "throw lots," astrology, and the reading of Tarot cards. In China, divination is common to many religious traditions and can be traced back to the text known as the *I Ching*, a diviner's manual at least three thousand years old that is still popular.

Some religious traditions have featured diviners, or officials thought to have the ability of reading signs. Ancient Greece featured, for instance, the oracle of Delphi and her priests, while ancient Rome's diviners were thought able to read the entrails of birds or other animals or understand the omens present in the cries of birds. The shamans of Native American or Central Asian religions, among others, are thought to have the ability to enter into trance states, sometimes with the help of drugs, and gain insight into the future.

SEE ALSO: African religions; Native American religions, North America; oracle bones

## Dome of the Rock

A building on Jerusalem's Temple Mount near Al-Aqsa Mosque, one of Islam's holiest sites. Also known as the Mosque of Omar, the domed structure covers the rock from which Muslims believe the prophet Muhammad ascended to heaven following a night journey from Mecca. Muslims also believe that the rock is the one from which the earth was founded and that it split on Muhammad's ascent, a piece of the rock following him to heaven. A footprint alleged to be Muhammad's can be seen on the rock.

SEE ALSO: Al-Aqsa Mosque; Jerusalem; Muhammad

## Druzes

An unorthodox religious sect whose beliefs are based in Shia Islam. Members of the Druze community, which numbers up to 1 million members, live primarily in Lebanon and Syria, with smaller groups in Jordan and Israel. Druze beliefs are derived primarily from the Ismaili branch of the Shia movement, with influences from other religions as well, including Judaism and Christianity. Its founders were the eleventh-century thinkers Hamza ibn Ali and Muhammad ad-Dirazi.

The Druzes are monotheists who believe also in the transmigration of the soul and pledge loyalty to Al-Hakim bi Amr-Allah (996–1021), the sixth caliph of the Egyptian Fatimid dynasty. Their long survival as a distinct sect is partly due to their closely knit community practices, which forbid conversion in and out of the faith as well as intermarriage. Many aspects of their beliefs and practices are kept hidden from all but an inner circle of believers known as uqqal, or "knowers," who are the only ones who have full knowledge of Druze scriptures and full participation in sacred rituals. Recent efforts to keep their communities distinct and strong have included involvement in Lebanon's civil war in the 1980s and political involvement in

*The Dome of the Rock, one of Islam's holiest sites, on Jerusalem's Temple Mount, from where is is believed that Muhammad ascended to heaven.* © Christine Osborne/Corbis

both Lebanon and Syria. Some Israeli Druzes have served in that nation's army.

See Also: caliphate; Ismailis; Shia Islam

## dukkha

A Pali word most commonly associated with Buddhism although some Hindus use it as well. It is usually translated as "suffering" though it also might mean "anguish," "unease," "dissatisfaction," or "frustration." All translations are meant to connote the transitory nature, and therefore the inevitable loss, of all earthly things, which is held to be the source of dukkha.

Buddhist thinkers have identified various forms of dukkha, notably in the Four Noble Truths where dukkha is described as taking five basic forms: birth, old age, and death; sorrow, despair, and physical or mental pain; involvement with things one dislikes; separation from what one likes; and not getting what one wants. Traditional Buddhism also holds that virtually all beings suffer from dukkha, even those described as enlightened or awakened beings. The main distinction is the level of dukkha; awakened ones have relatively less of it, while those in hell have the most. The purpose of Buddhism is the minimization and, ultimately, total liberation from dukkha, or entering the state known as nirvana.

See Also: Buddha; Four Noble Truths; Eightfold Path

## Durga

An important Hindu goddess. Her name means "she who is difficult to approach," yet her protective aspects are viewed by believers as positive since she is thought to represent the protective nature of Shiva's female consort, a deity whose other manifestations include Parvati and Kali. Hindu myths describe Durga as a slayer of the demons who threaten Creation. In one myth, Durga slays a buffalo demon who, knowing he could only be killed by a woman, felt himself free to attack the gods. The gods in response placed their creative energies into the form of a teenage girl, Durga, who was then able to slay the demon using the weapons of the gods. The slaying, however, proved to be an act of generosity. Durga freed the demon from his earthly, buffalo shape, thus allowing him to reach moksha.

In artwork, and in stark contrast to the often-frightening aspects of the destroyer goddess Kali, Durga is often depicted as a beautiful woman with a generous expression on her face. In images she has up to eighteen arms, although she is often referred to as the "ten-armed" goddess, in which she holds the weapons she uses to slay demons. She is also shown riding a lion or tiger. Durga is particularly popular in northeastern India, where believers celebrate an annual Durga-Puja every fall, which lasts several days and is centered in the city of Kolkata (Calcutta).

SEE ALSO: Kali; Shakti; Shiva

## Easter

The Christian holiday celebrating the resurrection of Jesus Christ. In the Roman Catholic and Protestant denominations, it is held on the first Sunday after the first full moon following the first day of spring (March 21,) although nuances in calendar systems mean that it can be celebrated on any Sunday from March 22 to April 25. Eastern Orthodox Christianity usually celebrates Easter one or more weeks later, although in some years the dates coincide. Easter is the oldest of all Christian holidays except for the weekly Sabbath, dating back to at least the second century.

Easter is the climax of Holy Week as well as the longer period of Lent. It is more central to the Christian calendar than Christmas, because the fathers of the early church designed the liturgy used during services around it. In addition, the holiday commemorates the central event in Christianity: Jesus Christ's resurrection from the dead. Like the Jewish holiday Passover, which may have influenced early Easter practices, the holiday is one of redemption and rebirth. Easter services generally include some form of a vigil (or "waiting,") consisting of prayers and Bible readings. Some denominations add an emphasis on baptisms, while Eastern Orthodox believers stage a ritual procession. All these observances are followed by more celebrations emphasizing the risen Christ.

Like Christmas, Easter has become a secular festival as well as a religious one. Such customs as the hiding of colored eggs and the giving of gift baskets are connected to fertility or springtime festivals from pre-Christian Europe or the Middle East. The English word *Easter*, in fact, is thought to be adapted from the name of an old Germanic fertility goddess, Eostre, or the festival dedicated to her, Eostara.

SEE ALSO: calendars; Christmas; Holy Week

## Eastern Orthodox Christianity

One of the major branches of Christianity along with Roman Catholicism and Protestantism, with an estimated 150 to 200 million adherents worldwide, including 6 million in the United States. Eastern Orthodox churches predominate in parts of southern and eastern Europe and in parts of the Middle East. No single overall church government exists; rather, numerous national churches are independently organized under four Christian patriarchates that date back to Christianity's earliest centuries and make up Eastern Orthodoxy's largest grouping. The four patriarchates are those of Jerusalem, Antioch, Constantinople (modem Istanbul), and Alexandria. The major national churches, each of which elects its own patriarchs, are those of Albania, Belarus, Bulgaria, Cyprus, Georgia, Greece, Romania, Russia, Serbia, and Ukraine. The patriarch of Constantinople is thought to have a somewhat greater degree of authority than other leaders, but he is in no way comparable to the Roman Catholic pope. Smaller Orthodox churches around the world remain linked to this larger grouping, including those in such far-reaching locations as China, Finland, and Alaska. The church designates itself as the Orthodox Catholic Church, but it has become common elsewhere to refer to it as the Eastern Orthodox Church to clarify the separation between it and the Roman Catholic Church. A further common English term for this institution is the Greek Orthodox Church. This is accurate insofar as the leading language of the church in its earlier years (and in much of its modern liturgy) was ancient Greek, but is also potentially misleading since the modern Greek Orthodox Church is but one of numerous national Orthodox churches.

With some variations, Eastern Orthodox Christianity is descended from the form of Christianity practiced in the Byzantine Empire, which dominated much of eastern Europe and large parts of the Middle East from the fourth century to 1453. The Byzantine Empire was the inheritor of the earlier Roman Empire, with which it shared many institutional features. Under Byzantine patronage, missionaries carried their form of Christianity to Russia and other portions of eastern Europe in the period from approximately 800 to 1200, bringing those areas into the Byzantine religious orbit.

### The Byzantine Empire and Its Heritage

The Eastern Orthodox Church adheres to the doctrinal decisions made by early Christian leaders at the first seven ecumenical councils. The last of these, the second Council of Nicaea, was held in A.D. 787. By that time the Western church, based in Rome, and the Byzantine church, based in Constantinople, had already begun to drill apart. The primary cause of friction was the insistence of the bishop of Rome, the pope, that he had authority over the bishops and later patriarchs of Jerusa-

lem, Antioch, Constantinople, and Alexandria, who refused to accept the pope's jurisdiction.

At Nicaea in 787, Eastern church officials addressed the complex issue of the use of icons in worship. An earlier Byzantine emperor, Leo III, had forbidden them. But the council concluded that icons could be venerated as long as God, not the icons themselves, was the primary object of adoration. In the decades that followed, Eastern Christians returned to their custom of investing icons with intrinsic sacred qualities and using them widely in worship. Western churchmen were uncomfortable with these practices.

The final split between Eastern and Western Christians came in 1054, but by the time of this Great Schism linguistic realities (Latin predominated in the West, Greek in the East) and political differences had made such a split likely. Conflicts had already arisen over doctrinal issues, but the greatest controversy was over church leadership. Eastern Christians held that their authority lay in their group of bishops and in the Byzantine emperor. By contrast, Western Christians continued to assert the primacy of the bishop of Rome. When Eastern Christian leaders rejected this claim, Pope Leo IX excommunicated the patriarch of Constantinople, who in turn excommunicated the pope. The breach deepened in 1204 when European crusaders en route to the Holy Land sacked Constantinople, pillaged its cathedral, and installed a representative of the pope on the patriarch's throne. Various attempts at reconciliation up to the modern day have not overcome the bitterness and mistrust surrounding that event, and true reunion is viewed as impossible unless the pope is prepared to accept equal status with Orthodox leaders (a very unlikely prospect).

*Beliefs and Practices* Aside from their disagreement over papal jurisdiction, the Eastern Orthodox Church and Roman Catholic Church have very similar doctrines. However, Orthodox theologians claim the Orthodoxy is the true, undistorted teaching of Jesus Christ, closest of all Christian communities to the version preached by Jesus' apostles without the additions of Roman Catholicism or the subtractions of Protestantism.

As in all Christianity, the Eastern Orthodox Church puts great importance on the Bible and the seven ecumenical councils of the early church. Veneration of the Virgin Mary and the Christian saints is also very important, and praying before icons—paintings or mosaics of Jesus and the saints—in homes and churches is widespread. Orthodox theology views humans as made in God's image, most fully human when most fully in natural communion with God. Sin is a barrier between God and human, so ever since sin entered the world, humankind exists in an unnatural state leading to death. (Orthodox Christians believe in heaven and hell but reject the Catholic concept of purgatory, for which they find no justification in scripture or tradition.) Salvation is seen as the way to reestablish the natural, right communion with God, who exists as the Trinity of Father, Son, and Holy Spirit. Orthodox theology differs from Roman Catholicism in rather technical interpretation of the Trinity, maintaining that both Son and Holy Spirit originate from the Father—Catholic doctrine emphasizes Jesus Christ's divinity as coexisting with, not originating from, the Father.

Orthodox Christians observe seven sacraments: baptism, confirmation, penance, the Eucharist (similar to Catholic Mass), holy orders, matrimony, and extreme unction. Orthodox rites and services are generally much longer than Roman Catholic rites—often three hours or more—and the Orthodox Church allowed the use of vernacular languages in worship services many centuries before the Roman Catholic Church (permitted only since 1963). Orthodox priests may be married (if they marry before their ordination), but Orthodox bishops must be celibate. The Orthodox Church observes the same holy days and abstinence from meat on Fridays as the Catholic Church, but the date of Orthodox Easter is calculated differently so this holiday rarely coincides with Roman Catholic Easter in the calendar.

SEE ALSO: councils, early Christian Church; papacy; Roman Catholicism

## ecumenism

The global movement to bring together all Christian denominations or, alternatively, to find ways that they might cooperate with one another. Believers in the movement emphasize the universality of Christian teachings rather than the differences that have arisen due to culture, history, and geography. The need for such a movement grew clearer in the period of religious wars following the Reformation, the split between Catholicism and Protestantism, in the 1500s and 1600s. After the Reformation, even if religious differences did not lead to war, followers of different Christian denominations often lived side by side without the unifying force of declarations of official state religions, with generally isolating effects.

Although ecumenical ideas first began circulating among European Protestants in the 1600s and 1700s, the formal movement originated in the twentieth century. In 1910, at an International Missionary Conference held in Edinburgh, Scotland, Protestant leaders urged the unification of certain church functions such as missionary work. Catholic leaders picked up on the idea by urging one another to be sympathetic to the needs of the other churches. Further conferences and discussions followed, and in 1948 the World Council of Churches was formed, which included Eastern Orthodox as well as Protestant and Catholic representatives. One result has been the removal of formal theological differences between churches, such as the anathemas (condemnations) that separated Roman Catholic and Orthodox churches for centuries. Another has been the rise of various national church unions in which sects within a denomination have been brought together under the umbrella of larger organizations. These include the United Churches of South and North India (two separate organizations), the Presbyterian Church, U.S.A., and the Evangelical Lutheran Church in America. The latter two now include most followers of those two mainstream Protestant denominations in the United States. The Roman Catholic Church, meanwhile, expressed its formal support for the movement in 1964 when the Second Vatican Council produced the "Decree on Ecumenism," one of the movement's most important statements. Catholic leaders followed this by initiating formal talks with Eastern Orthodox, Anglican, Lutheran, and other branches of Christianity aimed at reconciling theological or administrative differences.

Resistance to ecumenism has often emerged along ideological lines, as often within churches as between them. Many Christians reject, for instance, the ecumenical movement's support of liberation theology, a politicized movement most active in poor countries of the unindustrial-

ized world. Modern political and social issues, which sometimes intersect religious issues such as the ordination of women, have also fostered new religious divisions that counteract ecumenism. Indeed, one interpretation of the rise of evangelical movements in many churches is that it is a reaction to the perceived "liberalism" of the ecumenical movement.

SEE ALSO: evangelicalism; Vatican Councils

## Eid al'Fitr

An important Islamic festival. Eid al'Fitr, which means "breaking the fast," is held on the three days immediately after the end of Ramadan, the month of fasting. It therefore marks both the end of the fast and the beginning of the tenth month of the Islamic calendar. For Muslims, Eid al'Fitr starts with a communal prayer at the start of the first day, and is an occasion to visit friends, wear new clothes, exchange gifts, and visit the graves of loved ones.

Eid al'Fitr has a counterpart in a holiday known as Eid al'Adha ("Eid," also commonly spelled "Id," simply means holiday or festival). Eid al'Adha takes place during the final month of the Islamic calendar. It is intended to commemorate the prophet Abraham's intention to sacrifice his son Isaac. This festival also lasts a total of three days and begins with a morning communal prayer. It is an important part of the hajj, the ritual pilgrimage to Mecca. Together, Eid al'Fitr and Eid al'Adha are considered the two great festivals of the Islamic calendar.

SEE ALSO: calendars; hajj; Ramadan

## Eightfold Path

The path to enlightenment or awakening in Buddhism. It is at the heart of Buddhist

*A Buddha statue in Ayutthaya, Thailand. An end of suffering and entrance into nirvana awaits the follower of Eightfold Path, the fourth of the Buddha's Four Noble Truths.* © EVERTON MACDUFF/CORBIS

age wrong speech or action); right effort (maintaining the proper mental state); right mindfulness (full awareness of one's feelings, thoughts, and physical state); and right concentration (the practice of meditation). Here, "right" is sometimes translated as "perfected," since the Buddha was not describing a code of ethics but instead providing a set of behaviors that devotees should seek to perfect.

The Eightfold Path is also described using the three aspects of Buddhist practice. Right understanding and right thought connote wisdom, or prajna. Right action, right speech, and right livelihood make up conduct, or sila. Right effort, right mindfulness, and right concentration signal a disciplined mind, or samadhi. Perfected, possession of each of these three qualities will mark a believer as an arhat, a Buddhist saint. Pursuit of them, by metaphorically taking steps along the Eightfold Path, will help even the less ambitious by making it possible for them to avoid the accumulation of bad karma and takes them even further away from awakening.

The Eightfold Path is also known as the middle way, a reflection of the Buddhist emphasis on avoiding both the extremes of sensuality and materialism on the one hand and world-denying asceticism on the other.

SEE ALSO: Buddhism; Four Noble Truths; Siddhartha Gautama

teachings in virtually all schools of the faith. The Eightfold Path is thought to have been laid out in the Buddha's first sermons and appears in the Tripitaka, the key Buddhist scripture. The fourth of the Buddha's Four Noble Truths is that following the Eightfold Path is a means to bring about the end of suffering and entrance into nirvana. The path consists of right understanding (faith in the Buddhist view of the nature of truth); right thought (determination to follow the Buddhist path); right speech (telling the truth and avoiding insults); right action (avoiding criminal, abusive, or immoral behavior); right livelihood (avoiding jobs that encour-

## Elijah
### (9th century B.C.)

A prophet important in both the Jewish and Christian traditions. Elijah also appears among the prophets of Islam. In Judaism, where his story is told in books 1 and 2 Kings in the Hebrew Bible, Elijah is described as one of the leaders who helped early Hebrews to maintain their faith in the face of challenges from the nature religions of the ancient Near East, most notably the worship of Baal, the Canaanite fertility god. One famous story shows Elijah forcefully resisting the blandishments of a princess named Jezebel, wife of the son of an Israelite king and founder of a shrine devoted to Baal. After naming his son Elisha as his successor, Elijah ascended to heaven in a flaming chariot. Popular Jewish tradition holds that he reappears, symbolically, every Passover. It is customary to leave a door open for him and set a cup for him on the table of the seder, the ritual Passover meal. Among his roles then is to remind believers of their traditions, where he takes the role of a herald to the messiah. Jews came to view Elijah in apocalyptic as well as prophetic terms, seeing him as a figure who would return at the side of the messiah who will come at the time of God's final judgment to help resurrect the dead. Christians, meanwhile, adopted the tradition of Elijah as the herald of the messiah, and the New Testament Gospels report that John the Baptist appeared to be a reincarnation of him. Elijah was thought, therefore, to have prophesied the coming of Jesus Christ.

SEE ALSO: ancient Near East, religions of; New Testament; Passover

## Elohim

In Judaism, one of the names of God. In the Hebrew language, Elohim is a plural term. The plural form may have been meant literally among ancient Hebrews, indicating the "mighty ones," or gods, worshipped by the various peoples of the ancient Near East and of which the Hebrews worshipped one. In later years the term was taken to mean "One who is All" in a more nuanced understanding of the plu-

ral, and was differentiated from elelim, or "idols." During the reign of King David over ancient Israel during the tenth century B.C., Elohim and other names of God were replaced by Yahweh.

SEE ALSO: Exodus; Hebrew Bible; Yahweh

## *Engishiki*

An important text in the development of Shinto practices in Japan; in English, *Procedures of the Engi Era*. The *Engishiki* was compiled in the first decades of the tenth century by Japan's ruling emperors. It consists of two parts. One deals with secular governmental procedures. The other, the Jingi-kan, focuses on religious rites as practiced for the good of the nation, addressing such matters as the relationship between the state and the various *kami*, or Shinto deities, and the proper procedure for rites and ceremonies devoted to those *kami*. The Jingi-kan contains many special ritual prayers designed to be recited by shrine priests as well as descriptions of offerings. The sun goddess Amaterasu figures largely in many of the descriptions, and the *Engishiki* therefore likely played an important role in solidifying her as one of the central Shinto deities, especially with regard to her connections to the emperors.

SEE ALSO: Amaterasu; Nihon-Shoki; Shinto

## Epistles

The "letters" that make up nineteen of the books of the Christian New Testament. Biblical scholars and Christian denominations disagree on the authorship of the Epistles, but generally, thirteen of the Epistles are attributed to Paul of Tarsus, also known as Saint Paul the Apostle, and the remainder are attributed to James (the brother of Jesus), Jesus' disciples Peter and John (the author of the Gospel of John), and Jude, identified as a brother of James. Paul's letters are addressed to the Romans, Ephesians, Corinthians, and Hebrews; the remainder were presumably addressed to various Jewish Christian groups and individuals. Most were written sometime after the death of Jesus but before the destruction of the Jewish Temple in Jerusalem in A.D. 70, though some scholars believe several could have been written as late as 150.

The Epistles are the greatest source of Christian ethical and moral teachings next to those of Jesus Christ himself. The Epistles of Paul especially were intended to help guide early Christian communities in ways to lead a Christian life. They deal with such matters as marriage, celibacy, attitudes toward civil law and politics, and the importance of the avoidance of sin. A common thread through virtually all the Epistles is reminders of the need for Christians to seek to lead Christ-like lives.

SEE ALSO: Christianity; New Testament; Paul

## eschatology

The concern with and doctrine of "last days," or the final judgment of God and the end of history as well as humankind's ultimate fate. The term is derived from a Greek phrase meaning "last things." Elements of eschatology appear in most major religious traditions, as well as in many premodern religions. But it is most prominent in Judaism, Christianity, and Islam, all faiths that place emphasis on God's last judgment and which hold out the future hope for salvation, reward, or a kingdom of righteousness on earth. Jewish teachings hold that God has chosen the Jews to be his instrument for the redemption of the world. Provided they fulfill his commandments and live according to his will, they can reach a state of righteousness and at-

tain salvation. In Christianity, eschatology is based on the figure of Jesus Christ, said to herald the coming kingdom of God. Believers have differed, however, on whether the so-called end times will involve a great apocalypse or simply a return of the messiah to usher in God's kingdom. Islamic eschatology, which drew heavily on the Jewish and Christian ideas, envisions a final judgment of God upon humanity.

The fate of the individual soul is a common concern in eschatology. Both Christianity and Islam preach the immortality of the individual soul, and it is the individual upon whom God will pronounce his judgment. Those deemed worthy will enter a heavenly paradise, while those found wanting will receive their due punishment in an underworld. Understandings of the specific nature of this afterlife vary widely. In Judaism the picture is more complex, presenting the possibility of the raising of the dead and the establishment of an earthly kingdom of righteousness rather than an emphasis on an afterlife for the individual, although the Jewish tradition also preaches the immortality of the soul.

SEE ALSO: apocalypse; heaven; hell

## Essenes

An important Jewish sect that existed from about the second century B.C. to the first century B.C. The Essenes have received increased attention in recent decades because scholars suspect they are connected with the Dead Sea Scrolls, a collection of ancient manuscripts that shed light on the religious life of Judea during the period when Christianity appeared. The major source of knowledge about the Essenes is the first-century Jewish historian Josephus.

Most Essenes apparently lived an ascetic life in isolated communities, with all property shared and such matters as marriage closely regulated by elders. People who wanted to join the Essenes were put through three years of probation before they could join communal meals or participate in ceremonies. Women were forbidden from these communities, although accounts indicate that there were smaller groups of Essenes living in ordinary towns who practiced marriage. Believers took very seriously Jewish purity and dietary laws and observed the Sabbath, which was spent meditating on the Torah or in prayer. They disdained the Temple-based practices of most Jews, however, and preferred to live in isolation. Tenuous links with Christian beliefs among the Essenes' teachings include faith in eternal life or God's eternal punishment for sin and an emphasis on justice and equality among all in the eyes of God.

SEE ALSO: Dead Sea Scrolls; Judaism; Temple

## Eucharist

One of the fundamental sacramental rites in Christianity, commonly known in Roman Catholicism and Protestantism as Holy Communion. The Eucharist is designed to commemorate the Last Supper of Jesus of Nazareth and his twelve disciples. At that meal, held the night before he was crucified, Jesus (according to the Gospels of the New Testament) gave his disciples bread, saying "Here is my body," and wine, saying, "Here is my blood." Almost all Christian churches sacramentally replicate Jesus' act by offering believers bread and wine during worship services. Communion is one of the seven sacraments of the Roman Catholic Church and one of the two of those retained by Protestant churches. It is also a basic feature of Eastern Orthodox services. Only the Soci-

ety of Friends, or Quakers, among large-scale denominations, rejects it as they do other formal expressions of belief.

Though almost all Christians observe the Eucharist, they differ on its true form and significance. Official Roman Catholic doctrine holds that the essence of the Last Supper's bread and wine enters the bread and wine of weekly services through a process known as transubstantiation. That is, they are the true substance of the body and blood of Christ. Some Protestant churches agree, but others make somewhat lesser claims, namely that the bread and wine are symbols of faith and obedience or, at most, contain a spiritual presence rather than one of substance. In Eastern Orthodox Christianity, priests use only leavened bread and invoke the Holy Spirit during the Eucharist.

SEE ALSO: Gospels; sacraments

## evangelicalism

A movement in Protestant Christianity that developed in the United States but has spread around the world. It emerged in the twentieth century out of various controversies in mainstream Protestant denominations. These included the sense among some that the mainstream churches, such as Lutheranism and Presbyterianism, were allowing themselves to be too influenced by modern social movements and by a willingness to "relativize" biblical teachings through historical or textual scholarship. At the same time, early evangelicals rejected the crudeness and intolerance of the Christian fundamentalist movement, preferring instead to focus their efforts on evangelizing, or seeking converts.

Evangelical Christians emphasize personal conversion, in the form of the sincere acceptance of the redemption of Jesus

Christ on the Cross with Three Angels. *Roman Catholic doctrine holds that the ceremonial bread and wine dispensed during the eucharist are the true substance of the body and blood of Christ.*

Christ, as the road to salvation. They also emphasize the authority of the Bible, and generally adhere to a fairly literal interpretation of its teachings. Their efforts to gain converts, or to "save souls," have given rise to modern forms of mass revival meetings, which are sometimes televised; extensive missionary efforts; and the founding of huge churches, often located in suburban areas. Some members have also mastered the techniques of media and advertising, giving rise to so-called televangelism. Although evangelical leaders originally avoided active participation in politics, that has changed over the past twenty-five years, with evangelicalism becoming a major force in American politics. Evangelicals often take political positions based on their religious belief that the Bible offers absolute truths that apply to specific issues including school prayer, abortion, or homosexual rights. Some evangelicals, who have adopted a progressive rather than conservative approach to the movement, prefer to focus on the more positive aspects of biblical teachings rather than on the denial of rights or the attempt to impose evangelical doctrines on others.

SEE ALSO: fundamentalism, Christian; Great Awakenings; Protestantism

## excommunication

Broadly, the process of excluding someone from a religious community or from some of the practices of that community. Historically, the term is most closely associated with the Roman Catholic Church, in which excommunication processes are most formalized. Other Christian denominations generally prefer less legalistic versions of church discipline enforced within the church community itself.

In Catholicism, excommunication is used as a form of punishment for a believer who has transgressed a church law. Roman Catholic officials recognize two forms of excommunication: that which makes an offender one to be tolerated, and that which makes him or her one to avoid altogether. The latter is rarely imposed. In both cases, offenders are forbidden from taking part in church sacraments and are also denied a Christian burial. Offenses that warrant excommunication vary widely and include heresy, violation of the confessional, and abortion (among many others) and must be officially censured by a church official. Those who are excommunicated might be restored to the church by going through confession and absolution; in extreme cases such absolution can only be granted by a high official such as a bishop or even the pope himself.

SEE ALSO: Christian heresies; papacy; Roman Catholic Church

## Exodus

The second book of the Hebrew Bible, or Old Testament, and the source of some of the basic beliefs and most important stories of both Judaism and Christianity. Exodus describes the ancient Hebrews' escape from slavery in Egypt and the establishment of a revived covenant between the Hebrews, the people of Israel, and God. The major focus of the story is on the prophet Moses and his brother and sister, Aaron and Miriam. Jewish tradition also attributes the book to Moses, although recent scholarship suggests that it was compiled by numerous authors between the ninth and fifth centuries B.C.

Around the thirteenth century B.C., the Hebrews settled in Egypt, where they prospered. But a pharaoh arose who gave the order to enslave them and to kill the firstborn sons of all families. The infant Moses escaped this killing and grew up to be called by God to lead the Hebrews out of bondage. After a series of plagues convinced the pharaoh to let the Hebrews leave Egypt, Moses led them in a ritual later commemorated as Passover. As they fled, the Hebrews passed through a "Sea of Reeds," which closed over the pharaoh's pursuing troops. Then, the Hebrews entered the Sinai wilderness, which separated Egypt from the land of Canaan.

On Mount Sinai, God revealed the Ten Commandments to Moses as the symbol of the resealed covenant between God and the Hebrews, his chosen people. While Moses was away, the Hebrews persuaded Aaron to make a golden calf, an idol to probably an Egyptian god. When Moses returned, he ordered the golden calf melted down as an apostasy to the Jewish faith. The Hebrews proceeded to build a sort of portable shrine known as a tabernacle in order to worship God while they remained in the wilderness. The tabernacle contained the two stone tablets on which the Ten Commandments were inscribed. Uncertain of their devotion, God required the Hebrews to wander in the wilderness of the Sinai for forty years, but he also regularly demonstrated his forgiveness and generosity. In so doing, he assured the Jews that he would guide and protect them as well as lead them to his promised land. According to Exodus 8–14 in the Revised Standard Version of the Bible:

And Moses made haste to bow his head toward the earth and worshipped. And he said, "If now I have found favor in thy sight, O Lord, let the Lord, I pray thee go in the midst of us, although it is a stiff-necked people; and pardon our iniquities and our sin and take us for thy inheritance."

And he said, "Behold, I make a covenant. Before all your people I will do marvels, such as have not been wrought in all the earth or in any nation; and all the people among whom you are shall see the work of the LORD; for it is a terrible thing that I will do with you.

"Observe what I command you this day. Behold, I will drive out before you the Amorites, the Canaanites, the Hittites, the Per'izzites, the Hivites, and the Jeb'usites. Take heed to yourself lest you make a covenant with the inhabitants of the land whither you go, lest it become a snare in the midst of you. You shall tear down their altars, and break their pillars, and cut down their Ashe'rim. For you shall worship no other god, for the Lord, whose name is Jealous, is a jealous god."

For Jews, the Exodus remains at the heart of their religion, a symbol and confirmation of the relationship between God and his chosen people. For Christians, the Exodus is also a symbol of the power of God to grant freedom as well as guidance and forgiveness.

SEE ALSO: ark of the covenant; Moses; Ten Commandments

# Fa-hsien
## (ca. 388–422)

Chinese Buddhist monk who is credited with strengthening Buddhism in China and with providing an important, and for the time very unusual, link between China and the Buddhist centers of South Asia.

As a young man, Fa-hsien, whose name means roughly "splendor of religion," left his eastern Chinese kingdom to make a pilgrimage to India, where he ultimately spent ten years. He acted as a scholar as well as a devotee, and his accounts of the pilgrimage provide information on the Buddhist life of India that surpass even Indian records. He also brought back to China a number of Buddhist texts, which he later translated from Sanskrit into Chinese. Among them were a text on the nature of nirvana known as the Mahaparinirvana Sutra and a work on monastic discipline based on a version of the Tripitaka.

Fa-hsien traveled widely, visiting the most important Buddhist centers in India. These included Gandhara, a site in present-day Afghanistan whose Buddhist sculptures showed a great deal of Greek influence, and Peshawar, now in Pakistan. In northeastern India, the heartland of Indian Buddhism, Fa-hsien made pilgrimages to such sites as the Buddha's birthplace near the Nepal–India border and the outskirts of Varanasi, where the Buddha preached his first sermons. He also spent a great deal of time in the political and cultural center of Pataliputra, the site of much of his scholarly work. Returning to China by sea, Fa-hsien stopped in Sri Lanka, then the flourishing center of Theravada Buddhism.

SEE ALSO: councils, Buddhist; Mahayana Buddhism; Theravada Buddhism

# al-Fatiha

Literally "the Opening," al-Fatiha is the first sura, or verse, of the Qur'an, the holy book of Islam. Because this sura is said to embody the essence of the entire Qur'an, al-Fatiha is sometimes called "the mother of the book." It begins, "In the name of God, the Merciful, the Compassionate, Praise be to God, the Lord of the Worlds," and it has come to serve as the central part of many prayers and services, comparable to the Lord's Prayer in Christianity. More specifically and as a matter of course, al-Fatiha is recited at the beginning of a Muslim's daily prayers and in prayers for the sick or the dead.

SEE ALSO: Qur'an; suras

# Fatima
## (ca. 605–633)

The daughter of Muhammad, the prophet of Islam, and his wife, Khadija. Fatima was one of four children of the couple and the only one to survive the Prophet. She married Muhammad's nephew Ali and their experiences laid the foundation for the emergence of the Shia version of Islam. One of Fatima and Ali's sons was al-

*The Hand of Fatima, an Islamic good luck symbol, is found on door entrances, charms, and other places to ward off the "evil eye."*
© JOHN AND LISA MERRILL/CORBIS

Hussein, who died in battle in 680 and was considered the first Shia martyr. Hussein's followers then worked backward in time and claimed that only the descendants of Hussein, and therefore the descendants of Ali and Fatima, could lay a legitimate claim to being true caliphs, or followers of the Prophet as the heads of Islam. Fatima went on to hold a special, almost legendary status as a member of the holy family of Islam, especially among the Shia. Tradition claims that she was named by Muhammad as being one of the four women of special status in the Islamic paradise, the others being Maryam (Mary), Khadija, and the wife of the Egyptian pharaoh.

SEE ALSO: Ali; Muhammad; Shia Islam

# fatwa

A legal opinion based in Islamic law, or sharia. A fatwa is usually called for when a thorny issue leads people with questions or vested interests connected with that issue to consult a Muslim legal expert, or mufti. The mufti then pronounces his fatwa according to a particular school of Islamic law. Since they are pronounced according to one of a number of schools of law and since they can conceivably be contested, fatwas do not necessarily hold authority over all Muslims. They can also be ended or overturned. Nonetheless, fatwas generally hold, even across international boundaries, as long as they are perceived as well grounded in law and well explained by the issuing mufti. One fatwa of recent times that received global attention was pronounced in 1989 by the Ayatolla Khomeini, Iran's supreme religious leader: Khomeini's fatwa justified attacks on the life of British author Salman Rushdie, accused of apostasy, or rejecting and ridiculing the Islamic faith he was born into, in his novel *The Satanic Verses*. Rushdie lived under a guard provided him by the British government until 1998, when the fatwa was overturned.

SEE ALSO: Islam; mufti; sharia

# feng shui

A Chinese school of geomancy, or divination based on features of the natural world; the term means literally "wind-water." Feng shui is most commonly used in building and interior design and in the placement of grave sites. The idea is for buildings, objects, or graves to be positioned in accordance with natural forces and the landscape and therefore take advantage of the vital energy, or *qi*, that flows through all natural things. Among the factors feng shui masters take into account are those of yin and yang, which should be placed, respectively, to the left and right of proposed sites. They also consider the five elements of wood, fire, earth, metal, and water. Feng shui considerations underlay the planning and construction of such monuments as the Forbidden City, the palace complex of the emperors of the Ming and Qing dynasties in their capital city of Beijing. In the modern world, feng shui consultants are brought in to consult on such projects as office buildings and suburban homes.

SEE ALSO: divination; *qi*; yin-yang

## filial piety

A key idea in Confucianism as well as other Chinese and East Asian belief systems. It reflects the central place of the family in traditional Chinese culture, and the term implies a kind of reverence toward family relationships that is so fundamental and self-evident that not only do few question it, but it is one of the organizing principles of life. Relationships betweeen parents and children most clearly reflect the notion. Children are raised to obey and respect their parents while they live and to honor them after they die. Confucian rites exist, in fact, to honor dead parents. Parents, meanwhile, must care for and educate their children and be good examples of virtuous living. In a straightforward practical example, parents must provide for their children while they are young and, when parents grow old and are less able to work, children must provide for them. The most religiously strong form of filial piety is literal ancestor worship, a feature of many pre-Confucian Chinese cults and of later Chinese folk religion.

SEE ALSO: ancestor worship; Confucianism

## Five Classics

The collection of texts that constitutes the heart of ancient Chinese wisdom and the foundation of Confucian teachings. Of mostly mysterious authorship and chronological origin, the Five Classics were authoritative even when Confucius lived in the sixth and fifth centuries B.C. (although they had yet to be brought together as a collection). Also, since Confucius saw himself as a transmitter rather than an originator of wisdom, he urged their continued study. Tradition credits the authorship of the Five Classics to ancient sage-kings except for one, the *Spring and Autumn Annals*, which is attributed to Confucius himself. They were likely compiled in various versions throughout China's ancient Zhou dynasty period (1050–256 B.C.). The Five Classics are the *Classic of History*; the *Classic of Poetry*, the *Record of Rites*, the *Spring and Autumn Annals*, and the *Book of Changes* (or *I Ching*). Tradition also notes a sixth lost classic, the Classic of Music. The Five Classics were adopted as the core of China's system of advanced education during the Han dynasty (206 B.C.–A.D. 220) and remained there, with periodic alterations, until the twentieth century. Confucian scholar-officials were expected to master all of them.

The *Classic of History* is thought by some scholars to predate the Zhou dynasty, and parts of it may be among the earliest examples of Chinese writing. The text records the deeds and teachings of a sequence of ancient kings, legendary and actual, who ruled until 771 B.C. Some of them supposedly presided over a probably mythical lost golden age; thanks to the text, these kings continued to provide idealized examples for later rulers.

The *Classic of Poetry* is a collection of songs relating aspects of daily life and popular religion. Derived from both folk sources and the upper reaches of society, the poems were originally written to be sung and provided classical China with its dominant poetic forms, and therefore a sort of literary discipline.

The *Record of Rites* describes important rituals related to royal politics, education, and other areas of life. It contains mentions of the proper objects to be used as well as sacrifices for religious ceremonies. As such the *Record of Rites* underscores the importance of ritual to the Confucian system, and the sage himself is thought to have helped to compile the text. The text also notes the importance of the so-called doctrine of the mean, similarly expressed in ancient Greek philosophy, in which people are urged to follow moderation in every aspect of their lives as well as be sincere and truthful.

The *Spring and Autumn Annals* is an account of the twelve kings of Lu, Confucius's home state, from 772 B.C. to 479 B.C., tracing their lives month by month and noting important events or decisions. Interpreted by Confucian thinkers to emphasize good and bad governance, it was considered to ground the Confucian perspective on politics in actual events. For some readers the natural events mentioned in the texts, such as storms, were thought to be heavenly signs of good or bad leadership.

The *Book of Changes*, or *I-Ching*, is a divination manual popular not only in China but around the world. Its divination techniques involve the use of eight designs known as trigrams, broken or unbroken lines arranged in horizontal groups of three. The unbroken lines represent yang (male cosmic energy) and the number 9. Broken lines represent yin (female cosmic energy) and the number 6. Through various nearly random methods such as throwing sticks, the reader builds up the eight trigrams, using the text of the *I Ching* to interpret the meaning of both the lines and their combinations, which are thought to reflect all possible situations. The *I Ching* remains authoritative not only because of its divination techniques but because those techniques are symbolic of traditional Chinese cosmology. Confucius is credited with adding a commonly used commentary to the text.

SEE ALSO: Confucian scholar-officials; Confucianism; Four Books

# Five Pillars of Faith

The five acts that form the core of Islamic practice. According to sharia, Islamic law, the Five Pillars of Faith are compulsory for all adult male Muslims who are physically and financially capable of performing them; many other Muslims adhere to them as well. They are:

1. Profession of the faith by saying aloud the Shahada: "There is no God but Allah and Muhammad is his Prophet." The Shahada is also the key statement of conversion to Islam.

2. Prayer, or salat. Prayers are to be uttered five times daily facing in the direction of Mecca. The prayers themselves are given by the Qur'an, and each cycle of prayer begins with "Allahu akbar," ("God is great") and ends with the taslim, a statement commonly translated as "Peace be with you." Prayer is usually performed alone or in small groups aside from Fridays, when Muslim men are expected to attend midday prayers at a local mosque.

3. Charity, or almsgiving. Islamic texts describe this as the way Muslims take care of one another. Traditionally the proper amount of alms is calculated as a percentage of income donated to and then

distributed by an adherent's mosque. Islamic law recognizes that general guidelines should not apply to the poor, who might be unable to pay, or to the extremely wealthy, who might be expected to contribute more than average amounts.

4. Fasting during the month of Ramadan, the ninth month of the Islamic calendar. During daylight hours, Muslims are supposed to avoid food, drink, sexual activity, and smoking. Rules, again, are less strict for the young, the old, and the sick.

5. Pilgrimage to Mecca at least once in one's lifetime. Known as the hajj, the pilgrimage to Mecca is expected of Muslims who are able to afford the trip while caring for their families.

SEE ALSO: hajj; Qur'an; Ramadan

## five relationships

A Confucian vision of social order. The concept of five relationships first appeared in written form in a text known as the *Li Ji*, or *Record of Rites*, one of the Five Classics of Chinese civilization, but many parts of the book predated Confucius, and the notions behind these relationships may have as well. The concept is this: Society is derived from five fundamental relationships between two individuals. Each of the ten people involved must understand his or her role within these relationships and behave according to the obligations and expectations of this role. The result is social harmony, since each person would be acting according to the highest standards of character. The five relationships are father and son, elder brother and younger brother, husband and wife, elder and younger (or lesser) friend, and ruler and subject.

The Confucian vision of social harmony was hierarchical, and none of these relationships involves equality in the mod-

ern, Western sense. Fathers, for instance, are supposed to show kindness to their sons, who in turn are expected to observe the tenets of filial piety. Similarly, elder brothers are supposed to act with generosity toward their younger brothers, who in turn should show humility and respect. Husbands should behave in an upright and moral fashion toward their wives, whose proper role is one of obedience (the traditional Confucian vision is sexist by contemporary Western standards). For friends, among whom Confucians believed that no relationship was truly equal, the elder should be considerate and the younger (or lesser) properly deferential. Rulers should govern with wisdom and benevolence, a point on which Confucius elaborates in many of his teachings. Subjects, meanwhile, must demonstrate loyalty when their rulers show wisdom and benevolence.

SEE ALSO: Confucianism; filial piety; Five Classics

## Four Books

The collection of texts that, along with the Five Classics, makes up the core of the classical literature of Confucianism. The Four Books were designated as such during the era of Confucian revival and expansion known as neo-Confucianism, which began during China's Song dynasty (960–1127). The neo-Confucian thinker Chu-hsi (1130–1200) published the Four Books as a group, along with added commentary. For hundreds of years, until the practice officially ended in 1905, they formed the introduction to Confucian studies undertaken by those who wanted to pass China's civil service exams. The general pattern was for students to begin with the Four Books before moving to the more elaborate and authoritative (because older) Five Classics.

The best known of the Four Books is the *Analects* of Confucius, a collection of sayings and lessons allegedly written down by the sage's students and viewed as an authoritative source as close as possible to the teachings of Confucius himself. The others are the *Great Learning*, a short work focusing on the proper performance of rites as a reflection of a scholar or leader's honesty and self-cultivation; the *Doctrine of the Mean*, which describes in abstract terms the ways by which a scholar might cultivate himself in order to demonstrate the moral order of the universe; and the *Mencius*, the collection of teachings attributed to Mencius, who was considered the top early student of Confucianism.

SEE ALSO: Confucian scholar-officials; Five Classics; neo-Confucianism

## Four Noble Truths

The basis for all Buddhist teachings and practice. The Four Noble Truths were realized by the original Buddha, Siddhartha Gautama, during his period of trial and meditation and articulated in his first lessons after achieving enlightenment. They are: 1) the constant condition of life is suffering, or dhukka; 2) the source of suffering is attachment to impermanence or to the things of this world; 3) suffering can be brought to an end by ending such attachments; and 4) the way to achieve this end is by following the Buddhist Eightfold Path.

The Four Noble Truths provided the Buddha with a solution for the problems of suffering, decay, and impermanence, which he saw as the overarching facts of existence and the cause of people's sadness, discontent, and unease. By understanding the central realizations of the first three truths, people could achieve a true understanding of existence; by following

the fourth, the Eightfold Path, people could achieve nirvana, the state of contentment and bliss that is the goal of Buddhist enlightenment.

SEE ALSO: Buddhism; Eightfold Path; Siddhartha Gautama

## four stages of life

A Hindu concept first fully described in the Laws of Manu, compiled between 200 B.C. and A.D. 200. In this text, religious experts describe the four stages of life that men of the brahmin, or priestly, caste pass through on their way to achieving full religious knowledge. Historically, these four stages (especially the first three) have been broad enough to be applicable to much more of society than to brahmins alone. Thus extended, the concept of the four stages has emerged as a key component of Indian social ethics. Women are considered able to directly take part only in the first stage; they take part in the remaining stages only indirectly, through their husbands.

The first stage of life is the student's. According to the Laws of Manu, the stage begins for brahmins with a rite (still commonly observed) in which the young man drapes a sacred cord around his torso. He then studies the religious texts, the Vedas, with a teacher. More generally, young men in the student's stage are still supported by their families and are not expected to take any responsibilities seriously other than their studies and familial obligations.

The second stage is that of the householder. In the classical conception of the Laws of Manu, at this stage the brahmin leaves his teacher to return to his family, get married, take up a profession, and have children of his own. This was expected of all brahmins, partly since a son was necessary to carry out necessary funereal and other rites. More broadly, householders are considered the backbone of Hindu society and are fully justified in their pursuit of artha, or earthly power and wealth. Even the Laws of Manu asserts that, since householders support all other groups, they are the holiest of all.

The third stage of life begins when the householder, having fulfilled his responsibilities to his wife and children (or left them with enough wealth or opportunity that they are provided for), turns his thoughts and energies once again to religion. In the Laws of Manu this meant that the aging brahmin would retire as a hermit to the forest and achieve a state of detachment from worldly things and concerns. For many Hindus this has involved, instead, a slow but steady retreat from worldly concerns in favor of contemplation and meditation.

The fourth stage of life is the one most difficult to apply to the lives of nonbrahmins or even to brahmins unready to completely devote themselves to the religious life. It is to become a religious wanderer or sannyasin, possessing no earthly ties and surviving only through begging. In the classical sense described in the Laws of Manu, by becoming a sannyasin a devotee might complete the way of knowledge and achieve spiritual connection with the ultimate divine through constant meditation. In modern India thousands of believers actually take up this path every year, including a few women, and they are recognized as being legally "dead" by India's secular government. Technically, only members of the top three castes of the four social castes—the brahmin, kshatriya, and vaisya—are allowed to "take sannyas"; ironically, this means there is more social mobility in becoming a sannyasin than in other aspects of Hindu society.

SEE ALSO: caste; Laws of Manu; moksha

# fundamentalism, Christian

Christian fundamentalists are believers who advocate a return to what they view as the "fundamental" straightforward and simple teachings of Christianity, which they believe are threatened in the modern world by developments ranging from modern science to progressive social movements. The term was first used in this sense in 1920 in the United States, when members of some Protestant denominations mounted strong opposition to the teaching of the theory of evolution and the rise of so-called biblical criticism, a scholarly effort to place biblical teachings in a historical context and to apply literary analysis to biblical sayings, both of which amounted to these early fundamentalists to "questioning" the literal truth of holy scripture. An emphasis on the literal truth of the Bible has been central to fundamentalism ever since.

Christian fundamentalists also advocate a way of life away from what they see as corrupt modern life, in effect a return to a better age (which has never truly or fully existed). They tend to be patriarchal, believing that men should be the unchallenged heads of households, and they believe strongly in the importance of the nuclear family of one male parent, one female parent, and their children as the central unit of society. They vigorously oppose policies and practices that challenge this structure, which to most fundamentalists includes abortion, contraception, the women's rights movement, and homosexuality. Fundamentalists also believe very strongly in Bible-centered education that rejects the theory of evolution in favor of the biblical story of Creation and questions the constitutional separation of church and state. Fundamentalists advance their position through dedicated educational institutions and media networks and through political lobby.

Fundamentalists are often confused with evangelicals, and many do refer to themselves as conservative evangelicals to avoid connotations of dangerous extremism that are associated with radical Islamic fundamentalism. Unlike evangelicals, however, fundamentalists tend not to emphasize personal religious experience or the seeking out of converts. Instead, they encourage an unquestioned acceptance of what they consider to be correct religious truths. Evangelicals, for their part, do not always approve of fundamentalists' crudeness, intolerance, or desire to impose their beliefs on others.

SEE ALSO: fundamentalism, Islamic; Hindutva

## fundamentalism, Islamic

A fairly recent development in Islam that, like fundamentalist Christianity, seeks the restoration of what advocates see as "fundamental" religious beliefs and practices in the face of the challenges of the modern, secular world. Islamic fundamentalists believe in the literal truth of the Qur'an and the continued relevance of both scripture and Islamic law to people in modern times. Many Islamic fundamentalists are politically active, ranging from overt, legal participation in party politics to varying degrees of militancy up to covert, violent international terrorism. A common theme among Islamic fundamentalists is the need for the creation of Islamic states that reflect their view of Islamic teachings not only in religion but in politics, the law, education, and social norms.

There have been many different Islamic fundamentalist groups dating back to the early 1900s (some scholars date the

movement's origins even earlier), with considerable disagreement on beliefs, tactics, and visions of a future Islamic state. An early influential group is the Jama'at-i-Islami of Pakistan, founded by Abu'l-a'lal Mawdudi (1903–1979). Mawdudi wanted to "revitalize" Islam by urging believers to return to the example of the prophet Muhammad as a model for life. He also believed that the Qur'an and Hadith should be the basis for the political constitution of Pakistan, a goal he never achieved. Another early influence was the Egyptian Sayyid Qutb (1906–1966), one of the founders of the Muslim Brotherhood, a major fundamentalist group. Qutb deplored what he saw as the corrupting materialism and nationalism of the West and favored instead a return to "pure Islam." He believed that Islamic tradition provided all that was necessary for both individual and political life. Change (Islamic fundamentalists commonly accept certain aspects of the modern world such as technological advances) had to be reconciled with Islamic teachings and could not supplant or replace them.

Islamic fundamentalists often clash with Islamic leaders and other elites who favor modernization and secularization. In 1981, for instance, radical members of the Egyptian group known as Islamic Jihad assassinated Egyptial president Anwar Sadat for his willingness to negotiate with Israel and his crackdowns on various religious activities. In 1979, Shia fundamentalists in Iran staged a revolution against the pro-West, secular-style shah, Reza Pahlavi, and proceeded to create the first modern Islamic fundamentalist state. The Muslim Brotherhood, meanwhile, remains the largest political opposition force in Egypt, with branches in Syria and offshoots such as Hamas in Palestine. Hezbollah, a major militant fundamentalist organization based in Lebanon, is Shia and apparently maintains ties with Iran.

Both Hamas and Hezbollah have been labeled terrorist organizations in recent years; their activities are concentrated in the Middle East. In the West the Islamic fundamentalist movement has been increasingly associated with international terrorism, mainly in connection with al Qaeda, the radical fundamentalist organization led by Saudi Osama bin Laden that has claimed responsibility for the major terrorist attacks in the United States on September 11, 2001. Terrorist Islamic fundamentalist groups are likely influenced by social and economic developments in many Islamic countries as much as by religious beliefs: Many (but by no means all) rank-and-file modern fundamentalists come from middle- or lower-middle-class backgrounds and see few prospects in what remain poor countries dominated by narrow elites such as the Saudi royal family or its counterparts in the smaller Persian

Gulf states. They are willing to take extreme measures to change those circumstances. Other apparent inspirations for terrorist activity include the belief that the West is a threat to Islam, not simply a rival faith, and the insult to Islam that some believe is represented by the modern State of Israel. A measure of the willingness of Islamic fundamentalists to use modern technology, meanwhile, is their familiarity with computers, the Internet, and wireless devices such as mobile phones.

In theological terms, many Islamic fundamentalist groups take inspiration from salafism, the belief in the need to return to the Islam created by the "virtuous ancestors," namely Muhammad and his companions and successors. Free inquiry, or ijtihad, is permitted, but only when used in a proper way and only when Islam's earlier texts do not give clear answers.

SEE ALSO: fundamentalism, Christian; Hindutva; Islamic modernism

# Gandhi, Mohandas K. (1869–1948)

Indian nationalist and spiritual leader and one of the most recognizable figures of the twentieth century. Many Indians consider him the founder of their country thanks to his leadership in the independence movement that freed India from British rule in 1947. Gandhi is also revered for his advocacy of nonviolence and religious toleration, and his techniques of nonviolent civil disobedience have provided the model for social and political protests around the world, notably in the U.S. civil rights movement of the 1950s and 1960s and the South African anti-apartheid movement of the 1980s and 1990s. He is commonly and respectfully known as Mahatma Gandhi, from the Hindi word *mahatma*, meaning "great soul."

Gandhi was born into the Hindu tradition of Vaishnavism, or the worship of the god Vishnu. In his youth some of his best friends were Jains, members of a religious tradition thought to have influenced his later thinking. After taking a law degree in London, he went to South Africa to practice law. Always a devout Hindu and a practicing vegetarian, Gandhi expanded his religious education in South Africa, maintaining friendly contact with various Christian denominations and studying the Islamic Qur'an. His studies convinced him that all religions were fundamentally true; problems arose only when people misunderstood or misinterpreted religious teachings. Hinduism, however, remained Gandhi's strongest influence. He was inspired by the Bhagavad Gita to take up a simple life, with few possessions, and to maintain a sense of calm and detachment in the face of criticism or challenges.

South Africa was a British colony when Gandhi lived there, with populations of Europeans and Indians in addition to the local peoples. His political involvement began when he was shocked by the racial injustices suffered by non-Europeans. He led protests calling for reform (which sometimes landed him in jail) characterized by ahimsa, nonviolence. Gandhi had developed the idea that nonviolent protest was the only way to turn an opponent's mind and heart, and in the end was both a stronger force and the only way to effect lasting change. Opponents' violence, he argued, must be borne calmly and even cheerfully. He coined the word satyagraha, which he translated as "soul-force" or "truth-force," to refer to these techniques.

Gandhi returned to India and by 1919 was deeply involved in that country's independence movement. He quickly became a famous figure, beloved by the masses as a living example of his beliefs: For example, he took to wearing only a simple loincloth made from cloth he wove himself. He also practiced frequent fasts and other rites of self-purification, and he maintained a weekly "day of silence." His faith in human equality led him to reject most aspects of Hinduism's caste system, and he was a strong advocate of the rights of the so-called untouchables, India's poorest class. He called them harijans, or "children of God," and welcomed them into his ashram and into his larger political movement. Adding to his appeal was his calm demeanor and his cheerful, dry sense of humor. Gandhi helped turn the Indian independence movement into a mass movement, and he continued to advocate both nonviolent protest and noncooperation, or the simple refusal to observe laws or practices that are unjust or absurd. His 1931 salt march, a long walk to the sea in protest of the British monopoly on the salt trade, made him famous worldwide.

For Gandhi, nonviolence and noncooperation were ways to reveal the truth. His political activities and his life in general were based on the search for truth; at one point he claimed simply, "My life is my message." He believed that in all religions truth lay both outside and within every person and could be manifested in many ways. For Gandhi personally, truth lay in the attempt to live a simple and physically pure life. In societal terms, truth was the attempt to break down artificial barriers of race or caste. Gandhi also opposed modern industry and consumer society because in his view they drew people further from the truth; he favored instead a society of self-supporting villages and simple crafts. Gandhi rejected British rule in India not only because it was unjust but because it was artificial; India's ancient civilization could not realistically be governed by the inhabitants of a faraway island. Likewise, Gandhi was strongly opposed to the partition of British India into mostly Hindu India and mostly Muslim Pakistan because he believed the truth was that, regardless of their religious differences, Indian Hindus and Muslims were Indians first.

*One of the most popular of the Hindu gods, Ganesha represents good fortune, and is depicted with the head of an elephant, four arms, and a large belly.* © PHILADELPHIA MUSEUM OF ART/CORBIS

In early 1948 Gandhi was assassinated by a group of fanatical Hindu fundamentalists who found his religious openness and toleration unacceptable. The last word he uttered was "Ram," a name for the Hindu god Rama. He remains a worldwide symbol of nonviolence and spiritual ideals.

SEE ALSO: ahimsa; Bhagavad Gita; caste

## Ganesha

One of the most popular Hindu gods. Ganesha (or Lord Ganesh, also known as Ganapati) represents good fortune, learning, and the removal of obstacles. Many Hindus offer devotions to Ganesha when beginning new enterprises such as businesses or courses of study. He is often represented in artwork and other imagery as having the head of an elephant, a pot belly, and four arms, and images of him appear in some Buddhist temples as well as in many Hindu temples.

Ganesha is described in Hindu myth as the son of Shiva and his consort Parvati. He was created by Parvati so that she would have someone to guard her chamber while she bathed. Shiva, seeking to approach Parvati, mistook Ganesha for a more sinister figure and had him attacked. In the fight, Ganesha's head was cut off. Once Shiva discovered Ganesha's identity, he pledged to replace his head with that of the first creature he saw, an elephant.

SEE ALSO: Parvati; puja; Shiva

## Ganga River

The most sacred river in Hinduism. The Ganga, commonly known in English as the Ganges, starts in the Himalayas and traverses much of northern India. It splits into numerous, and ever-shifting, tributaries in the eastern Indian state of West Bengal before entering the Bay of Bengal. It passes through the sacred Hindu city of Varanasi (Benares), and at the city of Allah-abad, joins the river Jamuna. The meeting of the two is considered by many Hindus to be the holiest spot in India.

Hindus revere the Ganga as a presentation of the goddess Ganga, who is one of the wives of Shiva but is worshipped in her own right for her kindness and wisdom. The goddess is also sometimes depicted as a consort of Krishna, who is associated with the Jamuna. Water from the river serves to purify any ritual and wash away any sin; many Hindus seek to bathe in the water at some point in their lives or, alternatively, be cremated near the Ganga so that their ashes can be placed directly into the river.

SEE ALSO: Kumbh Mela; Shiva, Varanasi

## Garden of Eden

In Judaism and Christianity, the original earthly paradise and home of the first two humans, Adam and Eve. The name likely comes from an ancient Sumerian term meaning "plain." Referred to in Genesis, the first book in the Bible, the Garden of Eden is thought by scholars to refer to the formerly fertile riverine regions of southern Iraq. God expelled Adam and Eve, who gave in to temptation by the devil in the form of a serpent, from this paradise as punishment for their sin and disobedience, condemning them and all their descendants not only to the loss of paradise but to suffering and death. Christians believe that the Fall, as this biblical event is known, is the source of the original sin of which all humans are guilty. Islamic, as well as some Jewish, scholars regard the Garden of Eden as the ultimate destination of the righteous in the period following God's final judgment.

SEE ALSO: ancient Near East, religions of; Hebrew Bible; sin

## Garuda

A figure from both Hindu and Buddhist mythology, often depicted as either a bird or a flying creature with a human head. For Hindus, Garuda is usually associated with the god Vishnu. He is described in myth as the vehicle by which Krishna traveled between the earth and the heavens. In both Hindu and Buddhist traditions Garuda is depicted as the benign and heroic counterpart to the nagas, who are serpents representing evil and temptation.

SEE ALSO: Krishna; Vishnu

# al-Ghazali
## (1058–1111)

An important Islamic thinker whose reputation during his lifetime was such that many considered him a religious authority second only to the prophet Muhammad. Born in 1058 in Iran, al-Ghazali's full name is Abu Hamid Muhammad al-Ghazali. He was schooled in Iran, then went to work at an Islamic college in Baghdad, which during his lifetime was a major center of Islamic scholarship. He underwent a spiritual crisis in 1095, left his teaching job, and turned to Sufism, a mystical religious sect, seeking a deeper spiritual experience than his scholarly life had offered him. After some years of wandering that took him to Jerusalem and Mecca, he returned to Iran, where he joined a Sufi order. He returned to teaching in 1106, this time at an Islamic college in Nishapur in Iran. There he composed a number of works, most notably *The Revival of the Religious Sciences* and *The Confessions of al-Ghazali*; both texts are still widely read and consulted. One of his scholary works, *The Aims of the Philosophers*, which touched on the work of ancient Greeks as well as other thinkers, was highly influential in Christian Europe as well.

At the heart of al-Ghazali's teaching is the notion that reason alone is not enough to gain full religious understanding, although reason is very useful within its particular spheres. Revelation gained through mystical experiences was necessary as well, and helped the believer to grasp those elements of religious experience or teaching that reason could not explain. Philosophers or theologians whose speculations contradicted Islamic teachings, such as his near-contemporary Ibn Sina, had to be measured against those teachings and against religious faith. Al-Ghazali's efforts and reputation helped to reconcile the Sufi tradition with mainstream Sunni Islam, and established Sufism as a form of Islam, rather than a separate faith.

SEE ALSO: Ibn Sina; Sufism; al-Tabari

# Gnosticism

An early Christian heresy with roots in the mixture of Jewish, Greek, Egyptian, Roman, and Iranian thought and beliefs of the eastern Mediterranean region during the centuries before and after the time of Jesus of Nazareth. The term comes from the Greek word *gnosis*, which means "knowledge." One of the common beliefs associated with Gnosticism was the need for knowledge as a source of redemption, which separated it from the Christian emphasis on divine grace as the path to salvation. Some Gnostics also argued that Jesus was not God incarnated in human form, and therefore subject to human suffering, but was instead a less tangible avatar of God. Gnosticism is associated with versions of Christianity that failed to attract large-scale followings in the early years of the church, namely those forms associated with the Gospels of Thomas and Mary. The Gospel of Thomas was a collection of the teachings of Jesus. The Gospel of Mary was attributed to Mary Magdalene and raised her to the level of one of Jesus' chief apostles. Like Thomas, the Gospel of Mary emphasized Jesus' teachings rather than his suffering and redemption. These Gnostic Gospels were joined in 2006 by the newly published Gospel of Judas, which claimed that the disciple Judas had been instructed by Jesus to betray him.

SEE ALSO: Christian heresies; Gospels

*Located in Amritsar, India, the Golden Temple is the most important pilgrim site and shrine in Sikhism.* © BLAIN HARRINGTON III/CORBIS

## Golden Temple

The most important shrine and pilgrimage site in Sikhism. The Golden Temple is located in the city of Amritsar, named after amrit, the holy nectar found in both Sikh and Hindu lore, in the state of Punjab in northwestern India. It was built by Gurus Ramdas and Arjan, the fourth and fifth of the ten Sikh gurus of the sixteenth and seventeenth centuries credited with founding Sikhism. The Sikh maharajah (king) Ranjit Singh, who governed a large, independent state in the Punjab in the early 1800s, turned it into a striking structure with gold-plated domes and walls inlaid with jewels. In addition to serving as the central gurdwara (worship center) of the Sikh faith, the Golden Temple also features a library containing sacred texts and relics as well as meeting halls for Sikh el-

ders and scholars. Much of the complex was heavily damaged in 1984 during a battle between the Indian army and radical Sikh separatists who had seized and occupied the temple. The shrine, which stands in a complex of pools, has since been restored, and attracts some thirty thousand pilgrims and other visitors a day.

SEE ALSO: Sikh guru; Sikhism

## Gospels

Collections of Jesus of Nazareth's sayings and teachings and stories of his life. The Christian New Testament begins with the four Gospels according to Matthew, Mark, Luke, and John, their alleged authors. Each provides the "good news" of Christ; the word gospel comes from an Old English word meaning "good news." Each also tells similar stories of Jesus' life and teachings.

The first three are the most similar and are known collectively as the Synoptic Gospels. Matthew and Mark were likely written by the two original apostles of Jesus bearing those names. Luke and John, however, had no direct contact with Jesus. The Gospel of Mark is probably the oldest of the four, written between A.D. 65 and 70, more than thirty years after Jesus' death. According to tradition it was written using the recollections of not only Mark but also the apostle Peter. The Gospel of Mark emphasizes Jesus' status as the true messiah. The Gospel of Matthew was written about A.D. 85 for an early Christian community thought to exist in Alexandria, Egypt. It remains perhaps the most popular of the Gospels, emphasizing Jesus' divinity as well as his forgiveness and mercy. It also links the life of Jesus with the Old Testament prophecy of Isaiah. The Gospel of Luke was probably written around A.D. 70, and Luke is thought to have written the Acts of the Apostles around the same time. Luke appears to have been a worldly figure who traveled with Paul the Apostle. The Gospel of John, written sometime during the last quarter of the first century, provides the fullest explanation of the divinity of Jesus, true Son of God, sent to bring God's word to humankind. John was also the author of three of the New Testament's Epistles, or letters, as well as its last book, Revelation. John 35–40 of the New Revised Standard Version of the Bible summarize Christ's message:

> Jesus said to them, "I am the bread of life; he who comes to me shall not hunger, and he who believes in me shall never thirst. But I said to you that you have seen me and yet do not believe. All that the Father gives me will come to me; and him who comes to me I will not cast out. For I have come down from heaven, not to do my own will, but the will of him who sent me; and this is the will of him who sent me, that I should lose nothing of all that he has given men, but raise it up at the last day. For this is the will of my Father, that every one who sees the Son and believes in him should have eternal life; and I will raise him up at the last day."

The four New Testament Gospels were accepted as authoritative by the fifth century B.C. Numerous other Gospels exist beyond these four. They are known in general as apocryphal Gospels since they are not included in the authoritative Christian canon. Some, because of an esoteric interpretation of Jesus' ideas and experiences, are called the Gnostic Gospels. Among these are the Gospels of Thomas and of Judas, allegedly written by others among the Twelve Apostles, as well as the Gospel of Mary (Magdalene).

The word *gospel* also refers more generically to the good news of Christ as portrayed in, first, Jesus' message of salvation; second, the life of Jesus; and third, Christian teachings as a whole.

SEE ALSO: Acts of the Apostles; apostles; Jesus of Nazareth

# Great Awakenings

A series of religious revival movements mostly taking place in the British North American colonies, and after American independence, the United States. The Great Awakenings were based mainly in the Protestant traditions that dominated the colonies in the 1700s, particularly that of Congregationalism.

The first Great Awakening, taking place mostly in the American colonies from about 1720 to 1740, was largely an attempt to restore emotional content to religious traditions that had either become too reliant on reason or too bound by liturgical or ritual habits. Believers rejected traditional church authorities and flocked to hear revivalist preachers who emphasized both the love of God and the potential terrors of hell. Among them were the Anglican priest George Whitehead, who drew large audiences throughout the thirteen colonies, and Jonathan Edwards, who emphasized salvation by faith alone rather than by works or worship and encouraged evangelism, or new conversions. Throughout, believers established new congregations quite separate from established church organizations. Seeking alternatives to staid, established educational institutions such as Harvard and Yale, elites among those sympathetic to the Great Awakening started Princeton, Brown, and Rutgers universities and Dartmouth College.

The second Great Awakening took place in the 1790s. It was based in New England but spread to such newly opened up territories as Kentucky. Once again believers abandoned their established churches in favor of less formal, intensely emotional meetings, especially on the frontier. The second Great Awakening had an institutional legacy as well, with the founding of seminaries, religious colleges, and missionary movements. It was also a likely influence on the Southern Baptist movement and on the forms of Christianity that emerged among African American slaves. The event helped to establish revival meetings as a common feature of the American religious experience, especially in frontier or rural areas.

SEE ALSO: Congregationalism; evangelicalism; Protestantism

# guru

A term mostly associated with Hinduism although it is also used by Sikhs. A guru (the word is an ancient Sanskrit one implying "venerable and wise") is a respected personal tutor or teacher. The oral passage of religious wisdom from individual teacher to one student, or at most to a small group of students or "disciples," has been a tradition in Hinduism for several thousand years. The traditional pattern was for students to live with their guru at his ashram, or teaching center, and serve as well as learn from him. The bhakti movement of Hinduism gave even further status to some gurus by elevating them to the leadership of sects. Some gurus were even considered to be at least partly divine themselves.

The importance of gurus continues in the Hinduism of recent and modern times, and a number of gurus, both male and female, have attracted large followings not only in India but also in the West. Among them are the Maharishi Mahesh Yogi, who became famous in the 1960s thanks to his appeal to celebrities such as the Beatles, and Sathya Sai Baba, who in addition to being a guru is held by some to be an incarnation of the god Shiva.

In conventional Sikh doctrine, the term refers to the divine spirit made manifest. This divine spirit appeared in the persons of the ten gurus credited with founding Sikhism, and therefore these figures, from Guru Nanak (1469–1539) to Guru Gobind Singh (1666–1708) are considered to be spiritually elevated. This divine spirit is also found in the sacred scriptures of Sihism, the Adi Granth, as well as, in a more abstract sense, the community of Sikh believers.

SEE ALSO: ashram; Sai Baba, Sathya; Sikh gurus

# Guru Nanak
## (1469–1539)

The founder of Sikhism and the first of the ten Sikh gurus. He was born in the village of Nankana Sahib in the Punjab (northwestern India) in 1469, but little else is known for certain of his early life. He had a moment of spiritual epiphany in the town of Sultanpur sometime around 1499, after which he gave away his possessions and dedicated himself to a life of travel and preaching. During this epiphany he is said to have had a vision in which he was given the realization that neither Hindus nor Muslims, followers of India's two main religions, had a monopoly on religious belief and that the divisions between the two were not meaningful.

Over the next years Nanak traveled to many places, including both Hindu and Muslim centers, and engaged in philosophical debates with religious scholars and mystics. He may well have been influenced by the bhakti movement, which in its own ways was seeking to downplay the differences between Hinduism and Islam by focusing on God's formlessness and constant presence in all things. His teachings rejected asceticism, Hinduism's caste system, and other outward forms of faith, emphasizing instead the attainment of a state of inner purity through meditation. He did not reject earthly life, but asserted that believers must uphold their daily responsibilities while maintaining a state of detachment.

Nanak, who is usually portrayed in Sikh imagery as having a turban and a long, white beard, established the first Sikh community in the town of Karkarpur on the Ravi River. There followers lived and ate communally and engaged in hymn singing and ritual bathing. Nanak, meanwhile, assembled the Adi Granth, the central Sikh text, which consists of 974 hymns of his own composition. He is thought to have died in September 1539 after designating a follower known as Angad as his successor as guru in preference to any of his own sons.

SEE ALSO: Adi Granth; Sikh gurus; Sikhism

## Hachiman

The Shinto *kami*, or god, of war and one of the most popular of all kami. Hachiman was revered as early as the Nara period (710–784) of Japanese history and was the clan deity of the Minamotos, one of Japan's ruling families. He was extremely popular among Japan's warrior elites, the samurai, in later centuries. Hachiman is also considered by some Japanese Buddhists to be an enlightened soul or bodhisattva; Buddhists call him Hachiman Daibosatsu. Today, nearly half of all Shinto shrines in Japan are dedicated to Hachiman outright or contain special inner shrines devoted to him.

SEE ALSO: *kami*; Ryobu Shinto; Shinto

## Hadith

The main body of Islamic teachings and traditions outside of the Qur'an and therefore a fundamental part of the Islamic canon. Hadith consists of the sayings attributed to Muhammad and other early teachers whose reliability and authority have been established. It touches on matters of earthly rule and moral guidance about which the Qur'an itself often has little to say and is considered by most Muslims the second most important source for Islamic law after the Qu'ran.

The collections of Hadith began to take form in the eighth century. As the tradition developed, scholars recognized three general categories of them. The first, *sahih*, or "firm," are those whose authority is unquestioned and which do not overtly challenge orthodox belief. The second, *hasan*, or "good," are the product of "transmitters" (from Muhammad's time) who are not fully known or accepted. The third, *da'if*, or "weak," come from transmitters whose authority cannot be firmly established but are nevertheless useful.

There are six main collections of Hadith. The first two, and the ones given the most credence by believers, were assembled by the ninth-century scholars Muhammad al-Bukhari and Muslim ibn al-Hajjaj. The scholars reduced the number of sayings and teachings, which had originally been passed down orally, from over 500,000 to about 40,000 for each collection. Part of their purpose, apparently, was to codify the teachings considered legitimate and appropriate, since in the decades after the life of the Prophet many people invented teachings to justify various political or social agendas. These six collections are accepted as canonical by Sunni Muslims. Shia Muslims use them as well, but the most reliable Hadiths for the Shia are the collected sayings of the Shia imams.

SEE ALSO: companions of the Prophet; Muhammad; sharia

## hajj

Islamic pilgrimage to the sacred city of Mecca in Saudi Arabia. The hajj is one of the Five Pillars of Faith, the core of Islamic practice, and therefore all Muslims are enjoined to make the pilgrimage at least once in their lives. Islamic doctrine, however, recognizes that in many cases be-

*Pilgrims recite prayers while circling the Ka'aba seven times during the hajj.* Keystone
Features/Getty Images

lievers are too far away, lack the means, or for some other reason cannot make the journey, so the hajj is not an absolute requirement. For Muslims who do complete the pilgrimage, the hajj is often the high point of their religious lives. Those who do so are entitled to adopt the honorific title "hajji."

The hajj has its own season, generally the last month of the Islamic calendar, and lasts five days. It begins at a site outside of Mecca where pilgrims exchange their clothing for simple, uniform garments indicating the equality of every person. Men don a white robe made up of two sheets wrapped around the body; women generally wear modest black robes. This garb

also symbolizes entrance into a state of purity, or ihram. Pilgrims then enter Mecca proper and proceed on foot to the vast courtyard of the city's Great Mosque. At its center is the Ka'aba, Islam's holiest shrine, which pilgrims circle seven times in a counterclockwise direction while reciting ritual prayers. Touching the black stone at one corner of the Ka'aba is an especially moving experience in this stage of the pilgrimage. To complete this first stage, pilgrims then go back and forth seven times between the two sacred mountains Safa and Marwa and recommit themselves to the duties of Islamic believers. The remainder of the pilgrimage involves other important rituals, including visits to holy sites outside Mecca, the sacrifice of an animal, and a final circling of the Ka'aba.

Many Muslims believe that the hajj adds an element of community to a global religion practiced in widely separated parts of the world. On a more individual level the hajj is often a rite of passage, after which believers follow more literally and seriously the teachings of the faith such as the five daily prayers, avoidance of alcohol, and charity.

SEE ALSO: Five Pillars of Faith; Ka'aba; Mecca

## Hanukkah

The Jewish Festival of Light, which takes place in the Hebrew month of Kislev, which is generally the same as December in the Christian calendar. The festival is designed to commemorate the rededication of the second Temple in Jerusalem in 164 B.C. The rededication followed the desecration of the Temple by Antiochus Epiphanes, a Greek-speaking king of Syria who tried to impose Greek culture on the Jews. Hanukkah is also referred to as the Feast of Dedication, or the Feast of the Maccabees, the latter in honor of Judas Maccabeus, the head of the rebellion against Antiochus, and his descendants.

Hanukkah lasts for eight days, each of which is connoted by the lighting of a candle in a ceremonial holder called a menorah. In addition to the lighting of candles, the exchange of gifts is a regular feature of Hanukkah. For this reason, as well as the fact that the eight days of the festival are in December, Hanukkah joins Christmas (and, in small measure, Kwanzaa) in the "holiday" season of the United States. It is not, however, the Jewish equivalent of Christmas. Jewish tradition considers both Passover and the High Holy Days of Yom Kippur as more impor-

tant celebrations.

SEE ALSO: calendars; Passover; Yom Kippur

## Hanuman

A Hindu god representing mischief and irreverence as well as unwavering devotion. The central myths of Hanuman appear in the great epic Ramayana, where Hanuman uses his powers of strength and cunning to serve the god Rama in his efforts to find and rescue Sita, Rama's consort, from the clutches of the demon Ravana. These stories describe Hanuman as a monkey god, and he is therefore usually depicted in Hindu artwork as a long-tailed monkey, although he sometimes has a human body. He is also thought to have the ability to change size. Hanuman is among the most popular of Hindu deities, with many temples dedicated to him. Hanuman was thought to be the child of Vayu, a Hindu wind god, and a female monkey and is therefore a manifestation of the linking of the earthly and the divine.

SEE ALSO: Rama; Ramayana; Sita

## Hare Krishna

The familiar name for the International Society for Krishna Consciousness (ISKCON), a movement founded in the United States in 1965 by the Hindu guru A.C. Bhaktivedanta Swami Prabhpada. The Hare Krishna is a Westernized Hindu sect whose adherents are mostly Americans or Western Europeans; its popularity received a boost from the support of popular musician and former Beatle George Harrison, whose works suggested he saw himself as a follower of the god Krishna and helped to make familiar the "Hare Krishna" mantra.

The sect's teachings, which are based in Swami Prabhupada's translation of the Bhagavad Gita, require followers to practice vegetarianism and to give up alcohol and drugs. They are also supposed to disdain sexual contact except for the purposes of procreation within marriage. Unlike most other Hindu sects, moreover, members of ISKCON engage in proselytization, or active efforts to spread the word. Followers appear in public places, wearing distinctive robes and ringing bells while chanting and passing out pamphlets. Despite the dubious and corrupt acts of some of the gurus who have led the movement after Swami Prabhpada's death in 1977, the Hare Krishna movement has avoided cult status because some, but by no means all, Hindu scholars and teachers in the West and India consider it a legitimate Hindu sect.

SEE ALSO: Krishna; new religious movements, Western

## Hasidism

A Jewish religious movement that emerged in the late eighteenth century and grew popular among the large Jewish populations of Poland and Russia. It emphasizes mysticism, enthusiasm, and reverence for a leader, or rebbe. Among the early important rebbes were Israel ben Eliezer and Dov Baer, charismatic leaders who attracted large groups of followers. The appeal of these men and their teachings was also likely due to the fact that many ordinary Jews felt shut out of more of the conventional circles of scholarship and leadership maintained by learned Jewish elites. Israel ben Eliezer's sect, the Baal Shem Tov, taught that devotion to God is based in the emotions rather than in abstract scholarship or the accumulation of knowledge and that music and dancing could be forms of worship. After some hesitation, Orthodox Jewish leaders recognized Hasidism as a legitimate Jewish sect.

Jewish immigrants to western Europe and the United States in the late nineteenth and early twentieth centuries brought Hasidism with them, and the sect continues to thrive, especially in inner cities in the East. Hasidic Jews are recognizeable by their distinct appearance: Both men and women wear sober, dark clothes, and men and boys often grow curled sidelocks and eventually maintain full beards.

SEE ALSO: Judaism; Kabbalah; Orthodox Judaism

## heaven

The otherworldly paradise where devout believers dwell eternally after death in many religions, most prominently in Judaism, Christianity, and Islam. It is also commonly thought to be the dwelling place of God or the gods.

According to the Hebrew Bible, heaven is where Yahwah lives along with his angels. Judaism taught up to the second century B.C. that the dead went to a vague underworld known as Sheol. But later versions of the faith placed more emphasis on rewards for the righteous; Jews who were righteous enough would be resurrected after their death and go to heaven to be with God. The Christian concept of heaven is similar; heaven is considered the final destination of all those who have accepted God's salvation as granted by Jesus Christ. Roman Catholicism has traditionally added a realm known as purgatory for those who have died without the remission of their sins but who are basically good. In Islam, heaven is described as both a garden and a paradise. Descriptions of the specific nature of heaven, whether in biblical or Qur'anic scriptures or in other literature or folklore, have been highly controversial. Many argue that most of these descriptions should be understood allegorically, that heaven for Christians, for instance, will not necessarily involve clouds and pathways of gold, and that heaven for the devout Muslim will not necessarily be a paradise of sensual pleasures. In this view, the "bliss" of heaven is simply derived from one's closeness to God.

Heaven in other religious traditions includes the Chinese *t'ian*, which is more often portrayed as a distant deity who is the source of moral and physical law than as a destination for the dead. In this sense "heaven," as *t'ian* is often translated (traditional Chinese emperors were "sons of heaven"), is a reflection of divine will and of the divine order. Buddhism offers several heavens, including the Tusita heaven that is the home of the bodhisattva Maitreya as well as other Buddhas awaiting final release, and the Pure Land believed by some Mahayana Buddhists to be a place where the human soul can achieve final awakening, provided one reaches it. In Hinduism, the general understanding is that the heavens are the dwelling places of the gods, and they may exist either below the world or above it.

SEE ALSO: eschatology; hell

## Hebrew Bible

The holy scriptures of Judaism. The Hebrew Bible is also known as Tanakh, an acronym describing the three sections of the scriptures: Torah, Nevi'im (Prophets), and Ketuvim (Writings). The Torah, also known as the Pentateuch, consists of the five books of Genesis, Exodus, Leviticus, Numbers, and Deuteronomy. It is the most important part of the Hebrew Bible, providing the ancient history of the Hebrews as well as the original sources of Jewish belief and ritual. Inscribed separately on scrolls, the Torah itself is for many Jews an object of veneration. The Nevi'im includes the works of important prophets such as Joshua, Jeremiah, and 1 and 2 Isaiah, and thus provides a further source of Jewish thought and scholarship as well as historical and genealogical accounts. The varied Ketuvim consists of Psalms, Proverbs, the so-called five scrolls (the Song of Solomon, Ruth, Lamentations, Ecclesiastes, and Esther), 1 and 2 Chronicles, and the books of Job, Daniel, Ezra, and Nehemiah. As a whole these texts provide stories of worldly experience, prophecy, and various forms of religious devotion. This canon of texts was assembled by the second century B.C., with the Torah compiled first. Originally written in Hebrew, much of the Tanakh was translated into Greek and Aramaic before the first century A.D. The Tanakh is supplemented by a collection of texts not considered to be canonical but rather as attempts to fill in historical and theological gaps. This collection is known as the Apocrypha.

The Hebrew Bible is known as the Old Testament by Christians, who also consider the collection to be holy scripture. Early Christians used the Greek translation of the Hebrew, known as the Septuagint, which did not correspond exactly to the original Jewish collection. The Old Testaments used by Roman Catholic and Eastern Orthodox Christians continue to contain books and parts of books contained in the Septuagint. Protestants restrict themselves to the Hebrew canon, considering these other writings apocryphal.

SEE ALSO: Bible; New Testament; Torah

## hell

The place where the damned or evil, or their souls, go after death. The concept appears in various forms in the major monotheistic religions, Judaism, Christianity, and Islam, where it is most predominant as a feature of belief. It also appears in related forms in Zoroastrianism, Hinduism, Buddhism, and other traditions. The English word *hell* is derived from a common Germanic name for the home of the dead.

In Judaism, hell is associated with Gehenna, which was at first an actual site outside of Jerusalem where some followers of a pagan god known as Moloch practiced the fire sacrifice of children as late as the sixty century B.C. The word was later redefined to signify the place for punishment of evildoers. Christianity adapted the Jewish concept, describing hell as the abode of Satan and his demons as well as a place for the souls of those who reject God and live a willful life of sin. Several references in the New Testament refer to hell, or Gehenna, as the place where fire will destroy the evil. From the time of Christianity's beginnings, however, some thinkers have denied hell's literal existence, arguing that it is merely a metaphorical state of being separating the bad from the good, those who reject God's love and forgiveness from those who accept it. Much common understanding of the nature of hell in Christianity, meanwhile, comes from the work of medieval and Renaissance writers and artists such as the Italian writer Dante Alighieri, whose fourteenth-century *Inferno* describes a journey through hell.

Islam, likely influenced by Jewish and Christian ideas, describes hell as a huge pit of fire over which a bridge to paradise is suspended. All souls must cross the bridge to get to paradise but, unless God rules otherwise, the damned will fall into the fiery pit. The notion of a soul crossing the bridge may have come from Zoroastrianism, which preaches that each soul must have its deeds weighed on a so-called bridge of the requiter. If good deeds outweigh the bad, the soul finishes its passage across the bridge and enters paradise. If bad deeds outweigh the good, however, the soul falls into a hell that, in Zoroastrianism, is freezing cold. This idea of a final judgment in Zoroastrianism appears also in all three of the major monotheistic traditions.

In Hinduism and Buddhism, numerous hells exist as temporary states of being. They are generally the abode of those who have accumulated too much bad karma, too many misdeeds in too many previous existences. The reincarnation of souls, however, means that there will be eventual release from these hells, although this may take many lifetimes.

SEE ALSO: eschatology; heaven; sin

# hijra

The exile in A.D. 622 of the prophet Muhammad and his first community of followers from Mecca to Medina, an Arabian city some 270 miles from Mecca. Muhammad made the journey to escape religious persecution in Mecca, and subsequently the first true Islamic community, consisting of the Prophet himself, his fellow exiles, and a group of local helpers, was founded in Medina. This event marks the beginning of the Islamic calendar established by Omar, the second Islamic caliph, in 639.

SEE ALSO: calendars; Muhammad; Medina

# Hinayana Buddhism

The term used by Mahayana Buddhists, followers of the "greater vehicle," to describe those who adhere to the "smaller vehicle" of Theravada Buddhism. Hinayana is a somewhat derogatory term related to the allegedly selfish emphasis in Theravada Buddhism on individual enlightenment, of achieving the personal status of an arhat, or "one who hears," a kind of Buddhist saint. Mahayana believers, by contrast, emphasize the activities of bodhisattvas, or enlightened souls who delay nirvana in order to help others. For the Mahayana, Hinayana more specifically refers to both the oldest forms of Buddhism, which predated Mahayana notions, and what they see as the first stages of the Buddhist path.

Strictly speaking, Theravada Buddhism is the only survivor among the earlier Hinayana schools, the others having faded away by the first century B.C., although the two terms are sometimes used interchangeably. Theravada Buddhists deny that their "vehicle" is in any way more selfish or limited than the Mahayana alternative.

SEE ALSO: councils, Buddhist; Mahayana Buddhism; Theravada Buddhism

# Hinduism

The oldest of the major world religions. Although Hinduism mostly took shape during its classical period, between 500 B.C. and A.D. 500, elements of it existed more than a thousand years earlier. The religion mostly closely associated with the civilization of India, Hinduism provided the foundation for several other major religions, notably Buddhism, Jainism, and Sikhism. It is practiced by at least 850 million people on the Indian subcontinent as well as millions of Indians living in Africa, western Europe, North America, and elsewhere around the world.

*Origins and History* Classical Hinduism is the result of a long cultural evolution that began after 1500 B.C., when Indo-European immigrants entered northern India from central and western Asia. These Indo-Europeans, who were related to tribes that settled in Europe and the Middle East,

brought with them their religious beliefs and their languages. They found a large local population with religious traditions of its own. Over many centuries, and in a process that included much fighting among Indo-European clans, these newcomers established themselves as the dominant powers in India. Their religions, meanwhile, merged with those of the locals whom they subdued. The Indo-European, or Vedic, religion of fire gods and sacrificial rituals therefore became integrated with indigenous meditational practices and faith in various deities, included a central mother goddess. These may have been in place in India since the time of the mysterious Indus Valley civilization, which thrived in the third millennium B.C., long before the arrival of the Indo-Europeans. India's caste system also evolved as part of this process of integration. The caste system, which devout Hindus trace to the Creation of humanity by cosmic deities, divides society into a priestly caste, a military and rulership caste, a productive caste, and a laboring caste. Some people, the lowest in the system, were technically outcast, the "untouchables" who did the dirtiest, most unpleasant jobs.

By the first few centuries B.C., religious traditions arose that centered around the activities of the brahmins, the priestly caste. They conducted important rituals, maintained in oral form (and increasingly, written form) essential stories and lessons, and passed down their teachings as gurus to small groups of students. The Vedic and, in all likelihood, the Indus Valley deities evolved into the gods and goddesses who remain important to Hinduism even today, and ordinary people began to express their faith in household worship, at temples, and at large festivals. Hinduism's classical texts also acquired canonical versions. These include the Vedas, which were held to be of divine origin, and the Upanishads, which are largely lessons from gurus to disciples. Many other texts followed, including such commentaries on the Vedas as the Puranas and Brahmanas and the great epic poems *Mahabharata* and *Ramayana*. These texts were written in Sanskrit, the Indo-European tongue that is still the religious language of India.

During the first millennium A.D. Hinduism continued to grow more diverse. Among its major features was the appearance of a canon of literature in India's vernacular languages, notably the Tamil language of southern India. Much of this literature was in the form of bhakti, or devotional poetry, dedicated to a particular god or goddess. Certain deities became the focus of devotional cults, growing to be the most popular of a pantheon of hundreds. These were, most vividly, the trinity of Brahma, Vishnu, and Shiva. Other popular deities included Rama and Krishna, who were avatars, or different aspects, of Vishnu, and various forms of the "divine goddess" known as Shakti, who represented the feminine aspects of Creation. Among these representations were the goddesses Kali, Durga, and Parvati, as well as Sita, the wife of Rama, and Krishna's consort, Radha. Meanwhile Hindu scholars and teachers, such as Shankara (788–820) and Ramanuja (1017–1137) debated the true nature of divinity and its relationship to humanity. They differed on many specifics, but both helped to cement the Vedanta, or "way of the Vedas," as the mainstream form of Hinduism.

Muslim rulers controlled much of India from the twelfth through the eighteenth centuries, and although many Hindus converted to Islam during this period, especially those from lower castes seeking freedom from caste restrictions, the new religion had little impact on Hindu belief or practice. When the British began to take over parts of India, a process that began in 1757, they tried to introduce reforms into Hinduism relevant to Western morality and the modern world. In the early 1800s they banned the practice of sati, in which a widow chose to commit suicide by burning herself on her husband's funeral pyre. The reformer Ram Mohan Roy (1772–1833) approved of this and, heavily influenced by Islam and Christianity as well as modernism, urged an end to caste restrictions and some of the more esoteric Hindu rituals.

By the early twentieth century many Indians resented foreign rule and wanted India to gain its independence from Great Britain. At the head of the independence movement was another religious reformer, Mohandas K. Gandhi, whom followers revered as the Mahatma, the "great soul." Gandhi, like Roy, wanted to bring about an end to caste divisions, and he had a particular affection for untouchables, whom he called harijans, or "children of god." But he also was a living reminder of India's eternal religious traditions, dressing and living simply and trying to be an embodiment of Hindu ethics. When he was assassinated by Hindu extremists after Indian independence, his last words were "Ram, Ram," a version of Rama, one of the many names of God.

*Central Beliefs of Hinduism* Until fairly recently Hindus did not have a name for their religion; it was simply a central part of their culture and existence. Some called it by the Sanskrit words *sanatana dharma*, which might translate as "the one way." It was British scholars and their Indian counterparts who, beginning in the late 1700s, began using the word *Hinduism* to refer to the complex set of religious practices they found in India, but this word in fact means little more than "Indianism." The faith is extremely diverse and complex; beliefs vary according to social level, local traditions, scholarly and popular understanding of the natures of particular deities, and many other factors. Indeed, beliefs held by some Hindus might be directly contradicted by others. Yet there are a few beliefs that virtually all Hindus share.

Hindus believe that all life is divine and unified, that the godhead permeates every aspect of existence. Although Hindu tradition and literature are full of a complex and colorful pantheon of gods and goddesses, all of them are avatars of a single divine reality (in some sects individual deities are thought to be supreme beings). The common term for this single divine essence is Brahman. The purpose of Hindu faith and practice is for the individual soul, or atman, to regain union with Brahman. Hindu funerary practices, which involve cremation and then the placing of ashes into a river that ultimately joins the larger ocean, are a symbol of this spiritual process. A soul that has achieved full recognition of this union is said to have achieved moksha, or liberation from the cycle of birth and rebirth.

The concept of moksha is tied to another important Hindu concept, reincarnation, or the rebirth of the spirit over successive lifetimes. Achieving moksha requires hundreds if not thousands of reincarnations for most Hindus. Those who are thought to be closest to it are the members of the priestly caste, the brahmins. Those furthest from moksha are untouchables. All animals and objects, however, are thought to contain atman as well,

and the need to be reborn at higher levels. The best way for individual believers to ensure higher rebirths is to follow their particular dharma, translated as "path," "duty," "knowledge," or even simply "truth." One's dharma depends on his or her caste and on cultural traditions as well as religious beliefs. It is a parent's dharma, for example, to ensure that their children marry within the proper caste, and it is a child's dharma to accept those decisions. Brahmins and others who are considered closer to moksha have more expectations and restrictions placed upon them. Brahmins, for instance, are commonly vegetarians while those of lower castes are often not. Those of higher castes also were expected, until recently, to completely avoid physical contact with untouchables. Such contact was considered to be caste pollution, requiring elaborate rituals of purification. The main purpose of these and many other practices and beliefs is to ensure that the soul proceeds on its journey toward reunion with the ultimate godhead.

***Texts and Rituals*** Hinduism's classical texts—the Vedas, Upanishads, Puranas, Brahmanas, and other collections—are largely the domain of brahmin priests, although they provide the foundation for basic beliefs and ethics as well as for education and ritual practices. Far more popular are the texts which emphasize dharma. These include the *Mahabharata* and *Ramayana*. The first is based in the era when Indo-European clans vied for control over northern India. It contains an added section known, and often published separately, as the Bhagavad Gita. The Gita is popular Hinduism's most important text, emphasizing the importance of devotion, proper knowledge, and the need for right action. The *Ramayana*, meanwhile, provides exemplars of the ideal king and husband in the figure of Rama as well as the ideal devoted wife in the figure of Sita. The last few centuries B.C. and the first few centuries A.D. saw the appearance of numerous other central dharma-related texts. Among them were the Laws of Manu, a description of dharma mainly for young men of the priestly caste. The Laws of Manu also described the four stages of life that such men pass through: student, householder, dharma (religious devotion), and moksha, which here means a turn to asceticism, meditation, and wandering. Hindu thinkers did not shy away from earthly affairs, understanding that the profane and the sacred were closely linked. Texts focusing on these matters include the *Artha Shastra*, a manual of political power, and the *Kama Sutra*, a guide to pleasure, love, and etiquette. In the centuries following Hinduism's classical era, many works of philosophy and bhakti poetry, written in India's many languages, added to a diverse and deep canon of religious works.

Hindu worship, at its most basic level, is daily and constant. Believers commonly practice daily household rituals known as puja, which can take many forms. They also regularly visit temples, where brahmin priests maintain images of the deities that a particular temple is known for. Common features of these rites include the giving of offerings and the lighting of sacred fires. The diversity of these rituals reflects the belief among Hindus that every act of worship, no matter how small and no matter what god or goddess it is directed to, ultimately reaches the divine.

Hindu practice is also full of festivals. Among those practiced by most Hindus are Divali (Deepavali), a festival of light held in autumn, and Holi, a raucous celebration of the arrival of spring. Public festivals often include the procession of images of gods through the streets. Some festivals, such as the Kumbh Mela held every few years at several locations in India, are likely the largest religious gatherings in history. Many of these festivals, the Kumbh Mela included, are the destination of pilgrims; indeed, Hinduism has a rich tradition of pilgrimage. Believers often devote years to wandering among sacred sites. The primary destination of pilgrims is Hinduism's most sacred city, Varanasi, located on its most sacred river, the Ganga in northern India. Devotees who engage in ritual bathing there are thought to have their sins washed away, while those who die and are cremated there attain immediate release from the wheel of existence.

*Hinduism in the Modern World* Hindu practice and belief continue to lie at the center of life for millions of Indians both within India and around the world. India is modernizing rapidly, and in the view of some Indians taking on more and more of the materialistic and immoral aspects of Western culture, but Hinduism has proven to be supremely adaptable and open and will likely continue to be so. Modern India is a secular state in which the lower castes and untouchables, now known as the "scheduled castes," are granted full equality. Yet despite modernization and the secular nature of the Indian state, most Hindus continue to view traditional dharmas as the organizing principles of their lives. They continue to marry within their castes, often in traditional arranged marriages, and to try to live according to the guidelines appearing in ancient texts and to the customs those guidelines represent. Meanwhile, Hinduism's emphasis on the unity and divinity of all creation has proven increasingly popular among non-Indians. Outsiders cannot "convert" to Hinduism in any comfortable way; one must be born into the faith. Yet outsiders have adopted many Hindu practices, from meditation to study in ashrams to even the direct worship of Hindu deities such as Krishna. The "one way," sanatana dharma, continues to be perhaps the most diverse of all major religious traditions.

SEE ALSO: Bhagavad Gita; caste; mandir; Ramayana; Vedas

# Hindutva

A Sanskrit term meaning "Hindu-ness." The term came into common usage in the 1920s, during the Indian independence movement from the British Empire, and it has remained common since independence was achieved in 1947. In its most fundamental sense, Hindutva implies that there is a set of common religious and cultural characteristics shared by all Indian people who practice religions born in India: Hinduism, Buddhism, Sikhism, and Jainism. Those who practice foreign faiths, notably Islam and Christianity, are only truly "Indian" according to the extent to which they allow themselves to be absorbed into the "dominant" culture. The idea reflected the thinking of some independence leaders. Mahatma Gandhi took an extremely liberal view of Hindutva when he claimed that all Indians, even Muslims (whom he believed were mostly either converts from Hinduism or the descendants of converts), were truly Indian. Muhammad Ali Jinnah, the leader of India's Muslims, took the opposite view when he asserted that his fellow Muslims would never truly belong in an India controlled by the majority Hindus, that they were a truly separate "nation" deserving of their own state. In the event Jinnah, not Gandhi, got his wish. When the British left India they left be-

hind two new countries: mostly Muslim Pakistan and mostly Hindu India.

In more recent years Hindutva has served as a rallying cry for Hindu nationalist and fundamentalist groups. Some of the most vocal of these assert that India's religious minorities, most notably still Muslims, must accept a subordinate status within Indian society. The conflicts that have arisen from these notions have resulted in widespread communal violence, most recently in 1992 after Hindu nationalists destroyed a historic mosque in the northern Indian city of Ayodha, claiming that it stood on the site of the birthplace of the god Rama.

SEE ALSO: fundamentalism, Christian; fundamentalism, Islamic; Gandhi, Mohandas K.

# Holi

A spring holiday practiced by Hindus in northern India during a full-moon period in either February or March. Holi is generally associated with the god Krishna and his consort Radha. It is a festival of laughter, frivolity, and role reversals. The celebration features dousing people with colored water or powder and ignoring social mores as well as caste restrictions, at least for a short period. In modern India many celebrants add to the mood by drinking milkshakes laced with bhang, or hashish, a practice largely smiled upon by police and other authorities. The frivolity of Holi is thought to reflect such stories as Krishna's sporting with the Gopis, or female cowherds, while the turning over of conventional mores and practices might be seen in certain locales where female devotees of Radha attack their menfolk in make-believe combat. The festival ends when devotees exchange their color-splattered clothes for clean white ones and

*Part of the façade of the Eanna Temple of King Kara-indas in Uruk, which was dedicated to the city goddess Inanna.* BILDARCHIV PREUSSISCHER KULTURBESITZ/ART RESOURCE, NY

the gods create humans to use as laborers and thereby ensure that the work gets done.

SEE ALSO: Annunaki; Atrahasis; religion

## Inanna

A leading Sumerian goddess and the most popular deity in all of ancient Mesopotamia. Inanna (also Ishtar or Astarte) was known as the goddess of love and sexual passion, but she was also associated with war and was seen as a protector of kings and ruling dynasties. The great conqueror Sargon of Akkad, for instance, called on her to support him in battle. In addition, sometime in the third millennium B.C. she merged with a Semitic goddess, Ishtar, thereby becoming "queen of Heaven" and gaining an association with the planet Venus. As a result, one of her symbols was a star.

In her role as the sex goddess, Inanna was both selfish and inexhaustible, choosing, using, and discarding male lovers at will. Her chief lover, Dumuzi, for example, ended up spending half of his time in the dark reaches of the Underworld because of her, as told in the epic poem *The Descent of Inanna*. Not surprisingly, Inanna was a patron deity of prostitutes, and some of her priestesses may have served her as sacred prostitutes. Inanna had temples and shrines all across Mesopotamia, but her principal one was the Eanna, or "House of Heaven," at Uruk. Other important shrines were at Kish, also in Sumeria, and Nineveh, in Assyria.

Many hymns and other forms of written praise were composed for Inanna over the course of more than two millennia. The following example, phrased to make it sound as if the goddess herself is speaking, is Sumerian and dates from the late third millennium B.C.

> I am Inanna! Which god compares with me? [The chief god] Enlil gave me the heavens and he gave me the Earth. I am Innana! He gave me lordship, and he gave me queenship. He gave me battles and he gave me fighting. He gave me the storm-wind and he gave me the dust cloud. He placed the heavens on my head as a crown. He put the earth at my feet as sandals. He wrapped [a] holy . . . garment around my body. He put the holy scepter in my hand. The [other] gods are [like] small birds, but I am the falcon. . . . When I enter the Ekur, the house of Enlil, the gate-keeper does not lift his hand against my breast; the minister does not tell me, "Rise!" The heavens are mine and the Earth is mine. I am heroic! Which god compares with me?

SEE ALSO: *Descent of Inanna, The*; Dumuzi; sacred prostitution

## Indo-Europeans

Possibly the ancestors of a number of ancient peoples who inhabited Europe and western Asia, including Mesopotamia. The term *Indo-European* was initially mainly a linguistic one and referred to a proposed very ancient, ancestral language that may have given birth to many later languages. However, over time most scholars came to believe that there was also an ancestral Indo-European people, sometimes called the Proto-Indo-Europeans. If they did exist, the location of their original homeland is still a matter of considerable dispute. The two chief theories place that homeland either in southern Russia, just north and east of the Black Sea, or in Anatolia. Supposedly, sometime in the late Stone Age they spread outward in all directions and settled Europe, including Greece, Italy, and Germany; Anatolia; Armenia; Iran; and northern India. Noted University of Cambridge scholar Colin Renfrew recently suggested that the Indo-Europeans originated in Anatolia, where they invented agriculture and subsequently introduced it to neighboring peoples, including those who lived in the Fertile Crescent and later brought it to Mesopotamia. There may well be something to this idea. In the late 1990s Columbia University scientists William Ryan and Walter Pitman presented convincing evidence for a large-scale natural disaster in the Black Sea region north of Anatolia in the sixth millennium B.C. They believe that this catastrophe triggered the Indo-European migrations, including those into the Fertile Crescent. For the time being, however, the scholarly community as a whole remains uncertain about the origins of the Indo-Europeans.

SEE ALSO: Fertile Crescent; flood legends; languages

## inscriptions

Written words or messages cut or scratched into stone, metal, or other durable materials, of which tens of thousands have survived from ancient Mesopotamia. The study of ancient inscriptions is called epigraphy.

SEE ALSO: Behistun Rock; cuneiform; epigraphy

# Isaiah
## (flourished mid-700s B.C.)

A Hebrew prophet and the name of the book of the Old Testament he is credited with writing. Isaiah may have been related to the royal family of the Jewish kingdom of Judah and advised some of the rulers of that realm. He witnessed the invasion of the other Jewish kingdom, Israel, by the Assyrian kings Tiglathpileser III and Shalmaneser V and was opposed to the pro-Assyrian stance taken by Judah's king, Ahaz. Isaiah advised Ahaz's successor, Hezekiah, to resist the Assyrians, which he did. The unfortunate result was an invasion of Judah by Assyria's King Sennacherib. These events are told in passing in the book of Isaiah as well in two other Old Testament books, Second Kings and Second Chronicles.

SEE ALSO: Bible; Judah; Israel

# Ishbi-Erra
## (reigned ca. 2017–1985 B.C.)

A ruler of the Sumerian city-state of Isin, whose rebellious activities helped to weaken and bring about the collapse of the empire now called the Third Dynasty of Ur. Ishbi-Erra started out as a soldier and army officer in the empire. He must have acquitted himself well because King Ibbi-Sin (reigned ca. 2026–2004 B.C.) soon placed him in charge of the city of Isin. But Ishbi-Erra then betrayed the king's trust. The realm was already faltering under the strain of Amorite tribes migrating from the northwest and raids by the Elamites from the east; and Ishbi-Erra took advantage of the situation by declaring Isin independent from Ur. He also took control of the city of Nippur and even made alliances with some of Ur's enemies. After the Elamites sacked Ur, causing the fall of its

empire, Ishbi-Erra proclaimed himself the rightful heir to the Ur dynasts in the region; perhaps for this reason, the Sumerian King List lists him as the first monarch of a new line of rulers, the so-called First Dynasty of Isin.

SEE ALSO: Elam; Isin; Third Dynasty of Ur

# Ishkur

A major weather god worshipped by the Sumerians, the Assyrians, and the Babylonians as well as by some Semitic peoples as far west as Syria. He was also known as Adad or Hadad. Supposedly a son of the chief god, Enlil, Ishkur was thought to have the power to unleash terrible storms on cities or lands that had fallen out of favor with the gods. In contrast, he sometimes brought gentle rains that watered the crops of lands that were on good terms with divine forces. His chief symbol was lightning, and his most sacred animal was the bull.

SEE ALSO: Enlil; religion

# Ishme-Dagan
## (reigned ca. 1780–1741 B.C.)

An early Amorite king of Assyria and the stronger and more capable of the two sons of King Shamshi-Adad. The latter placed Ishme-Dagan on the throne of the city-state of Ekallatum, and surviving letters exchanged between father and son suggest that Ishme-Dagan was an effective ruler and military leader. After Shamshi-Adad died, Ishme-Dagan inherited the Assyrian throne and wrote a letter to his brother, Iasmah-Adad, then ruling the city of Mari. "Say to Iasmah-Adad: Thus says Ishme-Dagan, your brother," the letter begins.

> I have ascended the throne of my father's house. This is why I have been extremely busy, and have not been

able to send you news of my well-being. . . . You must not be anxious. Your throne is and will remain your throne. The gods Adad and Shamash I hold in my hand. . . . Let us swear a binding oath to each other . . . [and] maintain brotherly relationships with each other for all time.

Unfortunately for the brothers, their remaining reigns were short. Iasmah-Adad was soon overthrown by the brother of a former ruler of Mari, and a few years later Ishme-Dagan's small Assyrian realm was absorbed by the Babylonians under King Hammurabi.

SEE ALSO: Assyrian Empire; Iasmah-Adad; Shamshi-Adad

## Ishtar

Originally a local Semitic goddess associated with the planet Venus. Sometime in the third millennium B.C., the image of Ishtar (or Astarte) and her functions merged with those of the more important and popular Sumerian deity Inanna, goddess of love and sexual passion.

SEE ALSO: Inanna; religion; sacred prostitution

## Isin

A Sumerian, and later Babylonian, city lying in the lowlands between the Tigris and Euphrates rivers in southern Mesopotamia, about 125 miles (200km) southeast of modern Baghdad. Isin (modern Ishan Bahriyat) was inhabited at least from the fifth millennium B.C., but it did not rise to prominence until the fall of the Third Dynasty of Ur, at the close of the third millennium B.C. The first dynasty of Isin was founded circa 2017 B.C. by a ruler named Ishbi-Erra. The city was most

famous for its cult center and temple dedicated to Gula (or Ninisina), goddess of healing, which occupied the highest point in Isin. Mesopotamians came there from far and wide in hopes of achieving some sort of miraculous cure. Meanwhile, during the first two centuries of the second millennium B.C., Isin engaged in a lively and sometimes warlike rivalry with the neighboring city of Larsa, until both were captured by Babylonia's King Hammurabi and absorbed into his empire. Eventually the marshes reclaimed the site of Isin, and the locals came to call it Ishan Bahriyat, the "Monument Drowned by the Sea."

SEE ALSO: Hammurabi; Ishbi-Erra; Larsa

## Islam

The religion of the Muslims, based on the teachings of the prophet Muhammad and the holy book known as the Koran. Islam became the predominant faith of Mesopotamia following the Arab conquests of the region from A.D. 634 to 651.

SEE ALSO: Muslim period

## Israel

One of two Hebrew (Jewish) kingdoms situated in ancient Palestine and conquered by Mesopotamian kings. According to the Old Testament, Abraham, the first prophet not only of the Jews but also of the Christians and the Muslims, lived sometime in the 1800s B.C. His son, Jacob, was later renamed Israel. Jacob's twelve sons became the chiefs of the twelve tribes of Israel. Many biblical scholars suggest that these and other stories about the early Hebrews, including their sojourn in Egypt, may be either mythical or only loosely based on fact. What seems more certain is that by the eleventh century B.C. the first kingdom of Israel was established in Palestine. Instrumental in its creation was a war leader named Saul and his successor, King David, who made Jerusalem the capital circa 1000 B.C. David's own successor, Solomon, supposedly erected the first great Jewish house of worship—the First Temple—in Jerusalem. Following Solomon's death in the tenth century B.C., the kingdom split into two Hebrew states—Israel in the north and Judah in the south. Judah retained Jerusalem as its capital, and Samaria became the capital of Israel. Unfortunately for the inhabitants of both of these kingdoms, the Assyrian Empire was rising to prominence in this period. In the 720s B.C. the Assyrians conquered Israel, captured Samaria, and carried away most or all of the local nobles and resettled them in Assyria. Judah managed to survive for a little more than a century before it too fell prey to Assyrian aggression.

SEE ALSO: Jerusalem; Judah; Palestine

## Iter-Mer

The patron god of Mari, a city on the upper reaches of the Euphrates River that flourished in the early second millennium B.C. In ancient Akkadian, the language spoken by the Babylonians in that millennium, Iter-Mer translates as "Mer has Returned." *Mer* was the Sumerian word for "rain." So modern scholars assume that this deity was seen as the bringer of the seasonal rainfall essential for farming in the region.

SEE ALSO: farming; Mari; religion

## Jarmo

An important archaeological site in northern Iraq, where modern excavators found the remains of a prehistoric agricultural village dating to the seventh millennium B.C. Located in the foothills of the upper Zagros Mountains, just east of the Assyrian plains, Jarmo (or Qalat Jarmo) appears to have been one of the early villages set up by the inhabitants of the Fertile Crescent as they made their way southward onto the Mesopotamian plains. Excavations undertaken between 1948 and 1955 by Robert and Linda Braidwood of Chicago's Oriental Institute revealed that the village measured about 300 by 450 feet (92 by 135m) and supported a population of from one to two hundred. The diggers found the remains of twenty primitive houses with walls made of packed mud, a technique predating that of dried clay bricks. The villagers raised barley, emmer wheat, peas, sheep, and goats. Small clay tokens of varying geometric shapes found in the ruins may have been used to count livestock and measure quantities of harvested crops.

SEE ALSO: farming; Fertile Crescent; Ubaidian culture

## Jemdet Nasr

The name of the site of an early Sumerian town and of the last prehistoric period before the Sumerian cities entered their first great age of power and prosperity. Modern scholars usually date the Jemdet Nasr period to roughly 3200 to 3000 B.C. The site itself, located about 60 miles (97km) south of Baghdad, was first excavated in 1925 and again briefly in the late 1980s. Examples of pottery, cylinder seals, and clay tablets bearing cuneiform writing were found. The writing, dubbed proto-cuneiform by scholars, was used mainly for administrative purposes. Some tablets mention other Sumerian towns, including Ur, Larsa, Uruk, and Nippur, and evidence suggests that the Jemdet Nasr period was an era of cooperation among these cities.

SEE ALSO: cuneiform; pottery; Ur; Uruk

## Jericho

An important early archaeological site in the Fertile Crescent and later a Hebrew town captured, along with the rest of Palestine, by the Assyrians. Located just north of the Dead Sea, Jericho (modern Tell-es-Sultan) occupied a strategic spot

*A depiction of Jericho devastated by the Assyrians in the eighth century B.C.* MARY EVANS PICTURE LIBRARY. REPRODUCED BY PERMISSION

along a trade route running from the deserts west of Mesopotamia to coastal Palestine. The town was among the early agricultural settlements in the Fertile Crescent, which stretched northeastward into Syria and then eastward across the northern rim of Mesopotamia. Archaeologists divide prehistoric Jericho into three levels of habitation: pre-agricultural, before 9000 B.C.; pre-pottery A, ninth and eighth millennia B.C.; and pre-pottery B, seventh and sixth millennia B.C. The second of these towns had a stone defensive wall with a stone tower and several round mud-brick houses. The people grew barley, emmer wheat, and lentils. Much later Jericho became part of ancient Israel until that kingdom was absorbed by Assyria in the eighth century B.C. The book of Joshua in the Old Testament describes how the early Hebrews laid siege to Jericho and brought down its walls by shouting and blasting trumpets. Partly because of its importance for studies of the prehistoric Near East and also because of its prominence as an early Hebrew city, Jericho has been excavated numerous times. The first digs there were conducted by Charles Warren in 1868. Then came Carl Watzinger (1907–1909), John Garstang (1930–1936), Kathleen Kenyon (1952–1958), and Lorenzo Nigro (1997).

SEE ALSO: farming; Fertile Crescent; Palestine

## Jerusalem

An important Palestinian and Near Eastern city that, over the course of many centuries, fell under the control of numerous ancient conquerors, including several from Mesopotamia. According to the Old Testament, an early Hebrew king, David, made Jerusalem his capital around 1000 B.C. His successor, Solomon, erected the First Temple there, which became the principal focus of worship and religious and cultural identity for Jews in the region for many centuries to come. After early Israel split into two kingdoms—Israel and Judah—Jerusalem remained the capital of Judah. The Assyrian monarch Sennacherib besieged the city circa 701 B.C. but failed to take it. However, the Babylonians did manage to capture Jerusalem in about 597 B.C. and carried off King Jehoiachin and many other Jews into captivity. The Jews who remained in the city soon rebelled, and Babylonia's King Nebuchadnezzar II responded by destroying much of Jerusalem circa 587. Somewhat later Cyrus II, the Persian ruler who had defeated and absorbed Babylonia, allowed the Jews to return to Jerusalem, rebuild the walls, and erect the Second Temple. Subsequently, the city was ruled by Persians, Greeks, and finally, after a brief period of independence, the Romans, who installed a Jewish client king, Herod the Great. He renovated Jerusalem and embellished the Second Temple.

SEE ALSO: Israel; Judah; Sennacherib

## jewelry

Both men and women wore jewelry in ancient Mesopotamia, and jewelry items were also used to decorate statues of gods, were exchanged as gifts between rulers, were given as wedding gifts, were included in dowries and inheritances, and, of course, were stolen as loot during military campaigns. One of the largest archaeological finds of Mesopotamian jewelry occurred when noted excavator Charles Leonard Woolley explored the royal cemetery at Ur between 1926 and 1932. He uncovered sixteen tombs dating to the period of about 2900 to 2350 B.C., all containing considerable quantities of jewelry. Particularly impressive were the jewelry items of Queen Puabi, including a crown made of gold and lapis lazuli; necklaces of gold, silver, lapis lazuli, and agate; and gold and silver pins for fastening clothes. All of the tombs contained finely made earrings. Another important Mesopotamian jewelry find was made during excavations in 1988 and 1989 by Iraqi archaeologist Mazahim Mahmud Hussein in the ruins of the Assyrian city of Nimrud (Kalhu). Three royal tombs yielded some fifteen hundred pieces of jewelry weighing a total of 100 pounds (45kg).

Precious stones such as gold and silver and semiprecious ones such as jasper, agate, lapis lazuli, and crystal were fairly scarce in Mesopotamia, so many were imported. Gold and silver came from Anatolia and northern Iran and lapis lazuli from Afghanistan, for example. Valuable metals, as well as finished jewelry pieces, were also seized during raids of foreign lands, especially by the Assyrian kings. Once they had the proper raw materials, Mesopotamian jewelers produced many finely crafted items for both men and women. From Akkadian times, the early third millennium B.C., on, men commonly wore strings of beads and bracelets. In the first millennium B.C. Assyrian men and women wore earrings, bracelets, and amulets. Earrings were typically shaped like rings, crescents, grape clusters, cones, and animal and human heads.

No actual jewelry shops have yet been found, but a jar containing the tools of a jeweler named Ilsu-Ibnisu was excavated at Larsa. Included were a small anvil, bronze tweezers, a stone for grinding and smoothing jewelry, and beads of silver and gold that had yet to be fashioned into jewelry. The name of another Mesopotamian jeweler is also known. A letter found in the royal archive at Mari was written by a local priestess to a jeweler named Ili-iddinam; she complained that she had not received the necklace he had promised her even though he had been paid in advance. From studying Mesopotamian jewelry, modern experts have concluded that Ili-iddinam and other jewelers made most gold and silver items by cutting thin sheets of gold or silver into small pieces and using hammers and other tools to shape them.

SEE ALSO: crafts and craftspeople; Ur; Woolley, Charles Leonard

# Josephus
## (ca. 37 A.D.–100 A.D.)

A noted Jewish historian whose works provide important supplemental material for the history of ancient Palestine, including its invasion by various Mesopotamian monarchs. Josephus was among the leaders of the great Jewish rebellion against Rome between A.D. 66 and 70. He was captured and brought to Rome, where he gained the respect and patronage of the emperor Vespasian. Josephus's *Antiquities of the Jews*, completed circa 93, ambitiously covers the history of his people from the creation of the world to the time of the Roman vassal Herod the Great. It includes a retelling of the great flood and accounts of how the prophet Abraham originated in Mesopotamia, how Saul and David organized the first state of Israel, how the Babylonians besieged Jerusalem and took away many Hebrews into captivity, how the Hebrews returned to Palestine, how Alexander the Great invaded the region, and how Herod rebuilt the temple in Jerusalem. Josephus was a serious and skilled historian. But he was only as good as his sources, and most of the book up to the Babylonian captivity is based on myths and hearsay, mainly from the Old Testament. The rest, however, is of some value to modern historians. For instance, the following is part of Josephus's account of how the first Persian king, Cyrus II, allowed the Hebrews living in captivity in Mesopotamia to return to Palestine:

> In the first year of the reign of Cyrus, which was the seventieth from the day that our people were removed out of their own land into Babylon . . . Cyrus called for the most eminent Jews that were in Babylon and said to them that he gave them leave to go back to their own country, and to rebuild their city Jerusalem and the Temple of God. For [these endeavors] he would be their assistant, and he would write to the rulers and governors that were in [Palestine] that they should contribute to them [the returning Hebrews] gold and silver for the building of the Temple. . . . Cyrus also sent back to them the [sacrificial] vessels of God which [the Babylonian] king Nebuchadnezzar II had pillaged out of the Temple and carried to Babylon. (*Antiquities of the Jews* 6.1.1–2)

SEE ALSO: historical accounts; Israel; Jerusalem

# Judah

One of the two Hebrew (Jewish) kingdoms that flourished in ancient Palestine and were eventually attacked and absorbed by the Assyrians and the Babylonians. After King Solomon's death in the tenth century B.C., the first kingdom of Israel was divided into separate states—Israel in the north and Judah in the south. Jerusalem remained the capital of Judah. Judah survived the invasion of the Assyrians in the late 700s B.C. that brought about the destruction of Israel. But the Babylonians defeated Judah in 597 B.C. and deported its king and nobles to sites in Mesopotamia, marking the first stage of the Diaspora, the dispersion of Jews to areas outside of Palestine. In 537 B.C. the Persian king Cyrus II allowed the Jews to return to Judah, where they built the Second Temple between 520 and 515 B.C.. Judah was no longer an independent nation, however; it remained part of a Persian satrapy, or province, until Alexander the Great conquered the Persian Empire in the late fourth century B.C.

SEE ALSO: Israel; Jerusalem; Neo-Babylonian Empire

## Kalhu

One of the leading ancient Assyrian cities and one of the capitals of the Assyrian Empire. For details about Kalhu, see its Arabic and more commonly used name, Nimrud.

SEE ALSO: Ashurnasirpal II; Assyrian Empire; Layard, Austen Henry

## Kashtilash

The name of four rulers of the Kassite Babylonian dynasty (ca. 1729–1155 B.C.). The third member of the dynasty, Kashtilash (or Kastiliasu) I, who flourished during the early seventeenth century B.C., fought with Abi-esuh, grandson of Hammurabi, for control of Babylon. Little is known about Kashtilash II (late seventeenth century B.C.) and Kashtilash III (early sixteenth century B.C.). Kashtilash IV (mid-thirteenth century B.C.) attacked both Elam and Assyria but was unable to conquer either. The Assyrian king Tukulti-Ninurta I eventually ousted him and appointed three governors to rule Babylonia as an Assyrian dependency. The Kassites soon regained control of the region, however.

SEE ALSO: Elam; Kassites; Tukulti-Ninurta I

## Kassites

An ancient Mesopotamian people of unknown origins who entered the region from the east, across the Zagros Mountains, in the early second millennium B.C.

Their native language was unrelated to any other known tongue and is still not well understood. Mentions of the Kassites first appear in Babylonian records in the late 1700s B.C. They seem to have settled somewhere near the city of Sippar, and for the next few generations they were viewed as a threat to the stability of the surrounding region. In the early years of this period the Kassites established a ruling dynasty that is variously dated from ca. 1595 to 1155 B.C. or from 1729 to 1155 B.C. if one counts the kings who ruled before the Kassite occupation of Babylon.

That 1595 B.C. occupation was accomplished by the Hittites with the aid of the Kassites, in ways that are unclear. The Hittites soon departed and left the Kassites in control of Babylonia. Wasting little time, the Kassite ruler Ulam-Buriash defeated the king of Sealand in southernmost Mesopotamia, near the Persian Gulf. The Kassites transformed the loosely organized Babylonian lands into a strongly centralized state. Under their rule the countryside became more densely populated, with the creation of many new small towns and villages. They also respected existing religious traditions and encouraged the use of the Babylonian dialect of Akkadian across Mesopotamia. The Kassite period was largely peaceful, as the rulers showed little interest in foreign conquests. The Kassites did have an army, though; they bred horses and developed a lighter, faster version of the chariot.

Eventually the Kassite Babylonians fell

prey to the Elamites, who launched several attacks on Babylon in the early twelfth century B.C. The Kassite dynasty was terminated in 1155 B.C., but the Kassites continued to exist as a distinct group in the region for several more centuries. Some served in high positions in the governments of various Mesopotamian kingdoms.

SEE ALSO: Babylon; chariots; Hittites

## Khorsabad

The modern name for the ancient Assyrian city of Dur-Sharukkin. Modern scholars sometimes use the two names interchangeably. For details, see Dur-Sharukkin.

SEE ALSO: Assyrian Empire; Botta, Paul Emile

## king lists

Lists compiled by various Mesopotamian scribes over the course of many centuries in an effort to record the many rulers of the various kingdoms of the region. Also included in some lists are the names of rulers of neighboring regions. The scribes not only listed individual names but also grouped names into ruling dynasties. There were several such lists, beginning with the Sumerian King List, of which a number of versions have survived. These record rulers' names beginning with the handover of kingship from the gods to the humans in the dim past to about 1800 B.C. The following excerpt from the opening section of one version of the Sumerian King List shows how the earliest monarchs were given ridiculously long reigns:

> After the kingship descended from heaven, the kingship was in Eridu. In Eridu, Alulim became king; he ruled for 28,800 years. Alaljar ruled for

*The black Obelisk of Shalmaneser III, dating from 858–824 B.C., during the Neo-Assyrian era.* HIP/ART RESOURCE, NY

> 36,000 years. Two kings, they ruled for [a total of] 64,800 years. Then Eridu fell and the kingship was taken to Bad-tibira. In Bad-tibira, Enmenluana ruled for 43,200 years. Enmengalana ruled for 28,800 years. Dumuzi, the shepherd [also a god], ruled for 36,000 years.

These impossibly long reigns are reminiscent of, though longer, than the centuries-long lifetimes cited for the early patriarchs in the Old Testament book of Genesis. The earliest ruler in the Sumerian lists whose existence has been verified by archaeology is Enmebaragesi, a king of Kish. Gilgamesh, the hero of the famous myth and epic poem, is listed as the fifth ruler of the first dynasty of Uruk; he may or may not have been a real person. There were also Babylonian and Assyrian king lists.

In general, the Mesopotamian king lists have both strengths and weaknesses from the standpoint of history and scholarship. On the one hand, those overly long reigns in the Sumerian lists make dating early Sumerian political events next to impossible. On the other hand, there are many gaps and errors in the lists. Also, the dynasties are listed one after another, as if they followed one another chronologically; whereas in reality they sometimes overlapped, with one dynasty ruling in one city-state while another dynasty ruled in a neighboring city-state. On the positive side, the king lists do show which rulers came first in each dynasty and how many years each king reigned. Combined with other evidence, especially archaeological finds, therefore, the lists can be helpful.

SEE ALSO: government; historical accounts; kingship

## kingship

All of the city-states, kingdoms, and empires of ancient Mesopotamia were ruled by kings. Even when the Greeks, who had much experience with democracy, took over the region following the fall of the Persian Empire, they continued the local tradition of absolute monarchy. Going at least as far back as the third millennium B.C., kings justified their right to wield absolute power by citing one or another version of the myth of creation and how the institution of kingship was handed down from the gods. As told in the Babylonian *Epic of Creation*, for example, the ascendancy of the god Marduk as ruler of the universe and the other deities symbol-

ized the ascendancy of kings over their human subjects. Also, the Sumerian King List claimed that kingship was first handed down from the gods to humanity at Eridu.

To further reinforce this divine right to rule, Mesopotamian kings were often portrayed as somehow superhuman or semi-divine. Some ancient texts mention an aura or radiance surrounding the king's person, called the *melammu*, or "awe-inspiring luminosity." Also, it was common to refer to the king as the "son" of a certain god; to bestow on the king lofty, supernatural titles such as "king of heaven and Earth"; and to show the monarch standing with a god in artistic renderings.

However it was justified and reinforced, kingship brought with it duties and responsibilities as special and important as the king's titles and official images. Stemming from his unique relationship with the divine, he was often viewed as the highest of society's high priests. Among the words spoken during the crowning of an Assyrian king were these: "Before Ashur, your god, may your priesthood and the priesthood of your sons find favor." Although it varied from one time, place, and culture to another, a king's religious duties could include making sure that temples were built or maintained, appointing priests, leading various religious ceremonies and festivals, and consulting with official diviners and astrologers about the fate of the nation. The king was also the supreme commander of the army, with the authority to initiate wars at his will and to draw up plans for his military campaigns. In addition, he was the chief of state. In that capacity, he appointed government administrators and provincial governors, received and entertained foreign ambassadors, dispensed justice, and considered petitions from his subjects.

Most of these aspects of kingship in Mesopotamia were similar to those in many other places in the ancient world, from Egypt to Rome. There was one Mesopotamian royal custom that was unique and rather peculiar, however—that of the substitute king. In a number of Mesopotamian realms, if there seemed to be any sort of threat to the safety of the monarch, even an unfavorable omen, palace officials chose a temporary stand-in. The substitute, who had no real authority, was decked out in royal robes and was given quarters in the palace; meanwhile, the real king went into hiding. It was hoped that the stand-in would die in the king's place, thereby cheating fate. It appears that in some cases the substitute king was killed after the emergency had passed.

SEE ALSO: *Epic of Creation*; government; king lists

## Kirkuk

The modern and more frequently used name for Arrapha, a Hurrian and Assyrian city located on the Hasa River about 155 miles (250km) north of modern Baghdad. The site of Arappha was occupied as early as the fifth millennium B.C. At some point in the second millennium B.C., migrating Hurrians established a small kingdom or city-state centered on Arrapha, which seems to have been subject to the larger Hurrian state of Mitanni, situated to its west. By the tenth century B.C. Arappha had been absorbed by the Assyrians and remained part of the Assyrian Empire for several centuries.

SEE ALSO: Assyrian Empire; Hurrians; Mitanni

## Kish

One of the oldest and most venerable of the Sumerian cities and, according to the Sumerian King List, the place where the first royal dynasty arose following the great flood. Several mounds of ruins marking the site of ancient Kish lie about 8 miles (13km) east of the site of Babylon and some 85 miles (137km) south of modern Baghdad. The king list provides the names of many early kings of Kish, but Enmebaragesi and his son Agga were the first for whom archaeological evidence has been found. It appears that in the third millennium B.C. Kish was one of several prosperous and often competing Sumerian city-states, including Uruk, Ur, and Lagash; Kish may have enjoyed a brief period of dominance over the others around 2500 B.C. It is interesting that the king list gives credit for the establishment of the city's third and briefest dynasty (ca. 2450–2350 B.C.) to a woman named Kubaba since sole rule of Mesopotamian states by women was extremely rare. Kish also gained notoriety as the birthplace of the Akkadian conqueror Sargon in the late third millennium B.C. After the close of the Sumerian period, Kish remained an important center of learning. It was finally abandoned in the sixth century A.D.

Initial excavations at Kish were undertaken between 1912 and 1914 by a French team headed by Henri de Genouillac. An Anglo-American expedition under Stephen Langdon explored the site from 1923 to 1933. In addition to a royal cemetery similar to, but smaller than, the one found by Charles Leonard Woolley at Ur, they excavated the remains of a ziggurat dedicated to Kish's local warrior god, Zababa.

SEE ALSO: king lists; Ur; Woolley, Charles Leonard

## Koldewey, Robert (1855–1925)

A German archaeologist best known for

his pioneering excavations of the ancient city of Babylon. An architect by trade, Koldewey taught himself the rudiments of archaeology and honed his skills on a series of expeditions to ancient sites in Greece, Italy, and Anatolia. He went to Iraq in the late 1890s and soon introduced a new, more efficient technique for excavating mud-brick structures. Koldewey began digging at Babylon in 1899 and continued there every season until the outbreak of World War I in 1914. He uncovered the foundation of the temple of Marduk, a ziggurat, parts of the city's defensive walls, and much more. He thought he had also found the remains of the Hanging Gardens of Babylon, but since that time a number of other scholars have voiced their doubts.

SEE ALSO: Assyriology; Babylon; Hanging Gardens of Babylon

# Kramer, Samuel N. (1897–1990)

The twentieth century's leading archaeologist of Sumerian artifacts and translator of Sumerian documents. Long a scholar at the University of Pennsylvania, Kramer first began digging in Iraq in 1930. Over time he became increasingly adept at translating ancient Sumerian cuneiform texts and was particularly noted for his efforts to locate and translate neglected tablets lying in museums around the world. In one celebrated incident, he showed that pieces of a tablet in Istanbul, Turkey, were part of the same tablet to which pieces in Philadelphia belonged. He was also the first scholar to translate parts of the law code of Ur-Nammu, which predates the Babylonian king Hammurabi's law code. Kramer wrote many books, the most famous and influential of which is *History Begins at Sumer.*

SEE ALSO: languages; Sumerians; Ur-Nammu. And for one of Professor Kramer's translations, **see** farming

# Kurigalzu

The name of two noted Kassite rulers of Babylonia. Kurigalzu I (reigned in the late fifteenth century B.C.) was the first of the Kassite rulers to declare himself divine. He established a new capital, Dur-Kurigalzu (modern Aqar Quf), at a site about 18 miles (29km) west of modern Baghdad, which became an administrative center. The first Kurigalzu expanded the kingdom's diplomatic contacts with foreign lands, including exchanges of gifts with Egypt. He also sent one of his daughters to become part of the harem of the Egyptian pharaoh Amenhotep III.

Kurigalzu II (reigned ca. 1332–1308 B.C.) was placed on the Babylonian throne by the Assyrians, who had recently helped the Kassite monarchy depose a usurper. Kurigalzu, who seems to have been more warlike than most other Kassite monarchs, proceeded to attack the Elamites and defeat them in battle. Later, he turned on and attacked the Assyrians, although he was unable to achieve victory against them. The second Kurigalzu also gained prestige for his building projects, including the restoration of the temple of Inanna at Uruk and the expansion of the new Kassite city of Dur-Kurigalzu.

SEE ALSO: Babylonia; Dur-Kurigalzu; Kassites

## Lachish

An ancient Palestinian city captured by both the Assyrians and the Babylonians. By the early first millennium B.C. Lachish (modern Tell el-Duweir) was the second-most important town in the kingdom of Israel. As such it became a target of the Assyrian king Sennacherib, who took it in 701 B.C., although he failed to capture Jerusalem. Babylonia's King Nebuchadnezzar II seized Lachish circa 586 B.C.

SEE ALSO: Israel; Nebuchadnezzar II, weapons and warfare, siege

## Lagash

One of the more important Sumerian cities in the late fourth millennium B.C. and all through the third millennium B.C. Located about 120 miles (193km) northwest of modern Basra, Iraq, the main urban center of Lagash (modern Tell al-Hibba) was large for its time, covering at least 2 square miles (5 sq. km). The city-state also included two smaller urban centers, Girsu and Nin-Sirara. Apparently Lagash underwent sporadic periods of expanding power and influence. One occurred under a ruler named Ur-Nanshe (reigned ca. 2494–2465 B.C.), who built tall defensive walls and numerous temples, and his grandson, Eannatum, who defeated the king of Ur, situated south of Lagash. Another period of expansion and prosperity was in the late third millennium B.C., especially under a ruler named Gudea (ca. 2141–2122 B.C.). In the early second millennium B.C., Lagash went into decline.

The main site of Lagash was discovered in 1877 by Frenchman Ernest de Sarzec. Principal excavations were undertaken between 1929 and 1933 under the direction of two other French scholars, Henri de Genouillac and André Parrot. These investigators uncovered more than thirty thousand cuneiform tablets. They also found that the city's main temple had been dismantled during the Greek Seleucid period in the late first millennium B.C. and the bricks had been used to erect a fortress.

SEE ALSO: Girsu; Gudea; Sumerians

## Lama

A Sumerian goddess who was pictured in human form and thought to protect good, faithful people from harm. The term *lama* was also related to *lamassu*, the Assyrian term for the huge sculptures of winged bulls and lions placed at the entrances of Assyrian palaces. Like Lama, these images were thought to protect people, in this case those who lived and worked in the palaces.

SEE ALSO: palaces; sculpture

## Lamashtu

In ancient Babylonian mythology and tradition, a terrifying female demon who stole fetuses from the wombs of pregnant women and relished committing other evil deeds. Ancient Mesopotamians usually attributed incidents of crib death to Lamashtu. To thwart this dangerous creature, it was customary to wear amulets—charms

*A winged bull with a human face and a tiara, which represented protection to those in the palaces of Assyria.* ERICH LESSING/ART RESOURCE, NY

thought to have magical powers—or to hang an amulet near the door of one's home.

SEE ALSO: amulets; religion

## languages

Many languages were spoken over the course of the millennia in ancient Mesopotamia. The first widespread and important one was Sumerian, which modern experts have noted was unlike any other known tongue. Its original source remains uncertain, but sometime in the fourth millennium B.C. it replaced the existing language of southern Mesopotamia. That tongue, which scholars call Ubaidian and which was not written down, has survived in small part in the form of words adopted by the Sumerians; among them are the names of the great rivers—the Tigris and the Euphrates—along with the names of

some cities and the words for *date* and *palm*. Sumerian was written down, of course, in cuneiform characters on clay tablets. And it was the official language of administration and correspondence in Mesopotamia in the late third millennium B.C. In the early years of the following millennium, use of Sumerian began to wane, and by about 1600 to 1500 B.C. it was no longer spoken. However, it was retained as a "classical" language used by scholars for many centuries to come, in the same way that Europeans still used Latin for scholarly and religious purposes long after it had ceased to be spoken. Sumerian was eventually largely deciphered thanks to the existence of ancient dictionaries, in which scribes listed Sumerian synonyms for words in their own languages. A series of modern scholars, including Francois Thureau-Dangin, Arno Poebel, Thorkild Jacobsen, and Samuel N. Kramer, used these dictionaries, along with much ingenuity and patience, to make the world's first important language understandable.

Among the languages that replaced Sumerian for everyday use were Semitic tongues that entered Mesopotamia from the west. The first of these was Akkadian, which appeared in the early third millennium B.C. and over time evolved into various dialects. The two main ones were Assyrian, spoken mainly in northern Mesopotamia, and Babylonian, used primarily in the south. Akkadian was very different in structure from Sumerian, although many Sumerian words were absorbed into Akkadian. By about 1450 B.C., Akkadian had become the chief language of diplomacy and correspondence in Mesopotamia. Meanwhile, two languages of unknown origin—Elamite and Hurrian—continued to be used in some areas. Elamite was spoken mainly in Elam,

*The Greenhaven Encyclopedia of Ancient Mesopotamia*

in the southern reaches of the Zagros range, and in eastern sections of Mesopotamia, and Hurrian was spoken primarily in Mitanni and northern Mesopotamia.

Among the other Semitic languages that entered Mesopotamia after Akkadian were Amorite and Aramaic. The latter became the most widely spoken and written language of the region and well beyond. In the words of H.W.F. Saggs, a leading expert of the ancient languages of the region:

> The trading activities of the Aramaeans spread their language over much of the Near East, so that by the time of the Persian Empire (from 539 B.C.) it had become the international language of diplomacy. Indeed, it was already beginning to take on that role more than two centuries earlier, for when the Assyrians were besieging Jerusalem in 701 B.C., the Judean authorities requested that the Assyrian general should conduct negotiations in Aramaic, which they as diplomats understood. . . . Aramaic in its various dialects became the general language of much of the region from Palestine to Mesopotamia from the second half of the first millennium B.C. on, and had the same importance as a unifying force that was later enjoyed in the same region by Arabic, which displaced [Aramaic and other local languages] after the Islamic conquest in the seventh century A.D. (*Civilization Before Greece and Rome*, p. 18)

Meanwhile, in addition to Aramaic, some Indo-European languages were also used in Mesopotamia in the first millennium B.C. and early first millennium A.D. Notable among them were Old Persian and Greek, introduced after the conquests of Alexander the Great in the late fourth century B.C. But these never had the scope or staying power of Aramaic, nor later of Arabic.

SEE ALSO: Aramaeans; Behistun Rock; Grotefend, Georg F.; Kramer, Samuel N., literature; Rawlinson, Henry C.; writing

## Larsa

An important Sumerian, and later Babylonian, city in southern Mesopotamia, about 12 miles (20km) southeast of Uruk. Larsa (modern Tell Senkereh), which many scholars believe was the biblical city of Elassar, was continuously occupied from the fifth millennium B.C. to the third century A.D. Its heyday, however, was in the early second millennium B.C., when it engaged in a fierce rivalry with the city of Isin for control of southern Mesopotamia. By this time the rulers of both cities were Amorites, and Akkadian was in the process of replacing Sumerian as the main language of the area. The peak of Larsa's power came under a king named Gungunum (reigned ca. 1932–1906 B.C.), who defeated Isin, conquered Ur, and invaded Elam. The city's glory days were brief, though, as a later king, Rim-Sin (ca. 1822–1763 B.C.), was defeated by the Babylonian conqueror Hammurabi. Larsa was famous as a religious center. It housed a major temple and ziggurat of the sun god, Shamash (the Ebabbar, or "Shining House"), and shrines dedicated to the goddesses Inanna and Gula.

SEE ALSO: Gula; Hammurabi; Isin

## laws and justice

Fortunately for interested modern observers, a number of legal codes, individual laws, and trial records have survived from ancient Mesopotamia. These laws did not cover every aspect of life by any means, but they were often surprisingly comprehensive, touching on matters of property rights, wage and price controls, inheritance, and crimes against people.

The earliest-known laws were issued by a Sumerian king, Uruinimgina of Lagash (reigned ca. 2351–2342 B.C.). These dealt with taxation, burial fees, treatment of women and orphans, and more. Another Sumerian ruler, Ur-Nammu (ca. 2113–2096, B.C.), founder of the Third Dynasty of Ur, also issued a set of laws, saying that he wanted "to free the land from thieves, robbers, and rebels." Ur-Nammu's legal system was noteworthy for making no distinctions regarding the wealth or status of the accused; all people were to be judged and punished equally. The justice system was also unusually liberal for the ancient world, or even for many countries in the modern world, as most offenses, including rape and assault, were punished by monetary fines. Still another Sumerian king, Lipit-Ishtar of Isin (ca. 1934–1923 B.C.) issued a law code that contained rules guiding work and workers and the institution of debt enslavement (becoming someone's slave to pay him back for a debt).

The most famous and comprehensive law code issued in ancient Mesopotamia was that of the Babylonian king Hammurabi (ca. 1792–1750 B.C.). Much of the 8-foot (2.4m), black stone stele on which his scribes carved the code has survived. Hammurabi gave a rationale for creating his laws as follows:

> In order that the strong might not oppress the weak, that justice be given to the orphan and the widow ... for the pronouncement of judgments in the land ... and to give justice to the oppressed, my weighty words I have written upon my monument. ... Let a man who has been wronged and has a cause, go before my stele ... and let him have my words inscribed on the monument read out. ... And may my monument enlighten him as to his cause and may he understand his case!

Of the 282 laws listed on the stele, some deal with property rights, money, and the regulation of wages and trade. Others cover family and marriage issues, adoption, medical malpractice, and personal injury. Among the latter are these:

> If a son strikes his father, they shall cut off his hand. If a man destroys the eye of another man, they shall destroy his eye. If he break another man's bone, they shall break his bone. If he destroy the eye of a client or break the bone of a client, he shall pay one mina of silver. If he destroy the eye of a man's slave or break the bone of a man's slave, he shall pay one-half his price [i.e., half the amount the owner paid for the slave]. If a man strike another man in a quarrel and wound him, he shall swear, "I struck him without intent," and he shall pay for the physician. If he die as a result of the blow, he shall swear (as above), and if the man was a free man, he shall pay one-half mina of silver.

As these samples show, most of Hammurabi's laws carried heavy penalties. Indeed, the death penalty was imposed for a conviction for kidnapping, receiving stolen goods, breaking and entering, and even for poor performance of a government job. Also, Hammurabi's laws, unlike those of Ur-Nammu, made distinctions for the wealth and status of the accused. Three general classes were treated differently—nobles and big landowners (*amelu*); everyday people (*muskinu*); and slaves (*ardu*, either captured in war or sold into slavery to satisfy a debt). Interestingly, the *amelu* paid stiffer penalties than members of the lower classes, perhaps because a higher degree of honesty and dignity was expected of upper-class persons.

The manner in which the laws were enforced and justice was handed out varied somewhat from place to place. Specific empires came and went, but Mesopotamia was at its heart a conglomeration of local towns and villages that endured for millennia, and in general most matters of justice were handled on the local level. Typically town officials or elders either served as judges or chose judges from among their ranks. (In the towns ruled by Ur-Nammu there were four judges in each court case, chosen from the professional ranks, such as scribes, respected merchants, city elders, and so forth. The judges were assisted by a court clerk, or *mashkim*, who kept careful records of the proceedings.) There were no juries or lawyers. Instead, the litigants (the person bringing the case and the person he charged with wrongdoing) pleaded their own cases and presented their own witnesses. Both litigants and witnesses first swore an oath to the gods that they would tell the truth. To further impress on all involved the importance of honesty, most trials were held on the grounds of temples, which must have made many people think twice about lying under oath. After the judges had handed down the verdict, it was recorded in writing. A number of such verdicts have survived on cuneiform tablets.

Some people seeking justice went further and appealed to a higher authority, sometimes the king himself. Such a plea, actually a follow-up to some earlier ones, was recorded in a letter written by an Assyrian man to King Ashurbanipal (ca. 668–627 B.C.):

How does it happen that I, who have

*A painting depicting Austen Henry Layard, a 19th-century archaeologist who excavated several Assyrian sites.* © BETTMANN/CORBIS

made several appeals to Your Majesty, have never been questioned by anybody? . . . I have not committed a crime against Your Majesty. . . . I merely conveyed an order of the king to [a man]. Although I said, "I am on business for the palace," he [took] my property away. He even arrested me and put me in fetters [chains], and that in front of all the people. . . . Ever since last year, nobody has given me anything to eat. . . . Your majesty should know that the same two men who took the gold jewelry from around my neck still go on planning to destroy me and to ruin me.

SEE ALSO: crime and punishment; Hammurabi; Ur-Nammu

## Layard, Austen Henry (1817–1894)

A British diplomat and archaeologist who

was one of the major pioneers of Assyriology. While on an assignment in Iraq in 1845, Layard was drawn to the still largely unexplored ruins of ancient Assyrian cities. He later wrote:

These huge mounds of Assyria made a deep ... impression on me. .... A deep mystery hangs over Assyria, [and] Babylonia. ... With these names are linked great nations and great cities dimly shadowed forth in history; mighty ruins in the midst of deserts, defying, by their very desolation and lack of definite form, the description of the traveler; the remnants of the mighty races still roving over the land; the fulfilling ... of prophecies; the plains to which the Jew and the Gentile alike look as the cradle of their race. (*Nineveh and Its Remains*, vol. 1, pp. 2–3)

Layard first began digging at Nimrud, the site of the ancient Assyrian city of Kalhu. There he eventually unearthed nearly 2 miles (3.2km) of finely carved relief sculptures depicting the exploits of the Assyrian kings. One of the more exciting moments at Nimrud came when some of Layard's Arab workers discovered a huge carved stone head and were frightened because they thought they had dug up a mythical monster. "On reaching the ruins," Layard later recalled,

I descended into the newly opened trench, and found ... an enormous human head. .... [It was] the upper part of a figure, the remainder of which was still buried in the earth. I at once saw that the head must belong to a winged lion or bull. .... I was not surprised that the Arabs had been amazed and terrified at this apparition. ... This gigantic head ... rising from the bowels of the earth, might well have belonged to one of those fearful beings which are described in

the traditions of the country as appearing to mortals, slowly ascending from the regions below. One of the workmen, on catching the first glimpse of the monster, had thrown down his basket and run [away] as fast as his legs could carry him. (*A Popular Account of Discoveries at Nineveh*, pp. 47–48)

Later, Layard excavated at the mound of Kuyunjik, near modern Mosul, site of ancient Nineveh, and discovered the library-archive of Assyria's King Ashurbanipal, including some twenty-four thousand cuneiform tablets. Also at Nineveh, he revealed the magnificent palace of King Sennacherib.

Over the course of the next few years, Layard sent thousands of sculptures and artifacts to London's British Museum, where they became the core of that institution's impressive Assyrian collection. He published several books about his adventures and discoveries, most notably *Nineveh and Its Remains* (1849) and *Discoveries in the Ruins of Nineveh and Babylon* (1853). In time, Layard went back into public service and served as Britain's ambassador to Constantinople beginning in 1877.

SEE ALSO: Assyriology; Nimrud; Nineveh; palaces; Palace Without Rival

# letters

Some of the most important facts about political events and everyday life in ancient Mesopotamia have come from the contents of surviving letters. Unlike modern versions, these were not written on paper. Rather, the words were carved onto baked clay tablets, which explains why so many of them remain intact; if they had been written on paper they would have disintegrated long ago. The bulky clay letters were often placed within "envelopes," essentially carrying cases also made of baked clay, and delivered by servants or messengers. For the most part, letters were composed by scribes for kings, government officials, and members of the nobility. Most average people could not read and therefore had no use for letters, although there were undoubtedly occasional exceptions.

The setup of ancient Mesopotamian letters followed a standard, accepted formula, just as modern letters do. Today a typical letter begins with a salutation such as "Dear X" or "Dear Mr. X." The standard form for a Mesopotamian salutation was "X says the following: Tell Y that . . ." or words to that effect. After the salutation, the letter writer expressed wishes for the recipient's good health, then proceeded to get to the point of the letter. The social status of the correspondents also affected the style of the letter. If the letter writer belonged to a lower social class than the recipient, he took a subservient tone and used phrases such as "I grovel at your feet." If the two people were social equals, the letter writer addressed the recipient as "brother." If the letter writer was socially superior to the recipient, the tone of the letter might be very direct, even stern or cold.

There were numerous kinds of letters. One important category was royal correspondence—exchanges of letters between rulers. Hundreds of letters from the city of Mari, located on the upper Euphrates, dating to the early second millennium B.C. have survived, many of them written by King Zimri-Lim (reigned ca. 1775–1761 B.C.) and the early Assyrian monarch Shamshi-Adad (ca. 1813–1781 B.C.) and his sons. (For an example, see Ishme-Dagan.) Another important collection, the so-called *Amarna Letters*, consists of some

380 documents written in the 1300s B.C. by two Egyptian pharaohs to and from their royal counterparts in Hatti, Mitanni, Babylonia, and Assyria. Also, a number of later Assyrian letters were found in the ruins of the library of King Ashurbanipal at Nineveh.

Other common categories of letters included business correspondence, letters used as exercises for student scribes (generic letters copied and recopied), and those addressed to the gods. The latter were generally written by kings and were often read out loud before their assembled subjects. The ruler might thank the deity for sending divine aid or ask for guidance in a time of trouble. Letters were also written to praise the gods and thereby stay in their good graces, as in this example, addressed to the moon god, Nanna, from a Sumerian ruler:

> Say to Nanna . . . You, who are perfect in lordship and wear the legitimate headdress, the one with gleaming appearance and noble countenance, holy form endowed lavishly with beauty: Your greatness covers all countries. Your fearsome radiance overwhelms the holy sky. Your great awesomeness is imbued with terror. . . . You are indeed glorious from east to west. . . . You are the king of heaven and earth. It is you who decide their fate.

Some personal letters have also survived. The following example was written by a Babylonian student named Iddin-Sin to his mother, Zinu, in the eighteenth century B.C. It proves that modern students' concerns about looking fashionable in school are nothing new:

> Say to Zinu: Thus says Iddin-Sin. May the gods Shamash, Marduk, and Ilabrat preserve you safe and sound for my sake. The clothes of the other boys

[at my school] get better and better year by year. You let my clothes get plainer and plainer each year. By making my clothes plainer and fewer, you have enriched yourself. Although wool is used in our house like bread, you have made my clothes worse. Addad-iddinam's son ... [has just received] two new suits of clothes, but you are continually worried about merely one suit for me. While you actually brought me into the world, his mother adopted him. But the way in which his mother loves him, in such a way you do not by any means love me.

SEE ALSO: libraries; literature; Mari; writing

# libraries

The ancient Mesopotamians did not have libraries in the modern sense—that is, public institutions where people could go to borrow books. A Mesopotamian library was more of an archive, a collection of clay tablets usually kept in one or more rooms in a temple or a palace. Such archives began as a way of retaining records of official administrative, economic, or religious business. Over time, however, other kinds of literature, including letters, historical accounts, and epic poems, were also stored in archives. Among the earliest Mesopotamian archives discovered to date are those in Ur and Nippur, compiled when these cities were part of the Third Dynasty of Ur in the late third millennium B.C. A larger archive was found in the ruins of Mari. Dating to the nineteenth century B.C., it contains thousands of documents, including many letters written to and from Zimri-Lim and other rulers of Mari.

The largest and best-preserved Mesopotamian library-archive is that of the Assyrian king Ashurbanipal (reigned ca. 668–627 B.C.) at Nineveh. It was discovered in 1849 by pioneer Assyriologist Austen Henry Layard. Of the more than twenty thousand tablets in the original collection, about five thousand proved to be in good enough condition to translate. Beginning with translations by German scholar Carl Bezold between 1889 and 1899, experts have revealed the contents of some fifteen hundred complete texts covering a wide range of subjects. Some evidence suggests that the archive was originally divided into several rooms, each devoted to a specific subject.

SEE ALSO: Ashurbanipal; Layard, Austen Henry; literature

# literature

Thanks to the survival of thousands of clay tablets from many times and places in ancient Mesopotamia, it is clear that the civilizations of that region produced a large, varied, and rich collection of literature, some of it of high quality. Among the literary genres that developed were epic and other poetry, hymns and prayers, proverbs, social satires, laments, law codes, letters, astrological and divination texts, and historical accounts. Although examples of writing date back to the early third millennium B.C. or earlier in Mesopotamia, the earliest examples of literary texts date from about 2400 B.C. The Sumerians produced large amounts of literature. But few of the original versions have survived, and most of what exists today consists of later Babylonian and Assyrian copies. Particularly important are literary copies made by Kassite Babylonian scribes in the second half of the second millennium B.C.

*Epic Poems* The case of epic poetry is a clear example of this process. The Sumerians created several early epics, including the famous *Epic of Gilgamesh*. Babylonian and the divine. Besides the poems about Gilgamesh and Atrahasis, important epics included those about the goddess Inanna's descent into the Underworld, the romance between the deities Nergal and Ereshkigal, and the adventures of the heroes Adapa and Etana. The only Assyrian epic of which sections survive was the *Tukulti-Ninurta Epic*, which celebrates that Assyrian king's victory over the Babylonians in the thirteenth century B.C.

Mesopotamian poets also wrote shorter works, notably erotic poems that may have been intended as entertainment for royal courtiers at feasts, celebrations, and other gatherings. In one example, a man goes into a tavern and propositions a barmaid. The lyrics of these pieces are often sexually graphic. Yet their frequent use of similes and metaphors comparing lovers and their sexual organs to natural objects such as trees, wheat, and flowers make them literarily rich, even charming.

*Hymns and Prayers* Another important Mesopotamian literary genre consisted of hymns and prayers. This comes as no surprise since the people of the region were religiously devout, sometimes in the extreme. Most of the hymns were probably composed by priests and praised various gods. Consequently, modern scholars have learned much about these gods and the locations of their principal shrines by studying ancient hymns. This is part of a hymn to Inanna, goddess of love and sexual passion:

> The great-hearted mistress, the impetuous lady, proud among the gods and pre-eminent in all lands . . . the magnificent lady who gathers up the divine powers of heaven and earth and rivals great An, is mightiest among the great gods. She makes their verdicts final. . . . Her great awesomeness covers the great mountain and

*This hexagonal prism from the reign of King Sansu-Iluna is inscribed with a hymn honoring a Sumerian god.* ERICH LESSING/ART RESOURCE, NY

scribes later made copies of the original, which was subsequently lost. That original, like other written versions of epic poetry, was based on an oral tradition that likely stretched back to the period before the invention of writing. Just as Greek bards like Homer traveled around reciting stories about heroes, gods, and the Trojan War, early Mesopotamian poets told and retold tales about the heroes Gilgamesh, Enkidu, and Atrahasis and their encounters with the gods and fate. Epic poems were typically long, detailed, and dealt with universal, weighty themes, such as the meaning of life and death, the quest for immortality, and the relationship between humans levels the roads. At her loud cries, the gods of the Land become scared. . . . Wherever she [goes], cities become ruin mounds and haunted places, and shrines become waste land.

Other Mesopotamian hymns are like love songs and were probably recited in ceremonies in which kings enacted ritual marriages between themselves and Inanna. As Samuel N. Kramer and other noted scholars have pointed out, a number of such works resemble some of the psalms in the Old Testament; and indeed, the prevailing theory is that the writers of the biblical psalms were influenced to some degree by Mesopotamian models. Just as the psalms of the Hebrew king David were meant to be sung or recited to harp music, Mesopotamian hymns were likely accompanied by some kind of music. One striking example reads in part:

Bridegroom, let me caress you, my precious caress is sweeter than honey. In the bed-chamber, honey-filled, let me enjoy your goodly beauty. . . . Your spirit, I know here to cheer your spirit. Bridegroom, sleep in our house until dawn. Your heart, I know where to gladden your heart. Lion, sleep in our house until dawn.

*Proverbs and Laments* Another popular category of literature in ancient Mesopotamia was the proverb, a short, wise saying passed from one generation to the next. Like poems, proverbs were at first preserved by word of mouth, but in the second millennium B.C. scribes began to collect them and write them down. Often they would give the same proverb in both Sumerian and Akkadian, which turned out to be helpful for modern scholars trying to translate Sumerian. The main reason that proverbs were so popular was that change occurred only very slowly in Meso-

potamian society; so most people felt that the wisdom of past generations could still be applied to their own. The following are among the most enduring of the Mesopotamian proverbs: "The poor men are the silent men in Sumer"; "Friendship lasts a day, kingship forever"; "If you take the field of an enemy, the enemy will come and take your field"; "Conceiving is nice, but pregnancy is irksome"; and "For a man's pleasure there is marriage, while on thinking it over, there is divorce."

Another literary genre that involved short but pointed statements about life was social satire, made up mainly of brief, humorous tales. Each involved everyday people and/or animals and commented in some way on common social injustices, especially the exploitation of the weak by the strong. In one story, for example, a simple, uneducated gardener shows that he is far wiser than a highly educated doctor. Many satires were animal fables like those of the Greek writer Aesop, with dogs (symbolic of average people) outwitting lions (representing royalty) and so forth. There were also fictional letters and contracts, including a contract for a worthless piece of land drawn up by a bird and witnessed by other birds.

On a more serious note, almost all Mesopotamians knew about the ravages of war and famine and the loss of loved ones in such times of crisis. The strong emotions aroused by such events were frequently expressed in laments, or lamentations. These were sad works in which the writer, speaking for the people of a city, described the ills that had befallen the city and expressed grief, sorrow, and asked the gods for forgiveness. The Mesopotamian laments directly inspired the ones in the biblical book of Lamentations, inspired by the fall of Jerusalem to the Babylonians, including:

> The Lord has scorned his altar. . . . He has delivered into the hands of the enemy the walls of her palaces. . . . Cry aloud to the Lord! O daughter of Zion [Israel]! Let tears stream down like a torrent day and night! Give yourself no rest, your eyes no respite! (Lamentations 2.7, 2.18)

For excerpts from a lament attributed to the goddess Ningal, the *Lamentation Over the Destruction of Ur*, **see also** Ningal; Third Dynasty of Ur. For an excerpt from the Assyrian *Tukulti-Ninurta Epic*, **see also** Tukulti-Ninurta I. And for details about other kinds of Mesopotamian literature, **see also** divination; historical accounts; laws and justice; letters.

SEE ALSO: Bible; languages; libraries; writing; and the names of individual epic poems

## Lloyd, Seton (1902–1996)

A noted English archaeologist who supervised a number of important excavations at ancient Mesopotamian sites in the twentieth century. Lloyd began his career in 1928 on an expedition that investigated Tell el-Amarna, site of the city built by the maverick Egyptian pharaoh Akhenaten. From 1930 to 1937 he led a team from Chicago's Oriental Institute in digs at several sites near the Diyala River in northern Mesopotamia, including Tell Asmar (Eshnunna), Tell Agrab, and Khafajah. Later he acted as adviser to Iraqi archaeologists exploring the early Sumerian ceremonial center of Eridu. A specialist in mud-brick excavations, Lloyd wrote a number of important books about ancient Mesopotamia, of which *Foundations in the Dust* (1947) is the most famous.

SEE ALSO: Assyriology; Eridu; Eshnunna

## Loftus, William K. (1820–1858)

An English geologist who became an early pioneer of Assyriology when he excavated the site of the ancient Sumerian city of Uruk. Like many other European intellectuals of his day, Loftus hoped that excavations of ancient Mesopotamian cities would reveal artifacts and information that would confirm the authenticity of statements made about the region in the Bible. Building on work already done in the area by Danish scholar Karsten Niebuhr, Frenchman Paul Emile Botta, and another Englishman, Austen Henry Layard, Loftus searched for the city of Uruk, called Erech in the Old Testament. Loftus suspected that Uruk lay beneath the surface at a site the local Arabs called Warka. Sure enough, Warka did prove to be ancient Uruk, where he uncovered the remains of the city's defensive walls, many still intact and rising to a height of 50 feet (15m). Loftus later excavated the ruins of another Sumerian city, Larsa. There he unearthed a temple of the god Shamash. He published *Travels and Researches in Chaldea and Susiana* in 1857, a year before his untimely death.

SEE ALSO: Botta, Paul Emile; Layard, Austen Henry; Niebuhr, Karsten

## Lugalzagesi (reigned ca. 2340–2316 B.C.)

A Sumerian king who conquered most of Sumer shortly before the rise of the Akkadian Empire. Lugalzagesi began as the ruler of Umma, a city situated northwest of Lagash. He captured Uruk and Lagash and apparently planned to push westward to the Mediterranean Sea. But his ambitions were cut short by a greater imperialist, Sargon of Akkad, who defeated Lugalzagesi and took him prisoner.

SEE ALSO: Lagash; Sargon of Akkad; Sumerians

## Magi

A group or caste of religious experts in ancient Mesopotamia during the first millennium B.C. and perhaps later. According to Herodotus and other ancient Greek writers, the Magi (or Magians) originated under the Medes and were active in Zoroastrian worship during the years of the Persian Empire. The Greek geographer Strabo mentions Magi during the later Parthian period, and they existed in the Sassanian period, too. It appears that a Magus was not an ordinary priest but rather a special kind of priest who had expertise in interpreting omens and dreams and performing sacrifices involving fire. Herodotus writes about another peculiar Magian custom:

> There is a Persian practice concerning the burial of the dead, which is not spoken of openly and is something of a mystery. It is that a male Persian is never buried until the body has been torn by a bird or a dog. I know for certain that the Magians have this custom, for they are quite open about it. . . . [They] not only kill anything, except dogs and men, with their own hands but make a special point in doing so; ants, snakes, animals, birds—no matter what, they kill them indiscriminately. (*Histories* 1.140)

Today the Magi are remembered best in the traditional Christmas tale in which three of them, sometimes called wise men or kings, travel from Mesopotamia and visit the baby Jesus in Bethlehem.

SEE ALSO: Herodotus; Persian Empire; Zoroastrianism

## magic

The people of ancient Mesopotamia did not make a clear distinction between magic and normal religious beliefs and rituals. It was thought that the gods had the power to wield magic, for both good and ill, and some gods, notably Enlil and Marduk, were seen as skilled sorcerers. Magic always acknowledged the existence of evil, which was seen as a palpable force that lurked on the fringes of human society and was capable of "infecting" anyone at any time. This infection could take the form of illness, accidents, bad fortune, or death and was supposedly caused by demons, witchcraft, or gods seeking to punish the wicked. Any and all of these negative forces could be viewed as forms of black magic. White, or positive, magic existed to counter the effects of black magic. White magic consisted of spells, incantations, and physical actions, including burning effigies representing demons or evil spirits, that drove away demons and other aspects of black magic. Rituals of white magic were usually performed by a diviner or a spiritual doctor (*ashipu*). The white magician first had to determine what kind of demon or other evil was affecting the victim. To this end, he could consult special texts, the *Surpu* and the *Maqlu*, which contained lists of the various ills that could afflict people and numerous spells and cures for these ills. The ultimate goal was to rid the person of evil, when necessary by performing an exorcism. Practicing black magic or witchcraft was a crime, and the law codes of ancient Mesopotamia provided statutes dealing with it. The statute in Hammurabi's code reads:

> If a man charge a man with sorcery, but cannot convict him, he who is charged with sorcery shall go to the sacred river, and he shall throw himself into the river. If the river overcomes him, his prosecutor shall take to himself his house. If the river shows that man innocent and he comes forth unharmed, he that charged him with sorcery shall be put to death. He who threw himself into the river shall take to himself the house of his accuser.

SEE ALSO: divination; doctors and medicine; exorcism

## Mallowan, Max E.L. (1904–1978)

A renowned English archaeologist who significantly advanced modern studies of ancient Mesopotamia and the ancient cultures of neighboring regions. Mallowan received an education in classics at Oxford University and soon afterward launched his distinguished career by serving from 1925 to 1931 as an assistant to the great Charles Leonard Woolley in the groundbreaking excavations at the site of the major Sumerian city of Ur. It was while working at Ur that Mallowan met the famous English mystery writer Agatha Christie. Though she was fourteen years older than he, they fell in love and married. From 1932 to 1938, Mallowan directed excavations at several previously obscure ancient sites in Mesopotamia and then went on to work at the better-known ancient Assyrian site of Nimrud. Later,

between 1947 and 1961, he served as director of the prestigious British School of Archaeology. Mallowan was also knighted by the British queen in 1968. He wrote several important books, including *Twenty-Five Years of Mesopotamian Discovery* (1956).

SEE ALSO: Assyriology; Ur; Woolley, Charles Leonard

## Mamitu

An ancient Mesopotamian goddess who protected the sanctity of truth, particularly oaths made by one person to another or by a human to a god. In fact, the name Mamitu (sometimes written as Mami or Mame for short) came from an Akkadian word meaning "oath." This deity was also thought to punish people who committed perjury in court.

SEE ALSO: crime and punishment; laws and justice; religion

## map making

A number of maps have survived from ancient Mesopotamia. They were carved into clay tablets just as literary and other written texts were. Because it was difficult to carve rounded lines, most lines in maps were straight, even when denoting a road or boundary that actually curved. Maps were created to show the boundaries of estates and farms, the ground plans of temples and houses, the layout of cities or districts within cities, countries, and the world as a whole. All were drawn, like modern versions, as if looking down from above. Most maps were not drawn to scale; a notable exception is a map of the city of Nippur dating to the second millennium B.C., which is so accurate that it resembles the excavation charts prepared by modern

*Babylonian tablet showing an ancient map of the world, most likely from Sippar, in modern-day southern Iraq, between 700–500 B.C.* ERICH LESSING/ART RESOURCE, NY

the north. If so, the information likely came via thirdhand stories told by merchants who traded with the natives of what is now southern Russia.

SEE ALSO: Mesopotamia, geography of; Nippur; trade

## Marduk

The chief god of the Babylonian religious pantheon. Marduk was originally a local deity, the patron god of the city of Babylon. He was possibly conceived as an agricultural god because one of his symbols was a hoe. Over time, however, Marduk's status and prestige increased. The circumstances of his rise to power over the universe and the other gods were laid out in the Babylonian myth expressed in writing as the *Epic of Creation*. In that tale, Marduk defeats Tiamat, goddess of saltwater, who helped spawn the race of gods. From the eighteenth century B.C. on in Babylonia, Marduk began to supplant the Sumerian deity Enlil as chief god, a process that was completed in the twelfth century B.C.

Temples of Marduk existed all over Babylonia. And shrines to him and his son, Nabu, were also erected in many Assyrian cities. Marduk's main temple, however, was the Esagila in Babylon. There rested his primary cult statue, which was stolen by the Elamites circa 1185 B.C. and also by the Assyrians in the seventh century B.C. It was seen as essential to win back this sacred image because the prestige and prosperity of Babylon and its realm were tied directly to worship and appeasement of Marduk. Among the numerous hymns and praises written to and for Marduk over the centuries was this one, which invokes the deity's blessings for a person to live a long and peaceful life:

archaeologists. Canals were sometimes drawn as parallel lines with wavy crests between them to indicate water, and cities and villages were designated by small rectangles or circles. Streets and roads were indicated by lines with street names etched beside the lines. A Babylonian world map dating from roughly 600 B.C. shows the city of Babylon resting in the center. Around it stretch the known lands, which rest on a round disk surrounded by a circular outer ocean or great river. An accompanying text describes the "seven islands," which are indicated by triangles pointing outward from the edges of the outer ocean. One passage mentions the "land where the Sun is not seen," suggesting that by this time the Mesopotamians knew about the arctic region lying far to

May Marduk grant life! May he . . .

decree life for you! May he prolong your life, and may he let you keep it for everlasting days! May you live, and may you have peace! May it last forever! May life be your lot, and may a life of contentment be your share! When you lie down to sleep, may your dreams be propitious [promising], and when you rise, may your omens be favorable! Wherever you walk, may you be established in peace!

SEE ALSO: Babylon; *Epic of Creation*; Nabu

## Marduk-nadin-ahhe (reigned ca. 1100–1083 B.C.)

A Babylonian king who tried but failed to defeat the vigorous Assyrian king Tiglathpileser I (reigned ca. 1115–1076 B.C.). The sixth ruler of the Second Dynasty of Isin, Marduk-nadin-ahhe was a younger brother of King Nebuchadnezzar I, who had recently become a national hero by rescuing the stolen statue of the god Marduk from Elam. Perhaps trying to match the military stature of his brother, Marduk-nadin-ahhe launched a large-scale attack on Assyria. For several years the Babylonian campaigns were successful, but eventually the forceful Tiglathpileser got the upper hand. Marduk-nadin-ahhe was defeated, and his ultimate fate is unknown.

SEE ALSO: Babylonia; Elam; Tiglathpileser I

## Mari

Variously a city, city-state, and small kingdom situated along the upper reaches of the Euphrates River in what is now eastern Syria. The site of Mari (modern Tell al-Hariri) was occupied at least by the fourth millennium B.C., and a substantial town thrived there by the early third millennium B.C. In the late 2300s B.C. Sargon of Akkad used Mari as a base from which to launch some of his military campaigns. After the decline of Akkad, the city became subject to the Third Dynasty of Ur.

In the wake of the Third Dynasty of Ur's own decline at the close of the third millennium B.C., Amorites settled in Mari and ushered in its heyday of power and influence, spanning the period from about 2000 to 1800 B.C. During these years the city controlled one of the main trade routes leading from Mesopotamia into Syria-Palestine, and its kings had an effective army to enforce that control and to defend the city. Mari was also a center of art and culture in this period. Eventually Shamshi-Adad, an Amorite king of Assyria, captured Mari and installed his son, Iasmah-Adad, as king there. The last native king of Mari, Zimri-Lim (reigned ca. 1775–1761 B.C.), greatly expanded the local palace. But before he could expand the kingdom he was defeated by Babylonia's King Hammurabi, who burned and destroyed Mari.

The site of Mari then steadily faded from view until modern times. The city was rediscovered in 1933 by some Arab grave diggers, and soon a team of French archaeologists led by André Parrot began excavations. Another Frenchman, Jean-Claude Margueron, took over the digs in 1978. The excavators found that the fire set by Hammurabi's soldiers had preserved large sections of the city's mud-brick walls. The diggers also discovered more than twenty thousand clay tablets bearing writing in cuneiform, including many letters written by Zimri-Lim and other Marian rulers.

SEE ALSO: Iasmah-Adad; letters; Shamshi-Adad; Zimri-Lim

## marriage and divorce

In ancient Mesopotamia marriage was

viewed as a bond between a man and a woman designed primarily to produce children to perpetuate society and its traditions and civic order. Marriage, along with female fertility, was therefore seen as crucial to maintaining a viable society. Men seeking brides accordingly prized healthy young women, especially virgins. Although romantic love may have occasionally played a part in the choosing of mates, most marriages were arranged by relatives when the prospective brides were in their teens and the prospective grooms were about ten years older.

Because considerations of love usually did not enter into the marriage equation, a marriage was viewed in large part as a business arrangement. As such, it required a legal contract to be binding. One of the statutes in Hammurabi's law code states, "If a man takes a wife and does not arrange a contract for her, that woman is not a wife." The groom and/or leading members of his family negotiated with the bride's family about the upcoming union, especially regarding money matters. The bride's father produced a dowry, which consisted of valuable items for her upkeep in the marriage. Typical dowry items included jewelry, cooking utensils and dinnerware, furniture, slaves, and bars of silver or other rare metals. If the wife died, the dowry legally became the property of the children produced in the marriage, although the husband could utilize the dowry items if he wanted to. The father of the groom often gave the bride's family money or valuables, called the bride-price. Both the dowry and the bride-price could be paid in installments until the first child was born, at which time payment in full was due. These and other details of the marriage contract were sometimes set down in writing, but verbal contracts were

legal, too, and likely more common. The marriage was considered to officially begin at a feast held at the groom's father's house, although in some places and times it may not have been legal until the dowry and the bride-price were paid in full.

Marriage was usually monogamous. However, it was legal for a man to have another wife under certain special conditions. For example, when a wife could not bear children, her husband was allowed either to take a second wife or to father children with a female servant. Nevertheless, he remained legally bound to continue honoring and supporting his wife until her natural death, and a servant could not claim equality with the wife. One of Hammurabi's laws provided that if the servant "bears children and afterwards claims equal rank with her mistress," the wife "may not sell her," but "may reduce her to bondage and count her among the slaves."

Divorce was legal under a few circumstances, including abuse by the husband, the wife's infertility, or adultery on the part of the wife. Another of Hammurabi's laws stated, "If the wife of a man is caught lying with another man, they [the authorities] shall bind them and throw them into the water." It is unlikely, however, that husbands and local authorities resorted to such extreme punishments in all cases of adultery when divorce was a ready and more civilized option. Most scholars think that such harsh laws were meant to scare wives and thereby discourage them from having adultery. A divorce had to be approved in court by a judge. The judge made sure that the woman had some means of support after leaving her husband's house, and to that end the court might order the husband to give her back the dowry. The man also might have to

*Clay tablet showing a calculation of the surface of a terrain at Umma, Mesopotamia, from 2100 B.C.* ERICH LESSING/ART RESOURCE, NY

pay a fine. In Assyria, if a husband merely abandoned his wife and she had no living sons to support her, she was allowed to remarry after a waiting period of five years. If she did not wait the five years and had children by the second husband, the first husband could claim custody of those children.

SEE ALSO: laws and justice; women

## Martu

Another name for Amurru, chief god of the early Amorites, a Semitic people who settled in Mesopotamia in the second millennium B.C.

SEE ALSO: Amorites; Amurru; religion

## mathematics

The peoples of ancient Mesopotamia—particularly the Sumerians and the Babylonians—made important contributions to the early development of mathematics, and some of their mathematical ideas and systems are still used today. The early Sumerians had a simple decimal system, one based on the number 10, that they probably inherited from earlier peoples. That system used small clay tokens to indicate various numbers. One token stood for 1 sheep, 1 measure of grain, or, in the more general sense, the number 1. Another token stood for 10 sheep or the number 10. In this system, a number such as 23 was denoted by two number-10 tokens and three number-1 tokens.

Over time the Sumerians began writing numerical symbols on clay tablets, each symbol indicating a certain token and the number it represented. These symbols became very complex and are still not completely understood. By the last centuries of the third millennium B.C., however, the scribes had simplified the system, narrowing it down to just two symbols, a vertical wedge and a corner wedge. These had different meanings depending on their placement. In one configuration, they indicated 60 (6 x 10); in another, they stood for 3,600 (60 x 60), and so forth. All the multiples used either 6 or 10, which made it a rudimentary sexagesimal system (one based on the number 60). Everyday calculations, for commerce or construction, became somewhat less cumbersome when the Akkadians introduced the abacus in the late third millennium B.C.

Later, the Babylonians inherited and continued to use the Sumerian decimal system for counting, but only for numbers from 1 to 59. For higher numbers, the Babylonians expanded the Sumerian sexagesimal system into a more sophisticated version. Because the new system combined elements of decimal and sexagesimal schemes, it was rather clumsy in comparison to the simpler, strictly decimal version used in most of the world today. In Babylonia, for example, the number 3,832 was expressed as 1,3,52. Reading from right to left, the second number occupied an order of magnitude higher than the first, and the third an order higher than the second. Thus, the user understood that the 1 stood for $1 \times 60^2$ (or 3,600), the 3 for 3 x 60 (or 180), and the 52 for 52 single decimal

units. Adding the three numbers together therefore rendered 3,600 + 180 + 52 = 3,832. This shows that the Babylonians understood and used square roots. They also employed cube roots (for instance, $60^3$ = 60 x 60 x 60 = 216,000). The following is an actual surviving math problem from ancient Babylonia:

> Problem: If somebody asks you thus: As much as the side of the square which I made I dug deep, and I extracted one *musaru* [$60^3$] and a half of volume of earth. My base (ground) I made a square. How deep did I go? Solution: You, in your procedure, operate with 12. Take the reciprocal of 12 and multiply by 1,30,0,0 which is your volume. 7,30,0 you will see [i.e., will be the answer]. What is the cube root of 7,30,0? 30 is the cube root. Multiply 30 by 1, and 30 you [will] see. Multiply 30 by another 1, and 30 you [will] see. Multiply 30 by twelve, and 6,0 [360] you [will] see. 30 is the side of your square, and 6,0 [360] is your depth.

Some remnants of this sexagesimal system have survived. For instance, people still divide a circle into 360 degrees and count 60 seconds to a minute and 60 minutes to an hour in timekeeping, navigation, and astronomy.

The Babylonians also employed mathematical tables of various kinds to make some calculations easier. They had multiplication tables, tables of square roots and cube roots, and tables that listed monetary conversions, including the equivalents of the values of various goods to the value of given weights of silver. The Babylonians also developed a simple form of geometry for determining area and volume. This proved useful in constructing ziggurats and other large-scale buildings. Babylonian geometry eventually influenced early

Greek thinkers, who created a more sophisticated version by introducing provable theorems.

SEE ALSO: astrology and astronomy; weights and measures; writing materials

## Medes

The inhabitants of Media, in the western part of Iran, who played a key role in Mesopotamian history in the first millennium B.C. The Medes, who spoke an Indo-European language, began as a group of loosely organized but culturally related tribes that migrated southward from central Asia into Iran around 1000 B.C. or shortly thereafter. The reasons these tribes began to unite into a sort of national unit are unclear; one major factor may have been raids into western Media conducted by the Assyrians, who were rising to power in the early first millennium B.C. In any case, by the mid-700s B.C. the Medes were strong enough to return the favor and pose a moderate threat to the Assyrians. The annals of Assyria's King Tiglathpileser III (reigned 744–727 B.C.) and King Sargon (reigned 721–705 B.C.) record campaigns against the Medes, including carved reliefs showing Median fortresses with high battlements. These reliefs also depict the early Medes themselves. They wore their hair short and sported short, curled beards, tunics covered by sheepskin coats, and high-laced boots. Their weapons included a long spear and a rectangular wicker shield as well as bows employed with great skill by archers on horseback. These effective warriors, who gained the respect of the warlike Assyrians, soon became instrumental in the rise of the Median Empire, which eventually overcame Assyria and laid the groundwork for the larger Persian Empire.

SEE ALSO: Ecbatana; Media; Persian Empire

## Media

An ancient region and tribal kingdom that spanned the western and northwestern sectors of present-day Iran and bordered eastern Assyria. Media (Mada in Old Persian), which incorporated parts of the Zagros Mountains, was largely hilly but had several small, fertile plains as well. It was settled in the early first millennium B.C. by the Medes, an Indo-European-speaking group from farther north, and eventually became the focus of the short-lived but influential Median Empire, which helped bring about the fall of the Assyrian Empire in the seventh century B.C. Part of the reason that Media rose to prominence was that it controlled a major trade route running from Bactria and Parthia in the east, through Media, to Babylonia, Assyria, and Syria in the west. Even after the decline of the Median Empire, the region remained a populous, prosperous, and valuable part of the Persian, Seleucid, and Parthian realms that followed.

SEE ALSO: Medes; Median Empire; Persian Empire

## Median Empire

A powerful but short-lived imperial realm created by the Medes in the seventh century B.C. and one of the leading factors in both the demise of Assyria and the rise of the Persian Empire. Perhaps because of threats from the Assyrians, who dwelled directly west of Media in western Iran, by the late 700s B.C. the Medes had become organized under a series of war leaders. Their identities and deeds are now largely shrouded in the mists of time. The Greek historian Herodotus claimed that the key early figures in the creation of the Median nation, its capital of Ecbatana, and its empire were Deioces and Phraortes. "The achievement of Deioces, who reigned for fifty years," Herodotus writes,

> was to unite under his rule the people of Media—Busae, Parataceni, Struchates, Arazanti, Budii, Magi; beyond these he did not extend his empire. His son Phraortes, however, who succeeded to the throne on his father's death, was not content to be king only of Media; he carried his military operations further afield, and the first country he attacked and brought into subjection was Persia [in Fars, in southern Iran]. (*Histories* 1.105)

Modern scholars think that Deioces and Phraortes, as described by Herodotus, may have been composite characters based on confused secondhand accounts of several early Median rulers. There is no doubt that Cyaxares II (reigned ca. 625–585 B.C.) was a real person, however. And it appears that he was a dynamic ruler who almost single-handedly created the Median Empire. He reorganized the military and enlisted recruits from minor Iranian peoples whom Media held as vassals, including the Persians. When Cyaxares was confident in the size and abilities of his forces, he attacked Assyria in about 614 B.C. He was aided by the Babylonians, with whom he had made an alliance. The great Assyrian city of Nineveh fell to the combined Median and Babylonian assault in 612, and the once-mighty Assyrian Empire rapidly fell to pieces. To cement and celebrate the alliance that had brought down the Assyrians, Cyaxares gave his daughter Amytis in marriage to Nebuchadnezzar II, king of Babylonia.

The rise of Media and elimination of Assyria created a new balance of power in the Near East. The region was now dominated by four nations of approximately the same strength: Media, Babylonia, Lydia in Anatolia, and Egypt. But Cyaxares was not content with maintaining this balance of power. He launched a series of conquests that gained Media an empire stretching from the southern shores of the Caspian Sea in the east to Armenia (Urartu) in the west. Then, circa 589 B.C., he turned to the northwest and invaded Lydia, but he failed to conquer it.

Having established the Median Empire, Cyaxares died and was succeeded by Astyages (reigned ca. 585–550 B.C.). Not only was Astyages a mediocre ruler, he also faced major logistical difficulties in holding together the huge Median realm, including communication and transportation of soldiers and supplies over long distances. The threat of rebellions by subject peoples was another problem. Most of these peoples were discontented with Median rule and had to be kept in line by the use of force. The fact that many of the Median nobles resented Astyages was another factor in the overall weakness and vulnerability of the realm. These and other factors made Media a tempting target for would-be imperialists. And in about 553 B.C. Cyrus II, ruler of the Persian region of Fars, led a rebellion that soon toppled Astyages from his throne.

Thanks to Cyrus's foresight, however, Media was not destroyed but instead was absorbed into the new Persian Empire. He actually honored the Medes, appointing a number of Median nobles as courtiers and army officers. He also made the Median homeland the first satrapy (province) of his own realm, calling it Mada, and kept Ecbatana intact as his second capital. Thereafter, people routinely referred to the Persian realm as the empire of the Medes and Persians.

SEE ALSO: Astyages; Cyaxares II; Ecbatana; Media

## melammu

In the myths and lore associated with ancient Mesopotamian kingship, an aura or radiance surrounding the king's person. Sometimes translated as "awe-inspiring luminosity," *melammu* was an Akkadian word borrowed from the Sumerians. It is unknown where the concept came from, but it may have developed in the late fourth or early third millennia B.C. as a way of enhancing the image of kings by making them appear to be chosen or blessed by the gods. The Mesopotamian *melammu* was the partial basis for later artistic imagery of auras and halos surrounding the heads or bodies of Byzantine and Christian angels and saints.

SEE ALSO: kingship

## Merodach-Baladan (reigned ca. 721–710 B.C.)

A Babylonian nobleman who became king of Babylonia but was unable to hold onto his throne in the face of Assyrian aggressions. Although Merodach-Baladan (or Marduk-apal-iddina) was the name assigned to him in the Hebrew Old Testament rather than his actual Babylonian name, the biblical version stuck and is the one used most often today. Shortly after Merodach-Baladan became king of Babylonia, Assyria's King Sargon II attacked and forced him to flee to Elam. Seven years later, with the aid of the Elamites, Merodach-Baladan made a comeback and once more sat on the Babylonian throne. But then Sargon's son and successor, Sennacherib, drove Merodach-Baladan away again. The deposed ruler, whom the Assyrians labeled a "terrorist" in their annals, soon launched a rebellion in hopes of regaining power; he was unsuccessful, and not long afterward he died in exile. The biblical book of Isaiah (39.1–4) tells how Merodach-Baladan tried to get Hezekiah, king of the Hebrew kingdom of Judah, to help him fight the Assyrians, which turned out to be another failed effort. Despite his bad image in Assyrian writings, the Babylonians remembered Merodach-Baladan as a good ruler who bravely tried to defend his country against outside aggression.

SEE ALSO: Babylonia; Elam; Judah

## Mesopotamia, geography of

The geography of Mesopotamia—its topography, natural features and resources, and climate—and the geography of the regions surrounding Mesopotamia profoundly shaped the history of that ancient region and the lives of its inhabitants. First, Mesopotamia was located in the heart of what Europeans called the Near East (today referred to as the Middle East), centered mainly on what is now the nation of Iraq. The term *Mesopotamia* came from Greek words meaning "the Land Between the Rivers," a reference to the Tigris and Euphrates rivers, which run roughly from northwest to southeast through the region. In fact, much of that region consists of flat plains making up a vast river valley, and most of southwestern Mesopotamia was made up of the moist and marshy deltas of the two rivers. Today, the Tigris and the Euphrates join together at a point not far west of the Persian Gulf and then empty into the gulf. But in ancient times, the two rivers entered the gulf separately, forming two deltas that adjoined each other. That well-watered southeastern section of Mesopotamia was frequently referred to as Sumer because it is where the first major group of settlers, the Sumerians, erected the first cities in the region, and in the world. Later, after the decline of the Sumerians, the area was

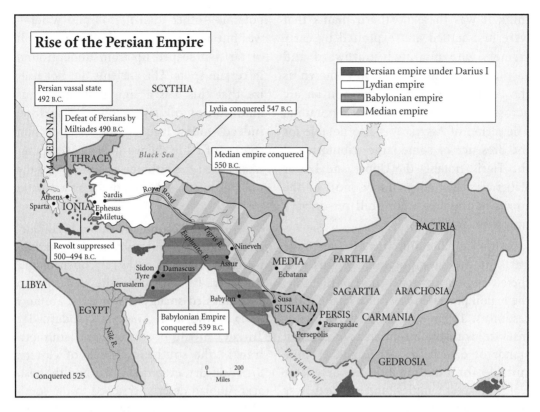

## Rise of the Persian Empire

Persian vassal state 492 B.C.

SCYTHIA

Defeat of Persians by Miltiades 490 B.C.

Lydia conquered 547 B.C.

**Legend:**
- Persian empire under Darius I
- Lydian empire
- Babylonian empire
- Median empire

MACEDONIA

THRACE

*Black Sea*

Median empire conquered 550 B.C.

Royal Road

Athens

Sardis

Sparta

IONIA

Ephesus

Miletus

*Euphrates R.*

*Tigris R.*

Nineveh

BACTRIA

Revolt suppressed 500–494 B.C.

Sidon

Damascus

Assur

MEDIA

PARTHIA

Tyre

Jerusalem

Ecbatana

SAGARTIA

ARACHOSIA

LIBYA

Babylon

Susa

SUSIANA

EGYPT

Babylonian Empire conquered 539 B.C.

PERSIS

Pasargadae

CARMANIA

Persepolis

Conquered 525

0    200

Miles

*Persian Gulf*

GEDROSIA

*Nile R.*

GALE

usually called Babylonia because the rulers of the city of Babylon often controlled it.

The section of Sumer/Babylonia that was situated closest to the Persian Gulf was appropriately called Sealand in ancient times. It should be noted that the original Sealand expanded in size over the centuries. In the heyday of the Sumerians, the gulf's coast lay more than 100 miles (161km) farther inland than it does now, so cities such as Ur and Eridu were almost seaports; over time, however, the coast receded southeastward, leaving these towns "high and dry," so to speak. In fact, there was usually less annual rainfall in Sumer than in other parts of Mesopotamia; average rainfall amounted to fewer than 10 inches (25cm) per year. And it was often very hot in the south, with temperatures reaching more than 100 degrees Fahrenheit

(38°C) fairly often. What made the area so fertile and tolerable was the presence of the rivers, with their rich network of tributaries and deltas. These were supplemented over time by many irrigation canals that the locals dug along the riverbanks.

Farther northwest, the moist alluvial plains of Sumer gave way to somewhat drier and slightly hillier plains. These so-called upper reaches of Mesopotamia were variously referred to collectively as Akkad, Assyria, and other names. Here, there was more annual rainfall, so the inhabitants needed fewer irrigation canals and relied more on wells for water. It was also somewhat less hot and in general more temperate in the northern parts of Mesopotamia. This made Assyria particularly suitable for growing grain. Most scholars think it was these northern plains that were first settled and exploited by early farmers who migrated southward and eastward from the region now known as the Fertile Crescent, stretching in an arc across the upper parts of Mesopotamia. The region of Assyria was also notable for the presence of some large tributaries of the Tigris, notably the Upper and Lower Zab rivers. Not surprisingly, most of the towns in the area were built on or very near these waterways.

Although the soil was rich in large parts of the Mesopotamian plains and there was plenty of water most of the time, the region possessed few other vital natural resources. There were very few trees, for instance, with the exception of occasional stands of date palms. Also, native stone suitable for building houses, defensive walls, palaces, temples, and so forth was scarce, especially in the south, in and around the river deltas. (In contrast, small amounts of gypsum, a soft, white or gray variety of stone, were available in selected places in Assyria.) It was because of this lack of building stone that the peoples of the region had to rely mostly on clay, or mud, to make bricks, which they dried in the sun or baked in ovens. Similarly, clay became the most common medium for making writing materials—in the form of dried-clay tablets. Mesopotamia also lacked sufficient quantities of metals, including copper and tin, which, when mixed together, made bronze; iron; silver; and gold. Thus, most timber, building stone, and metals had to be imported from neighboring lands.

Not surprisingly, therefore, the peoples of the region came to depend on trade; and many lucrative trade routes came to crisscross the plains. One exception to the general lack of natural resources in Meso-

potamia—other than its soil and water—was bitumen, a material similar to asphalt or tar that seeped up from underground in certain spots. The ancients did not realize that this was a sign that enormous amounts of oil lay below the surface; indeed, today Iraq is one of the chief sources of oil in the world. The Mesopotamians used the bitumen to waterproof the hulls of boats and sometimes as a mortar for bricks.

Ancient Mesopotamia's land, climate, and resources should not be characterized solely in terms of its largely open plains, however. In antiquity, the region also encompassed small parts of what are now Syria in the west, Anatolia (modern-day Turkey) in the northwest, and southern Iran in the southeast. Much of eastern Syria was dry, even desertlike; and the vast, arid Arabian deserts stretched to the south of the central plains. Meanwhile, northern Assyria blended into the foothills of the rugged mountain chains of Armenia (called Urartu in ancient times) and southeastern Anatolia. In these foothills, the winters were mild and the summers dry and pleasant, and the locals grazed goats, sheep, and other livestock on the well-vegetated hillsides. A similar terrain and climate existed in the foothills of the Zagros range lying northeast of Sumer and east of Assyria.

Moving outside of Mesopotamia proper, one entered even higher, more rugged, and more forested terrain in the regions of southern Iran, Armenia, and Anatolia. These areas were also much richer in metals than Mesopotamia was. This is one of the major reasons that the empire builders of ancient Mesopotamia—the Akkadians, Assyrians, Babylonians, Persians, and others—so often tried to raid or conquer these neighboring regions. In

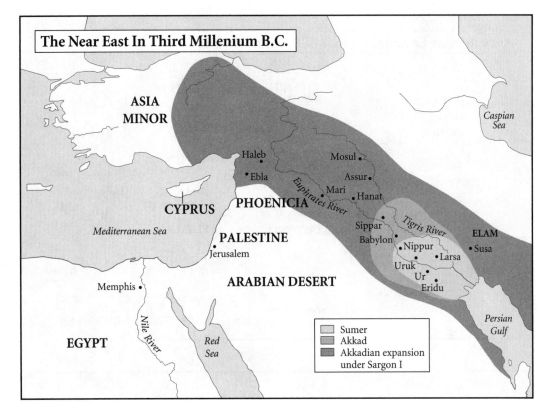

The Near East In Third Millenium B.C.

ASIA MINOR

Caspian Sea

Haleb
Ebla
Mosul
Assur
Mari
Hanat

CYPRUS PHOENICIA

Mediterranean Sea

PALESTINE
Jerusalem

Sippar
Babylon
Nippur
Uruk
Ur
Eridu
Larsa

Tigris River

Euphrates River

ELAM
Susa

ARABIAN DESERT

Memphis

EGYPT

Nile River

Red Sea

Persian Gulf

Sumer
Akkad
Akkadian expansion under Sargon I

short, they badly needed their natural resources. (They also frequently exploited their human resources by taxing their inhabitants or using them as soldiers or slaves.) Thus, it is impossible to discuss ancient Mesopotamia without considering the lands that bordered it and so often became incorporated into its political and cultural sphere.

SEE ALSO: Tigris and Euphrates; trade; transportation and travel

## Mesopotamia, history of

The history and cultural legacy of ancient Mesopotamia is central to the history and development of humanity in general, especially Western societies and those of the Middle East, called the Near East when used to describe ancient or medieval societies. This is partly because large-scale agriculture first developed in the Fertile Crescent, the arc-shaped region bordering Mesopotamia's northern rim sometime around 10,000 to 9000 B.C. Before this time there were likely no settled villages anywhere in the world. Historians generally refer to the long period of human culture before the advent of agriculture as the Paleolithic Age, or "Old Stone Age." The Neolithic Age, or "New Stone Age," when people in the area lived in villages but still used mainly stone tools and weapons, is usually dated from about 9000 to 6000 B.C. or somewhat later. Indeed, before farming began almost all people were nomads who moved from place to place, sustaining themselves through hunting, fishing, and gathering wild edible plants and fruits.

*The Emergence of Towns and Cities* Once

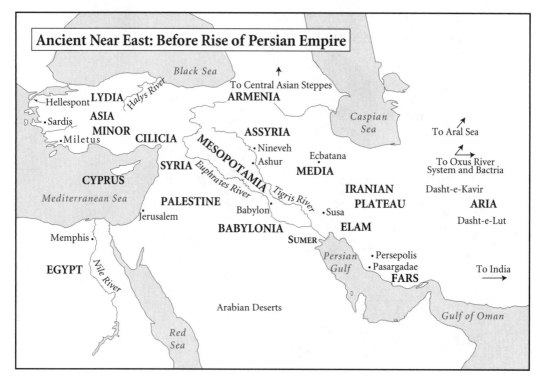

Ancient Near East: Before Rise of Persian Empire

GALE

farming began to develop in the Fertile Crescent, people settled into permanent villages; eventually, probably sometime between 6000 and 5000 B.C., some of them moved southward onto the Mesopotamian plains. There, agricultural villages were established. Some of these steadily grew into towns with populations of a few thousand people. Trade among these towns developed, stimulating increased cultural activities and still further expansion. Among the thriving communities were Tepe Gawra and Choga Mami, which featured the earliest-known irrigation canal, in northern Mesopotamia; and Ur, Eridu, Uruk, and Tell al-Ubaid in the south, near the Persian Gulf. Based on discoveries made at Tell al-Ubaid, modern scholars came to call the era lasting from roughly 5000 to 3500 B.C. the Ubaidian period.

Part of the importance of ancient Mesopotamia to world culture in general is the fact that these early villages and towns influenced people in neighboring regions to build similar settlements. In turn, the idea spread farther and farther, reaching many parts of Asia and Europe. Moreover, various logistical and cultural developments that originated in Mesopotamian towns—including artificial irrigation of crops, pottery making, and the erection of shrines and temples to honor the gods— also spread far and wide.

Meanwhile, within Mesopotamia itself, the march of civilization continued apace. Sometime in the late Ubaidian period, the first high culture arose in the southern part of the region, near the Persian Gulf. Its people, the Sumerians, may have been local Ubaidians who had reached a higher level of development; or they may have been outsiders who migrated into the region. Whatever their origins, they expanded some of their towns into full-fledged cities, some attaining populations in the tens of thousands. Though often referred to simply as cities, these were more accurately city-states, each consisting of a moderate-to-large expanse of farmland and villages controlled by a central urban area; the central city was usually surrounded by a large defensive wall made of dried mud-bricks. Among the leading Sumerian cities were Uruk, probably the first; Ur; Lagash; Sippar; and Nippur.

Each city-state thought of itself as a tiny nation. Other city-states, at the time mostly smaller, also emerged farther north, around the Tigris River and its tributaries. Each Mesopotamian city-state was ruled by a king who claimed to be somehow connected to or favored by the gods whom all Sumerians worshipped. These cities and their kings became quite territorial and frequently fought with one another. Fortunately for those involved, these early wars were not catastrophic and usually did not result in the complete destruction of population centers.

Meanwhile, when not fighting one another, these cities engaged in vigorous trade. Furthermore, commercial activities were not confined to Mesopotamia itself. Local merchants reached outward and either created or tapped into trade routes stretching far and wide. These routes were destined to keep the peoples of the Mesopotamian plains centrally connected, like the hub of a vast wheel, to a much greater world for many centuries to come. In the words of noted scholar A. Leo Oppenheim:

> During the nearly three millennia of its documented history, Mesopotamia was in continuous contact with adjacent civilizations and, at times, even

with distant civilizations. The region with which Mesopotamia was in contact, either directly or through [middlemen], stretched from the Indus Valley [i.e., India], across and at times even beyond Iran, Armenia, and Anatolia to the Mediterranean coast and into Egypt, with the immense coastline of the Arabian peninsula and whatever civilization it may have harbored. (*Ancient Mesopotamia*, p. 63)

Modern scholars call the era in which the Sumerian cities exploited this vast trade network and reached their height of power and influence the Early Dynastic Period, lasting from about 3000 to 2350 B.C.

*The First Empires* It was perhaps inevitable that one of these early, burgeoning city-states would take the next step and try to conquer and rule most or all of its neighbors. The first Mesopotamian ruler to do so—in the process creating the world's first empire—was Sargon of Akkad (a town lying north of the cities of Babylon and Kish in central Mesopotamia). During his reign (ca. 2340–2284 B.C.) he seized most of the cities in the region one by one and absorbed them into his growing realm. For the first time in history, the lower and upper halves of Mesopotamia had been united into one large political unit ruled by a central administration. Sargon's realm was successful for a while because he and his immediate successors used what are often termed *strong-arm tactics*. Not only did they maintain a strong, well-trained army, but they also dismantled parts of the defensive walls of captured cities so that these places could no longer adequately defend themselves. Sargon and his heirs also placed their own trusted nobles and other operatives in positions of power in the subject cities to discourage feelings of independence and rebellions among the locals. In addition, the Akkadian monarchs took effective control of foreign trade in the region.

Despite these measures, the Akkadian Empire was fairly short-lived compared to many other ancient empires. In addition to various political instabilities that set in over time, a warlike people from the foothills of the Zagros Mountains lying east of the plains—the Guti—invaded. As Akkadian control disappeared, many of the old Sumerian cities became independent again, and soon they drove out the Guti. From among the rulers who led the campaigns against the Guti arose a ruler of Ur, Ur-Nammu (reigned ca. 2113–2094 B.C.). Under his guidance, Ur became the major power in the region and there emerged the second Mesopotamian empire, today referred to as the Third Dynasty of Ur, or "Ur-III" for short. That realm expanded outward under Ur-Nammu's successors; however, like the Akkadian Empire, it proved to be short-lived, lasting from circa 2113 to circa 2004 B.C. The Ur dynasts felt themselves pressed from the northeast by the Elamites, whose center of power lay in southwestern Iran; and from the northwest by the Amorites, a Semitic-speaking people who originated in the Syrian highlands. The Elamites eventually besieged and captured Ur, and the empire quickly dissolved.

In the two centuries following the fall of Ur-III, some large individual city-states vied for power in various parts of Mesopotamia. Among the most successful were Isin and Larsa in the south, located in the region still widely called Sumer; Mari, a prosperous trading city on the upper Euphrates; and Ashur and Eshnunna, which fought each other for control of northern Mesopotamia, generally called Akkad or Assyria. At one point, an early Assyrian king, Shamshi-Adad (reigned ca. 1813–1781 B.C.) captured Mari and installed his son as its ruler. This marked the beginning of the first and shortest of three periods of Assyrian expansion in the region. Eventually the rightful king of Mari, Zimri-Lim (ca. 1775–1761 B.C.) made a comeback. But he and the other local rulers in the region soon had a rude awakening. A dynasty of Amorite kings had established themselves in the large city of Babylon in about 1900 B.C. The sixth member of that dynasty, Hammurabi (ca. 1792–1750 B.C.), turned out to be an avid imperialist and conqueror who, like Sargon and Ur-Nammu before him, dreamed of ruling all of Mesopotamia. Hammurabi's troops swept across the plains, capturing cities and carving out an empire almost as large as the Akkadian realm.

Although this new Babylonian superstate was also short-lived, it and its ruler established important precedents for future generations of Mesopotamians. In particular, after Hammurabi's reign Babylon permanently became the most envied and coveted city in the region. As scholar Karen R. Nemet-Nejat puts it:

> Hammurabi's reign left a lasting impression on future generations of Babylonians, thus making him one of the major figures of Mesopotamian history. . . . Hammurabi's nation-state did not survive him, but he did make Babylon the recognized [major] seat of kingship, a position that remained uncontested until the Greeks [took control of the region later and] built [the city of] Seleucia. Babylon even survived as a [premiere Mesopotamian] religious center until the first century A.D. (*Daily Life in Ancient Mesopotamia*, p. 31)

***Hatti, Mitanni, and Assyria*** Partly because of Babylon's ascendancy in these years, the period lasting from the fall of Ur-III, shortly before 2000 B.C. to roughly 1600 B.C. is often referred to as the Old Babylonian period. After Hammurabi's empire declined in the latter years of this period, a number of foreign peoples vied for control of parts of Mesopotamia. Among them were the Hurrians, the Kassites, and the Hittites. The Hurrians may have originated in the Asian region lying west of the Caspian Sea; the Kassites most likely entered Mesopotamia from the east, from or through the Zagros Mountains; and the land of the Hittites, called Hatti, was centered in Anatolia.

The Old Babylonian period ended when, in about 1595 B.C., the Hittites suddenly and boldly entered Mesopotamia, marched across the plains, and captured Babylon. For reasons that are still unclear, they did not follow up on this victory, however. Instead, they returned to Hatti, leaving a vacuum in central Mesopotamia that the Kassites swiftly filled. A Kassite dynasty now ruled Babylon and much of southern Mesopotamia from about 1595 to about 1155 B.C. The once culturally backward and unsophisticated Kassites very quickly adopted the local culture; like so many other Mesopotamian peoples over the course of time, they became "Babylonianized" in speech, dress, and political and religious customs.

Meanwhile, even as the Kassites were settling down in Babylon, many miles to the west the Hurrians were establishing their own strong foothold in the region. Located in the area lying between the upper reaches of the Tigris and Euphrates rivers, the new kingdom became known as Mitanni. The more well-to-do Mitannians raised horses and developed a formidable chariot corps, which they employed in their attempts to expand into southern

Syria. But these endeavors were largely fruitless. This is because the Mitannians increasingly found themselves part of a new and often dangerous political reality—an international balance of power in which at first four, and later five, major kingdoms vied for dominance in the Near East. In addition to Hatti to the north, Kassite Babylonia to the east, and Mitanni itself, there was Egypt, lying southwest of Palestine. The Egyptians had been invaded by a Near Eastern people of uncertain origins two centuries before, but they had expelled the intruders. And during Mitanni's formative years, Egypt was vigorously expanding its power and influence into the region of Syria-Palestine. This naturally brought the Egyptians into competition, and on occasion into armed conflict, with Hatti and Mitanni, both of which also had designs on Syria-Palestine. The climax of the Egyptian-Hittite rivalry was the great Battle of Kadesh, fought in Syria in about 1274 B.C.

The fifth member of the Near East's new major players, and the last to join the group, was Assyria. After the Babylonian king Hammurabi captured and absorbed the major towns of Assyria in the 1700s B.C., that area had fallen more or less into political obscurity. But the Assyrians were a proud and resilient people who retained their traditional culture during the centuries they were ruled by others. Under a strong and ambitious king, Ashur-uballit I (reigned ca. 1365–1330 B.C.), and his successors, they steadily began their second phase of expansion. By this time, Mitanni was already in decline, and some of its territories fell into Assyrian hands. Assyria also began moving into Armenia and developed a running rivalry with Babylonia, highlighted by the capture of Babylon by Assyria's King Tukulti-Ninurta I in the late 1200s B.C. In addition, the Assyrians launched many military expeditions into northern Syria.

*The Neo-Assyrian and Neo-Babylonian Empires* The Assyrian dominance of Babylon initiated by Tukulti-Ninurta turned out to be brief. This was because the era of the Near East's "big five," so to speak, was finally ending. Kassite rulers managed to regain power in Babylon, but soon afterward they were defeated and their dynasty was extinguished by the Elamites, who attacked in about 1155 B.C. Not long before this, the Hittites and the Assyrians had brought Mitanni to its knees, aided partly by civil disputes within Mitanni itself, which had weakened it and left it vulnerable to foreign enemies. The Hittites, too, were suddenly eliminated from the corridors of Near Eastern power. Sometime in the early 1200s B.C. large groups of peoples from southeastern Europe, and perhaps other areas, launched a massive folk migration that swept across Greece, the Aegean Islands, Syria-Palestine, and Anatolia. The invaders, whom modern historians collectively call the Sea Peoples, burned numerous cities to the ground, including the capital and other major population centers of Hatti. The Sea Peoples attacked Egypt as well. And only with a great deal of difficulty were the local pharaoh, Ramesses III, and his soldiers, able to repel them.

Fortunately for the Assyrians, their homeland was located far enough inland from the Mediterranean to keep them largely insulated from the main thrust of the Sea Peoples. Thus, while large portions of the Near East had undergone unprecedented upheaval, most of Mesopotamia survived. Still, interruptions in the flow of trade and other factors caused Assyria to suffer a period of serious decline. Mean-

while, in the years following Babylon's fall to the Elamites, Babylonia was equally hurt by disruptions in trade, as well as by internal political instability, and it, too, went into decline. Thus, by the early 900s B.C. all of Mesopotamia was politically fragmented and militarily weak. Historians sometimes call this Mesopotamia's "dark age."

As history has repeatedly demonstrated, such power vacuums in major centers of population and culture never last very long. Sure enough, before long a new imperial state rose to prominence in the already ancient Mesopotamian plains. Once more, it was the Assyrians who took the initiative. In their third and most successful period of expansion, they created the largest and most feared empire that Mesopotamia, and indeed the world, had witnessed to date. This realm is sometimes referred to as the Neo-Assyrian Empire to differentiate it from earlier phases of Assyrian empire building. The new drive for power began with two strong and ambitious kings—Ashur-dan II (reigned ca. 934–912 B.C.) and Adad-nirari II (ca. 911–891, B.C.). They and their successors seized all of Mesopotamia and many neighboring areas, including Babylonia, Elam, and parts of southern Iran, Armenia, southeastern Anatolia, Syria-Palestine, and eventually Egypt.

Particularly successful in their conquests were Ashurnasirpal II (reigned ca. 883–859 B.C.); his son, Shalmaneser III (ca. 858–824 B.C.); Tiglathpileser III (ca. 744–727 B.C.); and the four Sargonid rulers, so called because their dynasty was founded by the vigorous ruler Sargon II (ca. 721–705 B.C.). Sargon's son, Sennacherib (ca. 704–681 B.C.), was, like a number of Assyrian monarchs, both a ruthless conqueror and a great builder. When Babylon rebelled during his reign, Sennacherib swiftly and violently put down the insurrection and punished that city by laying waste to large sections of it, an act that people across the Near East remembered with horror for generations to come. Yet the same man who ordered this atrocity spent much time, effort, and money on domestic and cultural projects; most notably, he beautified the mighty Assyrian city of Nineveh and constructed a splendid new palace there. Sennacherib was succeeded by one of his sons, Esarhaddon (reigned ca. 680–669 B.C.), who, to the relief of the Babylonians, rebuilt much of Babylon. Then Esarhaddon's own son, Ashurbanipal (ca. 668–627 B.C.), brought Egypt into the Assyrian fold and defeated the Elamites, whose repeated attacks on Babylon and other cities on the plains had long plagued Mesopotamian rulers.

However, despite its strong start, Ashurbanipal's reign ended in abject failure. The last major ruler of the Assyrian Empire, he was defeated in the late 600s B.C. and his realm was torn asunder by a coalition of Babylonians and Medes, whose homeland was centered in western Iran. The Babylonians were led by a king named Nabopolassar; commanding the Medes was their talented ruler Cyaxares II.

The new empire established by Nabopolassar and expanded by his immediate successors is now often called the Neo-Babylonian Empire. Although it lasted less than a century—from about 626 to 539 B.C.—it was large and rich and witnessed Babylon's rise to a level of splendor and prestige greater than it had ever known or would ever know again. Nabopolassar's son, Nebuchadnezzar II (reigned ca. 605–562 B.C.), erected new palaces, temples, canals, and the famous Hanging Gardens of Babylon, built for his wife. This sumptuous monument came to be listed among the Seven Wonders of the Ancient World.

Though these efforts may have been partially inspired by the king's love of culture and finery, they also had an underlying political dimension. Nebuchadnezzar recognized that the key to success for the new Babylonia was for it to become a worthy successor to the now-defunct Assyrian realm. Thus, he must appear to be an even greater builder than Sennacherib and other accomplished Assyrian builders. "The Assyrians had always deployed vast sums in building themselves new palaces and administrative capitals," scholar Gwendolyn Leick points out.

> But Babylonia . . . had suffered neglect during the centuries of [Elamite and Assyrian] occupation. Now was the time to make good the scars of Assyrian aggression and Babylon was to eclipse the former glory of Nineveh, now in ruins. . . . The new [Babylonian] dynasty was seen not only as the avenger of Babylon's humiliation [by the Assyrians], but as the rightful heir of Assyrian power. [Nebuchadnezzar's great works were designed] to demonstrate the unrivaled position of Babylon as the capital of a world power which had triumphed over its rivals. (*The Babylonians*, pp. 63–64)

*The Sudden Rise of Persia* Nebuchadnezzar seems to have envisioned his efforts as the groundwork for a powerful and magnificent imperial realm that would rule Mesopotamia for centuries, perhaps forever. In fact the realm outlived him by only twenty-three years. The last Neo-Babylonian king, Nabonidus (reigned 555–539 B.C.), was defeated by Cyrus II of Persia, an event that permanently ended Babylonia's status as an independent nation-state.

One of the most talented, ambitious, and successful men ever to rule Mesopotamia and neighboring regions, Cyrus had become ruler of the Persian region of Fars, in southern Iran, in about 559 B.C. At the time Fars was a province of the Median Empire, which had coexisted with the Neo-Babylonian realm in the period following the destruction of Assyria. Under Cyrus, the Persians, who before this had been a fairly obscure people, suddenly rose to prominence as masters of the known world. They easily overthrew the Medes and then proceeded to conquer Anatolia, including the kingdom of Lydia and the Greek cities on the peninsula's western coast. The Persians next seized the regions of what are now eastern Iran and Afghanistan; Babylonia and the rest of southern Mesopotamia; and most of Palestine. Cyrus also planned to absorb Egypt, but he died in 530 B.C., before this dream could be realized. So his son, Cambyses (cam-BEE-seez), took on the task of defeating the Egyptians.

Under Cyrus, Cambyses, and the next major Persian ruler, Darius I (reigned ca. 522–486 B.C.), the Persian army was widely respected and feared, much as the Assyrian military had once been. In fact, the Persians modeled their military organization in a number of ways on the Assyrian army. The Persians also copied many of the Assyrians' best political and administrative ideas. Like the Assyrian Empire, for example, the Persian Empire, the largest imperial realm in the world to date, was divided into provinces, each run by a local governor who answered to the king.

Because Cyrus, Cambyses, and Darius were strong, skilled rulers, the Persian realm got off to a good start and for a while promised to grow even larger and more powerful. Darius had designs on Europe, and in 512 B.C. he led an expedition into the forests and steppes lying north of Greece and west of the Black Sea. But eventually the Persian monarch came face-to-face with an obstacle that was to become his realm's biggest nemesis and the eventual instrument of its destruction. This obstacle was Greece, at the time consisting of a collection of many small city-states rather than a coherent, unified nation. (In fact, Greece never became a unified country in ancient times.) First, the Anatolian Greeks rebelled against Persian rule, and it took Darius more than five years to put down the revolt, which ended in 494 B.C. Four years later he sent a Persian army to destroy Athens, on the Greek mainland, to punish the city for helping the Anatolian Greek rebels. But the much smaller Athenian army crushed the Persian invaders at Marathon, located northeast of Athens. After Darius's death, his son, Xerxes (ZERK-seez), sought revenge for the Marathon debacle. In 480 B.C. the new Persian king led an enormous army into Greece, but in a series of epic battles the Greeks inflicted heavy casualties on the invaders and drove them away.

In retrospect, the failure to capture Greece and use it as a base from which to conquer Europe proved a major turning point for Persia. Xerxes turned out to be a mediocre ruler. After he was assassinated in 465 B.C., almost all of his successors proved to be no better; in fact, some were downright corrupt and/or ineffectual. They were unable to effectively reverse the empire's steady decline, caused partly by internal power struggles as well as by rebellions by subject peoples and the increasing menace of the militarily more formidable Greeks. The last Persian king, Darius III, whose reign began in 336 B.C., simply folded under these mounting

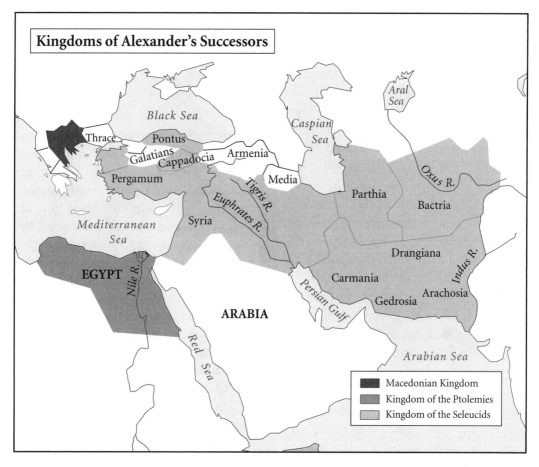

**Kingdoms of Alexander's Successors**

Macedonian Kingdom
Kingdom of the Ptolemies
Kingdom of the Seleucids

problems and pressures. Two years after he ascended the throne, Alexander III (later called "the Great"), the young king of Macedonia, a kingdom located in northern Greece, invaded Persia and swiftly defeated it. This initiated nearly two centuries of Greek rule in Mesopotamia and many of the lands on its borders.

*The Seleucid Empire* After the fall of Persia in the 320s B.C., Alexander's empire stretched from Greece in the west to the borders of India in the east, incorporating not only Iran, Mesopotamia, Syria-Palestine, and Anatolia but Egypt as well. However, Alexander died unexpectedly at age thirty-three, perhaps of alcohol poisoning, in Babylon in 323 B.C. His vast realm

quickly disintegrated as his leading generals (and some of their sons), the so-called Successors, vied with one another for its control. After many years of bloody warfare, most of the Successors were killed. The major survivors established three huge new Greek-ruled kingdoms: the Macedonian kingdom, centered in Greece; the Ptolemaic kingdom, centered in Egypt; and the Seleucid Empire, centered in Mesopotamia. The Seleucid realm also incorporated several other Near Eastern lands that had been part of the Persian Empire, including Syria and parts of Anatolia.

The founder of the Seleucid realm, Seleucus I (reigned 305–281 B.C.), and his successors worked hard to make Mesopotamia prosperous and successful in international relations. In particular, the Seleucids exploited all the old trade routes that ran through the region and attempted to open new ones. In this way, they became rich. They used the money partly to build new cities, the most important and splendid of which was Seleucia, located on the Tigris River not far north of Babylon. Due to its location, the city was sometimes literally called Seleucia-on-the-Tigris. Tens of thousands of administrators, soldiers, builders, artisans, and homesteaders migrated from Greece to Seleucia and other Mesopotamian cities and towns during these years. And Greeks came to form the upper crust of society on the plains. With a few exceptions, the local natives, especially those who could not speak Greek, were viewed and treated as inferiors.

Despite these successes, the Greeks were unable to maintain control of Mesopotamia and surrounding regions for very long. This was partly because the Seleucid rulers spent large portions of their great wealth on raising large armies, including many mercenary (hired) soldiers. These troops were used partly to prosecute costly border wars with the rulers of the Ptolemaic realm, mostly over possession of parts of Syria-Palestine. The Seleucid military was also used for defense because over time the realm came under increasing threats from outside powers. In the west, the Romans, masters of the Italian peninsula, conquered mainland Greece, the Aegean Islands, and most of Anatolia in the second century B.C. The Seleucid king Antiochus III (reigned 222–187 B.C.) was disastrously defeated by the Romans in western Anatolia. Meanwhile, in the east, the Parthians, who inhabited much of northern Iran, repeatedly attacked Seleucid towns and outposts, steadily capturing

and absorbing pieces of the empire. The Parthians also captured the main trade route that connected Mesopotamia to Afghanistan, India, and other eastern lands, a huge blow to the Seleucid economy.

***The Parthian and Sassanian Realms*** Eventually the Seleucid rulers lost so much territory, wealth, and power that their realm—which, at the end, consisted only of parts of Syria—simply ceased to exist. Mesopotamia and parts of the rest of the former Seleucid Empire came under Parthian control. The Parthians, who spoke an Indo-European language, built a new capital, Ctesiphon, located on the Tigris near the old Seleucid capital of Seleucia. Yet they made no effort to suppress Greek commerce, or even the Greek language, in Seleucia and other Mesopotamian cities. In fact, in some ways the local Parthian and Greek cultures merged, even though the Parthians were firmly in charge.

Unlike the Greeks, Persians, and Assyrians before them, however, the Parthians did not maintain a strong central administration, nor even a national standing army. Instead, local nobles oversaw large estates or tiny vassal kingdoms; they gave their allegiance to the Parthian king, seen as the chief noble, and supported him when necessary with money, goods, and troops. This feudal society, which resembled the one that existed centuries later in medieval Europe, worked well enough within the confines of Mesopotamia and other parts of the Parthian realm. And for a while the Parthian lords were able to effectively pool their resources when attacked by foreign powers. Parthian armies soundly defeated two large Roman forces that invaded Mesopotamia in the first century B.C., for example. These forces were commanded by Marcus Crassus, who lost his life in his treated with great reverence and respect by brahmin priests. The deities are symbolically awoken, bathed, dressed, entertained, and throughout the day showered with offerings by devotees. They are then "put to bed" at night. As with smaller shrines, worship at larger temples is individual rather than communal, and devotees can come at almost any time the image of the god or goddess is accessible. A major feature of many Hindu religious festivals is when the awakened deity is brought out of the "womb-house" and paraded through the streets. Among the most famous of these is the procession of the god Jagannath (Juggernaut) through the streets of Puri in eastern India in a large, ceremonial vehicle.

In some cases, large temples have enjoyed the patronage of the rich and powerful and, thanks both to this and to the scale and type of their offerings, these temples possess enough wealth to engage in extensive community and charitable activities. Prominent among these is the Tirumala-Tirupati mandir in India's Andhra Pradesh state, devoted to Vishnu. It is thought to be the wealthiest of India's temples. Meanwhile, in the United States and other nations where Indian immigrants have settled, community temples tend to be built to house the images of many deities rather than a single one in order to serve these diverse communities' needs.

SEE ALSO: church; mosque; puja

## Manichaeism

An important religious movement that arose in third-century Iran and, at various points, had adherents from Spain in the west to China in the east. At its heart Manichaeism emphasized the stark contrast between good and evil, and is therefore a dualistic religion. Its likely influences included Zoroastrianism, Judaism, Christianity, and Buddhism. Christian leaders considered it a heresy.

The founder of Manichaeism was the prophet Mani (ca. 216–274), a man from an Aramaic-speaking family living in a Jewish-Christian community in Mesopotamia. As a young man, Mani claimed to have been called to preach a new faith by an angel he referred to as the "Twin." Seeking converts, he then traveled throughout Iran's Sassanid Empire to perhaps as far east as India. He claimed to be the last in a line of prophets including Adam, Zoroaster, the Buddha, and Jesus. At first he was given complete freedom by the empire's rulers, but an autocratic king, listening to the complaints of orthodox Zoroastrian priests, imprisoned him. He suffered through twenty-six days of trials before he made a final statement and died. Mani's followers called him the "Illuminator" or "Apostle of Light," and his twenty-six days of suffering became known as the "passion of the Illuminator," in an echo of the passion of Jesus Christ on the cross.

Mani's teachings were based on the hope of a truly universal religion, one that would transcend national and linguistic boundaries. While he respected earlier religions, he saw them as too limited by time and space to be universally applicable. He and his followers hoped that Manichaeism would be able to replace them with a set of revelations that reflected simple religious realities understandable in any cultural setting.

At the heart of Manichaeism is the belief that the fundamental dualism of the universe is between spirit, which is divine and by definition good, and the body, which is evil. The soul, furthermore, has been corrupted by the body and other forms of matter. The goal of religion was to free the soul from the corruption of matter. To do this, one must reach the realization that one's soul is of the same spiritual nature as God. That was considered the only road to try salvation. Mani's writings described the history of the world in a way that expresses this process. During a past age, there was a complete separation of good and evil, light and dark. During the present age, good and evil are combined and in a state of tension. Provided one lives a righteous life by avoiding an excessive reliance on matter or things of the flesh, one's soul will enter paradise after death. If not, the soul will continue to be reborn in new, evil bodies. In practice, only a select group known as the elect were able to follow the "five commandments" (fasting, almsgiving, abstention from killing, vegetarianism, and poverty) and "three seals" (of the mouth, hands, and breast) led to true knowledge. Ordinary members of Manichaean congregations were known as "hearers" whose primary religious responsibilities were to support the elect and take part in such ceremonies as confession and the singing of hymns. Meanwhile, in the mythology of Manichaeism there appear such figures as Jesus, described as a supernatural teacher and guide, and a prince of darkness, who mingled evil with the "light" of divinity contained in the souls of the first humans.

Acting upon Mani's urging that this was a truly universal religion, Manichaean writings and teachings were quickly translated into many languages and followers set out across the old world to gain converts. By the fourth century Manichaeism had spread to the western edges of the Roman Empire and numbered, briefly, the great Christian theologian Augustine

among its followers. Christian leaders as well as political ones ruthlessly attacked it, though, and Manichaeism was mostly gone from the Mediterranean region by the sixth century. In Iran the faith remained strong even after the arrival of Islam until, in the tenth century, Muslim leaders persecuted the leaders of the faith, who moved their institution northward to the trade city of Samarkand, now in the central Asian nation of Uzbekistan. From Samarkand it eventually reached China, where Manichaean communities thrived until the fourteenth century.

SEE ALSO: Christian heresies; Zoroastrianism

## mantra

A verse, phrase, or group of syllables that, when spoken or chanted, is considered to have spiritual power in Hinduism, Buddhism, and other Indian religions, particularly when performed in direct imitation of a guru. The Vedas, Hinduism's first central group of texts, introduced mantras as a ritual technique and the hymns they contain are themselves considered mantras, although generally the word is applied to much shorter statements. The speaking or chanting of mantras can serve purposes from the propitiation of gods to being themselves the focus of meditation in the effort to make breath and sound part of the meditative process. There are three kinds of mantra. One is the use of actual words, such as the names of gods. A second is syllables with no literal meaning, most famously "om," properly pronounced "ah-oh-mm," which is thought by Hindus to be especially auspicious and is featured in most prayers. The third kind is a combination of actual words with syllables. The most famous of these mantras, common in Tibetan and other forms of Mahayana Buddhism, is "om mani padme hum." "Mani padme" means "jewel in the lotus"; "hum" is like "om" a sound without literal meaning. This mantra is generally dedicated to the bodhisattva Avalokitesvara and figures in the Lotus Sutra, one of the central texts of Mahayana Buddhism.

SEE ALSO: meditation; puja

## Mara

An Indian deity who appears in both Hinduism and Buddhism. He is most famous among Buddhists, where he is depicted as the lord of desire and the "tempter" of the Buddha during the latter's early meditations. While the Buddha was seeking enlightenment, Mara tried to entice him with political power, with challenges to his righteousness and, finally, with three "daughters" representing thirst, desire, and delight. The Buddha rejected them all. This story is one of the most familiar in Buddhism, the source of many stories and works of art. He continued to appear in Buddhist mythology even after the Buddha's enlightenment, as a continual source of temptation away from the path of enlightenment. Buddhist theologians often describe Mara as not necessarily evil or even as a personified deity, but rather as a representation of the many aspects of life which can draw one's focus away from the quest for enlightenment: desire, hunger, fear, doubt, even fatigue or psychological problems. Mara is far less common in Hindu lore, where he is the god of disease and warns of the dangers of attachment to the sensual life.

SEE ALSO: Eightfold Path; Siddhartha Gautama

## Mary
## (late 1st century B.C.–1st century A.D.)

The mother of Jesus and a central figure in Roman Catholic and Eastern Orthodox Christianity. Very little is known of her actual life. She plays a prominent role in the Gospels of the New Testament, particularly in the stories of the birth of Jesus contained in Matthew and Luke. Gospel accounts also suggest that she was present at Jesus' crucifixion and at various points of his teaching. In Luke, Mary is said to have accepted the role as guarantor of God's incarnation as a human being, which provided the basis for the doctrine of the virgin birth. The early organizers of Christian churches have enshrined the doctrine, and it has become common throughout Christianity. From it, some Christian thinkers have also derived the notion that Mary was completely without sin and was indeed a co-redeemer with Jesus. According to the Doctrine of the Immaculate Conception, for example, Mary was free from sin from the moment of her conception until her death. In 1950 the Catholic Church accepted as official dogma the ancient notion of Mary's Assumption—that is, that she was transported body and soul to heaven.

In Roman Catholicism and Eastern Orthodoxy, Mary is considered to stand above the saints, and there are special prayers and festival days devoted to her. Among the latter are Feast of the Nativity on September 8 and the Feast of the Assumption on August 15. She has also been the object of much popular devotion as the most prominent female figure in Christianity. Devotees make pilgrimages to sites where there are famous statues or other images of Mary, such as Guadalupe, Mexico, or where she has reportedly appeared in visions, such as Lourdes, France. The Protestant churches that were established from the 1500s rejected such "Mariolatry" as idolatry.

In Islam, Mary is known as Maryam, the mother of Isa (Jesus). She is held to be, along with Jesus, completely without sin and is considered one of the four best women of the Islamic paradise, along with Muhammad's wife Khadija, his daughter Fatima, and Asiya, the wife of Pharaoh.

SEE ALSO: Gospels; Jesus of Nazareth; Joseph

## Mary Magdalene
(A.D. 1st century)

The most prominent female follower of Jesus of Nazareth, and the woman mentioned most frequently in the New Testament Gospels next to the Virgin Mary, mother of Jesus. She is a Roman Catholic saint to whom numerous, probably speculative, stories have been attached. According to Gospels of Mark and John, she was the first person to see Jesus as the resurrected Christ.

She is first mentioned in the Gospels of Mark and Luke, which note Jesus cleansing her of demons. She subsequently became one of Jesus' followers, and she is mentioned in all four New Testament Gospels as having witnessed the crucifixion and burial of Jesus. Mark and John continue aspects of the story; according to their accounts, Mary Magdalene returned to Jesus' burial site on Easter morning to anoint his body according to the Jewish fashion. Finding him gone, she went to tell the apostles and returned to the tomb with Peter. Peter then left, and Christ appeared, telling her, in John 20:17, that he was ascending to heaven.

In addition to her Roman Catholic sainthood, the Eastern Orthodox tradition holds that she was a companion to John and died in Ephesus in modern-day Turkey. One of the esoteric Gnostic Gospels is also attributed to her. Other traditions grant her sacred powers and often confuse her (incorrectly) with other women attendants to Jesus. Medieval French tradition claimed that she brought early Christianity to the southern part of that country. Some Christian popular literature interprets her as a prostitute who was saved by Jesus, although there is no evidence for this in the New Testament Gospels.

SEE ALSO: Gnosticism; Jesus of Nazareth; New Testament

## Mass

In common usage, a mass is a regular worship service in Roman Catholic Christianity and Anglicanism. More precisely, the Catholic Mass is the Eucharist (or Holy Communion) in which worshippers commemorate the death and resurrection of Jesus Christ by accepting bread and wine as symbols of Jesus' body and blood. The Mass is therefore at the center of regular services in these denominations. It consists of two parts. The first is the liturgy of the word, which includes readings from holy scripture and a sermon, or homily. The second is the liturgy of the Eucharist, which offers special prayers and readings as well as the sacrament of the Eucharist itself. The term is derived from the Latin phrase *Ite, missa est*, which means "Go, it is ended."

SEE ALSO: Eucharist; sacraments; Roman Catholicism

## matsuri

A Shinto festival, although the Japanese term can also be used more broadly to refer to any holiday. There are many different kinds of matsuri; in Shinto their focus depends usually on the specific *kami*, or spirits, to be worshipped as well as the purpose of the festival itself. Celebration is usually neatly divided into two portions; religious rituals followed by a more relaxed public celebration. The rituals include purification ceremonies at the beginning as well as a procession featuring an image of whichever *kami* is the focus of the festival. Priests and laypeople also give offerings and recite prayers to the *kami*. The public celebration involves a feast, theatrical or other performances, and sometimes athletic contests. Frequently the *kami* makes a reappearance during this celebration within a mikoshi, or portable shrine. The frequent and varied matsuri are the most common public manifestation of Shinto faith in Japan.

SEE ALSO: Ise shrines; *kami*; Shinto

## maya

A concept with varied but overlapping meanings in Hinduism, Mahayana Buddhism, and Sikhism. Most simply, maya means illusion, in particular the illusion that the things of this world are meaningful in and of themselves.

The term was first used in the Hindu Vedas, texts written in the first millennium B.C. There it meant magic or tricks. According to the Bhagavad Gita, written later than the Vedas, maya is the power to give form to things. The Vedantic school of Hinduism expanded on the notion by associating maya with ignorance (of true reality). This ignorance was thought to produce undue reliance on the earthly form of things and even on their names. These things might even include individual personality and ego, which true knowledge would understand as part of the manifested reality of Brahman (the ultimate reality) rather than distinct entities. Some Hindus identified the cosmic illusion of maya with the goddess Durga.

In Mahayana Buddhism, the concept is similar. Maya there means an illusion such as those in magical performances. The things of the world themselves are such illusions, and have no distinct being of their own. For Sikhs, meanwhile, maya means the attractions of the things of the world. These things are real enough and part of God's creation, but their attractions are illusory and merely temporary.

SEE ALSO: Bhagavad Gita; Brahman; Vedas

## Mecca

The holiest city of Islam. Mecca was the birthplace of the prophet Muhammad, houses the great mosque containing the Ka'aba, Islam's holiest shrine, and is the focus of the pilgrimage that all Muslims are encouraged to make at least once during their lifetime.

Mecca lies some forty-five miles inland from the Red Sea port of Jiddah on the Arabian Peninsula, within the modern nation of Saudi Arabia, whose ruling family is charged with its protection and administration. A very old city, it stands on what in the ancient world were trade routes linking the eastern Mediterranean with the incense-producing areas of southern Arabia, and as an important trade center, it was multicultural in Muhammad's time. Local tribal elders rejected Muhammad's teaching once he had received his call from God on Mount Hira, outside the city, and the Prophet was forced to start the first Islamic community in Medina, to the north. He later returned to Mecca, where he cleansed the Ka'aba of its pagan idols and established it as the holiest of Islam's shrines.

About a half-million people reside in modern Mecca (non-Muslims are not allowed to live there), but during the annual pilgrimage season the population of the city swells by 2 to 3 million. Responsibility for the city, particularly its holy sites and the millions of pilgrims who make their way there every year, is taken very seriously by the Saudi government and gives the nation a special status among Muslim countries.

SEE ALSO: hajj; Medina; Muhammad

# Medina

Islam's second holiest city after Mecca, lying some 270 miles to the north in Saudi Arabia. Medina, then known as Yathrib, was where the prophet Muhammad established the first Islamic community in 622. The city's name is a variation of Madinat al-Nabi, which means "the City of the Prophet." Facing persecution in his hometown of Mecca, Muhammad led his followers to Medina in 622, an event known in Islamic history as the hijra. He subsequently took control of the city itself from the communities of Jewish merchants and landowners who were the standing elites, and established Medina as the administrative capital of Islam; this was all achieved peacefully, through the so-called constitutions of Medina, which placed Muhammad and his fellow exiles on an equal level with local tribes. The city retained that status until Muhammad's successors shifted their capital northward to the Syrian city of Damascus in 661.

Medina contains many holy sites, and Muslim pilgrims making the hajj to Mecca often travel to Medina as well. These include the tomb of Muhammad at the Prophet's Mosque. The first two caliphs, Abu Bakr and Omar, are also buried in Medina, as is Fatima, daughter of Muhammad, wife of the fourth caliph, Ali, and a revered figure among Shia Muslims. Aside from these tombs the city contains numerous mosques commemorating important events of Muhammad's lifetime and the early years of Islam. The sites are forbidden to non-Muslims although, unlike Mecca, non-Muslims are permitted to live in the city.

SEE ALSO: hijra; Mecca; Muhammad

# meditation

A form of religious practice in which the devotee maintains an inner focus, characterized more as a state of prayer than active thought or speculation. Its general purpose is to achieve clear understanding of something, whether it be a piece of scripture, an idea, an object, the relationship between the human and the divine, or even ultimate truth. Another goal of meditation, and sometimes one of its clearest features, is the attainment of calm and peace.

All major religious traditions have forms of meditation. In Hinduism, the various schools of yoga adopt different methods, but the general overall intention of meditation is the cleansing of the mind and soul so that the true nature of reality, and one's place in relation to it, might be grasped. Beyond yoga practices, Hindu worshippers commonly use forms of meditation in everyday worship. One frequent method is the repetition of a mantra. Hindu sannyasi, or holy men, might spend long periods, or even lifetimes, in modes of meditation. These might involve particular postures, such as sitting in the cross-legged lotus position, as well as the chanting of mantras. In the Tantric form of Hinduism, meditation is designed to awaken the divine energies that lie dormant within the body and, under the guidance of gurus, meditators are urged to visualize the release of those energies as well as use other methods. Some aspects of Tantric meditation have spilled over into popular Hinduism and into Tibetan Buddhism.

Meditation is most common in Buddhism, where the precedent for it was set by the Buddha himself, who gained his enlightenment and banished temptations while engaging in meditation. The Buddhist tradition likens the mind to a wild animal that is dangerous when untamed but very useful if it is properly trained, and meditation is training. The method is generally mental concentration on a particular memory, idea, or object; different schools make different recommendations. If practiced properly and under guidance, meditation in Buddhism is thought to lead the devotee through four stages of concentration: detachment from the material world, combined with a feeling of peace and happiness; consciousness of the spiritual limits of reason; the maintenance of peace but fading away of happiness; and the fading away of peace to a point of pure self-possession. This meditational progression will not result into entrance into the state of being known as nirvana, the Buddhist goal. Instead it will train the mind properly so that nirvana might possibly be reached through more advanced insight. Buddhist methods of meditation are not as varied as those found in Hinduism and involve sitting, calm, and sometimes chanting. In some schools, notably the Zen practice of zazen, or sitting, meditation plays a very central role.

In Judaism, Christianity, and Islam, meditation is considered a less mainstream approach to faith. Among Jews, meditation is used by those following the path of the Kabbalah as well as by Hasidic Jews. There,

the main method is concentration on the spiritual world in the attempt to gain awareness of the sefirot, the "emanations" of God. In Christianity, meditation is more common in the Eastern Orthodox and other eastern traditions than in Roman Catholicism or Protestantism. In Eastern Orthodoxy, monks use repetition of the Jesus Prayer, which runs simply, "Lord Jesus Christ, Son of God, have mercy on me, a sinner," in hopes of synchronizing the repetitions with breathing, thereby uniting the head and the heart. Mastery of this technique might lead to a vision of the "light" of God. Roman Catholic monasteries, meanwhile, often feature contemplative methods and practice that bear a close resemblance to meditation. In Islam, meditation is generally associated with Sufi mysticism, where devotees also seek an inner vision of the divine. There, contemplative methods are combined with often rather energetic spiritual exercises in pursuit of this vision. Among the important contemplative methods is ritual prayer or litany from the Qur'an known as a *dhikr* or "remembrance." By repeating it, the Sufi gains greater purity of the heart, although by itself it does not lead to divine visions. More broadly, the common practice in Islam of memorizing and reciting Qur'anic prayers might function also as a basic form of meditation.

SEE ALSO: monasticism; Sufism; Zen Buddhism

# Mencius
## (371 B.C.–289 B.C.)

Confucian philosopher who is generally considered the "second sage" of the faith due to his elaborations upon basic Confucian principles. Mencius is a Latin form of the Chinese name Mengzi. Of noble origin, Mencius was partly taught by a grandson of Confucius himself. He served briefly as an official in the state of Ch'i but spent most of his life traveling from state to state giving advice to rulers and lessons to followers. His greatest text, a collection of his statements and actions compiled by students, is known simply as *Mencius* and is one of the "four books" contained among the Confucian classics.

Mencius believed that human nature was fundamentally good, since humans are animated by heaven. Such qualities as humaneness and righteousness are innate, as can be seen by the natural love children have for their parents. These qualities, however, can be cultivated through proper guidance and moral reflection. By doing so, one aligns oneself with the will of heaven. Mencius also believed that filial piety was at the center of Chinese culture and society, and that to revere one's parents, through specific rites, was a sign of both inner goodness and cultivation.

Mencius was also highly concerned with good government, something which appeared to be in short supply during the so-called warring states period (475–221 B.C.) when he lived. The text of Mencius is in fact mostly oriented toward describing the features of good government. Leaders, he argued, must put the welfare of their people above all other matters, which involved both ensuring their material well-being and providing moral education. Moreover, leaders must provide examples of humaneness and righteousness, which signal that he is ruling in accordance with the will of heaven. If he fails to do these things, a ruler has lost the mandate of heaven, and it is perfectly justifiable for him to be replaced.

SEE ALSO: *Analects*; Confucianism; Four Books

# messiah

The "anointed one" whose appearance signifies God's intervention or salvation in Judaism and Christianity.

For Jews, the messiah is to be a member of the royal line of King David. Beliefs that became mainstream during the time of the second Temple (531 B.C.–A.D. 70) offered the hope that one day this "anointed one" would reestablish the kingdom of Israel. This hope has little basis in Jewish scripture, where references to the messiah are symbolic and open to a wide range of interpretations. Instead it is placed in the context of Jewish history, where most Jews have always lived under foreign and sometimes oppressive rulers. They have also lived with a sense of the loss of the original kingdom of Israel. The appearance of a messiah and the reestablishment of Israel would bring an end to this exile. It would also result in the establishment of God's kingdom on earth. This hope has resulted in the appearance of a number of "false" messiahs over the course of Jewish history, some of whom have built up substantial followings. It has also given rise to the branch of the faith known simply as messianic Judaism.

In Christianity, Jesus of Nazareth is commonly held to be the messiah hinted at in the Jewish scriptures of the Old Testament, the "anointed one" of the house of David. Christians also understand the term to mean "savior," the figure who provided humanity with a means of true salvation. One historical reading of the life of Jesus is that he appeared during a period of Jewish history when many Jews anticipated the imminent arrival of the messiah, a notion stated most clearly by John the Baptist. Some of Jesus' statements in the Gospels also suggest that he was thought to be the promised messiah, although the idea seems to be stronger among his apostles than in Jesus himself. In any case, early Christians accepted that Jesus was the means by which God provided humanity with salvation, and for that reason he was the messiah. This understanding was among the strongest features separating early Christianity from Judaism and marking it out as a completely different faith. For Jews the messiah was yet to appear, but for Christians the messianic prophecies had been fulfilled. The messianic aspect of hope, however, figures in a secondary way in Christianity when believers preach a "second coming" of Jesus at the time of the final judgment, when he will usher in an era of glory and righteousness.

SEE ALSO: Christianity; Judaism; millennialism

## middle path

A fundamental Buddhist teaching, described by the Buddha himself in some of his first sermons. The middle path lies between two extremes, either of which might lead one away from enlightenment. One extreme is that of excessive materialism, or focus on things of this world and of the flesh. For the Buddha such things were not in or of themselves bad, but they signal a continued attachment to desire and ignorance of the true nature of the universe. The other extreme was the world-denying asceticism the Buddha saw among some Hindus and which he himself had temporarily practiced. Asceticism, he argued, was also a sign of attachment to delusion, since to deny the world too energetically was to reinforce its power over you. Instead of either approach, Buddhists should seek the middle path, that of moderation in all things.

SEE ALSO: Eightfold Path; Siddhartha Gautama; Tripitaka

## midrash

The "investigation" of scripture in Judaism and a central form of Jewish scholarship. There are three important ways in which the term is used: 1) the process of scriptural interpretation itself; 2) through interpretation of specific scriptural passages; and 3) the compilation of such interpretations. Midrash is an ongoing process demonstrating by its very vitality the continued relevance of scripture to new generations and new historical circumstances. Its emphasis is not on philosophical speculation but on the relationship between scripture and social or cultural circumstances. Midrash is classified as either Halakhic or Aggadic. Halakhic texts focus on legal teachings (religious law as it works in the world) while Aggadic ones emphasize nonlegal matters such as theology and ethics. Midrashic texts continue to build on the ones produced during the second through seventh centuries, such as Genesis Rabbah, Leviticus Rabbah, and Esther Rabbah ("rabbah" means exegesis or explanation).

SEE ALSO: Judaism; Torah

## millennialism

In general, the belief in some sort of future period in which one group of believers will be privileged over others, or when an age of greatness and peace will start. Also known as millennarianism, millennialism is most often associated with Christianity. The Christian New Testament's final book, Revelation, claims that Jesus Christ will establish a thousand-year reign before the final judgment of God. This assertion has given rise to numerous Christian sects which emphasize millennialism and the human preparation for it. These are generally divided into pre-millennialists, who think that Christ will return before the millennium, and post-millennialists, who believe instead that he will return after it. It has also inspired a wide body of apocalyptic Christian beliefs about the nature of the "last days" prior to the beginning of Christ's thousand-year reign.

At the heart of Christian millennialism is a future transformation, and with it the hope for the end of suffering and a more righteous life. Although some Christians, taking Revelation literally, thought that Christ's reign would begin in the year A.D. 1000, and then A.D. 2000, the specific dates are relatively unimportant. Indeed, various Christian groups and leaders have used millennialist prophecies or ideas to give significance to events such as the Crusades. In the modern world, churches which emphasize millennialism are among the fastest growing in the Christian world; they include the Mormons, Seventh Day Adventists, and Jehovah's Witnesses. Meanwhile, fictionalized accounts of the so-called rapture of the last days (which are mostly based on nineteenth-century readings of Revelation) have grown popular among many evangelical or fundamentalist Christians.

The hope offered by millennialism has appeared in many other religious traditions, and millennialism is in fact a common feature of many of them. Judaism has at its center a kind of millennialist hope: the return to earth of a messiah who will usher in an age of righteousness. Jewish history has been full of "false messiahs" who have garnered huge followings, such as Shabbatai Zvi in the seventeenth century. Mainstream rabbinic Judaism has, however, tried to minimize the impact of

millennialist movements and ideas. In Islam, the Shia sect has a strong millennial component in its hope for the return of a last, "hidden" imam or prophet, the mahdi, while the religion as a whole retains, like Judaism and Christianity, a belief in a future last judgment. In Buddhism, the Pure Land school is built around future hopes of "salvation" in an ethereal place where one might attain final enlightenment, while the bodhisattva Maitreya is frequently depicted as a figure who will return to earth to renew the Buddha's teachings in a future, decadent age. Both Pure Land Buddhism and reverence for Maitreya have been extremely popular in East Asia, with Maitreya sometimes associated with peasant revolts.

Millennialism, with its sense that the world is imperfect, corrupt, or even evil, can develop destructive tendencies if "true believers" take it too seriously. In the mid-1800s, the millennialist Taiping Rebellion in China, begun by a Chinese man who believed himself to be the second coming of Jesus Christ, resulted in the deaths of millions. In the 1930s and 1940s, the "thousand-year Reich" proclaimed in Germany by Adolf Hitler's Nazis was an important factor in the start of World War II and, in its attempt to establish "purity," the Holocaust against European Jewry. In more recent years, but on a much smaller scale, millennialist cults have resulted in mass suicides among believers, such as Jim Jones's People's Temple movement in the 1970s and, in 1997, the Heaven's Gate movement near San Diego, California.

SEE ALSO: apocalypse; eschatology; new religious movements, Western

# mindfulness

A technique of meditation that lies at the heart of Buddhism and is the seventh component of the Buddha's Eightfold Path to enlightenment. By achieving true mindfulness, one moves beyond one's ego and the habits of understanding the things of the world according to the senses and conscious thought. It is a slightly paradoxical process, because only by divesting oneself of the mind can one achieve true mindfulness. Meditators are urged to perceive their interior lives by focusing on the four mindfulnesses: contemplation of the body, contemplation of feelings, contemplation of the mind, and contemplation of mental obstacles. Contemplation of the body is focused on gaining the understanding that the body is merely a temporary shell prone to death and decay, and therefore is not a "self." Contemplation of feelings involves observing one's emotional reactions to outside happenings or stimuli, and gaining the understanding that those reactions, too, are temporary. Contemplation of the mind asks the meditator to consider that his or her habits of thought—optimism, cynicism, desire, disdain, or any other quality—are unreal. Contemplation of mental obstacles, meanwhile, allows one to get beyond the laziness, ill will, and attachment to the senses which stand in the way of deeper understanding. With great practice, the meditator can develop the ability to only barely perceive the things of this world in ways he or she has commonly understood them, which is through the filter of the individual self. Then, the devotee can achieve a true understanding of the illusory nature of things.

SEE ALSO: Eightfold Path; meditation; vipassana

## moksha

The "liberation" from the cycle of birth and death that is the ultimate goal of Hindus. According to basic Hindu beliefs, the soul is trapped in a cycle of reincarnation, or transmigration, and must free itself from attachment to things and from ignorance before achieving moksha. For most believers, this will take rebirth through thousands of lifetimes, although it is also considered possible in most Hindu schools for people to achieve moksha within this lifetime, although this is quite rare. Hindus commonly describe moksha, furthermore, as the highest of four human endeavors, higher than (in ascending order) kama (pleasure), artha (worldly success and power), and dharma (duty and devotion). In attaining moksha, one's soul "rejoins" the ultimate reality of Brahman, as a drop of water in a river ultimately rejoins the broad ocean. Buddhists believe in a similar concept, although they generally refer to the ultimate goal as nirvana rather than moksha.

SEE ALSO: caste; nirvana; reincarnation

## monasticism

The practice of separating oneself from the larger community in order to live in a manner fully devoted to one's religion. Generally speaking, monasticism refers to the institutionalized forms of this way of life, the forming of monastic orders of monks or nuns. It more rarely signifies the single person who adopts the life of a wandering ascetic, as remains common in Hindu India, although many monastic forms began among such solitary ascetics. Full devotion to religious life might involve prayer, meditation, and study, often conducted according to a highly disciplined schedule. It might also involve education and other good works. Monasticism is most commonly seen in Christianity, and Buddhism, where monastic orders are a major feature of organized religion. It is not found as such in Judaism or Islam.

Muslims, in particular, reject the practice, since they believe that to deny the world is to deny the good things of God's creation. Orders of Sufi mystics, however, bear a superficial resemblance to monastic groups.

Christian monasticism began among small groups of ascetics living in third-century Egypt. These groups, which included both men and women, renounced their attachments to all worldly things, including families, and tried to live lives organized by continual prayer. They hoped that this would lead to true communion with God. The leaders of these 1st monastic orders were the hermit Antony (ca. 250–356), who is regarded as the father of monasticism in Christianity, and Pachomius (ca. 290–346), who organized eleven Egyptian monasteries. At the heart of their system was the idea that, in order to lead a life fully devoted to God, one had to avoid worldly temptations in whatever way possible. These so-called desert fathers had a continuing influence on monasticism in Eastern Orthodox Christianity. In the fourth century Basil the Great (329–379) and his sister Macrina (327–379) founded the first monastic communities in Asia Minor (modern-day Turkey), then close to the center of the Christian world. These orders advocated public works as well as separation. The major center of monasticism in Eastern Orthodoxy is Mount Athos in Greece, the site of numerous, male-only monasteries.

*The First Christian Monks* Farther west, Benedict of Nursia (ca. 480–547) is credited with institutionalizing monasticism. For the monastery he established at Monte Cassino near Rome, Benedict drew up a list of guidelines and rules that were to characterize monasticism in much of Western Christianity afterward, even for monks and nuns who were not members of the Benedictine order. Benedict's rule featured obedience to the head official of each monastery, known as an abbot or abbess, and a schedule of prayers and hymns to be carried out at specific times of the day. It rejected asceticism but required monks and nuns to live simply and humbly. Entrants into the order made three vows: obedience, remaining within the monastery, and the commitment to change one's habits. The third came to include the vows of poverty and chastity. Over the next centuries, as Germanic kingdoms replaced the territories of the Western Roman Empire, monasteries played important social, educational, and economic roles in addition to their religious roles. Until the revival of urban life in Europe after A.D. 1000, monasteries were community and market centers, and they kept alive what remained of Europe's literary culture. The monasteries also aided in the slow conversion of northern and western Europeans to Christianity. Noteworthy in all these efforts were the monasteries of Ireland, where monks took pains to preserve Latin and Greek texts and to evangelize the British Isles.

Roman Catholic monasticism became more diverse with the founding of the so-called mendicant orders, most notably the Franciscan order (begun under Francis of Assisi in 1210) and the Dominican order (founded in 1216). These orders began with the ideal that monks should neither own property nor remain in settled buildings. Instead they should live simply, and by the work of their hands, and therefore provide examples of "Christ-like" living. After some decades both orders, however, became institutionalized and established, with their own structures and hierarchies of officials. In the 1500s, Ignatius of Loyola (1495–1556) founded the Society of Jesus, or the Jesuit order. These were activist monks, involved especially in missionary and educational work. Among Protestants, meanwhile, only Anglicans have to any extent maintained monastic institutions.

*The Buddhist Order* In Buddhism, monastic orders are the main institutions of organized religion. Their origins date back to the teachings of the first Buddha and perhaps earlier, to India's tradition of wandering ascetics. The Buddha urged that the sangha, or monastic order, was one of the three "refuges" that Buddhists should seek. Meanwhile, by joining monastic orders, devotees could more easily follow the Eightfold Path designed to lead to enlightenment. Unlike Hinduism, however, the Buddha encouraged monks to disdain the extremes of asceticism. The Buddha himself is seen to be the "model" monk, and tradition holds that the basic rules for monasteries were presented in his teachings. Buddhist monks are known as bhikkus; the female variant is bhikkuni, although historically relatively few women have formally joined monasteries or served as nuns.

One of the major features of the Theravada school of Buddhism is the belief that its temples and monasteries remain close to the ideal set out in the first Buddhist teachings. Monks live simply on charity and donations, and are not permitted to eat after noon. They must spend most of their day in prayer or meditation. The religious life of monasteries and temples is directed by an abbot, generally a lifetime devotee whose presence provides stability and continuity; in Theravada Buddhism most monks serve only temporarily. Meanwhile, temples serve as centers of community life; in this tradition the term monastery is mostly applied to centers distant from lay populations and these

institutions are also known as retreat centers. Other Buddhist traditions where monasticism is strong include Tibetan Buddhism, where until the Chinese suppression of Buddhism beginning in the 1950s as many as one-quarter of the population served as monks, and Zen Buddhism. Japanese followers of Zen are urged to live frugally and to work as well as study and meditate. As in Theravada Buddhism, Zen monks often only serve as monks temporarily, although there are many who devote their entire lives to the practice.

SEE ALSO: Jesuits; meditation; sangha

# monotheism

The belief in one God, usually considered to be the Creator of the world and its moral systems as well as an omniscient, constant presence in people's lives. It is therefore contrasted with polytheism, the belief in many gods, and atheism, the belief in no god. The term is usually associated with the great monotheistic tradition that includes Judaism, Christianity, and Islam, which not only preach a single God but wholeheartedly reject the possibility of other gods, considering such beliefs to be idolatry.

The ancient Jewish scriptures suggest that Judaism was not originally monotheistic in the strictest sense. Instead, Jews believed in their one God while acknowledging that other peoples might have their own gods. Over time, however, the Jews' blanket rejection of other gods makes it accurate to speak of the faith as monotheistic. Zoroastrianism, which arose in Iran in the seventh and sixth centuries B.C., might also be able to lay a claim to being the first truly monotheistic faith. Christianity's monotheism is complicated by the doctrine of the Trinity, which preaches that God is three-in-one (Father,

*The Mormon Temple in Salt Lake City, Utah.* © Chris Rogers/Corbis

Son, and Holy Spirit); Islam's monotheism is much more literal and straightforward. Even Hinduism might in some senses be considered monotheistic. Its many colorful gods are considered by many Hindu theologians to be not separate entities but instead aspects of a single, universal divine essence.

See Also: atheism; polytheism

## Mormonism

A Christian sect that emerged in nineteenth-century America and has since spread around the world thanks to the evangelizing efforts of its members. Mormons are known more formally as the Church of Jesus Christ of Latter-Day Saints.

The sect was founded by the New Englander Joseph Smith (1805–1844). In 1822, Smith claimed, he was given a new, revealed truth by an angel named Moroni. This truth was written down to form the Book of Mormon, the sect's basic scripture aside from the Bible. According to the Book of Mormon, Jesus Christ reappeared to early immigrants in America, promising to found a new Jerusalem there. It is this aspect of the faith's teachings that leads some to refer to Mormonism as an Americanized, millennial version of Christianity. Mormons believe, furthermore, that Smith restored Christianity after the other, more established churches had fallen away from it.

Facing persecution, Smith's earliest groups of followers began to move west. Smith himself was arrested in Illinois and killed by an unruly mob. Meanwhile, early groups of Mormons began to disagree over fundamental principles, most notably one having to do with polygamy, or the right of a man to marry more than one wife. According to a revelation alleged to have occurred in 1943, Mormon men were granted that right as an echo of the polygamy of the prophet Abraham. Although schismatic sects appeared, the largest group of Mormons continued west under Brigham Young (1801–1877), where they settled in the area of the Salt Lake in the Utah territory. They considered this area to be the site of the new Jerusalem, a "Zion in the wilderness." The early settlers practiced polygamy, but the practice was officially ended by Mormon officials by the end of the 1800s (although individual polygamists continue to be reported).

The Church of Jesus Christ of Latter-Day Saints is governed by a complex and somewhat secretive hierarchy. It remains based in Salt Lake City, and its members are most numerous in the state of Utah. Young men are expected to devote two years of missionary or other service work to the church, and their efforts partly explain Mormonism's success in gaining converts around the world. These missionary efforts have been particularly focused on the Polynesian islands of the eastern Pacific, since (contrary to archaelogical, linguistic, and other evidence), the Mormons believe the Polynesian peoples are descended from Native American groups who, in turn, traced their descent to the lost tribes of Israel; the church maintains a strong presence in Hawaii for that reason. Mormons tend to follow conservative lifestyles, with young marriages and large families. Women are discouraged from working outside the home. Mormons avoid coffee, tea, and most soft drinks because they contain caffeine, and they disdain all other stimulants as well.

*Moses receiving the Ten Commandments (upper), and reading the Commandments to the Israelites (lower), a 9th-century manuscript page from the Bible of Charles the Bald.*

SEE ALSO: Great Awakenings; new religious movements, Western

## Moses
### (ca. 13th century B.C.)

The greatest prophet of Judaism, and an important prophet in Christianity and Islam as well. The predominant, rabbinic tradition of Judaism refers to him as "Moses, our Rabbi," noting his status as the first and greatest of the teachers of that tradition.

Moses' story appears in the book of Exodus in the Hebrew Bible, or Old Testament, and for Jews and Christians it is one of the most well known stories of their early religions. Ancient Egyptian records make note of him as well, giving Moses' existence a corroboration lacking for most other Hebrew Bible figures. According to Exodus, he was born to Amram and Jochabel, members of a Hebrew tribe with a long presence in Egypt, then the greatest empire of the Near East. In order to save the infant Moses from an order from the Pharaoh (the Egyptian emperor) to kill all the firstborn sons in Hebrew families, a direct strike at their lineages, Moses' parents hid him in a tangle of reeeds in the Nile River. There the pharaoh's daughter found and rescued him, and he grew up within the pharaoh's household. Moses' name comes from this episode. It is derived from the Hebrew *meshtihu*, which means roughly "I took him from the water."

Moses eventually grew to adulthood and married. While watching over a flock of sheep, he came across a burning bush, from which God called upon him to lead the Hebrew slaves out of Egypt, to end their exile away from the land of the Canaanites (roughly Palestine) that had been promised them in the original covenant between the Hebrews and Abraham. Following numerous challenges, most notably the pharaoh's resistance, Moses was finally able to gather the Hebrews together and lead them across a finger of the Red Sea to the Sinai Peninsula. They spent the next forty years "wandering" in the wilderness of that area.

On the peninsula's Mount Sinai, Moses was granted further revelations by God for, according to tradition, forty days. These revelations included the entire Torah or Pentateuch, the first five books of what was later to be the Hebrew Bible, as well as the oral tradition later referred to by rabbinic Jews as the Oral Torah. For most Jews the Pentateuch is an unchanging aspect of God's word to their people, while the Oral Torah is a source for inves-

tigation and debate. Another important part of God's revelation to Moses on Mount Sinai was the greatest symbol of a now reaffirmed covenant between God and the Jews, the Ten Commandments, inscribed on two stone tablets. It was also here that God insisted that his people worship him and no other God. Moses continued to lead the often contentious Hebrews on their wanderings until his death, at which time he named Joshua his successor.

In addition to his central position among Jewish prophets, Moses is considered by Christians to have appeared at the side of Jesus during the mountaintop event known as Jesus' transfiguration, when God revealed Jesus' divinity to some of his disciples, an account contained in the first three of the New Testament Gospels. Muslims call him Musa and consider him one of a long line of prophets leading from Abraham to the final prophet, Muhammad. According to the Qur'an, Musa predicted the coming of Muhammad.

See Also: Abraham; Exodus; Judaism

## mosque

The religious gathering place and house of worship for Muslims. According to the Qur'an, mosques are "houses which God has allowed to be built, that his name might be spoken in them." (Qur'an 24.36). Prayer and other forms of devotion in Islam frequently take place in other locations, and mosques are deemed desirable rather than absolutely necessary in Islamic communities. Many communities often have two types of mosques: large communal ones, which are the site of large-scale worship such as Friday prayers and are supported by the community as a whole; and smaller mosques established by different groups. The structures themselves generally have a large central hall where believers can gather. At one side of this hall is a niche where a special set of structures indicates the direction of Mecca. They include a pulpit for speakers and scripture readers and a stand on which to place the Qur'an. The floor of the hall itself is covered with mats or carpets for devotees; before entering, believers must remove their shoes and wash in a form of ritual ablution. Often a minaret or tower is attached to the mosque as an elevated spot from which criers called muezzin call the faithful to prayer. One clearly identifiable sign of a mosque is an Islamic crescent looming above the minaret. Paintings, statues, and other images are otherwise forbidden.

The Arabic word for this structure, *masjid*, is the commonly used term among Muslims. Among the most important of the masjids are the Masjid al-Haram in Mecca, the Masjid of the Prophet in Medina, and the Masjid al-Aqsa in Jerusalem. Other major mosques have been established outside the Arabic-speaking world, notably the Suleiman Mosque in Istanbul, Turkey, and the Jamma Masjid in Delhi, India. These mosques, like thousands of others, grew to serve community as well as religious functions, featuring madrasas (centers for Islamic education), lower-level schools, public hostels, hospitals, and even markets.

SEE ALSO: Al-Aqsa Mosque; church; mandir

## Mo-tzu
### (ca. 471 B.C.–391 B.C.)

Classical Chinese philosopher whose rejection of many aspects of Confucianism led to an alternative school of thought known as Mohism. Originally a Confucian student concerned with good government and social order, Mo-tzu came to believe that Confucian teachings placed far too much importance on the performance of rituals and on codes of behavior. They neglected, he felt, religious feeling, which for him was the true source of both social order and of human happiness. He argued for a return to simple virtues and for the practice of universal love. People must learn to view others' families and states as they would their own, and reject the temptations of selfishness and partisanship. For Mo-tzu, universal love would not only improve human life and human institutions, it was also the way of heaven. Practiced sincerely and conscientiously, universal love would allow one to live in accordance with the way of heaven, a basic goal of most Chinese schools of thought. Despite the abstraction of the notion of universal love, Mo-tzu believed that it was identifiable by its effects; if doctrines did not have an observable effect in improving people's well-being by granting serenity, generosity, and even prosperity, as universal love clearly did, they should be ignored.

Following Mo-tzu's death, disciples established Mohist churches where followers were urged to lead a simple and ascetic life. At the center of the church's teachings was a list of principles including not only universal love but respect for the virtuous and simplicity in one's material life and in rituals. Mohism attracted a wide following for many decades among a population suffering from the chaos of China's warring states period (475–221 B.C.), but it never grew popular enough to seriously challenge either Confucianism or Mohism's larger Daoist alternative.

SEE ALSO: Confucianism; Daoism; Mencius

## muezzin

The Muslim criers who call the faithful to their daily prayers and to the more public and formal Friday worship. Traditionally, the muezzin were mosque officials who, at the proper time for each prayer, took up a position at the mosque; at large mosques a muezzin stood on one of the minarets in order to be better heard. He would face toward the east and declaim, "Allah is great. I testify that there is no God but Allah; I testify that Muhammad is the prophet of Allah. Come to prayer. Come to salvation. Allah is great. There is no God but Allah." The muezzin would then face, in turn, toward the west, north, and south, and make the same cries. In the modern world, many living muezzin have been replaced by recordings and their calls broadcast via amplifiers and loudspeakers.

See Also: Five Pillars of Faith; mosque

## mufti

An Islamic legal scholar who is called upon to give opinions based on his knowledge of the Qur'an, the Hadith, and Islamic legal traditions. His opinions, known as fatwa, carry considerable weight and are usually issued in response to a particular query on a specific concern from an outside source. In today's world, when most Muslims live under bodies of civil, secular law, most mufti find themselves called to pronounce on personal matters such as marriage or inheritance. At other times they have played far more prominent roles, such as in the case of the Grand Mufti of Constantinople, who was one of the highest officials of the Turkish Ottoman Empire (ca. 1330–1921).

See Also: fatwa; sharia; ulema

## Muhammad
## (570–632)

The Prophet and founder of Islam. Muhammad is revered by over 1 billion Muslims around the world. Most consider him

to be God's final prophet, whose teachings were the culmination of God's message to humankind. His full name is Abu al-Qasim Muhammad ibn 'Abd al-Muttalib ibn Hashim. He is commonly known as the Prophet or the Messenger of God. Most of what is known of his life comes from stories in the Qur'an and Hadith, as well as later Muslim histories.

Muhammad was born in the Arabian city of Mecca in 570. He belonged to the Banu Hashim branch of the Quraysh tribe, one of the prominent tribes in southern Arabia and in Mecca particularly. While still very young he began to have experiences that he later identified as the visitations of angels, which inspired him to ponder religious questions. The Mecca of his day was polytheistic, and the center of religious activity there was a shrine known as the Ka'aba. Tribes of Jews were also important powers in parts of Arabia, and the peninsula had served for centuries as a sanctuary for Jews and for Christians whose views of the faith differed from those of religious authorities to the north and east. Judaism and Christianity were, therefore, known religions to Muhammad. Mecca was also a commercial center, where diverse peoples and goods moved in and out frequently, adding to the ferment of ideas. During Muhammad's early life, its trade had increasingly fallen under the control of a few of the city's wealthiest families, causing grumbling and discontent and threatening tribal unity.

Muhammad's father, 'Abd Allah, died before Muhammad was born. The boy was brought up by his mother and grandfather until their deaths, and then by his uncle, Abu Talib. At the age of twenty-five, and thanks to his success as a merchant, Muhammad married Khadija, a respected, prosperous widow with business interests of her own. Accounts suggest that Khadija was forty years old at the time of the marriage. The couple had six children: two sons who died in childhood and four daughters, one named Fatima.

*Muhammad and Khadija* Despite his growing wealth and entrance into Mecca's established society, Muhammad's questions about religion continued, in particular his confusion over whether there was one god or many gods. He developed the habit of going to Mount Hira, outside the city, to ponder these questions. There, in about 610, he perceived the presence of an entity he latered identified as the angel Jibreel (Gabriel). The angel pronounced Muhammad to be the Messenger of God and urged him three times to recite the words of God that were to enter him. Muhammad at first resisted, but he ultimately found himself compelled to accept the first of the "recitations" that were later to be compiled into the Qur'an, Islam's holy scripture. This first recitation was recorded as sura (verse) 96 of the Qur'an. It reads, "Recite: in the name of your Lord who created, who created Man from a blood clot." Muhammad continued to receive these revelations until his death in 632.

Still unsure that he had been called to be a prophet despite this first encounter with Jibreel, Muhammad questioned his own sanity. Khadija, however, convinced him to remain open to further visitations, to test whether they were true. By 613, if not before, Muhammad himself was convinced. He was now able to answer the most fundamental of his religious questions and, in doing so, he introduced the idea that is central to Islam: There is no God but God. There could not be separate gods for Jews and Christians if there was no God but God. Likewise, the question of Mecca's polytheism was absurd: Believers were worshipping idols rather than God, which could only be wrong. Since there was only one God who was the source of all Creation, all humankind should live in a single community of believers. The remainder of Muhammad's life was a quest to create that single community, as are many aspects of Islamic history since.

Muhammad, with Khadija's support, began preaching this message in 613, attracting a small group of devotees. The established families of Mecca mostly resisted him, however, finding his teachings an insulting challenge to their beliefs and ways of life, and they tried to quiet him using financial and peer pressure. In 619 Khadija died, as did his uncle Abu Talib. This meant that Muhammad, now considered a rebel and a maverick, could no longer rely on the protection of his clan. Unwilling or unable to remain in Mecca, Muhammad began preparations to migrate to the city of Yathrib (later Medina), some 270 miles to the north. He moved there in 622 with a small group of followers and established the first formal Islamic community. This event, known in Islamic history as the hijra, marks the beginning of the Islamic calendar.

*The Prophet's First Community* In Medina, whose name is a variant of Madinat al-Nabi, or "the City of the Prophet," Muhammad formalized his status as Prophet and as the leader of the community of believers. He devised different ways to bring together or attract to his community members of different groups: the migrants from Mecca, converts from Medina, Medinan Jews, and polytheistic Arabs. Through a series of negotiations concluded as the Constitution of Medina, Muhammad not only made beneficial arrangements with surrounding tribes, he also wrested control of the city from the Jewish tribes that had dominated Yathrib and gave himself the power to solve disputes and authoritatively address both religious and administrative concerns. His house, which he constructed for his new wives (although he could have done so, Muhammad did not take additional wives while he was married to Khadija), was the center of the burgeoning community. Meanwhile, he continued to receive revelations from God. These "Medinan suras," which address family, social, and religious issues, were later included in the Qur'an.

Muhammad gave his approval to those members of this community who, as was the common custom in Arabia, wanted to mount raids on Meccan caravans traveling past Medina. These raids ultimately led to Muhammad's first military encounter, the Battle of Badr, in 624. Muhammad's decisive victory there over the forces of his hometown convinced him further of his status as a prophet, and a defeat the next year, at the Battle of Uhud, was a sign to him only of insufficient trust in God, or Allah. The war between Mecca and Medina escalated with the 627 Battle of the Trench, when a vastly larger Meccan force mounted an unsuccessful siege of Medina. Meanwhile, Muhammad expanded his military power and the Islamic community by insisting, once he was strong enough, that any tribe seeking his support must convert to the new faith. He was also the beneficiary of faraway events: When the Sassanid Empire of Iran was defeated by the Christian Byzantine Empire in a series of battles in 627 and 628, many of the Arabian tribes that had formerly relied on the Sassanids turned to Muhammad for protection.

In 630 Muhammad returned to Mecca with a large military force. He captured the city and cleansed its shrines of their pagan idols, including the central Ka'aba shrine. Most Meccans converted to Islam, although the Prophet did not compel them to do so. His political and military power had also helped to establish another important precedent for Islamic states: Jews and Christians living in areas now under Islamic control accepted a subordinate, but free and protected, status. They remained free to practice their own faiths.

Muhammad died in Medina in 632 in the arms of A'isha, one of his wives. He was buried in a tomb near his original Medina mosque, in what was to remain an important pilgrimage site. Disagreements quickly arose over who was to be the Prophet's successor, or caliph, and these disagreements have divided Islam ever since. Abu Bakr, the father of A'isha and a close friend and military supporter of Muhammad, was ultimately chosen as the new leader of Islam. The major conflicting claim came from Ali, Muhammad's cousin and son-in-law, who was married to Fatima, daughter of the Prophet and Khadija. Ali ultimately became the fourth caliph in 656, but by then the Islamic community had split between supporters of Abu Bakr and his successors, later known as Sunni Muslims, and supporters of Ali and his descendants, or Shia (Shiite) Muslims.

*The "Seal of the Prophets"* For Muslims, Muhammad's status is unquestioned. He is considered the "seal of the prophets," the last in a long line of prophets sent by God to remind humankind of God's love and to prepare them for God's final judgment. This line of prophets includes Adam, Abraham, Moses, and Jesus, whom Muslims refer to as Isa. Since Muhammad's revelations are pure, uncorrupted, and complete, most Muslims do not consider it possible for another prophet to appear, although Shia Muslims commonly believe in the future arrival of a millennarian twelfth "imam" known as the mahdi. Although Muhammad was divinely ordained, he remained fully human, not a divine figure in his own right, and he insisted during his lifetime that he was merely a human channel for God's revelation. Later Muslim custom has embellished this somewhat by turning him into the perfect man, the ideal of the Prophet, philosopher, and earthly king. As a reflection of the general Islamic condemnation of the worship of idols, Muslims are forbidden from creating images of him in any form. Not only would such images encourage the inappropriate worship of a human being (only God can be worshipped in Islam), Muhammad cannot be justifiably "reduced" to an image.

Muslims commonly believe in two interrelated stories about Muhammad that both suggest his elevated status and connect him with the city of Jerusalem, although there is no evidence that he ever visited the city during his lifetime. The first, reported generally in Qur'an 17, is of a "night journey" from Mecca to Jerusalem Muhammad took in the company of Jibril, riding a winged creature known as Buraq. There he ascended through the seven levels of heaven, meeting along the way the other, earlier prophets, who confirmed Muhammad's status as the last and greatest of them all. This night journey, according to some mystics, took place just prior to the hijra, although Islamic tradition connects the night journey more closely to the second story, Muhammad's ascent to heaven and his meeting with God. In this story, God told Muhammad to perform the main Islamic prayer fifty times but agreed to reduce it to five after the Prophet argued that fifty daily prayers would be too difficult for most believers. Muslims ever afterward have thus been enjoined to

pray five times a day. Meanwhile Muhammad's ascent to heaven from Jerusalem rather than from Mecca assured that Jerusalem would remain Islam's third holiest city. While most Muslims accept these stories as fact, Sufis are particularly drawn to them, citing them as an example of the possibility of getting close to God and as a metaphor for the journey of the soul.

Sufis also see Muhammad as the exemplar of the visionary and mystic and the founder of all their orders. Meanwhile, for other Muslims, Muhammad's life and deeds are the source of the Hadith, the commentary on the Qur'an, as well as the Sunna, the basic source of Islamic law and customary practice. His life is commemorated by daily recitations of his name, commonly in the form of "Muhammad, peace be upon him" and in the five daily prayers. It is also commemorated during the fasting month of Ramadan, which recalls his divine revelations, as well as at festivals remembering his birth, death, and ascent to heaven.

SEE ALSO: Islam; Mecca; Qur'an

## Muharram

The first month of the Muslim calendar and a special period of commemoration for Shia Muslims. During the first ten days of Muharram, Shia Muslims remember the death of the martyr al-Hussein, the son of the first caliph (according to the Shia) Ali, during the Battle of Karbala in Iraq in 680. Rites include processions of men wearing black and sometimes mortifying, or beating, themselves to the point of drawing blood as a ritual of identification with past martyrs. On the tenth day of Muharram, a play is enacted reminding believers of the deaths of al-Hussein as well as his small son, who also died in the battle. Al-

Hussein's tomb in Karbala, a year-round pilgrimage site, is the focus of special celebrations during Muharram. Sunni Muslims also observe a holiday on the tenth day of Muharram, but as a celebration of the new year and recognition of blessings.

SEE ALSO: Ali; calendars; Shia (Shiite) Islam

## mullah

An honorific title in the Islamic world. Literally implying "lord," mullahs have historically been kings or other rulers, aristocrats, scholars, and religious leaders. This last has been the most common usage of the term in recent years, when men filling various religious posts have been designated as mullahs. These include teachers, prayer leaders in the mosques, or experts in Islamic law. Mullahs often have some training in or continued affiliation with the madrasas, the Islamic institutions of higher learning. In the West they are often identified with extremely conservative or even fundamentalist versions of Islam, although this understanding is not entirely accurate.

SEE ALSO: madrasa; mosque; ulema

# Nation of Islam

A Western sect of Islam founded by African Americans. It is also called the American Muslim Movement and the World Community of al-Islam in the West. Emerging out of various African nationalist movements in America in the early twentieth century, its first important leader was Elijah Muhammad (1897–1975). Elijah Muhammad was converted to Islam by a mysterious figure named Wallace Fard, who had tried to bring together several different Islamic movements in African

*Malcolm X, seen here in 1963, was a spokesman and Muslim minister for the Nation of Islam.* © Bettmann/Corbis

American communities in the early twentieth century and who claimed to be an incarnation of Allah. Fard argued that African Americans could reestablish their dignity by rejecting the dictates and leadership of "white slave masters." His first mosque was established in Detroit in 1930.

Elijah Muhammad founded the Nation of Islam's second mosque in Chicago in 1934. Both Chicago and Detroit were home to large African American populations, most of whom were recent migrants from the South, and he found a ready, if not large, audience. The Nation of Islam grew more popular in the 1950s and 1960s in the context of the modern civil rights movement, with groups forming in African American communities across America. It acheived its greatest fame in the mid-1960s, thanks to the efforts and charisma of Malcolm X (1925–1965). Malcom X, who was born Malcolm Little in Omaha, Nebraska, converted to the Nation of Islam while living in New York City in 1952. He served as the chief official of the main mosque in the Harlem section of New York and, in 1961, started the publication of a newspaper called *Muhammad Speaks*, which was to become the official mouthpiece of the movement. Malcolm X also served as the public spokesperson for the reclusive Elijah Muhammad.

The Nation of Islam's basic agenda under Elijah Muhammad was to urge African Americans to abandon Christianity as a "white" religion that perpetuated the oppression of blacks. Instead they should profess Islam, since Allah had selected people of African descent to be at the forefront of the global Islamic movement and, ultimately, of the leadership of the world. At its most extreme the movement argued that white people were inherently evil. Nation of Islam members also developed a prominent set of social programs as a manifestation of their faith in their moral superiority. The movement was active in trying to save those members of African American communities who suffered from crime, poverty, and drug addiction. Malcolm X, meanwhile, came to advocate African American separatism based on a sense of self-respect and self-reliance. He also advocated, when necessary, the use of violence for his own protection and for that of devout followers. For these reasons Malcolm X, and the Nation of Islam as a whole, remained at odds with those branches of the civil rights movement that advocated integration and nonviolence.

Various internal conflicts in the movement led to Malcolm's split from the Nation of Islam and the creation of his own branch of the faith. In 1964 he made the hajj pilgrimage to Mecca and declared his allegiance to Sunni Islam, a turn that softened his views somewhat toward separatism and the inherent evil of white people. He was assassinated in 1965 at a New York nightclub by members of an opposing group of Black Muslims. His experiences provided the inspiration for Alex Haley's 1965 book *The Autobiography of Malcolm X* and Spike Lee's 1992 film *Malcolm X*, cementing his place in American popular culture. Meanwhile, the Nation of Islam largely remained aloof from other black militancy movements of the late 1960s and early 1970s.

After Elijah Muhammad's death in 1975 the leadership of the Nation of Islam fell to his son, Walith Deen Muhammad. Under him, the movement changed its name officially to the American Muslim Mission and began to move toward incorporating itself into global Islam, denouncing any sense of race hierarchy or awareness as well as Fard's claim to divinity Muhammad dissolved the American Muslim Mission in 1985, although its mosques and other institutional elements remained in place performing various educational and social tasks. In recent years the Nation of Islam has been mostly associated, somewhat inaccurately, with the breakaway sect established in 1978 by Louis Farrakhan (1933–), a former associate of Malcolm X. Farrakhan continues to refer to his movement as the Nation of Islam and largely urges continued separation for African Americans; he is outspoken on various issues ranging from African American involvement in politics to drug abuse, and has been criticized for holding anti-Semitic attitudes. Farrakhan's Nation of Islam still publishes *Muhammad Speaks*, still urges clean living among its followers, and still appeals to African Americans. Islamic authorities elsewhere regard it as an illegitimate branch of the faith.

SEE ALSO: Afro-Caribbean religions; hajj; Islam

# Native American religions, North America

The Native American peoples of North America were and are extremely diverse in their ways of life and religious practices. Whether they were sedentary, practicing settled agriculture in some form, or nomadic had nearly as much to do with ritual and belief as with a tribe's geographical and natural resource constraints. Yet certain commonalities can be discerned across the continent, evolving from the earliest dispersal of indigenous North American peoples fifteen millennia ago. These experiences included migration and the hunt; prehistoric religions were animistic and included shamans who communicated with spirits and read omens and portents. Many traditions also professed belief in a supreme being or Great Spirit. Native American religions have tended to be very localized and place-oriented, require active daily participation, and involve communal ceremonies and shared benefits. Many feature rituals centered on stages of life, such as male initiation or death, or events such as the harvest or the hunt. Finally, Native American religions also have strong oral traditions of storytelling and teaching. At the heart of many of these is the theme of constant interaction between the human and the divine. Many Native American religious traditions have survived the arrival of European settlement and Christian conversion, and some tribal religious traditions have even enjoyed a revival in recent decades.

*Early Spiritual Centers Along the Mississippi and Ohio Rivers* Among the earliest and greatest religious monuments in North America are the ceremonial mounds built by the peoples who inhabited the Mississippi and Ohio River valleys. These mounds, built mostly of earth, served a variety of purposes. Some were secular, serving as the foundations for buildings, but many were religious. Mounds were used as burial sites and as platforms for large-scale rituals. The most well known, and probably the largest, of these mound-building societies was Cahokia, centered near the Mississippi in Illinois and thriving from about 950 to 1200. The Cahokia built dozens of mounds, with the largest, the so-called Monks Mound, more than

100 feet (30.5m) high and 1,000 feet (305m) long. A different group likely built the Great Serpent Mound in northern Ohio around A.D. 1000. Perhaps either a monument to a Serpent cult or a symbol of fertility or creation (since the serpent holds an egg in its mouth), the Great Serpent Mound uncoils over 1,300 feet (365m).

Some Native American religious traditions are reasonably well known because of written records compiled since the time of European arrival in the 1600s and because of their survival into the modern day. Among the most highly developed religions was that of the Iroquois Confederation. This was a confederation of five separate nations: the Seneca, Cayuga, Onandaga, Oneida, and Mohawk. By the 1700s the Iroquois controlled much of New York State and parts of neighboring Canada and the Ohio Valley. According to the Iroquois Creation myth, they descended from the Sky People who lived above the earth by means of a single pregnant woman, and women's status remained high in Iroquois villages. The Iroquois were basically monotheistic, professing faith in a Great Spirit responsible for the creation and maintenance of the earth and its people. The Great Spirit manifested itself through a group of lesser spirits often associated with a natural force such as the rain or a social phenomenon such as war. The Iroquois also believed in an evil spirit, the brother of the Great Spirit, who maintained his own group of lesser spirits. It was the responsibility of human beings to choose which group to listen to or follow; the wrong choice might result in punishment after death. Iroquois rituals were often seasonal, and they were presided over by elders rather than a distinct priestly caste. They consisted of feasts, dancing, singing and the giving of offerings to the proper spirits.

*Spirits of the Plains* West of the Mississippi, in the prairies and plains of Minnesota and the Dakotas, lived the Lakota people, also known as the Sioux. By the 1800s the Lakota were a large population with many tribal groups, but they remained seminomadic since at the heart of their economic life, and at the heart of their religious belief, was the hunting of the buffalo. The Lakota did not believe in any real separation between the earthly and divine realms, although human beings could not fully understand this unity outside of rituals. They believed also in a kind of force that animated all earthly things, filling them with "spirit." This force was known as Wakan Tanaka, and like the Iroquois Great Spirit, Wakan Tanaka employed lesser spirits to interact with human beings, with one of the most important being White Buffalo Woman. A special class of holy men, or medicine men as white Americans often called them, acted as guides, connecting human beings with these lesser spirits.

Important Lakota rituals involved both the perception of the unity of the universe and appeasement of the spirits in order to ensure successful buffalo hunts. Among the most common of these rites was the uses of the sweat lodge, a practice of many groups beyond the Lakota as well. Sweat lodges were usually temporary buildings filled with heated stones. There, under the supervision of an elder or leader who would pour water over the stones, devotees would pray, sing, and sometimes smoke a sacred pipe. The purposes of the ritual included purification as well as preparation for contact with spirits, including buffalo spirits. Another important ritual was the Sun Dance. In this annual ceremony performed before assemblies of tribal groups, certain individuals would come forward to perform the dance. These volunteers would build a special lodge, use a sacred pipe, and then perform the dance itself, which consisted of dancing while gazing into the sun and entering a trance and experiencing inner visions. The dance might last for several days. Sometimes, dancers who had pledged to do so put spikes through their chests that symbolically attached them to the sacred Sun Lodges. Performance of the Sun Dance not only gave the individual great spiritual power but helped to purify the entire tribe.

*The Sweat Lodge and the Vision Quest* Also common among the Lakota but practiced elsewhere as well was a set of rites known as the vision quest. Those embarking on the quest were usually young men, and the experience was both a rite of passage and a search for a personal guardian spirit. The vision quest started with the appearance of an omen, at which point the candidate, under the supervision of an elder, would purify himself through fasting, the sweat lodge, and other means. He would then go off on his own to an isolated place to pray for a spiritual vision. During this, and in order to prove his worth, he might also eat little or nothing, wound himself, or even perform more drastic forms of self-mortification. At length, a spirit might appear to him, often in the form of an animal. This spirit might give him special spiritual powers or grant him a so-called medicine bundle containing eagle feathers, bones, special herbs, or other objects as a symbol of the success of his quest. For the remainder of his life that guardian spirit would remain with the young man who set out on the quest.

Often associated with the Lakota, but actually originating among the Paiute peoples of northern Nevada, was a ritual known as the ghost dance. The ghost dance was a direct reaction to the arrival of large numbers of whites in the American West. The hope of its practitioners was that the dance would bring back the "ghosts" of dead ancestors, white Americans would be removed, and traditional lands and ways of life would be restored. The ritual lasted four or five days, during which dancers would sing songs and enter trances in which they had visions of the dead. During these visions dancers would receive solace and guidance that might help them in these troubled times. As the ghost dance tradition spread to other tribes such as the Arapahoe, the Cheyenne, and eventually the Lakota, it took on an even more millennialist tone, promising "ghost shirts" that would protect warriors from white men's bullets. To white settlers, meanwhile, it appeared to represent a militant threat, and the ghost dance was one of the reasons for the massacre of Lakota rebels at Wounded Knee, South Dakota, in 1890.

The Apache, another large tribal confederation, ranged throughout the American Southwest by the 1500s. Their religious beliefs were less fully articulated than those of the Iroquois or the Lakota because of the harshness of their environment and the challenges of survival. The Apache believed, however, in a central supernatural power that manifested itself everywhere in the form of lesser "supernaturals" or spirits. Individuals generally sought contact with their personal supernaturals through visionary experiences such as the sweat lodge. Through the proper rites, whether performed individually or with shamans or priests, people could manipulate the spirits for either good or evil. Larger ceremonies, known as "dances," commemorated rites of passage such as puberty or the invocation of natural forces such as rainfall or a good harvest. One of the most important of these, because it was thought to ensure the survival of the tribe, was the puberty ceremony for young girls, generally celebrated after her first menstruation. For related purposes curing rituals were also common. Those who conducted them were special shamans known as medicine men or women who were thought to have special spiritual powers.

*Totems and Trickster Heroes* Other distinct or common religious practices among Native American peoples include belief in a celestial spirit known as the thunderbird, believed to be in constant struggle with evil earthly spirits. The thunderbird appears frequently on the totem poles of the tribes of the Pacific Northwest as well as in the lore and ritual of tribes in the Northeast. The totem poles themselves were sacred ritual objects delineating a tribal or family connection with an animal spirit. Many tribal groups also featured stories and moral lessons connected with figures known generally as tricksters. These tricksters might be heroes, responsible for bringing a particular conflict to a good end or transmitting survival skills. They might also be lazy, stupid, or deceitful. Often they are considered to be divine and eternal in nature, messengers between the gods and humanity. Native American traditions frequently depicted them in animal form, such as the Coyote of the Southwest, the Raven or Blue Jay of the Northwest, or the Rabbit of the Southeast. Tricksters might also take human form, such as the Wisekedjak, or "Whiskey Jack" of the Ohio Valley and upper New York peoples.

The Native American Church, a modern variation, synthesizes Native American practices with Christianity and consciously seeks links among tribes. Organized formally in 1918 but featuring much older, traditional practices, the Native American Church is also known as the peyote religion. Today it numbers over 100,000 members from more than fifty tribes. Its central ritual is the use of a hallucinogenic substance, derived from the peyote plant, during organized, Saturday night meetings in a special spirit house. Peyote had been used by different Native American groups for thousands of years, but it only began to be employed in these distinct ceremonies among the Kiowa and Comanche tribes of Oklahoma in the late 1800s. Native Americans seeking unity among tribes as well as cultural integrity in the face of the loss of their traditional ways of life and their lands turned to religion in increasing numbers, inspiring the foundation of the formal Native American Church. Followers of the peyote rituals believe in a Great Spirit as well as messenger spirits such as the Thunderbird. Many of them also see visions of the peyote spirit, whom some term Jesus Christ, or at least Jesus as revealed to Native Americans. By following the so-called Peyote Road, members of the church hope to attain peace, maintain contact with spirits and with dead ancestors, and avoid alcoholism and other social problems. The Saturday peyote rites are followed by a communal breakfast on Sunday morning.

SEE ALSO: divination; pre-Columbian Mesoamerica, religions of; shamanism

## neo-Confucianism

A revival and reorientation of Confucian thought that took place during China's Song and Yuan dynasties (960–1279). Partly an adjustment of traditional Confucianism to Buddhist and Daoist influences, neo-Confucianism strengthened Confucianism's hold on China's elites and its place at the center of Chinese culture.

The key philosopher of neo-Confucianism was Zhu Xi (1130–1200). Like many Chinese thinkers, Zhu Xi based his work in tradition, writing commentaries on earlier texts, which described his main ideas and urging respect for both history and for classical authorities such as Confucius and Mencius. To the Confucian emphasis on logic and order he added the notion that the world is composed of two forces, *li* and *qi*. *Li* uses a different Chinese character here than the traditional *li*, or ritual, so therefore its meaning is different although pronunciation is the same. For Zhu Xi, *li* is the natural law or set of principles that make up and guide all things. It is fundamentally unchangeable. *Qi*, on the other hand, is the energy that flows through things, and its flow and makeup can be altered. While *li* is perfect, *qi* is not. Through education and respect for tradition, human beings can improve their *qi* and bring it more in alignment with *li*. Zhu Xi called further for a greater "investigation of things," by which he meant close study of the moral and ethical lessons provided by the Confucian classics. Those who improve their *qi* in this way demonstrate that they are qualified to govern. One practical effect of this new emphasis was a refinement and extension of the exams given to those who hoped to become Confucian scholar-officials. Other attempts to master *qi* involved the efforts of Song dynasty alchemists to discover a potion or some other substance that would provide immortality. The notion, meanwhile, that refinement of one's *qi* brings one into closer alignment with *li* is somewhat comparable to Daoism's urging that people seek to align themselves with "the way" of the universe.

A second school of neo-Confucian thought is represented by Liu Jiuyuan (1139–1193). Liu argued that only *li* exists, but that it is the same as mind. In order to understand *li*, one should try to investigate the mind through such means as meditation. Liu's neo-Confucianism, therefore, was more inwardly directed than Zhu Xi's. Liu is proverbially credited with the statement, "The classics are all footnotes to me."

SEE ALSO: Confucian scholar-officials; *li*; *qi*

## neo-paganism

A broad movement whose adherents seek to revive elements of pre-Christian European religions. Many believers have strong environmental and ecological concerns and spiritual connections to the natural world, decrying for example the continued destruction of natural phenomena such as forests and human beings' increased distance from the natural world in an urban, mechanized age. They seek to revive this connection with nature, often by reconstructing in modern forms ancient pagan celebrations and rituals. A common and familiar site for some of these events is the Stonehenge monument in southern England.

Neo-paganism is primarily a product of the 1960s, although its roots can be traced to the romantic and folkloric movements of the 1800s. Among the larger neo-pagan groups are those which revere mother or earth goddesses as aspects of the divinity of nature. These include the Church of All Worlds in the United States and Great Britain, whose followers worship a goddess named Feraferia, and the Pagan Way. Other large neo-pagan groups actively re-create the rites and even behaviors of pre-Christian religions. Among

them are the various Druid groups in the United States and Great Britain that admire the Celtic cultures of early northwestern Europe, and the Viking Brotherhood in Scandinavia, which emphasizes Nordic-German roots.

SEE ALSO: paganism; new religious movements, Western; pre-Christian Europe, religions of

## new religious movements, Japanese

A relatively recent religious phenomenon has been the rise of numerous religious movements—estimates range in the tens of thousands—in Japan, traditionally a center of religious syncretism. Some of these new religions are based in Shinto, some in Buddhism, and some on their own distinct combinations of religious ideas and practices both old and new. Most Japanese new religions are obscure, but adherents of a few number in the millions, such as Soka Gakkai or Tenrikyo.

Believers are drawn to the new religions for many reasons. Sects that emerged in the nineteenth century, such as Tenrikyo, provided personal spiritual satisfaction in a time of great social, political, and economic change. Many new religions that arose after World War II, such as Shinnyoen, attracted adherents who sought a new approach to spiritual life that could address the trauma of the war, the culture clash of American occupation, and Japan's rapid modernization, all of which threatened traditional ways of life. In both cases, established Buddhist or Shinto sects, associated as they often were with distant or discredited authorities, were no longer satisfactory. Membership in the new religions requires conscious choice, rather than simply adapting to existing customs. Few of the new religions have established institu-

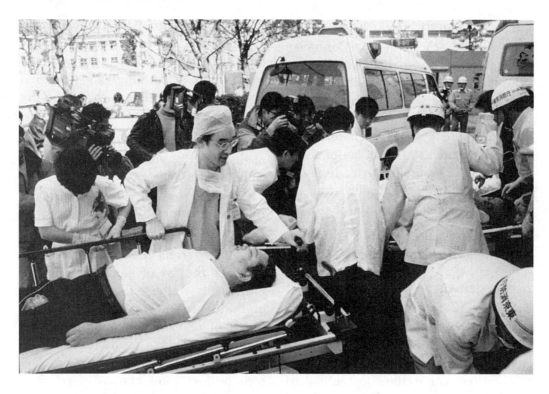

*Victims of the Tokyo subway system sarin gas attack are attended to by medics, March 20, 1995. Some members of the Japanese religion of Aum Shinrikyo were held responsible for the attack.* AP IMAGES

tional structures or clergy; members instead meet in small groups, often in homes. There, they share ideas and problems and establish and reinforce a sense of identity and community.

Tenrikyo is perhaps the oldest of these new religions, founded in the mid-1800s by a peasant named Nakayama Miki who claimed to have been possessed by a god. Through this possession, she was able to perform miracles and divination, and she attracted many followers. Her descendants have continued to play leading roles in the faith, which some consider a loosely Shinto sect. The goal of Tenrikyo belief is simple: a happy and healthy life. The sect claims some 2.5 million members today and maintains two hundred missionary centers worldwide. Another older new religion is

Konkokyo, the Religion of the Golden Light, founded in 1859. Believers focus on individual salvation using mediators between themselves and the gods, and they advocate social welfare work as a means to both express generosity and increase personal happiness.

The Sekai Kyuseikyo sect, or Religion for World Salvation, was founded by Okada Mokichi (1882–1955), who claimed to be a messiah and started a religion based on the worship of the Buddhist bodhisattva Avalokitesvara. Conflicts with Buddhist authorities, however, inspired him to break away and establish a separate religion. At the center of the faith are healing rituals using concentrations of divine light and the intent to live in harmony with nature. Believers think that heaven is possible on earth. Sekai Kyuseikyo achieved its greatest popularity in the years after World War II. Another very successful new religion that is closely related to Buddhism is Soka Gakkai, which has thousands of adherents around the world.

*Millennialism and the Golf Religion* Japanese new religions are still proliferating. Kofuku-no-kagaku, for example, was founded in 1986 and has gained thousands of members. It is also known as the Institute for the Research of Human Happiness. Devotees profess belief in an eternal Buddha, who has incarnated himself in forms ranging from Siddhartha Gautama in India to the Greek god Hermes. They are also urged to perform good deeds and to organize their lives around the "four principles of happiness": love, knowledge, reflection, and development. Like many of the new religions, Kofuku-no-kagaku has a millennialist element, predicting global wars and other disasters, the intervention of both gods and terrestrial beings, and other drastic changes. Another millennialist new religion, Aum Shinrikyo (Supreme Truth), made headlines worldwide when it was connected with poison gas attacks in the Tokyo subway system in 1995 that killed twelve people and injured five thousand. Aum Shinrikyo is based on a combination of Buddhist and Hindu beliefs, with a particular focus on the destructionist aspect of the Hindu god Shiva. Founded in the 1980s, its believers thought that the world would soon come to an end in a series of cataclysms, making way for a new cosmic cycle. Its founder, Shoko Asahara, believed that this process would begin in 1997. Despite stories of the use of drugs, sleep deprivation, and other questionable methods to keep recruits and new members in line, the sect grew widely. It was one of the few new religions to have a widespread following outside of Japan, with offices in Russia, Germany, and the United States. Asahara and others were imprisoned following the poison gas attacks and many of Aum Shinrikyo's groups disbanded. It continues to exist at a very small level.

Most of the Japanese new religions, and certainly the most popular ones, avoid the intellectual or societal excesses of the millennial cults. The Perfect Liberty Kyodan (PL Kyodan), which claims to have well over a million members worldwide, emphasizes instead personal happiness and self-expression. Descended from an earlier religion known as Hito-no-michi, PL Kyodan maintains a series of so-called patriarchs who, believers hold, can take on the troubles of members through a process of divine transference and with proper prayers. Believers are also urged to seek converts, mostly among overseas Japanese. PL Kyodan maintains a wide range of facilities at its base near the city of Osaka, including a hospital, a huge temple, and a 550-foot-tall (168m) Peace Tower. There are also several baseball diamonds at the complex, and because PL Kyodan maintains a large golf course there and features several churches with rooftop driving ranges, some Japanese people refer to it as the "golf religion."

SEE ALSO: new religious movements, Western; Shinto; Soka Gakkai

# new religious movements, Western

Recent decades have seen the emergence of numerous new religious movements in the Western world, and they have attracted many people who express dissatisfaction with, on the one hand, modern secularism and materialism and, on the other, established religious traditions such as Christianity or Judaism. They are an echo of

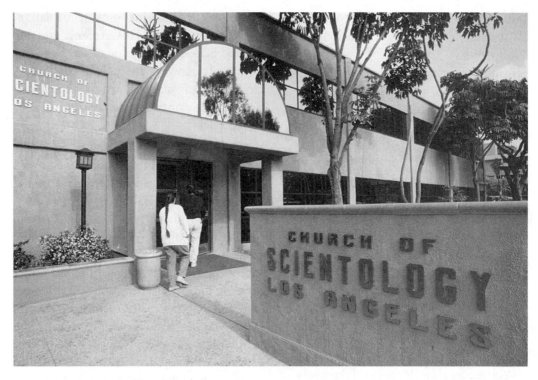

*A form of psychotherapy called dianetics is the main pillar of Scientology.* GETTY IMAGES

the new religious movements that have emerged around the world over the last century that number in the thousands and claim millions of adherents. The Western movement has ties to some of these: Soka Gakkai and other Japanese new religions, the Hare Krishna movement, theosophy. Indeed, many of the Western new religions maintain an emphasis on globalism rather than on standing national or cultural boundaries. A few, such as neopaganism, look back to earlier ages.

The new religious movements have some common characteristics. They tend to promise full self-realization for individual believers, and are largely egalitarian in practice. They often claim that each person carries a spark of the divine within him or herself. Practitioners are skilled in using modern technology, and such techniques as sales and public relations, to gain

converts and support. Many are also millennialist, preaching that the end of the "current era" is near and that believers must prepare for that event.

*Millennialism and Science Fiction* Among the largest new religious movements is the Unification Church, whose full name is the Holy Spirit Association for the Unification of World Christianity, founded by the South Korean Sun Myung Moon (b. 1920) in 1954. Moon claimed to have had, as a young man, visions of Jesus Christ, the Buddha, Moses, and other historical religious leaders, from whom he received a series of revelations. According to the church's doctrine, divine rule must be restored through the power of faithful marriages intended for procreation. Humanity's fall, what Christians refer to as original sin, was the result of the biblical Eve having had a spiritual relationship with the devil prior to her sexual union with Adam. Jesus might have restored holy marriage, but was prevented from doing so by his crucifixion. The Unification Church often stages mass weddings by which followers are freed from their fallen natures. The greatest symbols of these principles are the so-called Lord and Lady of the Second Advent, who some devotees claim are Moon and his wife, Hak Ja Han, and this restoration is thought to be nearly complete. The Unification Church is active worldwide, and claims membership in the hundreds of thousands. It is also highly active in missionary work, education, business interest such as newspaper publishing, and the building of political influence.

Scientology is another major new religious movement largely viewed with skepticism by outsiders. The Church of Scientology was founded in the 1950s by a science fiction writer named L. Ron Hubbard (1911–1986). Hubbard developed a form of psychotherapy that he called dianetics, which promised to liberate people from the bad effects of earlier experiences which had been implanted in the brain. Methods involved included long sessions with an "auditor" who guided the subject through various levels of memory. Those who successfully completed this procedure were considered to be fully "clear." As dianetics evolved into the Church of Scientology, Hubbard devised a system in which those who were "clear" were spiritually beyond most people. He believed that human beings were originally divine extraterrestrial entities known as thetans. While most people's divine nature lay trapped by ordinary existence, thetans had rediscovered their divinity, and were therefore clear thinking, confident, and morally righteous. Although it is concentrated in the United States, the Church of Scientology claims to

be active in 156 countries with millions of members, including some well-known entertainers and actors whose celebrity focuses attention on the church.

*Western Variations on Eastern Faiths* Some new religious movements in the West are derived from Buddhism and, especially, Hinduism. The Hare Krishna Society is perhaps the best known of these sects. Another, the Self-Realization Fellowship, was founded by an Indian teacher and immigrant to the United States, Paramahansa Yogananda (1893–1952), who had earlier been a member of the Theosophic Society. Yogananda argued that the practice of yoga enabled one to control the life energy that flowed both within and without. He also claimed that Jesus, Paul, and other religious teachers had both practiced yoga and understood this process. He founded the Self-Realization Fellowship in 1935, and it maintains important centers in Los Angeles and Encinitas, California, and in a few places elsewhere in the world. Members practice both spiritual development and charitable works, and hope to use their spiritual realizations to spread peace. Another Indian teacher, Bhagwan Shri Rajneesh (1931–1990), founded the Rajneesh International Foundation, which established a major ashram in Oregon in 1981. Rajneeshi teachings focused on a vulgarized understanding of Hindu Tantricism, arguing that members should seek self-expression, and therefore the unburdening of the soul, through "dynamic meditation." This included such features as yelling, dancing, and, sometimes, public sexual activity. Bhagwan was deported from the United States in 1985 for immigration fraud, and although his teachings dropped from the public eye, his movement continues to maintain a large ashram outside the Indian city of Pune.

In the late 1960s the teacher known as Maharishi Mahesh Yogi (b. 1911) achieved wide public attention because of the visits of the Beatles, the actress Mia Farrow, and other famous people ostensibly seeking spiritual wisdom to his ashram near Rishikesh, India. The Maharishi developed a movement known as the Spiritual Regeneration Movement, which focused on what he termed transcendental meditation (TM). This involved simplified methods of deep meditation that allowed the user to go beyond thought to a deeper level of consciousness. Having reached it, the user could then live a more relaxed, joyful, and creative life. TM, as a set of techniques and goals, grew extremely popular and in the 1970s and 1980s became a phenomenon of American and European popular culture. Many of those who undertook TM, or its variations, were also involved in the so-called New Age movement, which continues to thrive. The New Age movement at its core is optimistically millennialist, presuming that humanity is either at the beginning of or has already entered a "new age" of global awareness, egalitarianism, kindness, and generosity. Some believers, using astrological readings, call this new era the Age of Aquarius. New Age techniques are highly eclectic; believers use crystals, incense and other kinds of aromatherapies, and other aids to produce spiritual transformations, while others hope to add meaning and perspective by "channeling" past lives. New Agers reject the Jewish or Christian emphasis on sin, preferring instead an optimistic view of human character and possibilities.

Although the New Age movement and many of the Hindu-related schools are thought to be relatively harmless, some aspects of the new religious movements are considered by some to be dangerous and their believers are viewed as manipulated if not brainwashed members of cults. Indeed a few of the smaller movements, such as the millennialist Heaven's Gate, have promoted and even enacted mass suicides. Members of the Unification Church, for instance, are often called "moonies" as a reflection of their unquestioning obedience and devotion to the founder Moon. The church itself, meanwhile, has been criticized for some of its recruitment methods, which might include dietary deprivation. Scientology has been likewise criticized as a cult, with its recruits also subjected to manipulation and intimidation. Even followers of the Bhagwan Shri Rajneesh appeared to be members of a cult, all dressed in shades of orange with images of their leader around their necks. Fears about cult practices have given rise to various cult-watching groups ready to use such methods as "deprogramming" and "exit counseling" to get people to leave these movements.

SEE ALSO: cults; neo-paganism; new religions, Japanese

## New Testament

One of the two main parts of the Bible, the holy scripture of Christianity. Christians commonly believe the New Testament to be the word of God, although many differences exist as to how literally its messages should be interpreted. The text provides the fulfillment of the prophecies of the first part of the Bible, the Old Testament, also recognized as the Hebrew Bible in Judaism, which foresaw the coming of a messiah and describes the establishment of a new covenant between God and believers. This new covenant is characterized by the life, death, and resurrection of Jesus of Nazareth.

The New Testament consists of twenty-seven books. The first four are the Gospels attributed to Matthew, Mark, Luke, and John. These tell the story of the life and teachings of Jesus of Nazareth and contain many statements and teachings credited to Jesus. Next is the Acts of the Apostles, which provides a history of the first years of the Christian Church. Most of the remainder of the books are Epistles, letters written to early Christian communities or to early church leaders. Thirteen of the Epistles were written by Paul and another, the Epistle to the Hebrews, is attributed to him. Paul's Epistles are likely the books of the New Testament that were composed first chronologically. The Gospels were written later, between about A.D. 50 and 90. The final book of the New Testamant canon is Revelation, which suggests various forms of God's intervention in the world and is the source of most Christian eschatology. The books were originally written in Greek, the predominant language of the eastern portion of the Roman Empire.

The New Testament differs fundamentally from the Old Testament in that it is not designed to tell a historical story or delineate a tradition. Instead, the New Testament was composed and then compiled to provide witness to what Christians see as God's loving and forgiving actions and to both demonstrate and encourage faith. Neither the Christian Bible nor the New Testament in particular are themselves objects of veneration in the way the scrolls of the Jewish Torah or the Islamic Qur'an are venerated.

The authoritative collection of twenty-seven books that make up the New Testament emerged over a long period of time. The precise origins of some of its texts, especially the Gospels, is a matter of some dispute among biblical scholars. Jesus him-self did not write down his teachings. Scholars assume that, instead, his followers made note of them and also of their historical context and setting. These notes then formed a collection of sources that scholars refer to as "Q" (from the German word *Quelle*, or "source"). "Q" then became the main source of material used by the writers of the Gospels. The term "new testament" was first used by the early Christian thinker Tertullian in A.D. 160 to refer to a group of writings about Jesus and his teachings. Over the next centuries various church councils considered different versions of the collection. By the fifth century the canon in its modern form was accepted as authoritative by most Christians. Along the way, early church officials and theologians had considered and rejected several other Gospels as well as numerous "apocrypha": books that were thought to be important to spiritual development or the emergence of the church but could not be considered the products of divine revelation, the word of God.

SEE ALSO: Gospels; Hebrew Bible; Jesus of Nazareth

## Nicene Creed

A Christian statement of faith often used in religious services as part of the Eucharist. The Nicene Creed, which likely reached its final form at the Council of Constantinople in 381 rather than the 325 Council of Nicaea, is the only major statement of faith accepted, with minor variations, by all major branches of Christianity: Roman Catholicism, Eastern Orthodoxy, and Protestantism. The creed pronounces faith in the Trinity and concisely elucidates other basic Christian beliefs. The phrase "catholic and apostolic Church" uses the word *catholic* in the sense of "universal," not in reference to Catholicism as a formal institution. An English version of the Nicene Creed runs in part:

> We believe in one God,
> the father, the Almighty,
> maker of heaven and earth,
> of all that is seen and unseen.
> We believe in one Lord, Jesus Christ,
> the only son of God,
> eternally begotten of the Father,
> God from God, Light from Light
> true God from true God,
> begotten, not made, one in Being with
> the Father....
> We believe in the Holy Spirit, the
> Lord, the giver of life,
> who proceeds from the Father and the
> Son.
> With the Father and the Son he is
> worshipped and glorified.
> He has spoken through the Prophets.
> We _elieve in one holy catholic and
> apostolic Church.
> We acknowledge one baptism for the
> forgiveness of sins
> We look for the resurrection of the
> dead, and the life of the world to
> come.
> Amen.

# Nihon-Shoki

An important Shinto text. Written in Chinese in the early eighth century on the order of the Japanese imperial court, the Nihon-Shoki, or Chronicles of Japan, contains two sections. The first is a selection of myths and legends, many connecting Shinto deities such as the Sun Goddess Amaterasu with noble families as well as describing other elements of Shinto belief. The second is a genealogy of Japan's important clans from the fifth through seventh centuries. Among the important events that the text records is the introduction of Buddhism in Japan and its appeal to the ruling clans, who associated it with the more advanced culture of China.

SEE ALSO: Amaterasu; Kojiki; Shinto

# nirvana

The state of being that is the goal of all Buddhists. It means literally "extinction" or "blowing out" (as with a candle) but might better be translated from the Sanskrit as the "great peace." For Buddhists nirvana is the condition of being beyond all attachment, individuality, and ignorance about the true nature of life and the universe. To reach nirvana is often likened to achieving enlightenment, although the various Buddhist schools acknowledge differing degrees and kinds of enlightenment, not all of which reach nirvana. Indeed, there are degrees of nirvana as well. The state can be reached during one's physical lifetime, but one who has achieved that state in life only enters "complete" nirvana, or parinirvana, at death.

The term is used by Hindus as well, who generally associate nirvana with not only the end of worldly desires and attachments but also the union of the individual soul with the absolute. In this sense it is synonymous with moksha. To emphasize the difference Buddhists often use the term "nibbana," which is the equivalent of nirvana in Pali, an ancient Indian language in which many early Buddhist texts were written.

SEE ALSO: Buddha; moksha; Siddhartha Gautama

## Oceania, religions of

Oceania is the collective geographical name for the many islands of the Pacific Ocean, home to a diverse group of peoples, the descendants of waves of migrants moving eastward from Asia over the past three thousand years. Although the peoples of the region share many characteristics, mainly those having to do with migration, language, or trade, Oceania is conventionally divided into three culturally and ethnically distinct subregions. Melanesia is farthest west and south and consists of islands or island groups including the Solomons, Vanuatu, Fiji, and New Guinea. Micronesia lies farther north and east and comprises many small and isolated island groups such as the Marshalls and the Marianas as well as Guam, a U.S. possession. Polynesia is the largest of the regions, and among its island groups are Samoa, Tonga, Tahiti, the Marquesas, and the Hawaiian Islands. Greater Polynesia also includes the Maori people of New Zealand. Although these vast regions follow many distinct religions, most are polytheistic, and two characteristics common to many of them have become familiar outside the region. One of these is mana, a word connoting spiritual power and force. The other is taboo, referring to rules of behavior that must be maintained in order for the mana to flow in the most auspicious ways.

*Singsings and Cargo Cults* Melanesian religions tend to focus on nature worship and on reverence for the spirits of dead ances-

tors. Nature spirits, who are believed to inhabit trees, animals, or other natural elements, are thought to be the force that regulates the flow of mana across the lands, while ancestor spirits maintain peace of mind and community life. Through dreams and more formal ceremonies involving spirit mediums, individuals can come into contact with these spirits. Less apparent in regular worship, but also important, are the Melanesian gods. The gods are credited with creation and with giving tribal groups the means necessary to survive. Important rites in Melanesia include those associated with male initiation, birth, and marriage. Other rites are intended to ensure peace and tranquility between the spirit world and the world of the living. Villages commonly contain spirit houses where these rites take place, and ceremonies themselves can be very complex, involving dancing, retelling of histories and myths, and the exchange of goods. Since music is an important part of these ceremonies, Melanesian peoples often refer to them as "singsings." During these rites, the spirits are held to be present within objects such as drums and masks. In daily life, meanwhile, some animals, fish, and plants are considered to be totems with religious significance for specific clans or tribal groups.

Since 1800, with the arrival of Europeans in Melanesia, a new form of religion has arisen: the so-called cargo cults. These are vaguely millennial in nature, hoping for a future point at which Melanesians will be rejoined by their ancestors and enjoy full social and material equality with the richer outsiders. The symbol of these cargo cults, and the sign of the hoped-for fulfillment, will be the arrival of cargoes of goods brought by plane or ship and thought to be sent by the gods and spirits. Examples include the Vailala movement in Papua New Guinea and the Jon Frum movement in the outer islands of the Vanuatu archipelago. Although the cargo cults develop new rituals, and believers sometimes go so far as to build docks or airstrips, they still reflect the Melanesian emphasis on tribal ancestors. It has also been common for them to be incorporated into revivalist or missionary Christian churches in the area.

The population of Micronesia is much smaller than in the other two regions, and the majority of its population has converted to Christianity. Prior to the arrival of Christianity, Micronesians appear to have believed in a canon of high gods to whom annual devotions of fruits were given, as well as a panoply of spirits who were active in daily life. Many of these spirits were benign, such as the ones who guaranteed a sufficient supply of food or who guided the hands of boat builders. Others were malevolent, and needed to be avoided whenever possible. Micronesians also believed it was possible to commune with the spirits of dead ancestors or rulers, and a priestly caste emerged to handle the different ceremonies linked to these groups of gods and spirits.

The Polynesian islands were settled far later than Melanesia and Micronesia, with the major migrations to Hawaii beginning only thirteen hundred years ago. Nevertheless, the bigger islands of the region tended to support much larger populations as well as highly developed religious traditions with many common features.

Polynesians believe that the world was created by a mysterious force sometimes personified as a god named Tangaroa or Io (the names of gods have close variations across Polynesia). Tangaroa is surrounded by other high gods such as Rangi, the god of the sky, and Papa, the goddess of the earth. Their son, known as Tane, was the source of the first human being. Lono, the god of the harvest, and Tu, the god of war, are also high gods in the Polynesian tradition. Rites to them are officiated over by high priests known in Hawaii as kahunas (and elsewhere as tohungas) and are considered events charged with great spiritual significance. In addition to the high gods, Polynesians also worship lesser gods often associated with either natural forces or animals or as priests or tribal leaders who have been deified. Hawaiian examples of these include Pele, the goddess of the volcano, and Hi'iaka, the goddess of water. Polynesian religious lore, meanwhile, includes the stories of so-called culture heroes or demigods. These were human beings granted special powers by the gods but who also might lose their favor. One of these culture heroes was Maui, who supposedly created the Hawaiian Islands by fishing them from the sea by mistake. Maui died in the process of trying to assure immortality for ordinary people.

*Mana and Taboo in Polynesia* Prior to the arrival of Europeans in the 1700s and 1800s, everyday life in Polynesia was charged with religious significance from birth until death. For events such as the harvest or fishing expeditions, the gods were given offerings and chants were recited. Important rites of passage included male circumcision and the arrival of the age of sexual maturity, with the latter being an event sometimes celebrated publicly. Unusual events such as the construction of a new village, the arrival of an heir to the chief's throne, or the naming of a new high priest were marked by elaborate ceremonies, which sometimes involved the sacrifice of animals and, sometimes, humans of the slave class. The funeral of a high-ranking official or a beloved relation might be commemorated with feasting and sexual license or by self-mutilation. Virtually all major ceremonies were accompanied by feasting and music.

The flow of mana was a constant concern, as mana upheld not only the religious order but the social and political order as well. Mana was thought to flow from the gods to ancestral spirits to tribal chiefs and then to the people at large. Chiefs were thought to possess so much mana that, in some places, ordinary people who touched their shadow were punished by death for the offense of damaging the sacred force. Polynesians also believed that mana was present in material objects and in natural things. An elaborate system of taboos arose to protect the mana inherent in people or objects. Only priests and chiefs, for example, were allowed to enter temples or other locations deemed spiritually significant. Chiefs and all their possessions, meanwhile, were thought to be taboo to the general population. Men going to war or undertaking some other risky exercise, such as a long sea journey, had to undergo long periods of purification before setting out. They avoided certain kinds of food and contact with women in order to ensure that their mana remained strong and pure. Menstruating women were commonly considered taboo, and in some islands women were forbidden from entering canoes (themselves sacred objects) except in very unusual circumstances. Polynesians believed that taboos were enforced by the gods, and that those who broke them without the necessary rites of purification might suffer sickness and even death.

Among the most mysterious of Polynesian religious monuments are the dozens of monumental statues of masklike heads and torsoes on Easter Island, an isolated island nearly 1,300 miles (2,093km) east of its nearest neighbor, Pitcairn Island, and closer to South America than it is to the rest of Polynesia. Known in its own language as Rapa Nui, Easter Island's statues, or moai, were carved from porous stone between 1100 and 1600. Standing on average 13 feet (4m) high and numbering in the hundreds, they are thought to represent gods or deified ancestors such as dead chiefs or priests, and they may have been considered vehicles of mediation between the human and the divine. Although most scholars suspect that the statues were rolled to their sites on logs, some question this explanation based on the scarcity of trees on the island. Rapa Nui traditions, meanwhile, explain that it was the mana of the figures the statues represent which allowed them to "walk" to their current locations. Originally placed with their backs to the sea, many of the moai were damaged during a series of violent wars between the islands inhabitants in the fifteenth and sixteenth centuries.

SEE ALSO: animism; Australian aboriginal religions

# Omar
## (–644)

The second caliph of Islam, meaning the second successor to the prophet Muhammad as the leader of the faith. Omar, whose full name was Umar ibn al-Khattab (and is often rendered as Umar rather than Omar), is credited by Sunni Muslims as well as general historical scholarship with firmly establishing the basis for a large-scale Islamic Empire, and his contributions to the tradition were more administrative and political than religious.

A native of Mecca, Omar rejected Muhammad's teachings until 618, when he experienced a sudden conversion. He accompanied Muhammad on the hijra to Medina, where he proved to be both devout and an extremely able administrator and organizer. The Prophet called him Faruq, a name indicating that Omar was clearly able to tell the difference between truth and falsehood. Omar succeeded his predecessor, Abu Bakr, upon the latter's death in 634. The Shia tradition rejects Omar, whom they consider to have stood in the way of the claims of the rightful caliph, Ali.

Before he was assassinated by rivals in 644, apparently in retaliation for his ruthlessness, Omar contributed a number of elements that helped Islam establish itself as an institution. Among them were the canonization of the standard text of the Qur'an, the establishment of the 622 hijra as the beginning of the Islamic calendar, and regulations governing prayers, welfare for poor believers, and the treatment of non-Muslims within Islamic communities. He also established several military garrisons, such as Kufa in Iraq, which later became major cities.

SEE ALSO: caliph; companions of the Prophet; Muhammad

## oracle bones

Divination devices used by soothsayers of the Chinese Shang dynasty (ca. 1766–1050 B.C.). They were usually either the scapula (shoulder blade) or leg bones of cattle or sheep, although tortoise shells were also used. The practice was to use them in connection with a question requiring a simple "yes" or "no" answer. The questions themselves were usually addressed to dead ancestors thought to inhabit an unseen spirit world, although they were also asked of gods, including the high god Shangdi. After posing the question, the soothsayer would then place a heated rod on the bone, causing it to crack. The form and direction of the cracks would then provide the answer, which was then inscribed on the bone itself.

The inscriptions on the oracle bones provide a great deal of information on not only the Shang dynasty's religious beliefs but on genealogical, economic, and political practices as well. They therefore provide a great deal of insight into this first documented Chinese dynasty, especially its rulers, who used the bones for divination on many matters. They also provide the first examples of China's written language. The largest collections of oracle bones have been uncovered at Anyang in northeastern China.

SEE ALSO: divination; Five Classics

## Orthodox Judaism

The form of Judaism that most strictly adheres to Jewish traditions. In this it contrasts with the other main forms of the faith, Reform and Conservative. Unlike Reform or Conservative Jews, Orthodox believers argue that Jewish practice cannot be altered by historical events or developments. It is not an ongoing process but rather a settled and eternal tradition. This tradition was established by God's revelations to Moses on Mount Sinai, by the appearance of the oral and written Torah, and by the rabbis and elders who devised the Talmud. For the Orthodox, modern Jews must live their lives according to the commandments and strictures of that tradition in order to be true members of Is-

*Followers of Orthodox Judaism follow strict interpretations of the written and oral Torah, which they believe was handed down to Moses by God on Mount Sinai.* © RICHARD T. NOWITZ/CORBIS

rael. The name Orthodox Judaism was first used in 1795 by believers reacting against various reform movements, and the Orthodox came to see Reform or Conservative Jews as gentiles rather than practicing Jews.

Within the broad category of Orthodox Judaism there are important divisions. One of them is the divide between so-called integrationist Jews and segregationist Jews. Integrationists believe that it is possible to live fully in the secular world in economic, social, and political senses while maintaining the Torah. Most Orthodox Jews in the United States as well as Europe are integrationists. In the United States they maintain such institutions as the Union of Orthodox Jewish Congregations of America (which has the task of certifying kosher food, or food prepared according to religious dietary laws) and Chicago's Hebrew Theological College. Segregationist groups argue that Jews should live entirely apart from gentiles, and there are several important such groups in Israel, where they maintain their own educational systems and even political parties. Some of these reject even the secular nature of the Israeli state.

SEE ALSO: Conservative Judaism; Reform Judaism; Talmud

## paganism

A derogatory term used primarily in the Christian and Jewish traditions to refer to religious systems and peoples whose religions are not monotheistic. It is derived from the Latin word *pagan*, which means "villager." It was first used commonly to differentiate between the sophisticated people of Rome and the primitive "pagans" who inhabited northern and western Europe and followed various Germanic or Celtic faiths. Later usage of the term was generally meant to imply that monotheism was more advanced than polytheism and that pagans worshipped false gods. In Christian Europe both the Romans and Greeks (among others) were considered followers of paganism. A further implication of paganism is that followers practice nature religions, a feature of many of the neo-pagan practices that emerged in the twentieth century.

SEE ALSO: ancient Greece and Rome, religions of; neo-paganism; pre-Christian Europe; religions of

## Pa-hsien

The eight immortal saints in Daoism. These were originally mortal humans who achieved perfection and thus gained immortal life. Frequently the subject of Chinese art and folktales that identify them with symbolic objects, the Pa-hsien are often connected with the "eight conditions" found in religious Daoism and listed as opposites: youth and old age, poverty and wealth, high social rank and ordinary or common status, female and male. The eight are Li T'ieh Kuai, a grumpy wanderer who carries a container with magic potions; Chang Kuo-lao, who carries a drum; Ts'ao Kuo-chiu, who plays a Chinese version of the castanets; Han Hsiang-tzu, who is often portrayed with flowers, a peach, and a flute and is a mountain-dwelling sage; Lu Tung-pen, who hides from death using a magic sword granted him by a fire dragon; Lan Ts'ai-ho, another wanderer who carries flowers and is dressed in rags; Ho Hsien-ku, a female immortal often portrayed with Lan Ts'ai-ho; and Chung-li Ch'uan, a generous figure with a long beard whose fan symbolizes the ability to raise people from the dead. The Pa-hsien are connected furthermore with Hzi-wang-mu, the Daoist "Queen Mother of the West" and queen of immortals, who raises in her garden the peaches that bring immortality. Stories and portrayals of the Pa-hsien often depict them celebrating the queen's birthday with a festive banquet.

SEE ALSO: Chuang-tzu; Daoism

## Pali

The ancient Indian language in which early Buddhist texts were written. Meaning "scriptural text," Pali was derived from Maghadi, the language of numerous north Indian kingdoms in the first millennium B.C. and is a distant relative of Sanskrit, the religious language of Hinduism. Many scholars accept that the original Buddha himself spoke a Magadhi dialect. The Pali

*The Greenhaven Encyclopedia of World Religions*

texts are generally accepted to have been drawn from the oral teachings of the Buddha and his followers. These texts, most importantly the Tripitaka, were written down in final form in Sri Lanka in the first century B.C. Pali remains the language used by Theravada Buddhists in their study and devotion.

SEE ALSO: Sanskrit; Theravada Buddhism; Tripitaka

## panentheism

A variation of pantheism most clearly enunciated by European philosophers such as Georg F.W. Hegel and Alfred North Whitehead in the eighteenth and nineteenth centuries, although elements of panentheism can be found as far back as the works of the ancient Greeks. Panentheists reject the pantheistic notion that the divine permeates everything and exhausts all possibilities of experience. They hold instead that the divine is both immanent and transcendant, and that experiences, sense impressions, and other worldly attributes can occur separately from the divine.

SEE ALSO: pantheism; religion; theism

## pantheism

The belief that all of reality is divine, that, in effect, God and the world are identical. Pantheists reject the practice in most established religions of anthropomorphizing God (giving him or her human attributes), holding instead that the divine is immanent, or present and inseparable, in every aspect of nature. There are two basic forms of pantheism. The first holds that all of nature is divine, including such mundane aspects as sensory perceptions. The second holds that sensory perceptions are not truly real, that only the divine is real. Most

pantheistic schools of thought come out of the Western tradition, and such thinking can be traced back to the ancient Greeks. The seventeenth-century Jewish-Dutch philosopher Benedict Spinoza, meanwhile, argued that there could only be one true reality, although that reality could have many different manifestations or attributes. Therefore, God and the world must be one and there is no such thing as a true "individual." Most Christians and Jews reject the tradition on the grounds that God and humanity must remain separate and that God cannot be rendered abstract or impersonal.

SEE ALSO: panentheism; philosophy of religion; theism

## papacy

The institution of the bishop of Rome, the pope, head of the Roman Catholic Church and held by believers to be God's representative on earth. The words *papacy* and *pope* are both derived from *papa*, or "father," a word used by the Germanic kings of the early Middle Ages to refer to the bishop of Rome. According to the Vatican, the official seat of the church, there have been 265 popes from Saint Peter to the current pope, Benedict XVI. Many are among the most significant figures in world history, but individual popes' roles, and the influence of the papacy in general, have varied in accordance with personalities and with historical circumstance.

The authority of the bishops of Rome is traditionally based on their claim to be a direct line from Peter, an apostle of Jesus named by Jesus himself to lead the church. Over the first two centuries A.D. the status of the bishop of Rome was enhanced by several factors: the alleged location of the tombs of Peter and Paul in Rome, the fact that there were numerous martyrs to the church who died in Rome (including Peter himself in A.D. 67), and the fact that Rome was an imperial capital at or near the height of its power in Peter's day. By the second century most other Christian bishops recognized the special status of the bishop of Rome.

Over the history of the Roman Catholic Church, the papacy's authority has faced many challenges, notably the breaking away of the Eastern Orthodox branch of Christianity in the eleventh century, largely because eastern bishops demanded (and were refused) equal status, and the Protestant Reformation, when many Christians rejected the pope's authority entirely. Conversely, many popes have ambitiously sought to extend their power into political or military realms as well as spiritual ones. Under Pope Innocent III (1161–1216), for example, the papacy was the most powerful institution in Europe, with jurisdiction over kings and the ability to order Crusades against both Christian heretics in Europe and Muslims in the Holy Land. At the Council of Trent in the mid-1500s, however, the papacy restricted its role to being the "vicar of Christ" on earth and gave up much of its direct role in politics. Indirectly, of course, papal authority over the daily practices and beliefs of the faithful remained considerable.

In 1870 the First Vatican Council proclaimed papal infallibility to be official church dogma. This meant that the pope cannot err when he declares a dogmatic teaching on faith or morals in official pronouncements known as bulls or encyclicals. The council also reinforced the papacy's "ultramontane" jurisdiction over all Roman Catholics; "ultramontane" or "over the mountains" is a reference to churches across the Alps, or outside of Italy in general. In 1929 the papacy was granted political control over Vatican City, a small district in central Rome, making the popes once again temporal rulers. The Second Vatican Council in the 1960s modified papal claims somewhat by granting new responsibilities to other bishops and church organizations. This council also made the historically unprecedented gesture of papal acknowledgment of other branches of Christianity outside of Catholicism.

SEE ALSO: Peter; Roman Catholicism; Vatican Councils

## Parsis

The community of Zoroastrians living in India or descended from those living in India. Parsis make up the largest coherent group of Zoroastrians in the modern world, since few large Zoroastrian communities remain in mostly Muslim Iran. The word *Parsi* is a derivation of the Greek *Persian*, or Iranian.

The Parsis are descended from Iranian immigrants to India who first left Iran in large numbers in the tenth century. Apparently these migrants were seeking freedom from Islamic oppression, and their early experiences are noted in a text called the *Tale of Sanjan*. Most settled in the west-central state of Gujerat, an important commercial center on the Arabian Sea. They generally lived in peace with the majority Hindus, but suffered incidents of oppression under various Islamic rulers over the next centuries. When British imperialists began establishing their empire in India in the seventeenth century, many Parsis moved to Mumbai (Bombay) on India's west coast. There they gained prominence in commerce and the professions, giving the Parsi community a relatively privileged position in British India. Some Parsis also settled in other areas of the British Empire: Australia, Canada, Singapore, and South Africa being among their primary destinations. After India's independence in 1947, Parsis remained among Bombay's economic elites. But their numbers have begun to dwindle as younger Parsis marry outside the faith or adopt mostly secular ways of life. Estimates in recent years suggest the Parsi population, still concentrated in Mumbai, is fewer than 100,000. Meanwhile, the older communities of migrants have been joined by more recent Parsi newcomers, often highly skilled professionals, who have settled in the United States and Great Britain as well as the other, earlier destinations.

Their distance from Iran's Zoroastrian origins, their small numbers, and the pressures of the modern world have introduced numerous challenges to Parsis' religious practice and belief. As early as the fifteenth century Zoroastrian authorities in Iran sent the Parsis a series of letters intended to reinforce and standardize Parsi religious practice, and numerous institutions arose to fulfill that purpose. Ceremonies such as formal initiation into the faith, weddings, and religious services are held in special buildings open only to Parsis. Not all practices survive strongly, however. The traditional Parsi funeral, in which the body was laid out on an open platform to be consumed by vultures, has been falling out of favor due not only to modernization in general but to both public health concerns and the high value of real estate in Mumbai, where some of these burial grounds would be worth a fortune. In recent years the community has split between liberal believers, who are ready to adapt Parsi practices to the modern world (partly to ensure that younger people re-

main solidly within the faith) and the orthodox, who cling to more traditional rituals and, in some cases, belief in an occult form of the faith featuring reverence toward a mythical group of Iranian Zoroastrian masters and the recitation of prayers in an ancient language. Most Parsi immigrants to wealthy countries have been of the liberal branch.

SEE ALSO: Avesta; Zoroastrianism

## Parvati

A Hindu goddess known commonly as the devoted wife of Shiva. Her name means "daughter of the mountain," a reference to the location in the Himalayas where she fell in love with and won over Shiva, who was in the mountains to practice asceticism and meditation. Parvati gained Shiva's love by demonstrating her own asceticism and by promising to accompany Shiva in all his many forms: as deity, family man and ascetic. Their union has been described as both a parable of the ideal husband and wife, with Parvati playing a submissive role, and of the submissive relationship between humans and gods. Parvati also, however, is sometimes worshipped as a powerful aspect of the divine goddess. She and Shiva have two children, Ganesha and Karttikeya. She is also known as Uma, Gauri and, in her more formidable forms, Durga or Kali.

SEE ALSO: Durga; Shiva; Kali

## Passover

An important Jewish festival of remembrance and commemoration. Known as Peshach in Hebrew, Passover lasts for seven days in Israel and eight days in Jewish communities elsewhere. It is generally held during April according to the Western calendar. Passover commemorates the deliverance of the Hebrews from their bondage in Egypt during the period of Jewish history known as the Exodus.

The first and final days of Passover are holy days marked by the eating of unleavened bread, or matzoh; the eating of leavened bread, risen with yeast, is forbidden on those days. The festival also includes a communal meal, the seder, featuring both matzoh and sanctified wine (as well as a lavish dinner). Seder ceremonies also involve songs, stories, and a ceremonial retelling of the Exodus in which children and adults play set roles. Among the purposes of this retelling is to remind Jews of their heritage and to encourage them to see themselves as having personally been freed from bondage.

SEE ALSO: Exodus; seder; Yom Kippur

# patriarch

A title given to the bishops of the early Christian Church, which remains in use as a reference to the leaders of the various Eastern Orthodox churches. Originally thought to have derived from the use of the term for Old Testament leaders such as Abraham, the term patriarch was used for Christian bishops as early as the fourth century. By the late fifth century, the term was applied specifically to the bishops of the five main administrative divisions of the early church within the Roman Empire: Rome, Alexandria, Antioch, Constantinople, and Jerusalem. The split between the eastern (Orthodox) and western (Roman Catholic) churches, however, led to the bishop of Rome being more commonly known as the pope, and as Islam spread in the Middle East, only the patriarch of Constantinople enjoyed real power among the patriarchates. Indeed, this patriarch was usually an important official for the entire period of the Christian Byz-

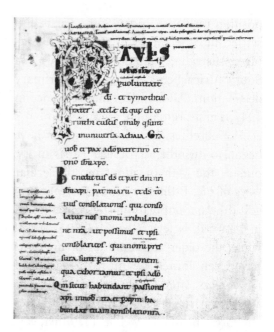

*Twelfth-century manuscript page of St. Paul's First Epistle (or letter) to the Corinthians.*

antine Empire, which lasted from the fall of Rome in 476 to 1453. During these centuries Eastern Orthodoxy spread westward and northward, and new, much less powerful patriarchates emerged in Russia. Today, there are nine patriarchs of Eastern Orthodoxy: Constantinople (Istanbul), Alexandria, Antioch, Jerusalem, Moscow, Georgia, Serbia, Bulgaria, and Romania. Each enjoys authority over autonomous church institutions; there is no single overarching authority for all Eastern Orthodox Christians.

SEE ALSO: Christianity; Eastern Orthodox Christianity; papacy

# Paul
## (−ca. 65 A.D.)

The most important early Christian thinker and missionary. Thanks to his development of a basic theology as well as his presentation of a number of ethical guidelines, Paul is commonly considered to be the second founder of Christianity after Jesus of Nazareth. His efforts greatly aided the establishment of Christianity as a faith separate from Judaism.

Most of what is known of Paul's life is contained in the New Testament Acts of the Apostles as well as in its Epistles, or letters, many of which are credited to Paul, who never personally knew or saw Jesus. Paul was born as Saul, a member of a prominent Jewish family living in Tarsus. Unlike most Jewish families, his had been granted full Roman citizenship. Paul also spoke Greek, the vernacular, or common language, of the eastern part of the Roman Empire. He was trained as a rabbi in Jerusalem, according to tradition, and belonged to the Pharisee sect, which urged complete fidelity to the laws of Moses. As such, he was much opposed to the teachings of Jesus at first.

While traveling to the city of Damascus around the year 33, apparently in order to arrest unruly Christians there, Paul experienced a conversion in the form of a vision of the risen Christ ascended to heaven. The vision convinced him that he must take up Jesus' message and to prepare humanity for Christ's return. He then began a long career of evangelizing, with his primary audiences being gentiles and Jews who did not live in Palestine. His fluency in Greek was no doubt a major advantage in this effort. Paul was accepted as a full apostle, a status equivalent to the original Twelve Apostles of Jesus, during a visit to Jerusalem where he met the apostle Peter and Jesus' brother James.

*Missionary Work Among the Gentiles*
Paul's missionary work began fully in Antioch, then the capital of Syria, in the 40s. There, Paul encouraged a clear break from Judaism by opposing other early Chris-

tians who had converted from the earlier faith. Some of these Jewish converts refused to share the Eucharist with gentile converts for fear of breaking Jewish purity laws. They also insisted on circumcision and on the adherence to other Jewish laws. Paul rejected these views. Using Antioch as a base, Paul went out to establish congregations on the island of Cyprus and in Greece, Turkey, and Syria. Most members of those congregations were gentiles. When Jerusalem Christians sent word to Paul that these converts should be circumcised and otherwise follow Jewish traditions, Paul went to Jerusalem to convince the locals that such measures were inappropriate for gentiles, that Christianity was in fact a separate faith from Judaism. Paul then returned to his missionary work and wrote some of his most important letters. In these he described further the ways in which Christianity was different from Judaism as well as ways in which Christians might seek to live their daily lives.

On a final visit to Jerusalem Paul was arrested for the crime of violating the Temple by allowing a gentile to accompany him inside. Local Jewish leaders treated him reasonably well on account of his Roman citizenship. But Paul did not want to be tried in Jerusalem as he had been harassed by Jewish authorities throughout his travels. He appealed to the Roman emperor for a trial in the capital, where he arrived in A.D. 60. He spent two years under house arrest, where he wrote further letters to early Christian communities, but little is known of his fate after that. One tradition holds that he was indeed tried but acquitted, and afterward went to preach in Spain before returning to Rome to be executed by the emperor Nero. The more common assumption, however, is that he was tried, found guilty, and then executed. A Roman church known as the Church of St. Paul Outside the Walls was built on his alleged burial site.

Paul's theology likely developed from both his original vision of Christ and his differences with conservative Jewish converts who disapproved of Paul's rejection of Jewish laws, which they thought would lead to immoral behavior. Paul argued that the sins of humanity had been redeemed by the grace of God, and that the intermediation of Jesus Christ—his teachings, suffering on the cross, death, and resurrection—was a manifestation of God's grace. Human beings must maintain faith in Christ's act of redemption rather than uphold Jewish laws. Christ had indeed replaced the Jewish law by introducing the Holy Spirit, and Christianity would be a "new Israel." Paul also believed that the return of Christ to earth was imminent. Paul's emphasis on God's grace and on justification by faith went on to be fundamental to Christianity, forcefully restated by Christian thinkers ranging from Augustine to Martin Luther.

SEE ALSO: Christianity; Epistles; New Testament

## Peoples of the Book

A phrase used in Islam to refer to Jews, Christians, and Zoroastrians under Islamic rulership and which provides the foundation for Islamic religious toleration. The Arabic term for such individuals is dhimmi, which means, roughly, "one under a protected status." Within Islamic states the Peoples of the Book are free to practice their own faiths and professions and to own property, although they might not be granted full citizenship status. The common restriction has been the placement of a special tax, the jizya, on the

dhimmi, although this has not been universal. The principle upon which the notion is based is that Jews, Christians, and Zoroastrians are monotheists who, in the case of the first two religions, revere many of the same prophets and holy texts as Muslims do.

SEE ALSO: Islam; jihad; Qur'an

## Peter
## (–64)

One of the original Twelve Apostles of Jesus of Nazareth and, by some accounts, their spokesman and leader. Originally known as Simon, Peter was working as a fisherman on the Sea of Galilee when he began to follow Jesus, who gave him the name of Peter. Gospel accounts indicate that he emerged as the leader among the apostles, particularly the Gospel of Matthew, which asserts that Peter will be the "rock" upon which the Christian community will be established.

After Jesus' death Peter served as the head of the first group of Christians in Jerusalem, and in the post he both defended his cobelievers against challenges from Jewish authorities and encouraged them to spread Jesus' message among both Jews and gentiles. Christian tradition holds that Peter went to Rome where he established a Christian community and led it for some twenty-five years before becoming a martyr during the reign of the persecuting emperor, Nero. Although this tradition has little foundation in either the New Testament or archaeological investigations, it is held nevertheless as the basis for the claim that Peter was the first bishop of Rome and that papal authority is derived from his. Many also hold that Peter's tomb in Rome is authentic, although archaeologists express doubts. Peter was also the author of two of the Epistles of the

New Testament. He remains among the most revered of the early Christians, and Roman Catholic tradition asserts that the popes, as bishops of Rome, are directly descended from Peter in his capacity as a church official and ultimately God's representative on earth.

SEE ALSO: apostles; Gospels; papacy

## Pharisees

An important group within Judaism during the era of the late second Temple, the first century B.C. and the first century A.D. They are generally accepted as the progenitors of the rabbinic Judaism, which became the main form of the faith after the destruction of the Temple in A.D. 70, and they are mentioned frequently in the New Testament Gospels, generally as opponents to the teachings of Jesus of Nazareth. Sources disagree on the exact origins of the movement. The Jewish historian Josephus describes them as a separatist political group unhappy with the tendency among many Jews to accept foreign, mostly Greek, influences. Rabbinic Jewish tradition, however, claims that they were a religious group seeking to uphold Jewish traditions and laws, the "traditions of the father," in the face of outside challenges. The Pharisees also seemed, generally, to reject the established rites and hierarchies of Temple-based Judaism, preferring simpler ceremonies and the opening of positions of leadership to all men. Rabbinic Jewish texts suggest that the Pharisees believed that the ideal rabbi was a man who had been trained first as a craftsman. They also argued that purity in behavior, such as the keeping of dietary laws, should be maintained everywhere, not just in the Temple. In theological terms, the Pharisees upheld belief in an "oral Torah" to accompany the written one and professed faith in an afterlife. Rabbinic Jewish custom has maintained that the Pharisees' emphasis on tradition, scholarship, and hope of a better life to come helped Judaism to survive after the destruction of the Temple showed that it could not be protected through military might.

SEE ALSO: Judaism; Temple; Torah

## philosophy of religion

Philosophical investigation into such religious matters as the origins of religion, the existence of God, the purpose of prayer, the relationship between God and humanity, the problem of evil, and the religious sources of morals. The philosophy of religion has been a part of the Western intellectual tradition since the ancient Greeks in the first few centuries B.C., but the term was not used until the so-called Age of Reason in the eighteenth century. The notion would be more difficult to define in such Eastern traditions as Hinduism and Buddhism, since they do not assert a strong difference between religion and philosophy and feel no need to "justify" or "explain" religious belief through rational means. Such a tension was clear in the West, however, since antiquity, and one of the main efforts of religious philosophers has been to reduce that tension, to reconcile religious faith with more strictly intellectual efforts. Among those prominent in this effort was Thomas Aquinas, one of the most prominent thinkers of the Roman Catholic tradition. More recently, nineteenth-century Danish philosopher Soren Kierkegaard, one of the founders of the existentialist school of philosophy, found it impossible to separate religious faith, in his case largely Protestant, with the attempt to solve philosophical problems. Most philosophers, however, have leaned in the other direction, toward rejecting religion as irrational and therefore not properly a subject of philosophical inquiry. Some philosophies, meanwhile, have served as secular substitutes for religion, notably Marxism and humanism in the Western world. Few philosophers seem satisfied with any version of the twentieth-century thinker Ludwig Wittgenstein's assertion that religious belief (ultimately a matter of faith, intuition, or tradition) cannot be understood as a matter of evidence or proof, although such a conclusion may simply lie in the nature of philosophical inquiry and in the existence of philosophy as a profession.

SEE ALSO: pantheism; religion; Thomas Aquinas, Saint

## pilgrimage

A religious journey, generally with a particular destination as the goal. Going on pilgrimages, sometimes at great personal cost, is commonly a sign of deep and sincere devotion, and virtually all major religions have pilgrimage traditions and sites. Underlying all pilgrimages is the assumption that certain sites have special spiritual importance, and going on a pilgrimage often serves as a rite of passage for believers.

In Judaism the common practice is a pilgrimage to Jerusalem known as 'aliyah. According to the Torah, Jewish men should make the 'aliyah three times a year on important festival days. The custom was generally impossible during the Diaspora centuries, but has been revived, particularly among Jews living in Israel. The main pilgrimage destination, visited year-round rather than on festival days in particular, is the so-called Wailing Wall, all that remains of the second Temple following its destruction in A.D. 70.

In Christianity pilgrimage has been most common among Roman Catholics and Eastern Orthodox believers; Protestants generally reject the practice. Records of pilgrimage to holy sites appear as early as the second century, when Christians made visits to such sites in and around Jerusalem as Golgotha (Calvary), the hillside where Jesus Christ was crucified. Rome is also a major pilgrimage site as visitors seek out the alleged tombs of Peter, Paul, and other saints. Meanwhile, devotees of particular saints often make pilgrimages to sites associated with these saints, such as Santiago de Compostela, where James was supposedly buried, and the tomb of the missionary St. Francis Xavier in Goa, India. Sites associated with the Virgin Mary, generally where devotees claim to have experienced visions of the Virgin, are also popular pilgrimage destinations. These include Lourdes in France, Fatima in Portugal, Medjugorje in Bosnia-Herzegovina (where visions of Mary were claimed very recently), and Guadaloupe in Mexico. Eastern Orthodox Christians, meanwhile, generally make pilgrimages to monasteries seeking guidance from holy men known in Russian as starets.

Pilgrimage is a major feature of Islamic practice. The hajj pilgrimage to Mecca is one of the Five Pillars of Faith in Islam and is expected of all adult males in a financial and personal position to go. Many women make the pilgrimage as well. Both often also travel to the city of Medina, which holds tombs of some of the early caliphs as well as other sites. Muslims may also perform the "minor" pilgrimage known as 'umra. Shia Muslims, for their part, might make pilgrimages to the tombs of Shia imams.

Pilgrimage is also important in Hinduism; indeed the Mahabharata contains a pilgrimage map of India depicting the entire subcontinent as a network of pilgrimage sites, which are to be visited by following a clockwise route. Most important among these are Hinduism's seven sacred cities, and the most commonly visited of these is Varanasi on the Ganga River. Many Hindus try to make pilgrimages to Varanasi at least once in their lives to bathe in the river's waters or to be cremated there, since cremation in Varanasi is thought to grant immediate release from the wheel of birth and death. Other rivers also serve as pilgrimage sites, and many of Hinduism's great religious festivals are in fact giant pilgrimages. One of these is the Kumbh Mela, thought to be the largest religious gathering on earth during the years when it is held at the confluence of the Ganga, the Jamuna, and the mythical Saraswati rivers. Pilgrimage sites in India are known as tirthas, or "fords," as when one fords a river from the profane to the sacred.

Buddhism maintains a wide variety of pilgrimage practices. Most common among all Buddhists are pilgrimages to Indian sites associated with the Buddha's life, such as the park outside Varanasi where he preached his first sermons. Another is the town of Bodh Gaya where the Buddha achieved enlightenment. Outside of India Buddhist pilgrims travel to a number of different kinds of sites. In Theravada Buddhist countries pilgrimage destinations often feature relics of the Buddha, such as a footprint, a fragment of the bohdi tree under which the Buddha meditated, or even a tooth, such as at the Temple of the Tooth in Kandy, Sri Lanka. In Mahayana Buddhist countries mountains and monasteries are common pilgrimage sites. China contains five sacred mountains, for instance: O'mei, Wu t'ai, P'u-t'o, Chiu-hua, and Tai. The first four are associated with bodhisattvas, while Mount Tai is a Daoist pilgrimage site. Many devout Chinese seek

to climb all five. Japanese Buddhists, meanwhile, may maintain the most elaborate pilgrimage traditions. In the Shikoku pilgrimage for instance, pilgrims must walk a route of over 700 miles (1,126km) and visit 88 temples. The climbing of Mount Fuji is also a form of pilgrimage undertaken by Shintoists as well as Buddhists.

A more abstract form of pilgrimage is the inner pilgrimage, taken through meditation and inward exploration. A metaphor reflecting the notion is that all life is a pilgrimage. The practice can be found in certain Christian traditions and in Hinduism, where devout yogis can "visit" the seven sacred cities through meditation alone. Sikhism also emphasizes inner pilgrimage, although Sikhs also commonly make visits to sites such as the Golden Temple in Amritsar, India.

SEE ALSO: hajj; Kumbh Mela; relics

## polytheism
Belief in many gods. Most religions in history have been polytheistic, including the dominant religions of the ancient world with which the practice is usually associated. Of the major modern world religions, only Hinduism and Shinto are polytheistic, although the case has been made that neither of these faiths is truly polytheistic since Hinduism's many gods and Shintoism's *kami* are actually aspects or avatars of the one ultimate reality. The case is also made that the major monotheistic religions retain elements of polytheism, such as the reverence for prophets and the messianism of Judaism, the Christian Trinity and veneration of Mary (particularly among Roman Catholics and Eastern Orthodox), and the devotion toward martyrs in Shia Islam.

SEE ALSO: monotheism; pantheism

## prana

The "vital energies" of Hindu philosophy. Prana is what separates the living from the dead. According to Vedic teachings, prana constitutes the "breath of life," from which the gods were created out of the "mouth" of a primal creator known as Prajapati, who later evolved into the god Brahma. The concept might also be read as the soul, since one's prana was thought to survive his or her physical death until it reached moksha or reappeared in a new incarnation. In yogic practices, some students are taught of the importance of controlling the "five pranas" in the body that affect breathing, nutrition, and digestion.

SEE ALSO: meditation; Tantricism; yoga

## pre-Christian Europe, religions of

North of the Mediterranean region, Europe was a wild and unsettled place until the Romans brought much of it within the orbit of their empire in the first century B.C. Its primary peoples were the Celts, who lived in permanent, if small, settlements in the western parts of Spain and France as well as the British Isles, and the seminomadic Germanic tribes who wandered much of the rest of the continent. Although these peoples were slowly Romanized and then converted to Christianity, Celtic and Germanic religious ideas and forms were a major influence on both European Christianity and on culture and folklore.

The Celtic peoples were the descendants of Indo-European migrants, distantly related to the peoples of Italy, Greece, and even India. They firmly established themselves in western Europe by 500 B.C., with the major centers being France, where the Celts were known as Gauls by the Romans, and Ireland. Most of the sources for Celtic religion are the writings of Romans, since the Celts did not have a writing system of their own. This religion was apparently based in nature, with guardian spirits thought to be present in various natural things such as trees, streams and hills. Because of this, the Celts believed that the landscape was "alive" and thus both accessible and sensitive to human activity. Their religious rites, officiated over by a priestly class known as Druids, focused on the relationships between people and these natural guardian spirits. The Druids believed in reincarnation, or the transmigration of souls, and they also conducted human sacrifices in times of war or hardship. Celts in Ireland, meanwhile, believed further in an afterlife known as the Land of the Young, accessible only to a few.

*The Gods of the Celts* The most commonly revered god of the Celts was known as Lugus or Lugh, both a warrior god and the Creator of all the arts. Perhaps even more powerful, however, was the great queen goddess Morrigan. Other important gods and goddesses reflected natural or social phenomena. Cernunnos, a deer god, was the lord of the animals and possessed shamanistic properties. A mare goddess, known variously as Epona, Macha, or Rhiannon, was thought to represent fertility. In both France and Ireland Celts believed in a trio of mother goddesses, known in Ireland as Brigits, who presided over poetry, healing, and crafts. The god of the ocean was known as Manannan.

The Celtic calendar contained several important feast days celebrating both seasonal changes and the activities of the gods. The spring festival, Beltane, was celebrated on May 1 with the lighting of huge bonfires. The beginning of the harvest, as well as the Marriage of Lugus, took place on August 1. The Celtic new year, Samhain, was celebrated on November 1, and it commemorated both the end of the summer and the day of the dead, the modern Halloween. Aspects of these festivals, such as the use of trees, bonfires, and dances, appeared in later European Christian celebrations. The Druid orders, meanwhile, developed a strong culture of learning at their isolated temple centers, with some developing the capability of memorizing and reciting very long stories and poems. This love of learning survived the suppression of Celtic culture by the Romans and the conversion of their territories to Christianity, with the latter taking place mostly after A.D. 400. Irish monks, of Celtic heritage, are thought to have kept much of classical Europe's culture alive at their isolated monasteries during the so-called dark age from roughly 500 to 800. An interest in Celtic religion was revived in the 1700s and remains today, with the founding of the Ancient Order of Druids in 1781. Modern adherents hold annual festivals at the Stonehenge monument in southern England (which actually predates Celtic culture) and at other sites considered sacred.

The Germanic peoples, also distantly related to the Indo-Europeans, originally inhabited a wide area of central, eastern, and northern Europe. But their migrations in the fourth and fifth centuries, inspired largely by conflict with the Roman Empire, extended their range of culture across Europe, from Spain to the Balkans and north and westward to Britain. After the fall of the Roman Empire in western Europe in the fifth century, Germanic kingdoms slowly took shape, and these Germanic kingdoms came to dominate the continent. The Germanic peoples slowly but steadily converted to Christianity, with

the last surge of pre-Christian Germanic culture taking place with the Viking invasions and migrations of the ninth, tenth, and eleventh centuries. The tales of their ancient religion remain alive in the sagas of Iceland as well as the "nordic" myths preserved elsewhere.

*Odin, Thor, and Valhalla* The primary Germanic god, the Creator of their culture, was Odin (also spelled Wotan). Odin presided over a blessed otherworldly kingdom known as Asgard, where he lived in a castle called Valhalla. Odin's wife Frea, or Frigg, was a flirtatious, unpredictable deity. One of their sons, Thor, was the most popular and widely worshipped of the Germanic deities. He is associated with warfare and with the rains, a combination indicated by his appellation as the god of thunder. His name lives on in the term Thursday, or Thor's day, as does Frigg's with Friday. Their other son, according to most Germanic traditions, was Balder. Loki was a mischievous and often dangerous figure, causing all sorts of trouble in Germanic myths. These deities were members of a group of "fair gods" known as Vanir. The Germanic peoples also maintained a secondary pantheon of gods, the Aesir, who were described in these myths as being at war with Odin, his sons, and their warriors. This secondary group, however, was ultimately accepted at Asgard after the two sides reached a peace. These deities included Frey, a father god, and his sister Freya, a goddess of love and fertility. Germanic religion also features lesser guardian spirits who were thought to live among men and women; elves and dwarves were among them, while "trolls" were thought to exercise a less beneficial influence.

Germanic religion is rich with myths and stories. Asgard, for instance, was the abode of other gods as well as Odin, and it was the final destination of all warriors killed in battle. There they live in eternal bliss. Killed warriors can only reach Asgard by crossing a bridge of ice, and in many myths they are escorted there by women known as Valkyries, either in flight or on horseback. While in Asgard the dead celebrate with the gods by drinking a sacred beverage known as mead, an alcoholic drink made from fermented honey. Mead was also considered the inspiration for poets. The gods' greatest opponents were known collectively as frost-giants who represented such forces as cold, stagnation, and sterility. These frost-giants, their allies, and evil spiritual forces were to engage in mortal combat with the Vanir and Aesir at the time of Ragnarok, a great millennial battle connoting the end of time. In this battle both Odin and Thor will be killed, but Balder will survive, as will all deserving humans, who will live in a great hall lined with gold.

In addition to the telling and retelling of these myths, which were thought to provide inspiration for warriors and for continued survival, Germanic religious rituals included sacrifices of animals and, occasionally, humans. There were separate temples or shrines for each of the gods, which were guarded by priests or chiefs responsible for reading omens and perform rites of propitiation to them. Families also regularly performed rituals to the gods in their homes. Funeral rites could be quite elaborate, especially for warrior elites or chiefs, who were often buried with ships or horses, and sometimes even with their wives or servants; many funeral sites remained hallowed ground, the sites for the giving of offerings and further sacrifices. Records suggest that, despite the myths, many Germanic peoples did not fully subscribe to belief in Asgard or limited it to warriors killed in battle. For ordinary people, the afterlife was darker and more mysterious.

*Summer and Winter Solstice* In general Germanic peoples celebrated four major seasonal festivals. The first was in mid-October and commemorated both dead ancestors and the beginning of winter. The second was the winter solstice, commonly known as Yule. In April the Germanic peoples celebrated the arrival of spring with Eostara, or Easter, and the most elaborate festival was a midsummer fertility festival in late June. All of these celebrations featured feasting, dancing, and the drinking of mead.

Even after the conversions of the Scandinavian peoples, who were the last of the Germanic peoples to accept Christianity, Germanic customs and rituals survived in new forms. They have experienced a resurgence in popularity in recent times, the inspiration for many of the operas of German composer Richard Wagner as well as, in a more sinister sense, the myths of a superior Germanic race propagated by Nazi Germany. In more benign examples, the Germanic gods live on, again, in the names of the days of the week and in aspects of festivals. In Norway and Sweden, for example, people still celebrate midsummer by dancing around a maypole, an ancient symbol of fertility.

SEE ALSO: ancient Greece and Rome, religions of; paganism; neo-paganism

# pre-Columbian Mesoamerica, religions of

Mesoamerica, the region consisting of modern-day central and southern Mexico and Central America, was the center of advanced civilizations and highly developed religious traditions long before the

*The Pyramid of the Sun looms over the ancient city of Teotihuacan, Mexico.* © CHARLES AND JOSETTE LENARS/CORBIS

arrival of Christopher Columbus and other Europeans in the late 1400s and 1500s. These civilizations generally built upon each other's accomplishments, with the earliest of them dating back to approximately 2000 B.C. Although the region was full of diverse and often very contentious tribal groups, many of them shared gods and religious customs. When Europeans arrived, they tried to convert Mesoamericans to Christianity, and in the process destroyed many monuments and other religious objects, notably the texts of the Mayans. But small groups of Mesoamericans still continue to practice aspects of their old faiths, and these have also seeped into both Mexican and Central American Catholicism.

***The Temples of Teotihuacan*** One of the prominent early civilizations of Mesoamerica was that centered on the city of Teotihuacan, whose massive ruins still stand some 100 miles (132km) north of modern Mexico City. Lying in the Valley of Mexico, an agriculturally rich region capable of supporting large populations, Teotihuacan housed a population of perhaps 200,000 people at its height in the period from A.D. 400 to A.D. 600. Its most prominent structures were two temple pyramids. At one end of a broad avenue stood the Pyramid of the Sun, larger than the largest pyramid still standing in Egypt. At the other end was the smaller Pyramid of the Moon. This layout was suggestive of the understanding of the order of the universe in Mesoamerica. The pyramids themselves, as well as other temples, were seen as connecting points between this world and the world of the gods, a common belief throughout the region. Under the center of the Pyramid of the Sun is a small shrine where the mother goddess was thought to dwell. The chief gods of Teotihuacan were two who were prominent throughout the Valley of Mexico, worshipped by many tribes. One was Tlaloc, the god of rain. His importance was great due to the necessity of rain for the purposes of growing crops, and as such he reflected fertility as well. For the purposes of ritual and storytelling, Tlaloc was often described as one of four Tlaloques, smaller figures thought to live at the peaks of tall mountains, each with his own special color and representing one of the four directions. To ensure fertility, Tlaloc was granted human sacrifices in solemn ceremonies. The other god popular in Teotihuacan was Quetzalcoatl, a feathered serpent who had many qualities: messenger between this world, the underworld, and the world of the gods; god of plant life and the earth; representative of time and the calendar; and the god of writing. Teotihuacan's priests and scholars developed a body of writings based on images developed by an earlier Mesoamerican civilization, the Olmecs. But aside from a few carvings, their texts disappeared or were destroyed during a series of military attacks in the seventh and eighth centuries, after which the city was abandoned.

To the south and east of the Valley of Mexico, in the rain forests and along the eastern coasts of Mesoamerica, the Mayan civilization thrived for over a thousand years, with the so-called classic Maya period lasting from about A.D. 300 to A.D. 900. This advanced civilization had a complex system of religious beliefs. The Mayans built dozens of ceremonial centers whose ruins still stand, among them Chichen Itza in Mexico's Yucatan Peninsula and Tikal in Guatemala. At the heart of Mayan religious belief was the cyclical

relationship among the gods, nature, and humanity. According to the Popol Vuh, the Mayan Creation myth, the gods created human beings out of the mixture of corn and water. To ensure that the gods maintained the growth of crops out of which humanity came, people needed to perform homages and sacrifices to them. The chief gods of the Mayans were Itzamna, creator of humankind and its arts and sciences; Yum Kaax, the god of agriculture; and Chac, the Mayan version of the rain god Tlatoc. The Mayans also revered Quetzalcoatl, whom they called Kukulcan. Also very important was the god of death, Ah Puch. Like other Mesoamerican peoples, the Mayans saw death not as a departure but as part of the cycle of life, as necessary to further growth as planting and harvesting. Beyond this pantheon of high gods were dozens of patron deities for specific purposes: farming, fishing, traveling, trade, war, even poetry and music.

*Sacrificial Rituals and the Mesoamerican Ball Game* Reverence to these gods often involved bloodletting rituals, since the Mayans believed that blood "carried" the properties of the gods and was essential to life. These rituals might include the sacrifice of war captives who, before they were beheaded, might be wounded in order for their blood to flow. The Mayans did not restrict such practices to captives, however. It was common for kings and other royalty to shed their own blood in special ceremonies, although rarely to the point of death. Another reflection of the importance of these bloodletting rituals was the Mayan ball game (versions of it were played elsewhere in Mesoamerica as well). The game involved putting a ball through a ring or onto a marker without using one's hands; some Mayan ruins contain more or less standing ball courts, where stone rings are placed perpendicular to the ground. Although the game was sometimes played simply for the sake of sport, in some contests losers were immediately sacrificed, with some ball courts containing racks for the skulls of these victims. Beyond these bloodletting rituals, Mayan religious ceremonies might also include dancing, feasting, and the drinking of an alcoholic beverage known as balche.

The Mayans had a complex view of the universe and of humanity's place within it. The heavens consisted of thirteen layers, the underworld nine layers, and the earth lay between, containing certain linking points such as the sacred core of temple pyramids, accessible only to royalty. In image they described the earth as the back of a giant reptile. In keeping with their cyclical view of the universe and of nature, the Mayans considered their world to be just one of many that had come before and would come after. They constructed elaborate calendar systems, informed by a sophisticated set of mathematics, to explain this order and to try to predict the future. The Mayans also developed the most advanced writing system of any early American civilization, with inscriptions and carvings mostly intended for religious purposes and prophecy.

The great Mayan centers fell into decline after A.D. 900, and Europeans destroyed almost all Mayan texts after their arrival on the Mexican mainland in the 1500s. But Mayan people continued to populate the region, speaking their own language and, sometimes, practicing the old faith. Chichen Itza and other sacred sites remained the destination of pilgrims, and even in the modern day it is not unheard of for small groups of Mayans to continue to practice sacrificial rituals involving animals.

The civilization that dominated the Valley of Mexico when Europeans arrived was that of the Aztecs. Originally a tribe from northern Mexico known as the Mexica, the Aztecs had migrated into the Valley of Mexico seeking work as mercenary soldiers. Unwelcomed by the settled, powerful tribes of the area such as the Toltecs and Tlaxcala, the Aztecs settled along the shores of a vast lake known as Texcoco. There, in the late 1300s, they began the construction of what was to be one of the great cities of its time: Tenochtitlan. Over the next decades their military might allowed the Aztecs to subdue many tribes and build a huge empire.

*Aztec Gods and Rites* Aztec religion adopted many of the practices of earlier Mesoamerican civilizations. They played a version of the ball game and used the Mayan calendar. Their main gods included Tlaloc the rain god and Quetzalcoatl, who to the Aztecs was the god of death and rebirth and the protector of craftsmen in addition to his other roles. But the most prominent god among the Aztecs was Huitzilopochtli, the god of war. Aztec warriors adopted him as their patron during their campaigns against other tribes, and their successes on the battlefield seemed to suggest that Huitzilopochtli approved. There were two great temple pyramids in Tenochtitlan, with the largest dedicated to Huitzilopochtli (the other was dedicated to Tlaloc). The war god's continual demands for human sacrifices meant that the temple was an active site. In addition to human sacrifices, commonly of war captives or slaves, rites to the war god included dancing and feasts. Meanwhile, like the Mayans, Aztec priests and warriors also let their own blood flow in order to ensure the continuance of the agricultural cycle.

The Aztecs believed that they lived in the "fifth world," with the previous four having been destroyed by the death of the sun, who was personified as another aspect of Huitzilopochtli. Their primary religious duty was to keep the sun alive. Warriors who died in battle or were sacrificed and women who died in childbirth were thought to go to heaven to accompany the sun. Others who died from less auspicious causes might go to the heaven of Tlaloc. A proper death, such as that in battle for a warrior, was important for the Aztecs, and nothing to fear since, as in the Maya view, death was essential to the maintenance of life. Those who did not die auspicious deaths were thought to travel aimlessly for four years in the realm of the death god, characterized variously as Tezcalipotla or Mictlantecuhtli. Afterward, they disappeared forever.

Tenochtitlan was conquered by Spanish invaders in the 1520s, who went on to construct modern Mexico City on the site. The Aztecs' two great temple pyramids were only uncovered in the 1970s. Nevertheless, many Aztec religious beliefs continue to survive, particularly in small villages.

SEE ALSO: Native American religions, North America; pre-Columbian Peru and the Andes, religions of

# pre-Columbian Peru and the Andes, religions of

Advanced civilizations and highly developed religions existed in the western portions of South America long before the arrival there of Europeans in the sixteenth century. The center of civilization in the region were the societies in what is now modern-day Peru, which emerged either in the valleys of the Andes or along the narrow strip of land between the Andes and the Pacific Ocean. Although these areas did not generally lend themselves to the construction of big cities comparable to those of the Valley of Mexico northward, they were rich enough in agriculture to support fairly large populations. Religious traditions arising in the region, even the complex religion of the Inca Empire, commonly featured objects, products, or animals that helped to sustain life: the sun, corn, squash, potatoes, and llamas. They also featured wild animals, notably the jaguar and the snake.

Relatively little is known about the earliest civilizations, or their religions, in Peru or the Andes. It seems that settled agriculture and permanent villages had appeared by about 1000 B.C., as well as routes for travel and communication between sites. The earliest major religion of the region was the so-called Chavin cult, whose origins date back to about 900 B.C. and which thrived for some seven hundred years. Although scholars disagree, many attribute its rise to the importance of corn growing and the subsequent need to guarantee fertility. The ruins of Chavin temples indicate that local peoples worshipped a wide variety of gods given both human and animal forms. The latter included jaguars, eagles, and snakes. The greatest of the Chavin deities appears to have been a human figure with snakes for hair and long fangs whom scholars have termed the Smiling God. Evidence also shows that animal sacrifice was a part of the cult. The ongoing need to assure rich harvests as population expanded partially explains the spread of the Chavin cult over a wide region. By 200 B.C. it had reached the substantial town of Tihuanaco near Lake Titicaca in modern day Bolivia. Temple ruins at Tihuanaco indicate a further belief in a spear-throwing deity scholars have named the Doorway God, since he seems to be fending off a group of winged invaders.

During the first millennium A.D., the Mochica state, based in northern Peru, was the largest in the region although Tihuanaco remained a regional power as well. Mochica's priestly caste presided over rites in temple-pyramids, the largest nearly 150 feet (46m) high, while its craftsmen produced very realistic depictions of daily life as well as images of the gods. Moche gods included a sky or sun god depicted on a mountaintop throne with the sun rising behind him and a jaguar god who lived along the coast and was considered the great, though unpredictable, protector. In the 10th century, a new state known as Chimu replaced Mochica, and its warriors conquered a substantial empire stretching over 500 miles (805km) along the Peruvian coast. In the Chimu capital of Chanchan stood a number of temple pyramids thought to have been devoted to deities similar to those of Mochica or even earlier peoples.

*Mysterious Lines and Patterns* Among the most mysterious of the religious monuments of early Peru are the so-called Nazca lines. These are either abstract patterns or geoglyphs, huge outlines, inscribed in the dry landscape of a high coastal plain in southern Peru. They are attributed to the Nazca people who lived there between 200 B.C. and A.D. 600. The outlines depict a variety of animals, or stylized versions of animals who might be gods. These geoglyphs are too big to be perceived from the ground, sometimes the length of two football fields, but they can be clearly identified from the air. Other lines form abstract patterns or shapes, or even straight pathways. The significance of the Nazca lines is unclear, and they have been the inspiration for many theories involving the occult or even visitations from outer space. Scholars generally suggest fairly simple and straightforward alternative explanations of their formation. The plain on which the lines were drawn is one of the driest on earth and sees very little wind. Furthermore, it is littered with small volcanic stones, which cover soil of a very different color. All the "builders" of the lines had to do was remove the stones and pile them along the sides using some sort of surveying method. The lines may have been "guides" to temples or other monuments or their purpose may have been for ritual processions or dances, but their specific purpose remains a mystery.

By the time Europeans came, the Inca civilization dominated Peru and the Andean region. From its base in the Cuzco valley, Inca warriors and diplomats, beginning in the fifteenth century, had constructed a huge empire stretching more than 2,500 miles (4,024km) along the South American coast and containing a population of over 11 million. Many of its citizens belonged to tribes other than the Incas, with the Chimu being one, and their religious influences combined with those of earlier groups to build a highly developed religion.

In Inca religion, a god known as Viracocha was the Creator of the universe and of humanity, able to transform himself into some of the heroes and inventors of Inca lore. Even more important was Inti, the god of the sun and the patron deity of the Inca ruling nobility, who thought of themselves as children of the sun. In the town of Cuzco, capital of the empire, stood a large Temple of the Sun devoted to Inti, and thousands of priests served Inti alone. Inca elites also maintained special orders of young women devoted to the service of Inti. These were known as Chosen Women or Maidens of the Sun. The tasks of these women, who were selected at a young age for their beauty, was to prepare ritual meals and to weave the cloth for royal garments. Sometimes, and once they were old enough, they were given as brides or concubines to non-Inca tribal elites, a sign of the generosity of the sun. A few were ritually sacrificed, although in general the Inca sacrificed animals such as llamas rather than humans. Notably, only women judged to be perfect were sacrificed.

*Popular Gods and Sacred Sites in Inca Worship* Inca religion also offered numerous patron deities popular among ordinary people. These included Apu Illapu, the god of rain and agriculture. His worship might involve pilgrimages to high temples, prayers, or human sacrifice in times of severe drought. Other popular deities included a pantheon of goddesses: Mama Coco, the goddess of health and joy and the subject of often racy folktales; Mama Zara, the goddess of grain; Mama Quilla, the moon goddess and wife of Inti; and Mama Pacha, a fertility goddess. Mama Pacha was the wife of Pachacamac, an earlier version of Viracocha.

A common feature of Inca religion, and a reflection of the Incas' sense of the divine order of the universe, was the huaca. Huacas were sites or objects where the earthly connected with the divine. Inca homes commonly contained icons or objects thought to have huaca properties. These were the focus of domestic rites. In addition to objects, huacas might even be mummified ancestors. More commonly, huaca locations were temples or small shrines where devotees might leave offerings or give prayers. The huacas provided well-defined means by which ordinary humans could connect with the divine forces that pervaded their lives. Believers also

used methods of divination, such as the drinking of an intoxicating beverage called ayahuasca, to try to communicate with the gods. Meanwhile, the proper observance of regular rituals was thought to maintain the divine order. If individuals failed to keep their rites, or if they otherwise failed in their duties to either the gods or the state, they were required to confess their sins and perform penance.

The Inca empire fell after the arrival of Spanish conquistadors in the 1530s, although Inca leaders put up a valiant fight for decades. Some of the fighting took place in the high mountain citadel of Machu Picchu, the site of one of the Inca world's largest and most mysterious sun temples; architectural investigations in the twentieth century showed that of the 135 skeletons found there, 109 were those of Maidens of the Sun. Inca religion, however, was the inheritor and keeper of long traditions, and even after the fall of the empire and dispersal of its tribes, people continued to practice aspects of the old faiths and to speak the Inca's Quechua language.

SEE ALSO: Native American religions, North America; pre-Columbian Mesoamerica, religions of

# Protestantism

The third major branch of Christianity, along with Eastern Orthodoxy and Roman Catholicism. The Protestant, or "protest" churches first emerged in the 1500s, when many western European Christians began questioning both the institutions, administration, and even basic doctrinal assumptions of the church of Rome in the Reformation movement. The combination of religious and political protest and the church's counterprotest movement yielded a century of religious wars that fractured

Europe into Protestant and Catholic areas. Protestantism took hold in England, Scotland, the Netherlands, northern Germany, and Scandinavia. European colonists and settlers later took it around the world. Of the approximately 1.5 billion Christians in the world today, at least 500 million are Protestants.

Although there are many different forms of Protestant Christianity, nearly all its denominations share a few common characteristics. Churches share the three basic principles first enunciated by Martin Luther, the German monk generally considered the founder of Protestantism. The first is that salvation can only be granted by the grace of God, and that believers can only open themselves to grace by maintaining faith in Jesus Christ's redemption, not by performing any acts or deeds. Second, the Bible is the ultimate source of all religious authority. Third, all believers are their own "priests," responsible for their own salvation and spiritual well-being. For all these reasons Protestants rejected the authority of the popes and the necessity for priestly leadership.

### Breaking from the Roman Catholic Church

In many ways these principles were reactions to traditional church practices, which required believers to perform sacraments and other acts with the intercession of a priest if they hoped to gain salvation. But Protestantism was more than a reaction to established practices. The Latin root word from which "protestantism" was derived also means to affirm or to avow, and Protestants wanted to worship in the pure, simple ways, open to all believers, that they thought the Bible intended. It was first used in the context of this spiritual revolt in 1529, twelve years after Luther's initial questions, when at a large meeting known as the Diet of Speyer, churchmen in Germany issued a formal "protestation" asserting that every person must stand alone before God. The meeting also established that each prince or other leader in German lands had the right to choose the religion that would apply in his territory.

Among the characteristics of Protestantism in practice is the equality of all believers, not only before God but institutionally. Although formal institutions and programs eventually arose for the training of Protestant clergy, the first were either rebellious Catholic priests, scholars, or even laypeople. Laypeople continue to play prominent roles in Protestant congregations. Protestant churches also disdain most of the decorations, artwork, and other ceremonial paraphernalia of Catholicism in favor of simple, unadorned structures and services. They also reduced the number of sacraments from seven to two: baptism and the Eucharist (Holy Communion), although relatively few Protestant denominations even perform the Eucharist at every weekly service. Aside from the Lutherans and Anglicans, Protestants consider the Eucharist to be a symbolic or memorial ritual; the bread and wine are not transformed or "transubstantiated" into the body and blood of Christ as Catholics believe. Likewise, and again aside from Lutheran and Anglican traditions, Protestants reject the veneration of saints, mysticism, and monasticism. In sum, Protestant churches try to be people-based and simple, rather than leadership or institution-based and at least partly mysterious.

Beyond these commonalities, the Protestant movement is extremely diverse, with some churches even asserting that the term "protestant" does not really apply to them. Among the major variations are Lutheranism, still the state church in Scandinavian countries, and Anglicanism (Episcopalianism), which is the branch of Protestantism closest to Catholicism in its rites and practices and which remains the official Church of England. The conservative Calvinist movement begun in the mid-1500s had such offshoots as Presbyterianism and Puritanism, while Methodism appeared in the 1600s as another attempt to bring religion directly to ordinary people. Protestant denominations differ in their methods of organization, with some branches having centralized administrations while others prefer locally run churches, such as many Baptists and Congregationalists. Esoteric variations of Protestantism include the Society of Friends, or Quakers, and Christian Science.

*Protestantism and Modern Controversy* A major feature of Protestantism in the modern world is the gap between liberal and conservative interpretations of theology and of the Christian life, a conflict which dates back to the so-called liberal Protestantism of the eighteenth century with its emphasis on reason, social concern, and personal religious experience and judgment. Many "mainstream" Protestant denominations, such as modern Lutheranism, Anglicanism, Methodism, and Presbyterianism, have taken a liberal stance on such social issues as female or homosexual clergy, divorce, abortion, and involvement in the ecumenical movement seeking to foster ties with all global Christians. A famous example of this sort of openness was the so-called social gospel preached by Reverend Martin Luther King Jr. (1929–1968), an ordained Baptist minister as well as a leader in the modern American civil rights movement. In contrast are the churches connected to the so-called evangelical and fundamentalist movements, which tend to be socially and politically conservative, sometimes to the extreme. In recent years evangelical and fundamentalist churches have grown increasingly popular and have attracted newcomers far more successfully than the mainstream denominations. Their popularity has spread even to areas formerly dominated by Roman Catholicism, such as Latin America. The evangelical movement stresses a literalist reading of holy scripture and rejects many of the social reforms that mainstream denominations are willing to consider.

SEE ALSO: Anglicanism; evangelicalism; Reformation

## puja

Hindu worship. Puja can take many forms, from solitary household devotions to elaborate temple festivals and ceremonies. There are no rules for puja, and its precise content varies greatly depending on such factors as which gods or goddesses are to be worshipped, Hindu sect, the texts used, the time of day, whether there are any special festivals taking place, and even geographic location. But there tend to be several common themes and features. One is that the god, depicted in an image or icon of some sort, is to be treated like an honored guest. He or she is awoken, bathed, dressed, fed, and put to rest in the evening. For this reason individual pujas often begin early in the morning, while in temples brahmin priests perform the honors as devotees come and go all day. Generally, offerings are presented and there is also some form of sacred fire. Another common form of puja is to walk around the image of the god or his or her shrine while chanting or singing. At the heart of many pujas, both household and temple ones, is a ritual known as the arati. Here, devotees use a lighted lamp. They first circle the lamp three times in a clockwise direction, chanting prayers or hymns. Then they wave the lamp before the image of the god or goddess, also in a circular motion. The arati might be granted to an honored human being as well as to a deity, and it is also commonly done through circular movements of the arms as they hold incense and offerings. Some pujas require the presence of a a brahmin priest, but most do not. Many devout Hindus maintain shrines in their homes for their regular pujas.

SEE ALSO: Hinduism; Kumbh Mela; mandir

## Puranas

A collection of Hindu religious texts written in Sanskrit. Meaning "ancient lore," the Puranas differ from the Vedas in that they are designed for all believers rather than the priestly brahmin caste; as such they are considered the primary source of knowledge of early popular Hinduism. They were also written much later, between A.D. 400 and 1500, although many of them contain material from earlier periods. There are two main groups of Puranas. The eighteen principal ones exalt either Brahma, Vishnu, or Shiva, and stress personal devotion as well as, in the form of myth, the miraculous actions of the gods. The most popular of these is the Bhagavata Purana, which tells of the early life of Krishna, avatar of Vishnu. The Devi Bhagavata Purana, meanwhile, contained in the larger Brahma-oriented Markandaya Purana, focuses particularly on the exploits of the divine Goddess (Shakti) and provides a clear example of the diversity of these texts. There are also eighteen lesser Puranas that serve to fill out the eighteen principal ones with more stories and lessons.

SEE ALSO: Smriti; trimurti; Vedas

## purdah

A Persian word translated variously as "veil," "screen," or "curtain." It refers to the practice of hiding women from public observation that is common in Islam and, until recently, Hinduism (where it is still practiced in isolated areas). In the home, purdah took the form of special rooms or quarters separated from the rest of the house by screens or high walls. In public, it takes the forms of veils or other concealing clothing, most notably the hijab, the black veil and robe common in some conservative Arab countries. The basic principles behind the practice were that only men of the family should be able to look directly at women, and that women should be protected as if they were hidden valuables.

Purdah is generally thought to be a relic of ancient Persian culture, which was taken up by Arabs after the Islamic conquest of modern Iraq and parts of Iran in the seventh century. It was later taken to India by Persian-speaking Muslim conquerors in the twelfth century, where many Hindus adopted it. Islamic teachings do not require the veil, although Qur'an 33.53 asserts that women must dress modestly.

SEE ALSO: Islam; Qur'an

## Pure Land Buddhism

One of the most popular forms of Mahayana Buddhism, especially in China and Japan. In Pure Land Buddhism, devotion is directed toward Amhitabha, the "Buddha of Infinite Light." Amhitabha is thought to preside over a "Western Paradise" known as Sukavati, which means "pure land" or "pure realm" in Sanskrit. In this Pure Land, features of life unite to make all aspects of Buddhist enlightenment possible, even inevitable. Therefore believers hope to be reborn in the Pure Land. For those reborn there, the next steps are enlightenment and the attainment of nirvana.

Pure Land Buddhism was initially one of many Buddhist cults that appeared in the centuries following the Buddha's death. Its roots appear to have been in a particular practice of early Buddhism, which encouraged concentration on the "Buddhas of the ten directions." A variety of sects arose that emphasized this inclusion of the cult of Amitabha, which was based on stories of a monk named Dharmakara contained in early Sanskrit texts. Dharmakara promised that, upon becoming a Buddha himself (the future Amitabha), it would be possible for those who invoked his name faithfully to be reborn in the Western Paradise. Two Pure Land sutras reinforced the cult, although they differed on the proper path for devotees. A larger Pure Land sutra noted that meditation and the accumulation of good karma were necessary for rebirth as well as calling upon Amitabha. The smaller one, meanwhile, proclaimed that all that was necessary was to call upon Amitabha at the time of death.

By the fourth century, Pure Land Buddhism had taken root in China thanks to the efforts of a monk named Huiyuan who, along with his followers, formed a sect that devoted itself to meditation on the name of Amitabha. Over the next centuries the faith became increasingly popular thanks to a series of evangelizers and system-builders. One, Shandao (613–681) created China's first body of organized Pure Land practice. It involved five precepts: meditating on Amitabha and the Pure Land; worshipping Amitabha; reciting scripture; chanting Amitabha's name; and making offerings to him. The simplic-

ity of these acts was likely one of the major attractions of Pure Land Buddhism, as was the promise of an otherworldly paradise rather than the more abstract and distant concept of enlightenment. Meanwhile, representations of Amitabha Buddha and of the Western Paradise began to appear in popular and devotional art, with one of Amitabha's attendants being Avalokitesvara, an important bodhisattva. Pure Land Buddhism was especially popular during China's Tang dynasty (618–907), when it enjoyed the patronage of some of the dynasty's emperors. A period of persecution in the 840s resulted in the destruction of many monasteries and a suppression of the faith. But by that time Pure Land Buddhism had taken hold among China's population, who found it congenial with their folk traditions and even with Confucianism and Daoism.

Pure Land Buddhism, along with many other Chinese imports, was taken to Japan by Buddhist monks in the period from approximately 700 to 1000. It grew increasingly popular after the tenth century and developed a distinctly Japanese form through the leadership of a monk named Honen (1133–1212). Honen reinforced the notion that ordinary people were incapable of achieving enlightenment by themselves; they were inherently too inadequate, too prone to evil actions. Instead they needed the assistance of Buddhas such as Amida (the Japanese name for Amitabha). The way to assure this was through the pronunciation of the nembutsu, a shortening of the Japanese phrase namu Amida butsu, which means "I put my faith in Amida Buddha" as well as the performance of other rites of devotion such as those introduced by Shandao in China. Honen's disciple Shinran (1173–1263), founded what was to become the largest Pure Land sect in Japan, the True Pure Land sect. The sect bears elements of monotheism, since devotees are encouraged to worship Amida alone, not any other Buddha or bodhisattva. It also bears an odd resemblance to Protestant Christianity, since believers are urged to focus on faith in Amida rather than in the act of reciting his name; a single "primal vow" of faith is enough rather than regular nembutsu. Further-more, priests of this sect are allowed to marry. True Pure Land Buddhism has become a key element of Japanese culture, as not only millions of devotees profess the faith but many of its practices, such as those connected with funerals, are performed commonly even by nonbelievers.

SEE ALSO: Amitabha; Mahayana Buddhism; sutra

## qadi

An Islamic judge. Historically the qadi, who must be an adult male Muslim of recognized good character, have been appointed by Islamic rulers due to their knowledge of sharia, Islamic religious law. Following the model of the second caliph Omar, who appointed the first qadi, rulers have considered it their religious duty to place the administration of justice in the hands of qadis. Their jurisdiction has been primarily in secular matters mentioned in the Qur'an, such as marriage, divorce, and inheritance. Sometimes, however, qadi have taken a role in the adjudication of criminal and civil law and have become important administrators in Islamic states. Traditionally the judgment of the qadis has been final, though in most modern Islamic states the right to appeal his decisions has been put in place. Some Islamic states have abolished the institution entirely.

SEE ALSO: fatwa; sharia; ulema

## qi

A Chinese word meaning "breath" or "force" that is often spelled phonetically as "chi." The concept appears in various branches of Chinese religion. Daoists claimed that *qi* was a vital force present in the breath and in bodily fluids. Control of this *qi* through various physical disciplines or meditation allowed one to manipulate this energy, which was thought in turn to allow one to attain spiritual power and even longer life. The manipulation or mas-

tery of *qi* is also a focus of traditional Chinese medicine and such exercises as Tai-chi.

The Neo-Confucianists of the Song and Yuan dynasties (960–1279) contrasted *qi* with *li*, the latter being the true underlying nature or reality of things. For them *qi* was the vital force that moved through things and might affect them positively or negatively. It was possible to manipulate *qi*, but *li* was permanent. More positive personal *qi* might be secured through such measures as diet or, most importantly, breath control. On a broader scale *qi* was thought to be the foundation of the five elements of wood, metal, earth, water, and fire, which are themselves the basis of physical nature. The concept appears throughout Chinese thought in various ways; a common one is the science of feng shui, which at its heart is the attempt to direct *qi* through physical structures in ways that might be beneficial.

SEE ALSO: feng shui; *li*; yin-yang

## qibla

The direction toward which Muslims are supposed to pray. The qibla is toward the Ka'aba shrine in Mecca, and regardless of where they are in the world, Muslims should pray facing in that direction in order for their daily prayers to be fully true. Each mosque contains a niche, known as a mihrab, that indicates the proper qibla, while in the modern world creative solutions such as taped arrows placed in windowless hotel rooms perform the same

*The Islamic holy book, the Qu'ran, with the left page in English and the right page in Arabic.* © JAMES MARSHALL/CORBIS

function. Originally the prophet Muhammad proclaimed that qibla was to be toward Jerusalem, probably influenced in this by the strong Jewish traditions in place in Medina. He later changed it to Mecca. Qibla is important not only for prayers; Muslim dead are buried facing Mecca while devout Muslims eat the meat of animals slaughtered according to halal practices, one feature of which is that the animals must be facing Mecca when killed.

SEE ALSO: Five Pillars of Faith; Ka'aba; Muhammad

## Qur'an

The holy scripture of Islam. Muslims believe that the Qur'an is the direct, perfect word of God, and its text an earthly manifestation of God's presence. Its message replaces or supersedes all previous divine revelations, although it also "confirms" them. The Qur'an is the ultimate source of all Islamic belief and provides the foundation for the interpretation of Islamic law.

The Qur'an is made up of revelations made by God to the prophet Muhammad. Muhammad, a merchant of the Arabian city of Mecca, began receiving these revelations, both directly from God and via an intermediary, the angel Jibreel (Gabriel), in 610. They continued intermittently until Muhammad's death in 632. The word *qur'an* means "recitation"; the revelations were at first recited to Muhammad and then by him. The Prophet's first followers memorized these recitations as he spoke them and began to use them in prayers. Some of them were eventually written down during Muhammad's lifetime using his dictation. The first Qur'anic collection was made in the 630s, after the Prophet's death, by his scribe Zayd Thabit, working under the instructions of Abu Bakr, Muhammad's successor as leader of the Islamic community. Zayd and others later compiled a more definitive collection during the reign of the third of Muhammad's successors, the caliph Uthman, in the 650s. Any other versions of the recitations were ordered destroyed. The Qur'an that exists today is this definitive compilation.

The Qur'an contains 114 chapters known as suras. These are commonly described as either Meccan or Medinan suras depending on where Muhammad received the revelations. The earlier Meccan suras are shorter and written with vivid imagery in rhymed prose. Their teachings are mostly those of basic Islamic principle. They recognize that God is the source of all Creation and urge the unity of humanity within a community of believers. Believers are enjoined to recognize God's forgiveness and compassion as well as his judgment, since God's final judgment will ultimately come. The Meccan suras also acknowledge Muhammad's role as Messenger of God. The Medinan suras are composed of revelations granted to Muhammad after the establishment of the first Islamic community in the city of Medina in 622. They are generally longer than the earlier suras, use more straightforward language, and focus on matters relating to religious, social, and moral order, on the actual workings of the community of believers. Warfare, marriage and divorce, and behavior are among the issues the suras touch upon. They also describe the fundamental duties of Islam including the Five Pillars of Faith: profession of the faith, prayer, charity, fasting during the month of Ramadan, and pilgrimage. The Qur'an does not place the suras in chronological order. Rather, they are organized more or less according to length, with the longest suras apppearing first. The exception to this is the first sura, known as al-Fatiha, "the opening," which is a brief devotional prayer commonly considered to contain the essence of the entire Qur'an.

*Only One God* An understanding of the Qur'an in its entirety provides the basis for the understanding of the Islamic faith. The scripture makes clear that only one God exists for the faithful: There is no other God but God. This God is the Creator of the perfect order of the universe and of all within it. He is separate from Creation but also constantly present within it. The Qur'an, God's revealed word, provides humanity with all the guidance it needs, and human beings must be prepared to accept that guidance, to submit to the will of God. Indeed, the word *islam* is generally accepted to mean such submission to God's will. The extent to which individuals do this will be the basis of God's final judgment of humanity. The Qur'an's verses emphasize that God is "compassionate and merciful," and indeed such a statement appears at the start of every sura. But he is also ready to pass strict judgments on his day of judgment. God has given human beings many qualities and the potential for greatness. But of all his creatures they are the only ones fully capable of evil, and only through "submission" will they be fully able to guard against their evil tendencies as well as completely open themselves to God's mercy and compassion.

The Islamic God, according to the Qur'an, is the same God worshipped by Jews and Christians, and indeed the text itself notes the line of the prophets that was eventually "sealed" by the final prophet, Muhammad. These include Adam, Abraham, Moses, and Jesus. But Jewish and Christian communities never completely accepted the teachings of these prophets as contained in such texts as the Hebrew Bible and Christian New Testament. Consequently these earlier revelations had become corrupted and impure. Only the Qur'an, God's final word, remains pure and perfect. Indeed, the Qur'an is not simply a compilation of God's revelations. It is an attribute of God, eternal and unchanging.

On many matters the Qur'an is indirect or ambiguous, a fact acknowledged by believers. Parts of it, for example, emphasize human free will while others assert that a "person's fate is hung about his shoulders" in a way that cannot be altered. The Qur'an also lacks specific information on Islamic law as well as the ritual requirements of the faithful beyond the Five Pillars of Faith. To address these features believers use, first, the Hadith, a living commentary on the Qur'an, as well as the Sunna, which provides more elaborate guidelines for the 90 percent of Muslims who belong to the Sunni branch of Islam. In addition, numerous schools of interpretation have arisen with different understandings of Islamic law, of free will, and of many other issues. The disputes that have arisen focus invariably on interpretation rather than on the Qur'an itself, the foundation for all interpretation.

*Uses of the Qur'an* Believers use the Qur'an in distinct ways, and in this sense it has acquired some of the coloring of a sacred ritual object. Muslims generally only approach the text while in a state of ritual purity, which requires washing beforehand. Some believe that the text itself has the power to heal or perform other miracles, as it conveys God's power and compassion. Unsurprisingly, the Qur'an has been the basis of Islamic education since its first appearance, and its often poetic writing encourages believers to memorize and recite its suras, an echo of the earliest groups of believers. Those who memorize the entire text to the extent of being able to recite it are granted the honorific title of hafiz. The suras have also been frequently set to music, and they have been chanted by Sufi mystics in search of divine visions.

Since the Qur'an is considered the eternal and unchangeable word of God, Islamic tradition has urged that believers read and recite it in the original Arabic language in which it was transmitted. Most of the faithful continue to do so, reciting Qur'anic prayers daily in Arabic even if they do not understand the language. Although translations into most languages are now commonly available, the scholarly or devout consider these translations to be only "paraphrases" or "interpretations" that believers might use to begin their understanding of the canonical Arabic text. One recent English "paraphrase" of sura 2, verse 255, the "Throne Verse," runs:

> God! There is no God but He, the living, the eternal, self-subsisting, ever sustaining. Neither does somnolence affect Him nor sleep. To Him belongs all that is in the heavens and the earth, and who can intercede with him except by His leave? Known to Him is all that is present before men and what is hidden and that which is to come upon them, and not even a little of His knowledge can they grasp except when He wills. His Throne extends over the heavens and the earth, and He tires not protecting them: He alone is high and supreme.

# rabbi

In general, a Jewish religious teacher. The Hebrew term can be translated as either "my teacher" or "my master." The term first came into usage during the late period of the second Temple, the first century B.C. to A.D. 70; before this Jewish religious experts were generally known as sages. As Rabbinical Judaism took shape over the centuries after the destruction of the second Temple, rabbis emerged as the spiritual leaders in the Jewish religion. In order to achieve the status of rabbi, one had to demonstrate thorough knowledge in both the oral and written Torah, or the Jewish spiritual tradition. In time, and especially among the Jewish communities of Europe, rabbis emerged as community leaders as well as spiritual guides.

In the modern world, and especially in Reformed and Conservative congregations, rabbbis have taken on roles closely approximating those of clergy in other faiths: preaching, providing pastoral counseling and presiding over such ceremonies as bar mitzvahs, weddings, and funerals. They do this while maintaining their status as teachers and maintainers of Jewish traditions and, indeed, it is not unheard-of for rabbis to profess atheism; in this case their goal is to preserve community traditions rather than perform religious duties. In the West, rabbis generally have to undertake a long period of both secular and spiritual education before they can be ordained as rabbis, while in Israel rabbis are trained in yeshivas, or Jewish schools.

SEE ALSO: synagogue; Torah; yeshiva

# Radha

The consort of the Hindu god Krishna and, in some traditions, a goddess in her own right. Radha was one of the gopis, or cowherdesses, among whom Krishna cavorts in one of the most famous Krishna stories, where he entertains and seduces the gopis in an allegory of divine love. The secular literary tradition, rather than any religious one, depicted her as Krishna's favorite lover in Hinduism's developmental centuries (i.e., before A.D. 1000). By the fourteenth and fifteenth centuries, however, Radha began to achieve a higher status in both secular and religious lore. For some, her love for Krishna was an allegory of the human love for the divine. More abstract theology focused on Krishna-worship held that she, like Krishna, was an embodiment of the ultimate reality, or Brahman. Her rise in status is attributed, at least in part, to a popular epic poem known as the *Gitagovinda*, written by Jayadeva in the twelfth century. The *Gitagovinda* is an erotically charged love poem that some choose to interpret, again, as an allegory of divine love. Adding to Radha's popularity is her frequent depiction at the side of Krishna in Hindu religious and popular art, making her a commonly known figure in popular Hinduism.

SEE ALSO: bhakti; Krishna; Shakti

# Rama

An important Hindu deity and, along with Krishna, an avatar of the god Vishnu.

Rama is best known as the hero of the great Sanskrit epic Ramayana, although he appears in the Mahabharatha as well. The Ramayana provides the common understanding of Rama's attributes. He is depicted there as the ideal man, the model for right conduct, reason, and for such qualities as loyalty and leadership. His chief consort is Sita, and the two are commonly held to be the ideal husband and wife. Along with Krishna, Rama was the focus of the bhakti, or devotional, cults that became common in Hinduism from the sixth century onwards. His popularity spread with the emergence of translations of the Ramayana into vernacular languages such as Hindi and Tamil in the following centuries, with some Hindu sects claiming that he was the supreme god.

Rama is most popular in northern India, where the town of Ayodhya, in Uttar Pradesh state, is held to be his birthplace. In 1992 Hindu fundamentalists destroyed an Islamic mosque thought to have been built on the site of his birthplace, inciting riots in many parts of India. Meanwhile, his name in the form of "Ram, Ram" is a common expression, even a greeting, among many Hindus. In art, Rama is generally depicted with blue skin, like Vishnu and Krishna, holding a bow and arrow. Common images show scenes derived from the Ramayana, with Sita accompanying Rama along with Hanuman, the monkey-god.

SEE ALSO: Ramayana; Sita; Vishnu

## Ramadan

The ninth month of the Islamic calendar and the month of fasting, according to Islam's Five Pillars of Faith. According to the Qur'an, Ramadan is a blessed month, when the holy text "was sent down as a guidance for the people" (Qur'an 2:185).

During Ramadan, Muslims are required to avoid food, drink, sexual activity, and smoking during daylight hours. Some are exempt, notably young children, sick people, travelers, soldiers, and women giving birth or menstruating; Islamic teachings do not require the faithful to sacrifice their health. Except in the case of the young, however, the exempt are expected to "make up" the fast at a later time when their condition allows.

Ramadan has also become an occasion for special attention to family or for more focused devotion to prayer and to God. Some choose to spend the final ten days of the month in retreat in a mosque. The fasting period ends when a reliable witness reports to the proper authorities that a new moon can be seen. A three-day festival, the Eid al-Fitr, follows.

SEE ALSO: calendars; Five Pillars of Faith; hajj; Qur'an

## Ramanuja
## (1017–1137)

An important Hindu philosopher of the Vaishnavite school, which focuses on the worship of Vishnu. In several important texts, notably a commentary on the Bhagavad Gita known as the *Bhagavadgita-bhasya*, Ramanuja provided an intellectual foundation and systematic theology for the bhakti, or devotional, practices then growing increasingly popular in India. He was born in the Tamil-speaking areas of southern India but during his lifetime traveled widely throughout the south, founding temples and even converting kings. According to tradition, he lived for 120 years.

Ramanuja's philosophy was centered around his sense that the world was real and had distinct characteristics; it was not

*A scene from Hindu epic poem* Ramayana, *bordered with Sanskrit text.* © BURSTEIN COLLECTION/CORBIS

an illusion or a negative force as some Hindu sects taught. Intellectual activity in the form of thought and discussion were not only themselves real, but helped the devotee to gain a better understanding of ultimate truth. Ramanuja charactized the world as the "body" of Vishnu, having a relationship to but not a separate existence from God. The soul, likewise, does not have a separate existence. The purpose of the body is to serve the soul, while the goal of the soul is to serve God. Furthermore, he argued, the world is a manifestation of God, and to criticize it or misunderstand it is to criticize or misunderstand God. Translated into the practices of worldly Hinduism, Ramanuja held that both bhakti practices and temple rituals, not one or the other, helped the devotee

to better understand God.

SEE ALSO: bhakti; Vishnu

## Ramayana

A great Hindu epic poem. Written in Sanskrit and containing some twenty-four thousand verses, the "Story of Rama" is attributed to the poet and sage Valmiki. It is also very old, dating back perhaps to 300 B.C. although some scholars hold that its current version may have been compiled as late as the first century A.D.

The Ramayana is the life story of Rama, a prince of the north Indian city of Ayodhya. Rama is educated by a religious sage, wins the heart and hand of Sita at a tournament, and becomes a warrior-king. After being banished from his homeland as the result of a family squabble, he spends fourteen years in exile in the forest along with Sita and Lakshmana, his half brother. While he and Lakshmana were away hunting, Sita was abducted by Ravana, the demon-king of Lanka (likely today's Sri Lanka). Rama then sets about rescuing her, enlisting the help of, among others, Hanuman, the dutiful monkey-god. After many adventures. Rama ends up killing Ravana and setting Sita free.

The stories of heroism turn to ones of morality when Sita finds it necessary to prove that she was faithful to Rama during her captivity. She passes through a trial by fire but, even then, the people of Ayodhya do not believe in her fidelity and Rama banishes her to the forest. There she meets the sage Valmiki and bears two children, the sons of Rama. Even though the family eventually reunites, Sita remains unable to fully clear her name and, at her own request, she is swallowed up by the earth.

The Ramayana is one of Hinduism's great sources of ethical teachings, particularly with regard to Rama and Sita, who are considered the ideal husband and wife. Rama, meanwhile, provides a model for the proper conduct of not only a husband but a leader and a man in general, while Hanuman is the epitome of loyalty. The poem does not shy away from conflict among these various teachings; despite his love for Sita, Rama places his duties as a king higher when he decides to banish her because of his people's charges of her infidelity. Meanwhile, religious interpretations of the poem focus on how the god Vishnu enters human affairs from time to time in order to protect the world from evil. According to these teachings Rama is the seventh incarnation of Vishnu, and not merely a heroic human figure.

The poem remains extremely popular, especially in its vernacular translations. For Hindus it can be the source of arcane religious lessons or meditative processes or, alternatively, a popular story of heroism and romance. In many parts of northern India, an annual month long festival known as the Ram-lila offers an enactment of the poem while in the south it provides the source for much dance and drama. The Ramayana spread to various parts of Southeast Asia where it contributed to the local folk culture, and Rama and Sita are renowned as ideal lovers in these regions as much as they are in India. The seventeenth- and eighteenth-century capital of the kingdom of Siam (now Thailand), was Ayutthaya (Ayodhya), named after Rama's birthplace and a sign of the enduring popularity of the tale.

SEE ALSO: Mahabaratha; Sita; Vishnu

## Rastafarianism

A religious and political movement that began in the 1950s among the descendants of African slaves on the Caribbean islands of Jamaica and Dominica and later spread around the world, although its adherents remain fairly small in number. Rastafarianism rejected both the Europeanized culture and the forms of Christianity that predominated in the Caribbean and was organized instead around a specialized interpretation of messianic Judaism. Rastafarians worship Hailie Selassie I, who was emperor of Ethiopia until his country was conquered by the Italians in 1935. Known as Ras (Prince) Tafari, before becoming emperor, Hailie Selassie went on to become a focus of both anti-imperialist and pro-African movements. Rastafarians believe that he was a divine being and the messiah of the black peoples. They hold furthermore that they are the descendants of the ancient Israelites, condemned for their sins to live under white domination for centuries. Their hope is to one day return to Africa, their true home. In this the Rastafarians were apparently influenced by the Back to Africa movement led by the American Marcus Garvey in the 1910s and 1920s.

In time the Rastafarian movement splintered into several groups. Their focus was less on a return to Africa than on more militant forms of black activism, or alternatively, mystical spirituality. During the 1970s Rastafarianism became widely known thanks to the reggae music of proponents Bob Marley, Peter Tosh, and others; when Marley died in 1981, he was given a reggae state funeral in Jamaica. Most Rastafarians today, outside of the Caribbean, are West Indian immigrants to the United States, Great Britain, or other countries, although the movement has had some appeal to other groups, such as the indigenous Maori of New Zealand. There is also a small community of Rastafarians in Ethiopia. The Rastafarian lifestyle encourages vegetarianism and the wearing of dreadlocks. The smoking of ganja, or marijuana, is also a common practice.

SEE ALSO: Afro-Brazilian religions; Afro-Caribbean religions; new religious movements, Western

## Reconstructionist Judaism

A modern Jewish movement based in the United States. Reconstructionism was founded by the rabbi Mordecai Kaplan, whose teachings were the inspiration behind the Society for the Advancement of Judaism, opened in New York City in 1922. Kaplan taught that Judaism was a continuously evolving civilization, not a time-bound or historical tradition requiring Jews to continually look backward. Recon-

structionist communities emphasize intensive and participatory study, allowing members to immerse themselves in Jewish religious thought and practice. According to the movement's main text, the Sabbath Prayer Book published in 1945, Jews should downplay such ideas as the Exodus and the belief that they are God's chosen people. As of 1998 there were some one hundred Reconstructionist groups, and the movement featured such institutions as the Reconstructionist Rabbinical College and the Reconstructionist Rabbinical Association, both based in Philadelphia.

SEE ALSO: Orthodox Judaism; Reform Judaism; Torah

## rectification of names

An important tenet of Confucian philosophy, especially as it applied to political leadership. The rectification of names is simply the argument that everything should be known by its proper name. When words are misused, only confusion and incorrect action result, and people might begin to feel resentment with their leaders, who they might feel are trying to mislead and manipulate them. Furthermore, Confucius argued, when words are not applied properly, this shows a lack of logic and clear thinking which is also harmful to social order. Rulers, he said, must be rulers, ministers must be ministers, and subjects must be subjects, and the precise meanings of those terms should be commonly understood and applied. Likewise, politics must remain politics and religion religion, and the separate spheres of the two should not be confused.

SEE ALSO: Confucianism; Five Classics; *li*

## Reformation

The movement in Christianity that resulted in Christian history's second great schism, or split: that between Roman Catholicism and Protestantism. The latter inspired the numerous "protest" churches that emerged in western Europe in the 1500s and after and rejected both Roman Catholic tradition and the authority of the popes.

This Protestant Reformation had its roots in the migivings of some Christians over some of the practices and theological assumptions of the established church of Rome. Few of the questions were new, but they were given new life in the early 1500s thanks to the intellectual habits of the Renaissance, which encouraged free inquiry into the "original" sources of all belief, and also thanks to the appearance of printing technology, which made the spread of ideas much easier. In 1517 the German monk Martin Luther (1465–1519) drew up a list known as the Ninety-five Theses. These "theses" were points of dispute, particular issues that Luther believed church authorities should examine. Many of them were concerned with indulgences, a common church practice by which one substituted cash payments for the ordinary penance offered by a priest for the forgiveness of sins. Although the story is probably anecdotal, popular Protestant tradition holds that the Reformation began when Luther nailed the Ninety-five Theses onto a church door in his hometown of Wittenburg. Luther went on to develop a simplified Christian theology based on three principles: salvation by faith alone; the priesthood of all believers; and the ultimate authority of scripture. Church authorities demanded that Luther, an officer of the church, withdraw his criticisms and objections. When he refused, he was excommunicated by the 1521 Edict of Worms. Luther was protected for the rest of his life by various German noblemen who had territorial or political axes to grind with the Roman Catholic Church.

An important feature of Luther's teachings was his desire to make Christian teachings readily available to ordinary people; prior to this time worship services were generally conducted in Latin, a language known only to the well educated. Luther's contributions included a German translation of the Bible, while other reformers used other methods to help devise a more "popular" Christianity. Among them were the German Philip Melanchthon (1497–1560) and the Swiss Ulrich Zwingli (1484–1531). Melancthon wanted to revise church rituals so that they would be more meaningful to ordinary people, while Zwingli's churches abolished the Mass as well as other ceremonial components of worship, such as incense, vestments, and decorations. Zwingli held that the demands of the people might just as well reflect the will of God as the dictates of religious elites. Another Swiss reformer, John Calvin (1509–1564), published an important text called the *Institutes of the Christian Religion* and, briefly, ran a theocratic government in the city of Geneva. Both were major influences in the development of Protestant institutions, with their preference for leaders who arose from the people and for lay officials. Calvin's teaching was also the basis for the conservative sects known variously as Puritans or Reformed Protestants, which took hold in the Netherlands, Scotland, and, for a short time, England.

*Politics and Religion* Political developments continued to reinforce church reforms. In 1529, at a meeting known as the Diet of Speyer attended by many important kings and princes from the German states, leaders granted the "protest" churches what amounted to official recognition by asserting that each prince had the right to choose which form of Christianity would be followed in his lands. Meanwhile in England, King Henry VIII broke with Rome in the 1520s and proclaimed himself the head of the renamed Anglican Church in England. Henry's motivation was largely his desire to end his first marriage so that he could marry again, a move opposed by Roman Catholic authorities. But the long-term result was the establishment of the Anglican form of Protestantism, the closest of the Protestant churches to Catholic ritual. Meanwhile, Henry's breakaway lent the authority of one of Europe's most powerful kings to the larger Protestant movement. In 1548, by which time Protestantism was spreading rapidly across Europe, the Peace of Augsburg, which ended numerous conflicts in the German states, gave further authority to the decisions originally taken in 1529.

In response to this threat, the Roman Catholic Church underwent a reformation of its own. This Counter-Reformation succeeded, at least partly, in arresting the spread of Protestantism, particularly in central and eastern Europe. The Reformation itself might be said to have ended in 1648. By then Protestantism had spread to the New World. But that year also saw the conclusion of an agreement known as the Peace of Westphalia. The Peace ended about a century of religious wars including, among other conflicts, a civil war in France, the war for the independence of the Netherlands, and the razing of much of the German states and the deaths of an estimated one-third of their population. The Reformation had split European Christendom in two.

SEE ALSO: Anglican (Episcopal) Church; Calvinism; Counter-Reformation

# Reform Judaism

A branch of Judaism that emerged in the context of the eighteenth-century Age of Reason in Europe and which, along with Conservative and Orthodox, is one of the main forms of Judaism in the modern world. Reform Jews are ready to adapt Jewish traditions to the modern world, or even when appropriate, to abandon them. At the core of this belief is the understanding that Judaism is an ongoing and developing entity, rather than a fixed body of beliefs and practices that was settled centuries ago.

Formally, Reform Judaism began in the early 1800s when German rabbis, fearful of losing members of their community to secularism and the attractions of modern science and assimilation into mainstream society, began to question the elements of traditional Jewish practice that set them apart from German gentiles, such as dietary prohibitions and the use of the Yiddish language in everyday life and the Hebrew language for prayer. In this they were inspired by the work of the German Jewish thinker Moses Mendelssohn (1729–1786), who created a German-Hebrew Bible and supported universal religious tolerance, claiming that Judaism and Christianity could comfortably coexist. In 1801 Israel Jacobsen established a school whose practices became a model for Reform Jews. Services were held in German rather than Hebrew, men and women sat together, references to a messiah were omitted, and the coming-of-age ceremony for boys, the bar mitzvah, was extended, as the bat mitzvah, to girls. As the Reform movement spread throughout Germany, other practices were abandoned as unmodern: wearing of prayer shawls, daily worship, and the prohibition of work on the Sabbath among them. Services were made more congenial through the use of music and hymn singing, and dietary restrictions were also abandoned

In 1841 the first Reform congregation in the United States was set up in Charleston, South Carolina. The movement continued to grow with the arrival of waves of German Jewish immigrants, especially after 1850. These newcomers published Reform prayer books, and established such Reform institutions as the Hebrew Union College in Cinncinnati and the Union of American Hebrew Congregations. Leaders and scholars established an official platform for American Reform Jews at a conference in Pittsburgh in 1885. Among its injunctions was that Reform Jews should no longer focus on an expected return to Israel in any geographical sense; this claim was later modified with the rise of the Zionist movement and the establishment of modern Israel in 1947. Meanwhile, Reform Jewish scholars maintain a variety of overall philosophical stances, with the most radical arguing for a wholesale abandoning of traditional rituals while others claim instead that Reform Judaism simply emphasizes the continual updating of Jewish practice to suit new historical circumstances.

Reform Judaism continues to debate adaptations to new circumstances. Recent concerns include whether or not single parents should be permitted as full members of congregations, attitudes toward homosexuality, and whether women should be accepted as rabbis (they have been). Among its most striking reforms is the giving up of the matrilineal requirement for membership in a Jewish community (outside of rather rigorous conversion procedures). Reform Jews say that a person is a Jew who is born of one Jewish parent (mother or father) and raised as a Jew. This might be a gesture toward the increasingly common practice of religious intermarriage among American and Canadian Jews, where as many as 50 percent of young people marry outside the faith. In modern Israel, meanwhile, Reform Judaism is not recognized officially although there are a few Reform groups there. Only Orthodox rabbis have official status and the Orthodox see the Jewish tradition as more settled and, among other things, do not recognize the ability of women to become rabbis.

SEE ALSO: Conservative Judaism; Orthodox Judaism; Reconstructionist Judaism

## reincarnation

The basic concept of life after death in Hinduism and Buddhism. It also appears in such smaller Indian religions as Jainism and Sikhism and in some modern religious movements, notably theosophy. Each of these traditions has its variations, but in general they hold that each person's soul is more or less permanent while their bodies are transient and temporary. After death, the soul is reincarnated into a new body. The Indian religions claim that the soul, furthermore, carries the burdens or rewards of present deeds, or karma, into future incarnations. Each religion provides a way for the soul to be released from this "wheel of birth and rebirth," or samsara, and this process is at the heart of these religious traditions. Reincarnation is also known as the transmigration of souls or metempsychosis.

SEE ALSO: karma; moksha; samsara

## relics

Physical objects held to have religious significance. In general the use of relics in religious ceremonies is an aspect of folk or popular religion rather than official theology and is similar to the worship of icons or images, although in Roman Catholic Christianity and Buddhism a theology and tradition of relics has arisen.

In Roman Catholicism, relics are usually associated with the saints, either objects thought to have been owned or used by a saint or pieces of his or her physical remains such as bones. The first mention of them in Christian history is of handkerchiefs taken from the body of Saint Paul and used to heal the sick. During the Middle Ages, a substantial market in (often false) relics arose as devotees sought closer physical identification with the saints as well as the hope that relics could encourage miracles. At the sixteenth-century Council of Trent Catholic officials made legitimate the veneration of relics, provided their authenticity was verified by the church. Among the most prized relics in years afterward were alleged fragments of the true cross or other objects not connected with a saint but with Jesus Christ himself. Among the most famous of these is the Shroud of Turin, alleged to be Jesus' burial cloth but proven by recent scientific investigation to be less than a thousand years old.

In Buddhism, relics are generally physical remnants thought to come from the Buddha himself. Often temples or stupas were built around these relics, which might range from bones to teeth to even the ashes from his funeral pyre. A Temple of the Tooth at Kandy, in Sri Lanka, supposedly contains one of the Buddha's canine teeth. Even alleged footprints of the Buddha have been the source of veneration and stupa-building. Similarly to Catholic veneration, Buddhists also revere the relics of saints, heroes, and bodhisattvas.

SEE ALSO: iconoclasm; pilgrimage

# religion

In general, the systems of thought, belief, and practice that emphasize gods or a supernatural world and which underlie the ethical mores of given, identified communities. Religion is a fundamental element of human experience, and features of religion, such as funeral rites, can be found even among the small bands of hunter-gatherers who wandered parts of the earth two or three hundred thousand years ago. Philosophers, scientists, and scholars, primarily in the West, have suggested a wide range of definitions for and explanations of religion. The British philosopher Alfred North Whitehead, for example, claimed that "Religion is what the individual does with his own solitariness," while German economist and political thinker Karl Marx famously asserted that "Religion is the sigh of the oppressed creature … it is the opiate of the masses." The anthropologist Clifford Geertz saw religion as primarily a set of symbols that explained the world to people, while Austrian psychoanalyst Sigmund Freud wrote that "religious beliefs correspond closely with the fantasies of infantile life." In a more abstract sense that does not easily lend itself to rational explanation, many scholars explain religion as the sense of something outside ordinary experience, of a divine "presence" known as the numinous, a term derived from the Latin word *numen*, or "divine power."

No definition of the features of religion is completely applicable to all of the established faiths, although a few generalizations are possible. Most religions have founders, and their development can be traced historically. They rest on a specified canon of texts. Beliefs and community mores are expressed in regular and well-defined rituals. They ultimately rest on faith rather than empirical and systematic proofs. Other systems of belief, such as humanism or even fascism or Marxism, have these features also (and might therefore be considered religions in some respects). But only "religions" emphasize the numinous. Hinduism does not have a founder, but offers many gods and many sacred texts. Buddhism preaches no supreme being or beings but offers believers the attainment of spiritual understandings well beyond established norms. Confucianism centers on a vision of an ideal society as well as reverence for a past and present which might include ancestral spirits. Daoism, like Buddhism, offers no gods but rather a richer spiritual life and has identifiable founders and canonical texts. Shinto's origins and texts are vague, but it connects believers closely with the world of the spirits and with nature. Judaism, Christianity, and Islam share all of these defining features.

SEE ALSO: philosophy of religion; theism

## resurrection

The raising to life of a person or divine being believed to be dead. The phenomenon is most closely associated with Christianity but it can also be found in Judaism and Islam.

The central event of Christianity is the resurrection of Jesus Christ three days after his death by crucifixion. Christian theology holds that, through the resurrection, Christ conquered death, and in so doing provided the example of how believers might also conquer death by professing sincere faith in his sacrifice. These believers, following death, will be raised again to bodily life in heaven. The celebration of Christ's resurrection, or Easter, is the greatest Christian festival.

The Hebrew Bible, meanwhile, mentions the resurrection of the dead in sev-

eral of its books. In general these early Jewish writers put forward the idea that the nation of Israelites will rise from the dead upon achieving true righteousness following a period of judgment. Rabbinic Jewish belief took up the idea, and since it holds that the body and soul are inseparable, both will be resurrected as long as, again, they are of a person of righteousness. Some Jewish sects later abandoned the notion, preferring instead the doctrine of immortality of the soul.

Islam also preaches of a time of judgment at which point all people will die and then be resurrected. Then, depending on the deeds of his life as recorded in two separate books, one a record of good actions, the other a record of evil ones, he or she will be sent to heaven or hell.

SEE ALSO: heaven; hell; Jesus of Nazareth

## Revelation

The final book of the Christian New Testament, and the primary statement of early Christian eschatology. The text is also commonly known as the Book of Revelation or Revelation to John, after its author, who also wrote the New Testament Gospel that bears his name. Tradition holds that it was composed at a location in modern-day Turkey known as Patmos. Scholars suspect, however, that the book had several authors and was not actually compiled until the last decades of the first century. It is unique among New Testament texts in that it is neither historical nor didactic (instructional) in nature. Instead Revelation is apocalyptic, using various literary methods, most commonly descriptions of visions, to describe aspects of the final judgment of the Christian God.

The text is divided into two parts. In the first, its author or authors write letters to early Christian communities admonish-

*The Four Horsemen of the Apocalypse: War, Fire, Pestilence, and Death, who, according to the Book of Revelations, will ride the earth during the apocalypse.*

ing them to remain true to their faith. The second contains numerous allegories and symbols related to God's intervention in history and of the fates of peoples who have resisted God's injunctions. These include mentions of Satan and of the Christian hell, although few of the statements are explained fully and it is unclear whether their authors intended them to be taken literally; certainly Christians and scholars have differed widely on ways to interpret Revelation since it appeared.

When the text is placed within its historical context, it seems to reflect a kind of crisis of faith brought on by the persecution of early Christians by the Roman Em-

pire or by Jewish authorities. Christians are reminded that, if they remain steadfast in their faith, God will lead them to triumph over their enemies. These enemies might not only include the Roman Empire but other, perhaps more figurative or metaphorical, forces of evil or bad faith. Provided Christians hold true, they will be protected and God will have his final victory at the end of time. One verse of Revelations refers to a thousand-year period of trial and testing, inspiring millennialist sentiments among some Christians.

SEE ALSO: apocalypse; eschatology; New Testament

## Roman Catholicism

One of the three main branches of Christianity, along with Eastern Orthodoxy and Protestantism. Roman Catholicism is by far the largest of the three, with nearly one billion adherents. The church's institutions are based in the Vatican in Rome, and believers are concentrated in Europe and in North, South, and Central America. But Roman Catholic congregations can be found around the world. Catholics are governed institutionally by over two thousand church districts known as dioceses, and they are ministered to by over 400,000 priests. The head of the institutional church, the pope, is one of the most recognizable and powerful individuals in the world, and the church either directly administers or is affiliated with a number of other bodies ranging from schools and universities to charitable organizations. Meanwhile, Catholic community and missionary organizations remain active around the world. Historically, the Roman Catholic Church has been a primary patron of the arts, particularly in Europe.

In basic terms, Roman Catholic belief and practice differs from that of other

Christians in clearly visible ways. Catholics accept the authority of the popes and the infallibility of their official decisions on matters of faith and morals. They also accept the religious authority of Roman Catholic tradition in addition to that of holy scripture, believing that both are vehicles of God's grace. The Catholic service, commonly known as the Mass, follows well-defined liturgical patterns and until fairly recently was performed regularly in Latin, the official language of the church. Recent reforms based on the insistence of Catholic communities have resulted in the official sanction of masses conducted in modern everyday, or vernacular, languages. Believers, meanwhile, take part in seven sacraments, or deeds that are thought to confer the grace of God. These are baptism, the Eucharist, confirmation, confession and penance, marriage, priestly ordination, and extreme unction (commonly known as last rites). Many Catholics also take part in the reverence of the Virgin Mary or of the saints, practices which have inspired some of the church's most colorful festivals and works of art.

The word *catholic* means "universal," and the Catholic Church traces its roots to the "Universal [Christian] Church of Rome" that emerged in the first centuries after the life and death of Jesus. This era is known as the "patristic" era after a Latin term for the early church fathers. From a small Jewish sect located in the Roman province of Judea, early Christianity spread widely. Nearly from the beginning it established its presence in Rome thanks to the efforts of Peter, one of Jesus' apostles, and Paul, early Christianity's great evangelizer to the gentiles (non-Jews). Although Roman authorities initially rejected the new religion, many ordinary citizens were attracted by its focus on charity, morality,

and community life. By the third century the early Christian church was beginning to develop the institutions that would survive as Roman Catholicism. These included an authoritative scripture (The New and Old Testaments), and a structure roughly modeled on that of the Roman army. This included the division of Roman Christendom into administrative divisions known as dioceses, with each headed by an official known as a bishop. The bishop of Rome (later, the pope), who traced his institutional lineage to Peter, would have rough primacy over the other bishops (although this custom was often disputed). Christian communities, meanwhile, would be ministered by layers of priests and deacons answerable to the bishops.

*The Universal Church of Rome* These institutional elements helped to stabilize and perpetuate the church and perhaps even made the new religion more attractive to non-Christians, as the Roman Empire slowly collapsed in the fourth and fifth centuries. In 313 the Roman emperor Constantine ended any official suppression of the church by declaring it a legal religion; Constantine himself was the first Christian emperor. And by the end of the fourth century, Christianity had become the state religion. Administrative conflict was brewing, however, as the effective capital of the Roman Empire had shifted eastward to Constantinople (now Istanbul in Turkey). This provided the eastern bishops with greater authority than they had exercised earlier, and they often challenged the place of the bishops of Rome.

Meanwhile, a number of early church councils further established Roman Catholic doctrine and practice as well as condemning as heresies alternative ideas and approaches to Christianity. These included the Council of Chalcedon in 451, which established the Nicene Creed as a basic statement of faith and asserted that, contrary to opposing opinions, Jesus Christ had both a divine and human nature. In this same era the Christian theologian Augustine contributed such essential ideas to developing Roman Catholic doctrine as original sin, the notion that all human beings are guilty of sin and can only be saved by God's grace.

Another important development in these centuries was the rise of the monastic movement, which is far more prominent in Roman Catholicism than Eastern Orthodoxy and outside of the Anglican movement, does not appear in Protestantism at all. The first major monastic order in the Roman world was the Benedictine order. Its founder, Benedict of Nursia (ca. 480–547), founded a monastery near Rome that established the basic pattern for later orders. Entrants to the order (monks) made lifelong commitments that could only be broken in rare instances. All monks and nuns (women were included in Benedict's early scheme) took vows of charity, poverty, and obedience. They had to fully recognize the authority of monastery leaders, whether abbots or abbesses, and adhere to a strict daily course of prayer, hymns, and study. Later orders built upon this model but offered approaches to monasticism ranging from mendicancy and asceticism to more assertive missionary and educational work. Versions of these vows are also taken by Roman Catholic priests who, along with monks and nuns and in contrast to the clergy of other faiths, are not permitted to marry.

The city of Rome, and therefore the Western Roman Empire, fell to Germanic warlords in 476. This left the church as the main source of stability in those regions, further increasing the power of the bishops of Rome. Over the next centuries, most of the Germanic peoples converted to Christianity and officially recognized the authority of the bishops of Rome, whom they called "papa," or pope. Thanks to this military and political support, the popes were now comfortable in continuing to claim authority over Christians in the still-existing Eastern Roman Empire (commonly called the Byzantine Empire). In the East, however, bishops maintained a greater sense of authority over their jurisdictions, and at the Council of Chalcedon had recognized a group of "primates" or patriarchs who had authority over the bishops. Except for the pope, all the primates were eastern bishops: those of Constantinople, Alexandria, Jerusalem, and Antioch.

*Europe's Church* In 1054 the Roman Church formally split with the eastern churches, which went on to represent Eastern Orthodoxy. Soon after, the popes formally asserted their authority over western European kings by insisting, among other things, on the authority to select bishops and on their power over all matters related to religion. In 1095 Pope Urban II called for a Crusade to the Holy Land using western Europe's military might. Its ostensible purpose was to protect Christians and holy pilgrimage sites in and near Jerusalem, but Urban also wanted to try to bring all Christians, even those in the east, under his jurisdiction. The period of Crusades was to last for nearly two hundred years, but only served to widen the breach between the Roman Catholic and Eastern churches.

In Europe, meanwhile, the church was the dominant institution, controlling or influencing virtually every aspect of life. Beyond its influence in politics, the church started the first universities and ran almost every educational institution. Monasteries often served as commercial and community centers as well as religious ones, and almost all art, architecture, and music was religious art, architecture, and music. During the fourteenth century, the influence of the church waned when the papacy was moved to Avignon in southern France (1307–1371) thanks to the scheming of French kings and other nobles, but it reasserted itself in the fifteenth century. Then, the church served as both a political patron and an artistic one, beginning the construction of its greatest monument, St. Peter's Basilica in Rome. It was also a political power in its own right, as the popes ruled a collection of Papal States in central Italy.

In the sixteenth century, the Roman Catholic Church was challenged by the Protestant Reformation, when numerous reformers rejected the authority of the popes and the other elements of the Roman Catholic infrastructure, as well as some of its doctrine. The Reformation broke the church's hold on all European Christians, splitting European Christendom into two branches. In response, the Roman Catholic Church initiated the Counter-Reformation, characterized by the Council of Trent (1545–1563). At this council the Catholic bureaucracy was made more efficient and the popes were discouraged from direct political intervention. The council also reinforced the importance of a new, militant monastic order known familiarly as the Jesuits. At the same time, Catholic leaders insisted upon their traditional doctrinal stance, that Christian authority came not only from holy scripture, as Protestants claimed, but

from Roman Catholic tradition and papal edicts. In this same era of European exploration and colonization, Roman Catholic missionaries took their faith across the globe, establishing the church in Latin America and North America.

Although Roman Catholicism remained the dominant religion in much of Europe, the primacy of religion in European life in general declined in the eighteenth and nineteenth centuries with the rise of modern science and increasingly secular ways of life. At first, the church's response was to reject modernity. Church officials insisted on complete and continued obedience to church authority and strict adherence to traditional doctrine. The Papal States were lost in 1870 to a newly unified Italian state, and in the first Vatican Council of 1869–1870, church leaders both failed to respond to new social concerns, such as the welfare of industrial workers, and affirmed papal infallibility, the concept that there could be no error in official pronouncements of the popes on matters of faith and morality. Italy established Vatican City as a fairly independent entity in 1929, but in those years the influence of the church was at a low ebb. At the Second Vatican Council, from 1962 to 1965, church leaders tried to make their peace with the modern world. This included certain sympathetic gestures toward the ecumenical movement, which has tried to bridge the differences among the different branches of Christianity and minimize what many saw as the elitism of the Latin Mass, as opposed to services in devotees' everyday spoken languages.

The papacy of the late twentieth and early twenty-first century remains essentially conservative, however. Both Polish Pope John Paul II and his successor, Benedict XVI, have firmly maintained the church's traditional opposition to abortion, birth control, and divorce; condemnation of homosexuality; prohibition of female clergy; and mandatory celibacy of the priesthood. The Roman Catholic Church today is faced with challenges to these controversial positions both from within its official ranks and from parishioners. The church's reputation has also been tarnished by scandals involving charges of sexual abuse by priests. Dealing with these issues, and revitalizing the faith amid Western secularization on one hand and the global spread of Islam on the other, are the challenges it faces in the twenty-first century.

SEE ALSO: councils, Roman Catholic Church; papacy; Vatican

## Rosh Hashanah

The Jewish New Year festival. It takes place on either Tishri 1 or 2 of the Jewish calendar, which is in September or October. Among its features is the blowing of a ram's horn, or shofar, as a call to spiritual awakening and reminder of Moses and the Exodus. Rosh Hashanah, which means "beginning of the year" in Hebrew, is also known as the Day of Judgment or Day of Remembrance since Jews are asked to recommit themselves to their faith and traditions. For many Jews Rosh Hashanah is marked by a ten-day period of self-examination and penitence. Along with Yom Kippur, it is part of the High Holy Days of every autumn.

SEE ALSO: Moses; Yom Kippur

## Ryobu Shinto

The form of Shinto that arose under the extensive influence of Buddhism in Japan beginning in the eighth century. The term might be translated as "double Shinto." Its key feature is the identification of many of the important Shinto *kami*, or gods, with Buddhas or bodhisattvas, thereby simplifying a connection between the two faiths. The Sun Goddess Amaterasu, for instance, was identified with a Buddha known in Japanese as Dainichi, and both were worshipped at Amaterasu's shrine at Ise. Japanese emperors, meanwhile, came to be considered as embodiments of both Amaterasu and Dainichi. The development of Ryobu Shinto helped Buddhism to take hold in rural areas, as it enabled the established *kami* to accommodate "newcomer spirits," and on a larger scale it reflects Japan's openness to religious syncretism. The official rituals of Ryobu Shinto was officially forbidden during the era of State Shinto (ca. 1868–1945), when leaders wanted to downplay "foreign" influences such as Buddhism and thought of the school as a form of degraded Shinto.

SEE ALSO: Buddhism; *kami*; Shinto

## sacraments

In Christianity, ritual acts meant to convey God's grace. Christian theology holds that in order for such an act to be valid, it must have the proper form, administration, and intention. In addition, the recipient must be receptive to grace by being in a proper state of faith. There are seven sacraments according to Christian tradition. These are baptism (the ritual entrance into Christ's community), confirmation (generally an adolescent reaffirmation of the baptismal commitment); Eucharist (or Holy Communion, the taking of bread and wine as the transubstantiated body and blood of Christ), penance (or acts signifying forgiveness of sins), extreme unction (the anointment of oil during last rites); the taking of holy orders (joining the priesthood or a monastic order); and marriage. Baptism and the Eucharist are considered the most important, and they were the sacraments retained by most Protestant churches after the Reformation, although the performance of the sacraments varies widely. Only the Quakers and Salvation Army, among large or well-known denominations, reject the performance of sacraments entirely.

SEE ALSO: baptism; Eucharist; Reformation

## saddhu

A Hindu holy person who has renounced the world and lives independently, free of any particular order or sect. The Sanskrit term comes from a root word for "accomplish," and what a saddhu has accomplished is the renunciation of the senses and of worldly things. There are many varieties of saddhus engaged in very different activities, but the general pattern is that they wander through India, often on a route of pilgrimage sites, and survive on charity. They are highly respected among Hindus as being far along a path toward union with god. Saddhus are also known as "sants" or saints. The female equivalent is sadhvi.

SEE ALSO: four stages of life; Hinduism; sannyasi

## Sai Baba, Sathya (1926)

A renowned Indian guru who claims to be the incarnation of the god Shiva. Born Sathya Nrayana Raju, he allegedly began performing miracles at age fourteen and started his first ashram in 1960. Devotees consider him possessed of much spiritual power, with the ability to heal the sick, read minds, and materialize sacred ash, or vibhuti, from apparent nothingness. His numerous followers include not only Indians but thousands from around the world. There are many Sathya Sai Baba centers around the globe, but the guru's main ashram is at Puttaparthi in India's Andhra Pradesh state, near Sai Baba's birthplace. Tens of thousands make the pilgrimage every year with the hope of experiencing darshan, or the spiritual benefits of nearness to the guru. The ashram sponsors schools and hospitals and engages in other charitable work.

See Also: ashram; guru; new religious movements, Western

## saint

A person thought to have great closeness to the sacred or to possess special spiritual powers. All religions have such figures, whether recognized by popular acclaim or in a more official manner, but the tradition of saint veneration is most highly formalized in Christianity. The early Christian Church began to use the term in reference to deceased holy people who were recognized as saints by the church in the sixth century. In the twelfth century, the Roman Catholic Church established formal procedures for the canonization (selection) of saints by placing the responsibility on the popes. These procedures made official practices that were already a feature of popular Christianity, such as the use of the stories of the saints' lives as moral lessons or pilgrimages to visit the relics of saints. Meanwhile, the Eastern Orthodox Church put in place canonization processes of its own, with the bishops of each separate national Orthodox church making its own decisions. In both traditions those canonized included martyrs, great thinkers or mystics, and holy virgins. Protestant denominations except the Anglican Church reject the cult of saints.

Most other major traditions have their own forms of saints. In Islam as well as Judaism, the English word *saint* is often used to refer to great teachers or lawgivers, and the practice finds its expression most commonly in popular worship rather than orthodox theology. In Buddhism, those considered close to full awakening are saints, most notably the arhats of the Theravada tradition. In Hinduism, the concept is similar to that of saddhus (holy persons).

See Also: arhat; Roman Catholicism; saddhu

## *samadhi*

A high state of mind and being thought possible in both Hinduism and Buddhism. A Sanskrit term that might be translated as "total concentration." *samadhi* is the highest state of spiritual absorption one can achieve while still inhabiting a human body. It is thought to involve nearly perfect contemplation of the ultimate reality without interference from the ego, from desire, from emotion, and even from hunger or thirst. Such a state is often the goal of meditation of yogic practices, which are generally accepted as the only paths by which one can achieve it. In Hinduism, one who has reached *samadhi* is sometimes considered to be close to moksha, or release from the wheel of birth and death. The shrines of past *samadhin* are often pilgrimage sites. In Buddhism, *samadhi* is thought to be essential to the goal of attaining enlightenment, and the various Buddhist schools prescribe different techniques to help one achieve it; in Zen Buddhism, for instance, meditative concentration on a single object is considered useful in overcoming the sensory belief that there are differences among things. The one common factor, as in Hinduism, is an ascetic life.

See Also: meditation; yoga

## samsara

The process of reincarnation in Hinduism, Buddhism, and other Indian religions. A Sanskrit term meaning "wandering," samsara is popularly described as a circular process, the "wheel" of birth and death. The soul is considered to be lost in samsara, burdened by desires and attachments or by karma, the consequence of action

278 The Greenhaven Encyclopedia of World Religions

known. The soul, furthermore, is reincarnated lifetime after lifetime in forms ranging from inanimate objects to gods. Release from samsara, known as moksha in Hinduism and the attainment of nirvana in Buddhism, is the goal of these religions.

SEE ALSO: moksha; nirvana; reincarnation

## sangha

A Buddhist monastic order. Within their sangha monks (bhikku) or nuns (bhikkuni) live according to a monastic code laid out by sacred texts requiring, for instance, specific times for meditation and no eating or drinking after noon. The model was set by the original Buddha and his first followers, and some claim that the Buddha had in mind the creation of a monastic movement rather than a widespread popular religion. Along with the Buddha and the dharma, the sangha is one of the "three jewels" in which devout Buddhists pledge to seek refuge. Their general purpose is to allow believers a means to leave the world, if only temporarily, to focus themselves on meditation and the dhamma path.

There are three main forms of sangha: the Theravada, northern (Tibetan), and eastern (Chinese, Japanese, Korean). The Theravada tradition is likely closest to the form of monasticism that emerged in India in the era immediately following the Buddha's death. In all traditions the sangha and lay community are supposed to live in a mutually beneficial relationship. The laypeople provide the sangha with its means of support (in the Theravada tradition especially, monks are discouraged from engaging in conventional work of any sort), while the sangha provides the community with access to the dharma as well as more conventional pastoral benefits such as education and counseling. Sangha hierarchies

are determined by both seniority and extreme devotion, although in some countries there are official national sangha offices.

SEE ALSO: Buddhism; Eightfold Path; monasticism

## sannyasin

A Hindu religious ascetic, from a Sanskrit word meaning "abandoning" and also spelled sannyasi. The female equivalent is sannyasini. Conventionally sannyasin are considered those who have entered the fourth stage of existence described in Hindu texts: kama (pleasure), artha (power or worldly achievement, and dharma (religious devotion) are the first three, and while many higher-caste Hindus live according to these initial stages, few become sannyasin. These figures renounce worldly life, leave their families and homes, and as an important ritual separation, perform their own symbolic funerals. Like other Hindu holy persons, sannyasin are not cremated (the common Hindu practice) but are buried, usually seated in a meditative posture. More narrowly, sannyasin commonly are ascetics who pledge devotion to the god Shiva, and there are distinct orders of these devotees.

SEE ALSO: four stages of life; dharma; saddhu

## Sanskrit

Ancient language of India in which Hinduism's classic texts were written. Sanskrit was originally a spoken language, brought in an early form to India by Indo-European migrants in the second millennium B.C.; it bears some similarities to other languages of the Indo-European family, including ancient Greek, Latin, and modern tongues such as English and the

Hindi spoken in northern India. The sacred Sanskrit used by Brahmin priests in ceremonies was eventually written down to form such texts as the Vedas, Upanishads, and Puranas, and in time Hindu thinkers used the language to write down the great epics Mahabharata and Ramayana, the Laws of Manu, and many other texts. Sanskrit eventually ceased to be a spoken language among the larger population, although Brahmin priests continued to learn it and employ it in rituals, as they continue to today. Many of the original Buddhist teachings were also composed using Sanskrit, although the canonic versions of those texts were eventually written in Pali, a related language.

SEE ALSO: brahmin; Pali; Vedas

# Sarah
# (ca. 2000 B.C.)

The wife of Abraham (patriarch of the early Hebrews and a prophet of Judaism, Christianity, and Islam). Her story appears in the book of Genesis in the Old Testament. Although in their original covenant God had promised Abraham that Sarah would be "a mother of nations," Sarah remained childless until she was ninety years old. Doubting her ability to fulfill God's promise, Sarah gave Abraham her servant, Hagar, in the hopes that Hagar would bear Abraham's child. Hagar indeed conceived and gave birth to Ishmael. But Sarah was also eventually able to conceive and gave birth to Isaac, the fulfillment of God's promise and a great joy to his mother. Hagar and Ishmael were banished, and Isaac followed Abraham as the Hebrew's patriarch. Sarah's tomb, meanwhile, at Hebron in modern-day Israel, is accepted by Jews as a sign that God will keep his promise of a promised land, just as he kept his

promise that Sarah would be "a mother of nations."

SEE ALSO: Abraham; covenant; Hebrew Bible

# Satan

The chief adversary of God in the Jewish and Christian traditions. Satan also appears in Islam, where he is known by the Arabic version of his name, Shaitan. Satan is commonly accepted as the Prince of Evil, or simply the devil, although the term "devils" is also used to refer to evil spirits in general.

In the Hebrew Bible or Old Testament, the word *satan* first appears in reference to human opponents. In later books, notably Job, Satan is described as a figure who, with the permission of God, comes to earth to test Job and the extent of human goodness in general. In later Rabbinic Judaism, Satan is described as the source of all sins, and a highlight of the Jewish Rosh Hashanah holiday is the blowing of a shofar, a ram's horn, in order to confuse him.

In the book of Revelation in the Christian New Testament, Satan is described as a fallen angel named Lucifer, who "fell" because his pride refused to allow him to submit to God. He possesses the ability to fool people into thinking him an angel of light and, with the use of demons or other spirits, can possess human beings and force them to oppose God. The New Testament also refers to him as Beelzebub, a name derived from a "lord of flies" in the Old Testament book of 1 Kings: Baalzebub. In later Christian writings as well as popular culture, the four terms Satan, devil, Lucifer, and Beelzebub are mostly synonymous.

In the Islamic Qur'an, Satan is mentioned often as the opponent of God. His descendants are described as jinn ("genies") who go bad and use various means to tempt people away from God. Ordinarily, jinn are generally merely rebellious or impudent spirits.

SEE ALSO: angels; heaven; hell

## sati

The Hindu practice, now almost entirely extinct, of a widow burning herself to death, either on the funeral pyre of her husband or shortly afterwards. Strictly speaking sati, or suttee, refers to the woman herself rather than the practice: *sati* is Sanskrit for "virtuous woman." Women who made the choice to follow their husbands into the fire were thought to possess great loyalty, devotion, and virtue, and the action brought honor to their families. The practice was documented by Greek visitors to India as early as the first century B.C., and the Mahabharatha mentions it as well. Some satis have had memorial stones erected in their name and many of these "sati shrines" still stand; the earliest dates back to 510. In some towns, particularly in the western Indian region of Rajasthan where the practice seems to have been most common, "sati gates" commemorate the passing through of many women on their way to the funeral pyre. The gates are marked by handprints of the sati women.

Sati has never been particularly widespread and has usually been very controversial. Opponents note that frequently women did not freely choose to burn themselves but went to the fire while on drugs or were otherwise forced. Moreover, widows in Hindu India are figures of very low status not allowed to marry again and to live with their husband's families, who might not welcome them, so sati might have been considered by some to be a way

out of this life rather than an expression of virtue. The Islamic Mughal Empire tried to ban the practice in the sixteenth century and in 1829 the British, who then ruled India, also tried to abolish it. Instances of sati, however, were still reported for decades and still may take place. An infamous instance of sati took place in Rajasthan as recently as 1987.

SEE ALSO: caste; Hinduism; Laws of Manu

## satori

The word for enlightenment in Zen Buddhism, and as such the goal of Zen teaching and meditation. In Zen satori is thought to occur either suddenly and nearly spontaneously, but only after the devotee has prepared himself or herself with meditation or other exercises, or as a slow realization. Zen Buddhists believe that both methods reflect the experience of the original Buddha during his period of meditation under the bodhi tree. The Soto sect of Zen believes that zazen, or "quiet sitting," (i.e., meditation) might bring about the transformative flash of insight that satori represents, while the Rinzai sect urges a more active approach involving not only meditation but discussion and even earthly activities such as daily chores. Either way, Zen practitioners believe that satori cannot be fully explained, described, nor understood. It can only be experienced.

SEE ALSO: Buddhism; meditation; Zen Buddhism

## Saul
### (ca. 11th century B.C.)

The first king of Israel. Saul's troublesome reign, lasting from approximately 1021 to 1000 B.C., marks the appearance of Israel and the first instance of the ancient Hebrews establishing possession of the land they believed God had promised them. According to the Hebrew Bible book of 1 Samuel, the main source for stories of his life, Saul became king of the Hebrews by accclamation after leading an expedition to rescue the oppressed town of Jahesh-Gilead. As king, Saul continued to win military victories but had a falling out with the prophet Samuel himself. Apparently, Saul was inconsistent in his religious duties, offering unauthorized sacrifices before battles for example, and Samuel withdrew his support from the king. Without Samuel's religious sanction and the popular support that resulted, Saul was unable to rule effectively. With the arrival of David at court, a challenger whom Saul pledged to kill (unsuccessfully), the king began to lose his mental faculties. Saul died during a battle with the Philistines, and he was succeeded by David. The lesson of Samuel's account of Saul is generally held to be the need for political leaders to follow religious practice and dictates.

SEE ALSO: David; Judaism; Solomon

# seder

A ritual meal that serves a centerpiece of the springtime Passover festival in Judaism. A commemoration of the Exodus, seder takes place on the first night of Passover for Jews living in Israel and on both the first and second nights for Jews living elsewhere. The word means "order" in Hebrew, and the foods served and sequence of events during seder are prescribed by sacred texts.

Taking place in households rather than synagogues or temples, seder begins with a blessing of wine, known as the kiddush, by the head of the household. This "leader" of the seder also recites a sacred liturgy taken from a text known as the Hagaddah.

The features of this liturgy include statements that unleavened bread will be served, just as it was to the early Hebrews before their departure from Egypt, and the wish that all who partake in the ceremony will maintain freedom. Following is a set of four questions, commonly asked by a young child. They begin, "Why does this night differ from all other nights?" and continue with questions as to why celebrants eat unleavened bread and bitter herbs. The answers allow celebrants to recall the story of the Exodus.

The next stage of seder is the Passover meal, which is preceded by a ceremony in which bitter herbs, symbols of slavery, are dipped into a mixture of wine and crushed fruit. This step is to demonstrate that suffering leads to spiritual progress and other rewards. Following the meal proper, many celebrants conclude the ceremony with the recitation of verses condemning those nations who oppress Israel and with a call to the prophet Elijah. The presence of Elijah is held to signify the coming of the messiah.

SEE ALSO: Elijah; Exodus; Passover

# Sephardim

Jews who trace their descent to the Jewish communities of Spain and Portugal, where during the Middle Ages (ca. 650–1250) Jewish communities thrived under Islamic kings. Meaning "Spanish" Jews, the Sephardim are distinct from the Ashkenazim ("German" Jews) not only in their history but in their language and forms of ritual. On a larger but less accurate scale, the Sephardim are Jews whose background is North African or otherwise "Oriental" (non-European).

The Sephardim were expelled from

Spain and Portugal by Christian kings, who completed their reconquest of those areas by 1500. They resettled in various areas around the Mediterranean, although small but important communities of Sephardim settled in France, Holland, and England as well. They carried with them the advanced intellectual and commercial culture their Iberian ancestors had developed, and they remained distinct communities, recognized as such by the Ashkenazim who made up most European Jewish groups. The Sephardim spoke a language known as Ladino and followed a tradition of Jewish ritual that dated back to the Babylonian Exile, markedly different from the Palestinian ritual of the Ashkenazim. Today, many of the estimated 700,000 Sephardic Jews live in Israel.

SEE ALSO: Ashkenazim; Diaspora; Judaism

## Septuagint

The term for the Greek-language translation of the Hebrew Bible (Old Testament). The translation was made in the third and second centuries B.C. at the then Greek-speaking city of Alexandria in Egypt, likely for the Jewish communities in Egypt. The term is derived from the Latin word for 70, *septuaginta*, and appears to be based on the likely false story that the translation was done by seventy-two translators, six each from the twelve Hebrew tribes. The Torah or Pentateuch, the first five books, were translated first, with the rest completed over a number of decades.

The historical importance of the Septuagint lies in the Christian rather than Jewish traditions. This was the version used by early Christians seeking to find prophecies of Jesus in the Hebrew Bible (an exercise condemned by Jewish scholars) and it went on to be the basis for the translation of the Hebrew Bible

into Latin as well as the languages of other early Christian communities in Armenia, Egypt, and elsewhere. The Septuagint remains the accepted edition of the Hebrew Bible in the Eastern Orthodox Church. It contains a number of books, the Apocrypha, which are not part of the Hebrew Bible but which most Christians accept as part of their canon of scripture.

SEE ALSO: Apocrypha; Hebrew Bible; New Testament

## Shabbat

The Jewish sabbath or weekly holy day, aspects of whose traditions were later adopted by Christianity and Islam. The term is Hebrew for "rest." The weekly Shabbat in Judaism is intended not only as a day of rest but of commemoration. Shabbat commemorates God's Creation of the world in seven days, as recorded in the book of Genesis, as well as the covenant between God and the Jews. It serves as a weekly reminder to Jews of who they are and of their relationship to God and their traditions.

Like many Jewish festivals a household rather than temple ritual, Shabbat begins at sundown on Friday with the lighting of two candles by women of the household. Other rituals include the eating of two loaves of bread as symbols of God's generosity to the stricken and the reading of the Kiddush, a prayer of sanctification pronounced over wine on Friday evenings and again on Saturday; one should not eat during Shabbat until the Kiddush has been said. The festival ends on Saturday evening with a ceremony of separation.

For Christians, the Sabbath is on a Sunday, and rituals are generally held in churches rather than in the home. Early

Christian leaders made the switch in the fourth century, although they emphasized that the Sabbath was to be a day for worship rather than of rest. Many Christian denominations, nevertheless, have maintained that Sunday should be a day of rest (although this custom has been increasingly ignored in recent times). In Islam the main echo of Shabbat is the importance of the Friday noontime prayers, during which all men are urged to go to mosques and hear speakers rather than perform their prayers at home or in small groups.

SEE ALSO: calendars

# Shakti

A Hindu term meaning "divine power" but which is broadly understood as the feminine aspects of divine power or, simply, "the goddess." Hindus consider the dualistic relationship between the female and male essential to universal order on all levels, and the notion underlies worship, ritual, and the stories and lessons in sacred texts. All Hindu gods, for instance, are not thought to be fully active or complete without the complementary qualities of their wives or consorts, thus the pairs of Shiva and Durga, Krishna and Radha, Rama and Sita, and many others. Shakti is described in many, sometimes contradictory, ways. It might be the ultimate source of all things or the power of illusion. It might be the fickle, destructive qualities of nature or the nurturing qualities of the ideal mother. Shakti might even be a queen or a prostitute.

Scholars customarily trace the importance of Shakti to the, strictly speaking, pre-Hindu Harappan civilization that dominated northwestern India some four thousand years ago. Archaeological investi-

gations have found many signs of worship of female divine figures from that era. As Hinduism evolved in the first millennium B.C. and first millennium A.D., goddess worship continued to feature prominently, and even the male-dominated Vedas acknowledged the important roles of such goddesses as Aditi, the goddess of space and Usha, the goddess of the dawn. Even today the power of Durga, Kali, Parvati, Lakshmi, and other manifestations of Shakti is acknowledged throughout Hinduism.

Worship of Shakti proper, or Shaktism, is one of the three main, overlapping currents of Hinduism, the others being Shaivism (worship of Shiva) and Vaishnavism (the worship of Vishnu). Shaktism is based on the fundamental belief that all goddesses are manifestations of a single great "Goddess," or mahadevi, who stands on a level at least comparable to that of Shiva and Vishnu. Mahadevi is worshipped not only as a goddess but as a symbol of primal power, including the power that animates human beings. In this sense she, or her force, is thought to inhabit a region at the base of the spine in the form of a snake known as Kundalini. Through meditation or ritual Kundalini can be awakened and encouraged to rise through the five energy centers, or chakras, thought to be located along the spine and head. The passage through the uppermost chakra, when Shakti is thought to be "reunited" with her husband Shiva, is a mystical, ecstatic release, which is the goal of some devotees. There are, comparatively speaking, far fewer followers of Shaktism than of its two alternatives, and it retains its status as a somewhat esoteric form of Hinduism. Far more common, and in fact a basic feature of Hinduism, is the worship of the "divine female" in the form of a goddess such as Kali or Parvati.

*A shaman in costume from Onitsha, Nigeria.* © PAUL ALMASY/CORBIS

SEE ALSO: Kali; Shiva; Vishnu

## shamanism

A form of religious practice emphasizing the work of shamans, people who are thought to be able to read divine signs, heal the sick, and perform other spiritual tasks. Although elements of shamanism appear in most major religious traditions, the notion is most commonly associated with premodern religions or those outside the major faiths. There, shamans are thought to be intermediaries between the earth and the spirit world, and they often also serve as community storytellers and keepers of lore. They might use various natural objects, such as plants, or ritual devils to perform readings and ceremonies.

SEE ALSO: African religions; divination; Native American religions, North America

## Shangdi

Also spelled Shang-ti, the highest god or "supreme ruler" of the formative Shang dynasty of China (ca. 1760–1027 B.C.). Shangdi was thought to possess such powers as presiding over the changing of the seasons and the harvest, the weather, and success in battle. He was apparently too distant to be worshipped directly, and archaeologists and scholars have found little evidence of rituals devoted specifically to his worship. His aloofness may have reflected or even reinforced the belief that one's dead ancestors could be used as intermediaries in his spirit world, a characteristic of ancestor worship. After the Shang dynasty fell to the Zhou Dynasty, (1027–256 B.C.), Shangdi's characteristics melded into those of the even more abstract great deity known as *t'ian*, or heaven.

SEE ALSO: filial piety; Five Classics

## Shankara
## (ca. 788–820)

Important Hindu philosopher. Shankara was born into the brahmin caste in southern India. He turned early to a life of asceticism and wandering and, according to tradition, became a student of Govindapada, a disciple of the great sage Gaudapada, in a cave on the banks of the Narmada River in central India. Gaudapada is credited with being among the founders of the Advaita Vedanta school of Hinduism, and the young Shankara took up the Vedanta approach. Along the way he fully dedicated himself to the life of a renunciant, eventually travelling to Varanasi on the Ganga River in northern India, where he began to teach and write and attract students of his own, and to the foothills of the Himalayas. Shankara's life ended with a "tour of victory" in which he walked throughout India engaging all comers, successfully, in debate, before walking northward to the god Shiva's abode in the Himalayas.

At the heart of Advaita Vedanta, propounded in such texts as Shankara's commentary on the Brahmasutra (a text seeking to explain Brahma), is the argument that Brahman, the ultimate reality, underlies everything. People's tendency to differentiate between the things they see and experience, and to consider them as distinct from the ultimate reality, only takes them further away from understanding this underlying unity. Religious training and ritual should be designed to help people realize that these distinctions are illusory, that there is not even any real difference between the self and Brahman, that "they are that," as the Sanskrit mantra *tat tvam asi* puts it.

SEE ALSO: Brahman; mantra; Ramanuja

## sharia

Islamic law. Most Muslims consider sharia to be God's law for humankind and of divine rather than human origin. At its heart are the means by which and degree to which Muslims obey God's laws in their earthly lives, and in addition to being a straightforward set of instructions, its authority must be based on the believer's sincere faith and good intentions. Beyond the Five Pillars of Faith, which stand at its center, sharia laws divide human activities according to five categories: obligatory, recommended, legally indifferent, disapproved, and prohibited.

The main Islamic sects view the sources of sharia differently. In Sunni Islam, sharia is derived from the Qur'an and Hadith, the examples of the prophet Muhammad and other early Muslims, and community traditions. It might also be informed by further interpretation, especially when the other methods provide no clear path.

*Four Schools* The Sunni tradition bases its understanding of sharia on one of four accepted schools of law. These provide flexibility in interpretation while assuring that the law reflects accepted authority and the general consensus of most Muslims. Their uses also partially explaining the differing Islamic practices around the world. The Hanbalite school, the most conservative of the four, was founded in Baghdad by the legal scholar Ibn Hanbal (780–855). It is based on a literalist reading of the Qur'an and Hadith and rejects free speculation on the law as likely to lead to misinterpretation and sinful behavior. The Hanbalite school informs the legal structure of modern-day Saudi Arabia. The Malikite school, which predominates in Egypt, Sudan, and elsewhere in North Africa as well as in some of the smaller Persian Gulf states, was founded by Malik Ibn Anas (ca. 715–795) in Medina. It bases its interpretations on three graded steps. First, and most authoritative, were the Qur'an and Hadith. Second was the consensus of legal and religious scholars based in seventh- and eighth-century Medina specifically. Third, and a method only to be used in rare cases when the others did not apply, was an understanding of "public advantage." The third school, the Shafi'ite school, was based on the teachings of the prominent scholar al-Shafi'i, (767–820), a distant descendant of the Prophet who lived in Cairo in Egypt. It also places primary authority in the Qur'an and Hadith, but recognizes that in some instances the Hadith might take precedence. The school also accepts reasoning by analogy, or hypothetical comparisons, but rejects personal opinion. The Shafi'ite school is most predominant in Indonesia, Malaysia, southern India, parts of Arabia and East Africa.

The fourth school, the Hanifite school, was founded in Iraq by Abu Hanifa (ca.

700–767), is more open-ended than the others. It makes room for personal interpretation and opinion, provided that opinion is based on careful consideration of Islamic traditions as well as of the cultural or historical context. In some cases these interpretations might even contradict the teachings of the Qur'an. For example, the Qur'an says that convicted thieves should have their right hand cut off, a punishment accepted by the Hanbalite school. The Hanifite school, by contrast, acknowledges that such a punishment might not have been appropriate in the diverse setting of Iraq, and that other punishments must be deduced from other teachings from the Qur'an or Hadith. The school provided the official basis for the legal systems of the Islamic empires of the Abbasids and Ottomans and thus became the most widespread of the four. In the modern world Muslims in Pakistan, Bangladesh, India, Central Asia, Turkey, Syria, parts of Iraq, and southeastern Europe adhere to the Hanifite school, especially in such personal matters as divorce and inheritance.

Shia Islam generally offers no such variety of interpretations. For the purposes of legal authority believers emphasize the Qur'an, the traditions of Ali and the other Shia imams, and conclusions reached by Shia legal thinkers known as mujtahids. Sufis, meanwhile, see sharia as little more than a foundation for a mystical approach to Islam.

The relationship between sharia and civil or secular law has been complicated in Islamic history, and it continues to be so. Most Islamic states historically maintained bodies of secular law alongside sharia, and their ways were informed by local, nonreligious customs as well. In the modern world the nations of Saudi Arabia

(Sunni) and Iran (Shia) make their understandings of sharia the law of the land, while most other Muslim countries possess codes of secular or civil law. Even in those cases, however, many localities continue to solve specific issues, especially personal ones, with interpretations of sharia.

SEE ALSO: Five Pillars of Faith; Shia Islam; Sunni Islam

## Shia (Shiite) Islam

One of the two main branches of Islam. Its adherents are far smaller in number than those of the mainstream Sunni branch but greater than those of the mystical Sufi movement. In the modern world up to 100 million Muslims are Shia, the majority of whom live in Iran and Iraq, both of which have Shia majorities. Minority Shia concentrations can be found in Bahrain, Yemen, Oman, Syria, Lebanon, East Africa, Pakistan, and India, and smaller groups are scattered in many other countries around the world.

Shia Islam traces its origins to the decades following the death of the Muhammad in 632. They claim that the Prophet had selected Ali, his cousin and son-in-law, to be his successor as the leader of the Islamic religion and the rising Islamic state. Records of this are inconclusive, however, and early Muslims chose Abu Bakr, an associate of Muhammad's but not a relative, to be the first such leader, the first caliph. Ali only became caliph in 656, after Abu Bakr had been succeeded in turn by Omar and Uthman. Devout Shiites consider the three to be not only illegitimate caliphs but actual usurpers to be condemned.

By the 650s competing factions had arisen in Islam, and Ali was linked with the rebels who had murdered Uthman. For this and other reasons he never had the full support of the Muslim community, and he was raised to the caliphate only in the face of strong opposition from other candidates. He was forced to fight a number of wars to maintain an increasingly shaky position and in 661 he was assassinated by the Ummayads. He left behind the two sons that he had had with Fatima, Muhammad's daughter. These sons, al-Hassan and al-Hussein, were the Prophet's only direct male heirs.

Ali had moved the base of the caliphate to the city of Kufa in Iraq, whose southern regions were a majority Sufi area. There al-Hassan and al-Hussein took on the status of imam, which for the Shia is a term that has meaning beyond its general definition as an Islamic theologian. For the Shia, the imams were divinely anointed successors to the Prophet. Al-Hassan ultimately rejected the status, dying soon after. Al-Hussein, along with his small son, died in a battle at Karbala, Iraq, in 680. He was seeking to gain the caliphate by defeating Yazid I, who represented the Sunni Ummayads. Al-Hassan, who was thought to have been poisoned, and al-Hussein became the first Shia martyrs, and continue to be revered by the Shia faithful.

*Imams and Martyrs* The Shia community as a whole, meanwhile, continued to cling to the notion that only those who were direct male descendants of Muhammad could be imams, and they also condemned what they saw as the worldliness of Sunni Muslims. Shia thought asserted that the imams demonstrated qualities of sinlessness and perfect judgment with regard to legal and other interpretation; they were said to have possessed a kind of "special knowledge" which gave their decisions the weight of authority. Added to this, according to the extensive tradition of Shia scholarship, was that the imams provided a link in a chain of prophecy that stretched through Muhammad all the way back in time to Jesus, Abraham, and even Adam. They therefore embodied the will of God and commanded the obedience of all humankind.

Central to the traditions of most Shiites is that there were a total of twelve imams, with Ali, al-Hassan, and al-Hussein the first three. The line continued until the death of the twelfth imam, Muhammad al-Muntazar, in 878. Then only five years old, and therefore without any sons of his own, Muhammad al-Muntazar is said to have disappeared into a cave hidden within a mosque in the Iraqi city of Samarra. Unready to believe that God had then withdrawn His guidance in the form of these divinely inspired leaders, the Shia hold that this twelfth, "hidden" imam will someday return. He will be known then as the mahdi, and he will establish a realm of peace and righteousness on earth prior to God's final judgment. Because of their solid faith in these twelve imams, the largest branch of Shia Islam are called Twelvers. Other descendants of Fatima and Ali, or even members of the Banu Hashim branch of the Quraysh tribe meanwhile, are granted honorific titles such as sayyid or sharif, both references to their origins.

Shia Islam in practice differs markedly from Sunni Islam in important respects. The main Shia authorities, for instance, are religious experts known as mujtahids, and their decisions are binding in religious matters. Believers also place special emphasis on martyrs and on the process of martyrdom. The tomb of al-Hussein at Karbala is a major pilgrimage site reflecting this emphasis, and other tombs commemorate other martyrs. During the important Shia festival known as Muharram (the word actually refers to the month of the Islamic calendar in which it takes place), many Shiites recall the martyrdom of al-Hussein with self-flagellation and other painful rituals. For the Shia, reverence for martyrs and pilgrimages to tombs are forms of worship.

Figures such as al-Hussein might not only be considered martyrs but saints, and the existence of saints in Shia Islam is another feature that separates it from Sunnism. The Shia believe that the imams represented human perfection and that other figures come close to reaching that state. Among them are the members of the Banu Hashim, most notably the sharifs of Mecca, whose heavy responsibility is the care and maintenance of the Ka'aba, Islam's holiest shrine. Sunni Islam, by contrast, does not recognize the perfectability of any human being following Muhammad.

*Twelvers and Seveners* Although the Twelvers are the largest Shia group, numerous other sects have arisen. One is the Seveners, who are also known as the Ismaili. They hold that the line of imams stopped with the seventh, Ismail (the Twelvers recognize a different figure, Musa al-Kazim, as the seventh imam). Ismaili communities are scattered across the world today, and their status as a recognized sect was confirmed by the Ismaili Fatimid dynasty, which ruled Egypt from 909 to 1171. A branch of the Ismailis known as the Nizaris follows a figure known as the Aga Khan, or "chief commander," a title given the line of Ismaili imams by a nineteenth-century Iranian emperor. The modern-day Nizaris are very active in business, finance, and philanthropy, and are urged to integrate themselves into the cultures of the countries where they live. Beyond the Druzes, a secretive sect based in Lebanon, Israel, and Syria, most other Shia sects are quite small.

In the modern world, the Shia-Sunni split is the most visible divide in Islam, and it has spilled over into politics in recent decades. In 1979 Shia religious leaders in Iran overthrew a pro-Western, modernizing leader known as the shah, who to their minds was too inclined to bringing Western styles of life to their country. Iran's government and legal system continue to be based on a strict reading of Shia Islam, although much of the country's population expresses a quiet frustration with its restrictions. Shia political influence in the Islamic world was also reflected by the militancy of believers in the Lebanese conflicts of the 1980s and 1990s and, in the twenty-first century, by the rise to power of Shia leaders in parts of Iraq. The general Sunni view of Shia Muslims is complex. The orthodox view is that Shia Islam is an "exaggeration" of the faith rather than an outright heresy. While some conservatives criticize the Shia alternative for dividing Islam, others respect it for keeping alive some of the religion's earliest ideas and features.

SEE ALSO: Ismailis; Muhammad; Sunni Islam

## Shinto

The indigenous religion of Japan. Shinto is not only a religion but a way of life. It offers believers a sense of the relationships between themselves and the divine, as well as between human beings and nature, and it organizes the year with a rich variety of festivals and ceremonies. Japan is a nation of religious syncretism, where Shinto has been joined by Buddhism, Confucianism, Christianity, and dozens of new religions, and where people see few contradictions in belonging to more than one faith. But Shinto is the oldest of these and the one that is most distinctly Japanese. Some 125

million people practice elements of Shinto in both Japan and among communities of Japanese immigrants worldwide.

*Origins and History* Shinto's origins are mysterious. It has no specific founder and no defined body of scriptural texts. It probably emerged out of groups of Japanese folk traditions and beliefs dating back over two thousand years. As was the case with many ancient peoples, these customs were often associated with the agricultural year and with the encouragement or appeasement of nature spirits. As Japan became a settled civilization in the middle of the first millennium A.D., some of these beliefs were used to support rulership and state organization. The Yamato clan, which by the sixth century had come to control much of central Japan, claimed descent from the sun goddess Amaterasu, while other important Japanese families also maintained patron deities, or ujigami.

The rise of centralized political control in Japan coincided with the arrival in the country of many Chinese influences, often by way of Korea. Among these influences was Buddhism, which was attractive to Japan's elite families. They did not reject Shinto in favor of Buddhism, however. Instead, Shinto and Buddhism began a long era of reconciliation and coexistence, which still continues and is sometimes referred to in general as Ryobu Shinto, or "double Shinto."

Meanwhile, Shinto mythology and ritual became codified, at least at the elite levels of society. During the Heian period of Japanese history (794–1185) two important texts appeared, the Kohiki (712) and Nihon-Shoki (or Nihongi, 720), which were written using Chinese characters. In addition to being the chronicles of Japan's great clans, these texts portrayed Japan's origins using elements of Shinto myth. They described how the Japanese islands appeared during a prehistoric "age of the gods," when the earth was a formless chaos characterized by generations of *kami* (gods or spirits). During the eight generations of these invisible spirits two of them, Izanagi and Izanami, created the Japanese islands by dipping a spear to this formless chaos. The children of the two included the sun goddess Amaterasu, who later rose to be the leading figure among all the *kami*. The age of the gods came to an end when Amaterasu's legendary human descendant, Jimmu Tenno, became emperor around 660 B.C. The Yamato clan claimed to be descendants of Jimmu Tenno, as does the Japanese imperial line today. Another important text, the *Engishiki* (tenth century), described the proper performance of important Shinto rites and provided important prayers. At the center of these rites for emperors was the care of three sacred objects considered symbols of divine favor: a sword, a jewel, and a mirror.

Following the Heian period, Japan's rulers often preferred Buddhism to Shinto, but aspects of Shinto remained important to them. In the effort to reconcile the two, many of the Shinto *kami* were also classified as bodhisattvas, or "little Buddhas." Meanwhile, groups within Japanese society continued to revere their own personal *kami*. The samurai, for instance, Japan's warrior elite from the twelfth through nineteenth centuries, were particularly fond of Hachiman, the *kami* of war. The Japanese also continued to associate the *kami* with natural forces, an area about which Buddhism has little to say. In the late thirteenth century, for example, the Japanese claim to have been saved by these nature *kami* from seaborne invasions from the warlike Mongol Empire. The Mongols

had been stopped, people believed, by kamikaze, or "divine winds," which had scattered their ships across violent, stormy seas. Shinto beliefs also remained predominant among Japan's ordinary people. *Kami* who received much popular devotion included Daikukoten and Ebisu, who represented wealth, and Jurojin, who represented long life and good health.

Following over two centuries of being mostly closed off from the outside world, Japan was opened up again by Western imperialists in the mid-1800s. In response to the Western challenge Japanese leaders began a rapid period of modernization, and an important element of this modernization was the appearance of state Shinto. Beginning with the restoration of the Meiji emperor in 1868, and lasting until Japan's defeat in World War II in 1945, Japan was once again dominated by Shinto. Leaders used it to reinforce a sense of Japan's distinctness and nationalism. Japanese emperors were once again revered as gods, Shinto shrines were placed under state authority, and Buddhism was marginalized. Following Japan's defeat, the institutions of state Shinto were dismantled and shrine Shinto, in which emphasis is placed on local shrines and their patron *kami*, replaced it.

*Central Shinto Beliefs* The Japanese often refer to Shinto as their life religion and Buddhism as their death religion. In this they mean that, while Buddhist belief and ritual tend to emphasize future lives or the afterworld, Shinto is a religion of the here and now, of life passages, and of the cycles of nature. These are echoes of Shinto's origins in early Japan, when people perceived that the forces of nature were animated by divine spirits. From that belief, it was only a short jump to the sense that divine spirits are also apparent in the daily lives of human beings. At the heart of Shinto belief is the attempt to create a balance between the human and natural worlds and the sense that the human and divine are in constant interaction.

These divine spirts, the *kami*, are too numerous to be counted. They range from "high gods" such as Amaterasu, Hachiman, Ebisu, or Susano (the ruler of the underworld) to mischevious deities like the rice god Inari to thousands of guardian deities and ancestor spirits in villages and among families. Each of the *kami* is thought to have a distinct personality and to possess a life force known as tama. This life force might be expressed in beneficial or harmful ways, so believers take care to bring forth the nigimitama, or helpful aspects, of a *kami*'s energies and to minimize its aramitama, or harmful aspects. By establishing a good relationship with the kami, believers can create harmony or even develop special spiritual powers.

Shinto beliefs also encourage good behavior and social harmony. Believers are encouraged to maintain a "true heart" and to live with honesty, sincerity, uprightness. Those who live this way, and who maintain proper levels of spiritual purity, can be fully open to the will of the *kami* and to the blessings and gifts the *kami* might provide. Living in a pure way might involve things as simple as a daily bath and taking off one's shoes before entering a house. The sense that one is living in a world full of active spirits also inspires good behavior in a public sense; the Japanese traditionally feel great shame when they fail to maintain proper behavioral norms. In this they "lose face" not only among the peers but with the *kami*. The word the Japanese use for harmony, whether between humanity and nature or within human society, is wa. One of the main purposes of Shinto belief is to maintain wa.

*Rituals and Sacred Space* The wide variety of Shinto rituals reflect the belief that there are innumerable *kami* to be praised, worshipped, or called upon for help or guidance, as well as the fact that Shinto in practice is local, aside from state cults connected to the imperial family. The primary public rituals are festivals known as matsuri, of which there are two basic forms. "Big festivals," or taisai, take place generally every three years, and are dedicated to the *kami* worshipped in local shrines. In them, processions take place in which images of the *kami* are transported in portable shrines known as mikoshi. "Ordinary festivals" take place more frequently, and are as much community celebrations as religious festivals. In addition to mikoshi processions, these festivals involve feasting, games, performances, and other events. Beyond these, Shinto shrines hold seasonal festivals as well.

Many Shinto rituals commemorate rites of passage. The Shinto birth ritual is a major event taking place some months after a child's birth. Generally, extended family members accompany the parents and infant to a local shrine, where the child is blessed by a priest. Children return to the shrines to give thanks and pray for healthy lives at the ages of five for boys and three and seven for girls. Weddings also require the blessings of priests and the making of vows to *kami*, although they generally do not take place in shrines. The Buddhist day of the return of the dead, or Obon, is also an event of Shinto significance. Often during household rituals, believers make prayers to ancestral spirits, worshipping them as domestic *kami*. Funerals themselves, meanwhile, are often conducted according to Buddhist rites in keeping with the sense that Buddhism is the "death religion."

It is common for believers to visit shrines individually in search of blessings or guidance. Before doing this, believers take steps to spiritually purify themselves. Common purification rituals include the waving of a sacred branch of the sakaki tree, prayers, and chants by Shinto priests. Believers will then enter the shrine to pray and give offerings. To make their presence known to the *kami*, devotees will either clap or ring a bell, and will then make their specific requests. A second clap or tinging of a bell will signify the end of the ceremony. If the request is granted, and in order to uphold wa, the believer will return to the shrine to thank his or her *kami*.

Shinto shrines are known as jinja in Japanese, and are differentiated from tera, or temples, which is the term used for Buddhist centers. Villages and neighborhoods maintain shrines that are the focus of local celebrations dedicated to local *kami*, but Japan also contains national shrines. These include the Ise shrines near Kyoto, where the inner shrine is dedicated to Amaterasu while the outer shrine is dedicated to Toyouke, a harvest god. Ise is the greatest Shinto pilgrimage site. Another national shrine is the Yasukuni shrine in Tokyo, dedicated to the *kami* of over the more than 2 million people who died defending Japan in its wars from 1853 to 1945.

Shrines are considered sacred space, inherently different from earthly space because they are the realms of the *kami*. One enters them by going through a gateway known as a torii, which is generally painted red with black or gold ornamentation. The torii symbolizes the place where one passes from the earthly realm to the realm of the divine. Some torii stand alone but perform the same symbolic function, as some natural sites are considered themselves sacred, the realm of the *kami*. Prominent among these is Mount Fuji near Tokyo. Climbing the mountain is itself considered a religious rite. A variation on the conventional jinja is the temporary shrine, which might be constructed on a roadside, in an office, or another convenient location.

*Shinto in the Modern World* Shinto beliefs and customs remain central to Japanese life, although participation in Shinto festivals and rites appears to be declining, as does faith in individual *kami*. The main reasons for this are probably the secular emphasis of the modern world and Japan's continued religious syncretism, which has given rise to many new religions influenced by Shinto or Buddhism but different in many fundamental respects. Nevertheless, Shinto has adapted to the modern world in vivid ways. In recent years, for example, male Shinto priests have been joined by female ones; women often played a central role in earlier shrine rituals, but until these changes only as miko, or shrine attendants. It is also possible to find Shinto shrines on the Internet, since sacred space does not necessarily imply location but rather a shift in perception. Meanwhile, millions of Japanese continue to take part in New Year's and springtime festivals related to ancient Shinto festivals, and Japanese emperors and their families remain enmeshed in Shinto tradition. Each new emperor comes to the throne in an ancient rite known as the daijosai, in which he eats specially grown new rice as a symbol of his link to Amaterasu, the goddess of the sun.

SEE ALSO: Amaterasu; Izanagi and Izanami; kami; Nihon-Shoki; torii

# Shiva

One of the chief Hindu gods and probably the most widely worshipped of them all. Shiva, whose name means "Auspicious One" in Sanskrit, is part of the central trinity of Hindu deities along with Brahma and Vishnu. Engravings from the pre-Hindu Harappan civilization (ca. 2800–1800 B.C.), which show a yogi in meditation, suggest that early versions of Shiva were revered even then. He appears in the Vedas under the name Rudra, and later in the Mahabharata and Ramayana as one of the most powerful of all deities.

Shiva takes many aspects. He is the destroyer, clearing the way for new life and new energies. He is the great ascetic or yogi, often portrayed as meditating high in the Himalayan mountains. Shiva is also considered a representation of sensuality, and a symbol of the belief that spiritual worship and sensuality come from the same source. Other common aspects of Shiva are as the great avenger or as the cosmic dancer Nataraja, presiding over the eternal dance of death, rebirth and the promise of release. Shiva's female consorts are aspects of the divine feminine force, or Shakti, and their names include Durga, Kali, Parvati, and Uma. Their children are Kartikeya and, more famously, Ganesha.

Worship of Shiva often centers around a symbol known as a linga, which is often taken to be phallic. Other ritual objects associated with him are the trident and holy ash, which are common features of ascetic cults devoted to him. The Ganga River in northern India is said to flow through his hair, while Mount Kailasa in the Himalayas is his meditation retreat. In religious and popular art, Shiva is often portrayed as a wandering ascetic, or sadhu, wearing little and with his hair coiled up on his head. His skin might be white, black, red, or blue, and around his neck he has both a snake and a necklace of skulls. He carries his trident (or in South India, an axe), and a small drum. In his forehead there is a third eye. When directed inward it connotes spiritual vision, but it can be destructive when focused outward. Some images of Shiva depict him as not one among many but as the supreme god Madeva: destroyer, creator, and preserver. Devotees of Shiva in this form, who are commonly known as Shaivites, might place three verticle marks on their foreheads to represent these three aspects.

SEE ALSO: Durga; Ganesha; Vishnu

# Shrine Shinto

The predominant form of Shinto in post-World War II Japan, although it had existed as a formal category of Shinto for many centuries previously. The end of the war in 1945 and the subsequent American occupation brought about the end of State Shinto, in which the religion and politics were closely intertwined. Shrine Shinto, by contrast, mostly disdains any connection with politics, focusing instead on ritual worship in shrines. In this it may be contrasted also with various forms of folk worship. At the center of Shrine Shinto stand the more than eighty thousand shrines that are part of an Association of Shinto Shrines and which feature a wide variety of emphases and forms of ritual often associated with local gods and customs. They remain independent of the Japanese government, relying on voluntary or organizational donations for their support.

SEE ALSO: new religions, Japanese; State Shinto; Yasukuni shrine

# Siddhartha Gautama
## (ca. 6th–5th centuries B.C.)

The founder of Buddhism, considered to be the first person to achieve enlightenment or awakening in the current historical era. Siddhartha Gautama was his human name, and he is known by many other formulations, Buddha Gautama (or Gotama) and Shakyamuni among them. Gautama was the name of his clan, while his tribe were the Shakya. Shakymuni means, simply, sage of the Shakyas. Although the word *Buddha*, meaning enlightened or awakened one, is a title rather than a proper name, in general usage Buddha is understood to mean the founder. Most Buddhists believe that he lived many lifetimes prior to the one in which he became awakened, and that there are numerous other past or even present Buddhas.

Siddhartha Gautama was born in Lumphini in modern Nepal, although during his time it was part of an Indian kingdom. The major Buddhist traditions differ as to the dates of his life, with Theravada Buddhists holding that he lived from 523 to 543 B.C. and Mahayana Buddhists claiming 565 to 486 B.C. Modern scholars, meanwhile, suspect it may have been even later. Nevertheless, the main aspects of the legends of his life, enlightenment, and teachings are accepted by all Buddhists. The classic account of his life, the *Acts of the Buddha*, was written by Asvaghosa in the first century A.D.

*A Princely Life* Siddhartha's parents, Suddhodana and Maya, were members of India's ruling kshatriya caste, and the young Siddhartha was brought up as a prince. His mother died when Siddhartha was seven days old, and his father then married Maya's sister, Prajapati, who guided Siddhartha's upbringing. He led a life of great luxury filled with preparation in military and governmental arts, but it was also a life of seclusion. His father wanted to shelter him from the suffering and sorrow of the outside world. Upon growing up, he was married to Yasodhara, a bride chosen by his father. The two eventually had a son, Rahula. Stories of this and all stages of Siddhartha's life have been much embellished with legend and folklore. Maya, for example, was claimed to have seen in a dream a vision of a white elephant entering her womb from the side the day before he was born. Asked to interpret this, priests told her that she would have a son with a great destiny, either as a universal prince or an enlightened soul. Suddhodana, meanwhile, is said to have tried to keep Siddhartha within his luxurious palace compound and shelter him further by surrounding him with dancing girls, celebrations, and every other pleasure that a young man could desire, in addition to his wife and child.

Siddhartha chose a different course, however, as a result of three trips outside the walls of the compound. On the first, he saw a weak, old man. When he asked a servant about him, the servant replied that all men were subject to such a fate. On the second trip, he saw a sick man, and wondered how people could celebrate and be happy when faced with the constant threat of illness. On the third trip he saw a dead person for the first time. The servant reminded him that death was the fate of all people. Contrasting this with his luxurious life of pleasure, Siddhartha wondered how people could ignore the fear of death. Now entirely curious about life outside his palace walls, he traveled about and observed the toil of peasants and the suffering of animals. Finally meeting up with a Hindu ascetic who appeared peaceful, Siddhartha made up his mind to renounce his worldly existence and seek the cause of suffering and whether any possible cure for it might be found. Late one night, he took a last look at his sleeping wife and son and rode out with his loyal servant. After some distance he sent his servant back with a message and his ornaments of status. Siddhartha then cut his hair, put on a tattered robe, and adopted the life of a religious ascetic. He was then about twenty-nine years old.

Over the next six years Siddhartha studied under important gurus, learned various forms of meditation, and undertook many austerities. In a final fast, he was joined by five other ascetics and allowed his body to become extremely weak and thin. Realizing, despite his weakness, that he was no closer to his goal than before, Siddhartha finally allowed a young servant girl, Sujata, to give him food. His five companions abandoned him for this indulgence, but Siddhartha had come to the realizations that, not only did austerities lead one away from enlightenment, a healthy body was necessary for the pursuit in the first place. Now suspecting he was on the proper path, and having dreamt that he was soon to become awakened, Siddhartha sat down under a bodhi tree, accepted a final meal from Sujata, and pledged to meditate until he had achieved enlightenment.

*Meditation and Awakening* During that night of meditation, and according to legends that were apparently added fairly late to the overall story, Siddhartha was tempted away from his path by Mara, the Buddhist Lord of the Senses, who used fear, intimidation, and even the promise of the fulfillment of lust to distract Siddhartha from his meditation. He was able to withstand these temptations, and after a series of increasingly deep trances, Siddhartha awoke with full knowledge of the Four Noble Truths. He had found the answer to his questions about the source of suffering and the way to overcome it. He had become an enlightened one, a Buddha.

Having found five disciples, the Buddha then gave his first lessons at Sarnath, near the north Indian city of Varanasi. There he delineated the Four Noble Truths: that life is full of suffering; that this suffering is caused by desire and ignorance of the transitory nature of things; that it is possible to be liberated from this state; and that the way to do this is to follow the Eightfold Path: right understanding, right thought, right action, right speech, right livelihood, right effort, right mindfulness, and right concentration. The Eightfold Path was the middle path between the extremes of asceticism and sensual overindulgence. It encouraged moderation and, properly perfected, led to the state of being known as nirvana.

The Buddha's five original disciples formed the core of the first sangha, or order of Buddhist monks. They, and their followers, went on to write the first important Buddhist texts, which were later compiled into a collection known as the Tripitaka. The Buddha himself lived forty-five more years, teaching his message to whomever was ready to listen. During a final journey at the age of seventy-nine, he fell ill and was once again visited by Mara. Mara informed him that it was time for him to achieve final nirvana. The Buddha agreed, and he died three months later to enter the final nirvana, or parinirvana. A Buddhist stupa, or memorial tower, was erected at the site of his death in the town of Kusinagara, as other stupas were later erected at the sites of his birth, his enlightenment, and his first sermons. Although he was cremated on the order of the local ruling family, supposed relics of the Buddha were dispersed far and wide to become venerated objects themselves.

SEE ALSO: Buddhism; Confucius; Jesus of Nazareth

## Sikh gurus

Ten historical figures considered both the founders of Sikhism and mediators of the divine in that religion. Each made distinct contributions to the early development of Sikhism, helping to define it as a faith separate from both the Hinduism and Islam of sixteenth- and seventeenth-century India. For Sikhs the term *guru* means "holy preceptor."

The first guru was Nanak (1569–1539). Guru Nanak urged devotion to a God whose love was for all peoples, and he was the author of many of the verses later compiled into the Adi Granth, the Sikh scripture. The second guru, Angad (1504–1552) was one of Nanak's earliest disciples in the Punjab region of India, Sikhism's home. The third guru, Amar Das (1479–1574), worked to devise many of the organizational and ritual aspects of Sikhism while his son-in-law Ram Das (1534–1581), the fourth guru, founded the town of Amritsar, still the holiest city of Sikhism. The Adi Granth began to be compiled by the fith guru, Arjan (1563–1606), and Arjan was also the first of the gurus to come to the attention of the Islamic Mughal overlords who then ruled India. He died while a prisoner of the Mughals, who targeted the Sikhs for the next century not so much for their religious beliefs as their growing presence and power in the Punjab. The sixth guru, Hargobind (1595–1644), led the now-militant Sikhs in a number of conflicts with the Mughals. The seventh and eighth gurus, Hari Rai (1630–1661) and Hari Kishan (1656–1664), who

did not survive to adulthood, presided over an era of peace. A new era of wars resulted in the Mughal execution of the ninth guru, Tegh Bahadur (1621–1675). The tenth and last guru, Gobind Singh (1666–1708), Tegh Bahadur's son, continued to lead Sikh warriors against the Mughals. He also began the so-called Khalsa order, calling on all Sikhs to remain not only devout but militant and visible. Gobind Singh's death brought about the end of the line of specific human gurus, with the status of guru passing to both the Sikh community as a whole and to the scripture itself, the Adi Granth.

SEE ALSO: Golden Temple; Duru Nanak; khalsa

## Sikhism

A major Indian religion, practiced by some 16 million people in India and another 2 million in the United Kingdom, North America, and elsewhere. Sikhism is a monotheistic faith, centered on belief in a Creator God whose governing principles are unity, justice, and grace. It remains the third largest religion in India after Hinduism and Islam, and it likely arose as an acknowledgement of the common ground shared by those two faiths.

Sikhism was founded by Guru Nanak (1469–1539), who was born a Hindu in the fertile agricultural region of the Punjab in northwestern India. Turning to a religious life in his twenties, Nanak eventually heard a call from God claiming that the religious differences between Hinduism and Islam were irrelevant, a notion also propounded by some of India's bhakti (devotional) poets. After a further period of wandering, contemplation, and discussions with religious experts and gurus, Nanak founded his first community at Kartarpur. There he served as the "preceptor" of this new, syncretic faith. Among his innovations were the composition of poems and sermons, many of which were later included in the Adi Granth, the Sikh scripture. He also instituted communal prayers and meals for men and women, in defiance of Hindu caste restrictions and Muslim customs, on the principle that all people were equal in both an earthly sense and in the eyes of God.

Nanak designated one of his followers, Angad, as his successor, beginning the line of ten Sikh gurus who were to turn this new faith into not only a major religion but a distinct community and political force. These gurus compiled a canonic version of the Adi Granth, established the Golden Temple of Sikhism in the Punjabi city of Amritsar, and, in the seventeenth century, turned to militant resistance to defend themselves against India's Islamic Mughal Empire, which considered them a threat.

The tenth and final guru, Gobind Singh (1666–1708) designated the Sikh community as the khalsa, which means "pure." In an initiation ceremony, water was turned into holy nectar by being stirred with a sword symbolizing God's justice. Those who took the nectar, who joined the khalsa, dedicated themselves to both God's service and the preservation of their community. This was reflected in their appearance, designed to leave no doubts in the minds of anyone that believers were members of the khalsa. Sikh men do not cut their hair or beards (commonly wrapping their hair in turbans). They wear special undergarments and carry a comb, a small dagger, and a steel bracelet, which they wear around their right wrist. They also take the name Singh, which means "lion." In the first half of the nineteenth century Sikh power in the Punjab reached its greatest extent under the maharajah Ranjit Singh (1780–1839), who presided over a powerful Sikh kingdom that was eventually subdued by the British in two violent wars. Any residual bitterness between the two faded away quickly, however, and Sikhs played a major part in both the armed forces of British colonial India as well as its police and civil administration. Following Indian independence in 1947, some Sikhs wanted to establish a separate Sikh state in the Punjab to be known as Khalistan. This movement was especially militant in the 1980s and resulted in much communal violence between Hindus and Sikhs. The movement has waned and the current prime minister of India, as of 2005 and 2006, is Manmohan Singh, a Sikh.

*The Sikh Sense of God* Sikh religious belief is based on the principle that God can be found within, not in ritual, philosophy, or even behavior (although behavior reflects God's grace). Neither Nanak nor his successors wanted to integrate Hinduism and Islam, but rather to emphasize their common ground, which was love of God and respect for his power. At the center of Sikh worship is meditation on the name of God and on scripture, often through repetition, in order to perceive and then live according to God's will. Guru Nanak argued that believers pass through successive stages of realization. People first come to understand that God's Creation is governed by God alone and that he is the sole judge of humanity. Then they realize the complexity of this Creation and the need to be humble in the face of these realities. The believer is then ready to receive God's grace and to be liberated from the cycle of birth and death to become united with God. The main obstacle to this path is selfishness or self-centeredness, which can be overcome by maintaining openness to God's love and respect for his power and justice.

Sikhs place great emphasis on family and community life, on the sharing of benefits, on daily work, and on involvement with earthly matters. They do not, like Hindus, seek asceticism or renunciation. This emphasis derived from Nanak's teaching that believers must work for communal liberation in addition to individual liberation. Daily worship includes three daily prayers and, often, readings and recitations from the Adi Granth. Daily rites of singing and prayer also take place at Sikh temples, which are known as *gurdwaras* ("gateways of the Gurus"), at which Sikhs consider the preparation and serving of communal meals to all visitors a religious duty. These are also the sites for birth rites, marriages, and social activities. Local communities are known as sangat, while the larger community of Sikhs is the panth. Sikhs, unlike Hindus or Muslims, do not maintain dietary restrictions, although initiated members of the khalsa are supposed to avoid alcohol and tobacco and some meats.

Following the teachings of Guru Gobind Singh, living gurus were replaced by the Adi Granth following his death, and Sikhs see the text as a living thing and object of reverence and respect. It lies in places of honor, whether in homes or in gurdwaras and is known, in this context, as Guru Granth Sahib, which means "honorable Guru in book form."

SEE ALSO: Adi Granth; Guru Nank; Sikh gurus

## sin

Most generally, bad or evil actions considered from a religious standpoint, although in some religious traditions to live in a state of sin is simply to live separately from God. According to most religions sin is the result of deliberate decisions or intentions rather than involuntary action.

The theology of sin is most apparent in Judaism, Christianity, and Islam, where sin is considered the intentional flouting of God's will. In Judaism, sin is thought to be the result of bad tendencies or inclinations. Most basically, these tendencies cause defiance of God's laws and commandments. Rabbinic Judaism refers to sin as the "passing over" or "rejection" of the will of God which in its course damages one's relationship to God. Sins can be forgiven, however, through rituals of atonement. In early Judaism these included animal sacrifices but since the beginning of the Diaspora most gain atonement through prayer, fasting, and the maintenance of spiritual purity.

*Original Sin and Actual Sin* In Christianity, the term and concept of sin are used in several ways, leading to a variety of interpretations on the magnitude and meaning of sin. According to Paul, sin was one of the major features of worldly life, and Christians should struggle to avoid it. In other writings sin was associated with a lack of faith or belief in Jesus Christ. Both of these ideas are common in Protestant Christianity. The notion of original sin, which appears in Judaism as well, is central to Christian thinking. According to the doctrine of original sin, all human beings find themselves in a state of sin as descendants of Adam and Eve, who committed the first sin by turning away from God in the Garden of Eden. Christian theologians differentiate original sin from "actual" sin, which are thoughts, words, or deed, committed by individuals. The life, death, and resurrection of Jesus Christ, provided the believer has sufficient faith in them, provide Christians with atonement, although teachers are careful to note that true faith includes the avoidance of future sins and is not a blanket "forgiveness" for them all, past, present and future.

The theology of the Roman Catholic Church divides actual sin into two further categories. Mortal sins, for example, are grave sins committed in full knowledge that the actions were sinful and with full intention. They are thought to cut the believer off from God's grace until he or she confesses those sins and performs rites of redemption. Venial sins, the second category, are lesser offenses whose motivations are less deliberate. They do not necessarily require confession and penitence. In terms of specific "actual" sins, the recent Christian guide has been the Ten Commandments, although most Christian traditions maintain lists of the actions considered sinful. One of the purposes of Christian belief is to overcome sin, whether original or actual. Those who fail to overcome sin are condemned to hell after their death, a feature which some interpret as simply an insurmountable separation from God.

In Islam, sins might be committed against God or against other human beings. Muslims do not believe in original sin, but do recognize people's constant tendency to fall into sin. The Qur'an and other writings provide ways to avoid that in asserting what devotees should believe and do. Furthermore, since Muslims believe that God is always compassionate and merciful, the way out of sin is always open. For most Muslims, the greatest motivation for following a sinless life is the final judgment of God as well as one's personal conscience and role in the community. The greatest sin in historical Islam has been apostasy, or the intentional rejection of the Islamic faith after one has been born into it or converted to it. Muslims do not believe that the followers of other religions live in a state of sin but rather in a state of ignorance.

In Hinduism and Buddhism, it is ignorance that has to be overcome rather than bad actions themselves. Bad actions, especially intentional ones, have been divided up into various categories by Hindu and Buddhist thinkers, and Hindus have also often added the deeds or rituals that are necessary to atone for them. But at the root of bad actions is always ignorance of one's dharma, for Hindus, or of the true nature of life and the universe, for Buddhists. A life full of bad actions will only result in further entangling oneself in the cycle of birth and death.

SEE ALSO: dharma; eschatology; reincarnation

## Sita

Hindu goddess and consort of Rama in the great epic poem Ramayana. According to the poem, she was created from a furrow plowed by King Janaka, her father, and religious tradition considers her an incarnation of Lakshmi, the consort of Vishnu. Prince Rama won her hand in marriage but then lost her as she was kidnapped by Ravana, the demon-king. Even though he rescued her Rama later lost her again as she was unable to prove that, during her captivity, she had remained chaste and faithful to her husband to the satisfaction of public opinion. Thinking he was following his duty as a king, Rama banished Sita to the forest, where she bore and raised their two sons Kusa and Lava. After the sons grew up and were acknowledged by Rama, Sita was swallowed up by the earth, at her request. For this reason, as well as her origins out of a plowed furrow, Sita is often identified with the notion of the earth as mother.

Sita is among the most popular of all Hindu deities, with some surveys suggesting that she is more widely revered than any other. She is held to be the embodiment of loyalty, self-sacrifice, and devotion to her family, although her appeal also likely comes from her sense of strength and independence.

SEE ALSO: Lakshmi; Rama; Ramayana

## Smriti

A designation for a particular group of Hindu texts. Smriti is the Sanskrit word for "recollection," and the Smriti texts are those thought to have been composed from human memory as opposed to having been "revealed" in a more mysterious fashion, as were sruti texts such as the Vedas. Since the Smriti literature was derived from the sruti literature, however, it is considered to have divine authority.

In popular Hinduism the Smriti texts stand at the center of the canon of sacred literature. The major texts are the Puranas (a collection of ancient myths and legends), the epics Ramayana and Mahabharata, and the Bhagavad Gita. The Laws of Manu, the early Hindu guide to ethics and behavior, is also considered one of the Smriti. These texts remain authoritative for most Hindus because of their age, their supposed origins, and the fact that they were originally written in Sanskrit, which to some Hindu thinkers is the language of the gods. Later Hindu sacred literature, such as the devotional poems that appeared in many of India's everyday languages, does not generally carry the same authority as the Smriti texts.

SEE ALSO: Bhagavad Gita; Laws of Manu; Puranas

## Society of Friends (Quakers)

A distinct Protestant Christian sect that arose in England in the mid-1600s. Members of the Society of Friends seek to devote themselves to God without the assistance or interference of ministers, churches, or the other institutional aspects of organized religion. They are commonly known as Quakers, a name given them by outsiders whom believers told to "quake" in the presence of God.

The Quakers were originally known as Seekers, members of meetings of small groups of people disillusioned with the religious ferment among Catholics, Anglicans, Puritans, and various other Protestant groups in the England of the mid-1600s. This upheaval had played a major part in bringing the country to civil war in the 1640s, an episode that ended up in the unprecedented step, taken by victorious Puritans, of beheading King Charles I. The Seekers were further inspired by the rise to prominence of a preacher named George Fox, who urged personal contact with God without any kind of institutional mediation. By 1660, after an unsatisfactory interlude of Puritan government in England and the restoration of the monarchy under Charles II, there were as many as sixty thousand members of Quaker meetings. All faced persecution from England's more established religions and their governmental allies. In the same years Quakerism crossed the Atlantic, taking root in the English colonies of Massachusetts and Rhode Island. In 1681, with the approval of Charles II, Pennsylvania was chartered as a full Quaker colony under the leadership of the preacher William Penn.

Despite periods of persecution on both sides of the Atlantic, and the ultimate end of Penn's "holy experiment" in Pennsylvania, Quaker meetings, as their communities became known, continued to flourish. Members have commonly taken leading roles in philanthropic movements and other forms of charity work, factors contributing to the award of the Nobel Peace Prize of 1947 to Society of Friends groups in the United States and Great Britain. Their roles in such movements as the abolition of slavery has given them a historical importance that outweighs their numbers.

Common to the numerous sects of Quakerism that have arisen since the 1600s is George Fox's teaching that all people have access to the "Inward Light." A full sense of the Inward Light, of God's presence, allowed one to live a sinless life and is the source of the movement's pacifism. Quaker meetings are conducted in such a way as to aid believers to realize the presence of the Inward Light: There is silence as members await its presence, and only when one senses it fully does he or she speak. That person then "ministers" to the meeting by means of this "testimony." A few people, whose testimony has been recognized as authoritative, are considered Recorded Ministers free to travel to other meetings should the Light guide them there. A few groups, known as "programmed" meetings, have worship ceremonies that are a little more planned. There are an estimated 210,000 members of the Society of Friends around the world, with substantial membership in Africa and Latin America as well as Britain and the United States.

SEE ALSO: Anglican (Episcopalian) Church; Great Awakenings; Protestantism

## Soka Gakkai

A religious group in Japan associated with the Nichiren sect of Japanese Buddhism. Soka Gakkai, whose name translates

roughly as "Association for Creating Values," was first formed in the 1930s and became an organized sect in 1952. Its teachings are derived from those of a thirteenth-century Buddhist monk, Nichiren. Nichiren sought not only individual enlightenment but social transformation and earthly well-being, and he urged that the Japanese live solely by the teachings of the Lotus Sutra, which he thought provided all essential moral law. His followers considered Nichiren to be a reincarnation of the bodhisattva to whom the original Buddha had given the Lotus Sutra.

Soka Gakkai practiced extensive outreach from the beginning, and its membership grew rapidly. By the late twentieth century there were more than 6 million members and the organization's political party, the Ko-meito or "Clean Government Party," was the third largest in Japan. Members also built Japan's largest temple on the slopes of Mount Fuji. Soka Gakkai's appeal, which is based on the teaching that happiness is possible in this life through goodness and prosperity, has led to the rise of congregations in the United States and Europe as well as Japan.

SEE ALSO: Lotus Sutra; new religions, Japanese; new religious movements, Western

## Solomon
## (ca. mid-10th century B.C.)

The third king of ancient Israel, and son of King David and his wife Bathsheba. Under Solomon's rule Israel reached its greatest size, stretching from the borders of Egypt to the Euphrates River in Iraq. His reign is thought to have lasted from 967 to 928 B.C. Most accounts of his life and accomplishments come from the biblical books of 1 Kings and 2 Chronicles.

Solomon's kingly accomplishments were great. He defended Israel with great military skill and established colonies beyond its borders. He also completed the great Hebrew Temple in his capital, Jerusalem, as part of a massive building program. A skilled diplomat, Solomon also tried to secure Israel by arranging alliances with other powers, often through marriage (biblical accounts provide him with seven hundred wives and three hundred concubines, no doubt an exaggeration). Solomon also came to be considered a sage, renowned for his wisdom. Indeed, he was chosen to succeed David by the prophet Nathan, who anointed him in preference to several older brothers. Much of the biblical book of Proverbs is attributed to him, although the Song of Solomon is not his work. He was criticized by some later Jewish leaders for having tolerated idolatry, the worship of other, non-Jewish gods, particularly by his wives.

Israel split into two separate kingdoms during the reign of Solomon's son Rehoboam. One reason is thought to have been unrest among some of the Hebrew tribes caused by Solomon's granting special treatment to his own tribe, the Judah. A group of northern tribes seceded to form a smaller kingdom of Israel, while Solomon's descendants ruled over the remaining kingdom of Judah.

SEE ALSO: David; Saul; Temple

## State Shinto

The predominant form of Shinto in Japan from the time of the Meiji restoration in 1868 to the end of World War II in 1945. State Shinto was highly nationalistic, featuring a reverence for the Japanese emperor as a divine being and government-organized ceremonies at state-managed shrines.

The roots of State Shinto reach deep into Japanese history, which has often claimed a connection between imperial rulers and the gods, who work together for such purposes as a healthy harvest and national order. Much of this emphasis, however, fell into disuse during the centuries from approximately 1000 to 1800, when Japan's ruling classes were heavily influenced by Buddhism and Confucianism. After the Meiji emperor was restored, and Japan's new leaders sought to unify the nation for the purposes of rapid modernization, Shinto was used as a focus of Japanese distinction and separateness. State institutions tried to instill this by taking control of all Shinto shrines, establishing a national Shinto Ministry as a major government office, and trying to marginalize both Buddhism and wayward Shinto sects (despite official proclamations of religious freedom). Schools, meanwhile, were forced to teach Shinto morality and the Japanese public was urged to see religious holidays also as occasions for nationalist celebrations. Much reverence was devoted to emperors, who again were seen as divine and as the focus of national unity and the national quest for strength, prosperity, and global power.

State Shinto was abolished in 1945 by the Allied powers who defeated Japan in World War II. The divinity of the emperor, also, was repudiated. Japan since has practiced almost complete separation of church and state, although critics have called into question politicians' commemorative visits to the Shinto war shrine at Yasukuni, seeing it as an echo of State Shinto.

SEE ALSO: kami; Shrine Shinto; Yasukuni shrine

## stupa

A Buddhist structure designed to commemorate either the original Buddha himself or a revered Buddhist saint. Stupas are generally built as a symbol of parinirvana, the final death and release from existence of the Buddha. Frequently containing relics, stupas are often sites of worship or pilgrimage. Those in India, where the oldest stupas stand, likely were modeled on earlier burial mounds and consist of a domelike structure with a sculpted umbrella at the top, surrounded by gateways symbolizing the boundary between sacred and earthly space. Stupas in other parts of Asia have taken various forms, from bell-like structures to pyramids. In China, Korea, and Japan stupas are also known as pagodas. Pagodas are easily identifiable because they are structured as multistory buildings, with each story progressively smaller. Worship at stupas involves walking around them in the direction of the sun, while smaller models of them can be found in household and other small shrines.

SEE ALSO: Buddhism; pilgrimage; torii

## Sufism

The mystical branch of Islam and, along with Sunni and Shia Islam, the third major form of the faith. Sufi practice and belief is based on trying to attain a direct experience of or "vision" of God on the personal level and, on a larger level, manifesting divine love in the wider world. Sufis use such methods as meditation, music, poetry, and a variety of spiritual exercises designed to invoke this direct experience of the divine.

The term "Sufi" is derived from an Arabic word for wool and is probably a reference to the rough woolen clothes worn by early Islamic mystics. Most Sufis view their approach toward faith not as outside of mainstream Islam but rather as a separate dimension of it. They cite the ascetic lifestyle of the Prophet Muhammad

as an example of their own approach, as well as the Prophet's emphasis on inner spirituality. In Islamic records Sufis are often referred to as "friends" (awliya), since their forms of worship are manifestations of the idea of "friendship" with God that appears in the Qur'an.

Groups of Sufis began to take shape early in Islamic history, when some believers rejected the worldliness of the Ummayad caliphate (661–750). These early Sufis found the institutional emphasis of early Islam, with its continual encouragement to obey sharia laws and other dictates, unsatisfactory; although they believed that observance of sharia was necessary, it could not be a substitute for the personal experience of God. They also found the legalistic arguments of Islamic scholars dry and impersonal. As a reaction, they emphasized a personal, inner theology. At its core was an ascetic approach to living and an instinctive and unwavering trust and love in God. Among the early Sufi thinkers was Jafar al-Sadiq (?–765), who went on to become one of the Shia imams. According to Jafar, God was like a "ray of light" that Muhammad helped bring into the world.

Most early Sufi groups were small circles of teachers or guides known as "sheikhs" and their students. But the movement grew in the tenth and eleventh centuries with the rise of Sufi orders and so-called Sufi lodges, which were likely influenced by monastic practices among Eastern Orthodox Christians as well as Greek and other philosophical traditions. The first large Sufi order was the Qadiriya, begun in Baghdad by Abd al-Qadir al-Jilani (1078–1166). The Qadiriya, which continues in today's Baghdad, ultimately spread widely across the Islamic world. Its adherents performed philosophical work along with their inner spiritual explorations. The Qadiriya adopted a moderate approach to Sufism exemplified by one of the great Sufi thinkers of this era, Abu Hamid al-Ghazali (1058–1111). Al-Ghazali was an Islamic teacher and, originally, upholder of the orthodox Sunni tradition of Islam. He ultimately turned to Sufism in order to fulfill unmet spiritual needs, joining Sufi groups in Syria for two years of meditation and prayer. One result was a book called *The Revival of the Religious Sciences*, in which al-Ghazali sought to reconcile Sunni orthodoxy with Sufi mysticism. He claimed that it was possible for a person to be profoundly religious and at the same time be ignorant of the sharia or Islamic scholarship. One should simply practice religion by trying to fill the heart with God and repent of sin. Sufi methods such as meditation helped in this, and they ensured that other Islamic practices, such as the Five Pillars of Faith, were performed in the right, sincere spirit.

*A Spiritual Journey* Sufism expanded as Islam itself spread beyond its Arab and Iranian roots to include Turkish and Indian populations. In India, for example, many people brought up in Hindu traditions found Sufi mysticism congenial. The influence may have been mutual, as some believers began, in partial opposition to the teachings of al-Ghazali, to break away from any strict or necessary adherence to Islamic law. Ibn al-Arabi (1165–1240), an Arab philosopher and mystic whose ideas were extremely popular in India and points east, was a leader in this regard. Al-Arabi combined Islamic with Greek, Iranian, and Indian ideas in a philosophy that emphasized the unity of all existence. He claimed that all of Creation was a manifestation of the divine, and that people could gain access to that understanding through inner explorations. In such a journey, Islamic law was largely irrelevant. Although he was a controversial figure, considered a heretic by some of the orthodox, al-Arabi was thought to be a great teacher and spiritual master by many others. Among Turks, meanwhile, a number of so-called Dervish orders arose. The Dervishes emphasized the attainment of hypnotic states of mind where believers could gain a "glimpse" of the divine. These states could be reached through energetic whirling or dancing exercises or through the dhikr, which is the repeating of the name of God or of phrases from the Qur'an until the repetitions become habitual and unconscious, part of the rhythm of the body.

Another form of Sufi practice common among the dervishes was the use of music and poetry. The great Sufi poet Jalal al-Din al-Rumi (1207–1273) was associated with the dervishes. Rumi's Mawlawiya order of Sufi mystics thrived in Turkey until the twentieth century, and remains in existence today. Related orders emerged in India and Indonesia, and they developed their own poetical and musical traditions. Among them are the ghazals, songs of religious devotion, sung in earlier Islamic empires in India and by such popular singers as the Pakistani Nusrat Fateh Ali Khan in modern times. These various Sufi methods helped to spread Islam in not only India and Southeast Asia, but in Africa and Central Asia as well.

SEE ALSO: Jalal al-Din al-Rumi; meditation; Qur'an

## Sunni Islam

The largest of the three major branches of Islam—Sunni, Shia, and Sufi—comprising approximately 90 percent of the world's Muslims. Sunni is the mainstream form of Islam, according to its adherents, who

*Sunni Iraqi girls at prayer in Baghdad, August 2003. Sunni Islam is practiced by 90 percent of the world's Muslims.* © LYNSEY ADDARIO/CORBIS

number up to 1 billion worldwide. It is the majority approach to the faith in all mostly Islamic nations except for Iraq and Iran and also in Europe, Australia, North America, and other nations where Islam is a minority religion. Although it is the mainstream form of the faith, Sunni Islam is not an established, firm, orthodoxy. Instead, it provides room for a variety of interpretations and approaches.

Several interrelated features of Sunni Islam mark it out from other branches of the faith. One is a declared loyalty to the sunna, a term referring to Islamic customs or accepted codes of belief and practice as introduced in the Hadith and other Islamic traditions apart from the Qur'an. The best examples of sunna in practice were set by Muhammad and the companions of the Prophet during the seventh-century decades of Islam's origins. Sunni Muslims use the term sunnat al-nabi, which means "example of the Prophet," as a guide in their daily lives. Taken as a whole, the sunna forms an authoritative, living commentary on the ultimate authority, the Qur'an. The word Sunni is simply a shortened form of Ahl al-Sunna w'l-jama'a, or the "people of the Sunna." For many believers, conformity to the sunna amounts to living as a devout Muslim and assures entrance into the Islamic heaven after death.

***Sunni Flexibility*** In specific regions Sunna is generally formed by the consensus of a community, provided that consensus is based in the Qur'an, Hadith, and other traditions. It is therefore broad enough to make acceptable a reasonably wide range of Islamic practices, and another important feature of Sunni Islam is its readiness to incorporate a variety of different ethnic and linguistic traditions into the global community of Islam. The Sunni approach accepts that varied practices will occur when Islam comes into contact with existing social and cultural traditions. Thus, Islam in practice is not expected to be exactly the same in Saudi Arabia and Indonesia. On the issue of women in Islam, for example, both cultural traditions and a strict interpretation of the sunna encourage women to wear the veil in Saudi Arabia. In Indonesia, by contrast, women traditionally held greater social freedoms and responsibilities prior to the arrival of Islam and the sunna is interpreted more broadly, resulting in women commonly wearing a hijab (the traditional black gown) but leaving their faces uncovered. Neither approach is necessarily orthodox, and both are acceptable. This same openness of interpretation applies to many other issues as well, and is likely a major aspect of Sunni Islam's appeal and success around the world.

The notion of community consensus as the authority for local practice is an echo of the historical evolution of Sunni Islam. Sunnism emerged as a result of the larger attempt to create a kind of orthodox, or mainstream, Islam in the centuries following the death of the Prophet. The effort was partly a reaction to the rise of different branches of the faith that elders and scholars did not entirely approve of or see as true to the teachings of Muhammad and his companions. Most notably among these was Shia Islam, but as the religion spread rapidly in the seventh and eighth centuries, many local communities had vastly different understandings of the teachings of the Prophet, and in some places teachings were simply made up. Moreover, as Islam moved beyond Arabia, leaders found that some of these teachings were not entirely appropriate or applicable. Islamic scholars responded to these challenges by creating set lines of religious authority or bases for interpretation. Among them was al-Shafi'i (767–820), a legal scholar living in Cairo, Egypt, who was a distant descendant of the Prophet. Al-Shafi'i established that the sunna was formed by the lives, words, and deeds of Muhammad and his companions and that only the Qur'an itself had greater authority.

*Different Interpretations of the Successors to the Prophet* Other prominent Islamic scholars added to al-Shafi'i's contributions over the next centuries, thus giving greater weight to the sunna. They developed such methods as tafsir, which was a kind of study of interpretation of the Qur'an and Hadith. By the tenth century, a systematic tafsir had evolved that worked through the Qur'an verse by verse and explained many of the implications of the text when they were not apparent. This effort was partly due to tendency among some Muslims to interpret the Qur'an and Hadith according to personal speculation or intuition, or alternatively to add to these sources stories from other religious traditions or from folklore. Another important development was the rise of four accepted schools of legal interpretation in order to allow for some flexibility in understanding sharia or Islamic law. These were the Shafite (based on al-Shafi'i's teachings), the Hanifite, the Malikite, and the Hanbalite. The early culmination of all these teachings came with the work of the scholar al-Tabari (839–923), whose *Qur'an Commentary* remains a basic source for the interpretation of sunna and represented the consensus of Islamic scholars during these formative centuries.

A clear differentiation between Sunni and Shia Islam, and a reflection of its relative openness, appears in the two branches' understanding of the origins of the caliphs, or successors to the Prophet. Sunni Muslims accept the first three caliphs, Abu Bakr, Omar, and Uthman, as legitimate caliphs even though they were not relatives of Muhammad. Shia Muslims only accept the line of caliphs beginning with the fourth, Ali, who was Muhammad's cousin and son-in-law. The basis of these different interpretations was the Sunni belief that the caliph was an earthly ruler only, since no figure after Muhammad could be anything other than human. Shia Muslims argue, by contrast, that true caliphs must be divinely ordained. Meanwhile, and in accordance with the general principles of sunna, Sunni Muslims also acknowledge that the caliphate had to reflect political reality and that there needed to be some flexibility in the selection of these figures. Ostensibly, Sunni Muslims hold that caliphs must be members of the Quraysh tribe that Muhammad belonged to. But historically they have also accepted members of leading families of Mecca and even, after the Turks replaced the Arabs as the dominant powers in the Islamic heartland of the middle east, the Turkish sultans of the Ottoman Empire.

SEE ALSO: Islam; sharia; Shia Islam

## sura

A chapter of the Qur'an, the holy book of Islam. The Qur'an contains a total of 114 suras of varying lengths. Each one is thought to contain revelations given directly by God to the prophet Muhammad. All except one of them starts with a statement known as the bismallah: "In the name of God, the Compassionate, the merciful," and all but three of them are written as either direct, first-person statements or imperative commands. One of those three exceptions is the first sura, known as al-Fatiha, "the opening" of the Qur'an; following al-Fatiha, the suras are mostly arranged in order of descending length. Traditionally, each is also noted as either Meccan or Medinan, allegedly signifying the period of the Prophet's life when he received them. The content of the suras varies widely, from prayers to stories of prophets to codes of ethics to eschatology. Many Muslims seek to memorize complete suras, and they are grouped in thirty sections so that the entire Qur'an may be recited in a month.

SEE ALSO: al-Fatiha; Muhammad; Qur'an

## sutra

A form of sacred text found in both Hinduism and Buddhism. Their general purpose is exposition or commentary on beliefs or practices, or description of the meaning of religion in earthly life. The need for such texts arose when, in Hindu India in the centuries after 1000 B.C., religious teachers refused to work with written texts in their daily lives, necessitating the production of brief written works which could be committed to memory. The practice of using written sutras became common after 500 B.C., and virtually every school of Hindu thought has its own collection of them (which often overlap with other collections). Among the more well-known sutras in Hinduism are the Artha Shastra, a discourse on earthly power, and the Kama Sutra, a guidebook of etiquette and sexuality designed for upper-caste young men. In Buddhism, some sutras have achieved the status of holy texts themselves, such as the Lotus Sutra and Diamond Sutra, both central to the Mayahana tradition.

SEE ALSO: canon; Lotus Sutra; Puranas

## synagogue

A Jewish temple and public space. In Judaism synagogues are used not only for religious ceremonies but for meetings, for study, and especially in the modern world, for community activities.

Jewish tradition holds that the first synagogues were established during the sixth-century B.C. Babylonian Exile, when they were necessary for Jews to carry on their worship away from the now-destroyed Jerusalem Temple. Even after the exile and restoration of the Temple, synagogues continued to play a part in religious life, especially outside Jerusalem, when religious leaders could only make occasional visits to the main Temple ceremonies. After the second Temple was destroyed in A.D. 70, synagogues became the focus of community religious life, and one of the institutions that helped allow Judaism to survive. Documents from that era note that they existed not only in Judea but throughout the Eastern Roman Empire, in Asia Minor (Turkey) and Mesopotamia (Iraq).

Modern synagogues are run entirely by elected lay officers and maintain no established clergy. They are thus reflections of the Jewish communities in their localities. Typical features include an ark where the Torah scrolls are kept along the wall of the building facing Jerusalem, as well as a raised platform where the scrolls are placed and read (or sung) from during services by a person known as a cantor. There might also be an "eternal light" kept burning in front of the ark. In Orthodox synagogues in the West, women and men still sit in separate sections of pews while in Reformed and Conservative congregations they sit together.

SEE ALSO: church; mandir; mosque

## al-Tabari
## (ca. 839–923)

An important Islamic scholar and thinker whose works continue to influence Sunni Islam. Born in Iran but writing most of his major works in Baghdad, the capital of the Abbasid caliphate and center of Islamic thought in his day, al-Tabari's full name is Abu Ja-far, Muhammad ibn Jarir al-Tabari. His major works are the *Qur'an Commentary* and *History of the Prophets and Kings*. The *Qur'an Commentary* connected the words of the Qur'an with explanatory material attributed to the prophet Muhammad and his original companions as well as other early Muslim thinkers. It remains an important reference for Islamic thinkers. The *History of the Prophets and Kings* attempted a full history of the world focusing on prophecy, and it featured an account of Muhammad's life as the culmination of that history of prophecy. To assemble it, al-Tabari used a variety of sources ranging from earlier biographies and accounts to poetry and tribal genealogies. Very popular from the time of its first appearance, al-Tabari's *History* depicted the course of history as the playing out of God's divine will.

SEE ALSO: al-Ghazali; Qur'an; Sunni Islam

## Talmud

One of the main texts of Judaism and the focus of the Rabbinic Judaism that has dominated the faith since the early decades of the Diaspora. In its narrowest sense Talmud is a textual commentary on the Mish-nah, the original text of Rabbinic Judaism. There are actually two Talmuds: the Palestinian Talmud, compiled around the end of the fourth century, and the Babylonian Talmud from about a century later. For most Jews the Babylonian Talmud is the more authoritative, and its commentary is much more wide-ranging than its counterpart. Both texts can be divided, in general, into Halakhah, which focuses on rituals and laws, and Aggadah, which is concerned with ethics and stories. The two Talmuds were originally written in the Semitic language of Aramaic.

In a broader sense the term Talmud refers to the study of Jewish laws, rituals, ethics and history, and such study is fundamental to the rabbinic Jewish tradition. It analyzes not only the Mishnah but the Torah and other texts as well, and it was originally thought to have been handed down by God to Moses during the Exodus and then preserved orally by an inner circle of elders for many centuries. Believers are still encouraged to enter into this study and dialogue with the past.

SEE ALSO: Judaism; Mishnah; Torah

## tanha

A Pali word meaning "thirst." In Buddhism, the term is used to refer to the source of all human suffering, the "thirst" or craving for worldy objects ranging from material goods to experience to fame. This thirst implies a clinging to the world, to "becoming" in an earthly sense, and it is the root cause of not only suffering but also of continual rebirths. The primary goal of Buddhism is to gain release from tanha. The state of nirvana connotes the cessation of all clinging, of all "thirst."

SEE ALSO: dhukka; Four Noble Truths; nirvana

# Tantricism

An esoteric school, or rather collection of schools, in Hinduism and Buddhism that has exercised a profound influence on both. In general, Tantricism shares with Hinduism and Buddhism the notion that the goal of life is moksha, release from the wheel of birth and death or, alternatively, enlightenment and entrance into nirvana. It differs from most mainstream forms of the other two faiths by not rejecting the body, the motions, or other aspects of the individual self. Tantric worshippers see the body as a microcosm of the universe and try to work through it and transform it in pursuit of larger religious goals.

In Hindu Tantra, aspects of which are probably as old as Hinduism itself, the body is thought to mirror the universe. Believers hold that the universe was created from top to bottom, in a set of successively lesser or more vulgar forms: mind, space, air, water, fire, and finally earth. The body contains counterparts of those levels, and their energies are known as chakras. The lowest chakra, that of earth, is at the base of the spine, while mind, the highest, is located between the eyebrows. There is also a chakra hovering above the head, the sahasrara chakra. The chakras are connected by three channels of energy that lie in the middle of the spine and at the body's two sides. The purpose of Tantric rites is to awaken an energy force known as kundalini, which is generally described as a snake. Kundalini lies asleep in the lowest chakra for the uniniti-

ated or unenlightened. Adepts will try to awaken it so that it passes through all of the chakras via the three channels and ultimately passes outside the body to enter the sahasrara chakra. This is done through various yogic practices, some of which may be sexual in nature, and requires training, concentration, and the guidance of a guru.

The above process is also described using Shiva as a male force and Shakti as a female force, which exist separately in each of the chakras. Kundalini is Shakti, and in its sleeping form is wrapped around Shiva in the form of a linga, or phallic image. Once kundalini is awakened and passes through the various chakras, Shakti is reunited with Shiva in the sahsrara chakra, which is also described as a thousand-petaled lotus. This happy reunion, or explosion of enlightenment to use another metaphor, constitutes the realization of the unity of the cosmos.

Devotees of Tantricism are generally disapproved of by mainstream Hindus. Their emphasis on the "energies" of the body and on the spiritual nature of certain, and admittedly rarely employed, sexual practices contradicts much traditional Hindu thought as well as conservative social norms, and these ideas and practices are easily misunderstood or vulgarized. Moreover, Tantra rejects asceticism, caste, and the inequality of women; all women are thought to be embodiments of Shakti. Although Hindu Tantric schools probably reached their height around 1000 A.D., many still exist, and Tantricism has again been an important influence on various other sects.

In Buddhism, Tantricism is associated with some Mahayana traditions in Tibet, India, China, and Japan. It is generally considered to have arisen in the later centuries of the first millennium. An alternative term for it is vajrayana, or "intedestructible vehicle." Buddhist Tantra's most distinguishing characteristic is that it offers devotees the possibility of enlightenment in this lifetime, and it added numerous Buddhas and bodhisattvas, ones who had accomplished this, to the ones that already existed in the Mahayana traditions. These included a number of female ones. Although Buddhist Tantric texts include very sophisticated philosophical discourse, its greatest focus is on method and practice, a feature it shares with its Hindu counterpart. These include the use of mantras, the ritual deployment of images, icons, and devices, such as the mandalas characteristic of much of Tibetan Buddhism, and, rarely, sexual practices. Performed consistently, properly, and with the right guidance, these might lead to enlightenment. Alternatively, believers might use these practices in order to use sacred power for less exalted purposes. Meanwhile, Buddhist Tantra also shares with Hindu versions a conception of the need to bring together opposites, which are often depicted in artwork in male-female and sexual terms.

SEE ALSO: Hinduism; meditation; Tibetan Buddhism

## Temples, Jerusalem

Two successive structures in Jerusalem that served as the geographical focal point of early Judaism and, after the second Temple was destroyed and never replaced, as the symbol of the worldwide Jewish community's hope that they might one day return to Jerusalem.

The first Temple was built by Kings David and Solomon in the mid-tenth century B.C. At that time David and Solomon ruled over a unified kingdom of Israel, and built the large and elaborately decorated

temple to reflect their power and status among the nations of the ancient Near East. It was built in a style common to that time and place, with a main entrance that faced east and through which one entered a courtyard. At the center of the Temple stood the "Holy of Holies," a small shrine where the ark of the covenant was kept and to which only high priests had access. The Temple was destroyed by the Babylonian Empire in 587 B.C., after a long siege of Jerusalem and after the final conquest of Judah, the rump area of what remained of the kingdom of Israel. A later Jewish festival, 9 Av, partly commemorates the event.

The Temple grounds, or Temple Mount as the area is commonly known, remained strewn with rubble for some seventy years until Jewish leaders returned from their exile in Babylon. They built a smaller temple under the guidance of a figure known as Zerubbabel; the construction was performed by the permission of the Persian emperor, who had conquered Babylon and who now controlled Jerusalem and its surrounding territories. The second Temple, about which far more is known than the first Temple thanks to a greater quantity of surviving records, was the site of the most important Jewish rites and ceremonies of the era, many of which included animal sacrifices. Leaders of Jewish communities living outside the city walls were commonly expected to go to the Temple for important events.

In 167 B.C. the Temple's sacred status was desecrated by a new king of Greek heritage, Antiochus IV, working together with Jews sympathetic to the introduction of Greek ideas into the faith. Following a violent rebellion, Jewish leaders rejected this Greek-inspired movement and rededicated the Temple in 164, an event commemorated by the festival of Hanukkah. Under the Romans, in the first century B.C. local leaders, notably Herod, enlarged the Temple. All contained within walls, this enlarged Temple maintained a series of separate "courts." The large Temple court was accessible to all visitors, and it was in this area that Jesus of Nazareth met with Jerusalem's Jewish leaders in the early first century A.D.. Further within, in a consecrated area accessible only to Jews, was a court of women and the court of the Israelites, which could only be visited by adult male Jews. From it, devotees could see the sacrifices performed in the court of the priests. At the center of this complex was the Temple's inner sanctuary, holding an altar with ritual objects such as a menorah and a new, symbolic, "holy of holies."

The second Temple was destroyed by the Romans in A.D. 70, after a further desecration and another major Jewish rebellion. All that remains of the structure is the Temple Mount's Wailing Wall, a pilgrimage site for Jews. The destruction marked the beginning of the Jewish Diaspora, when communities scattered and no longer had a focal point for their faith. After the Islamic conquest of Jerusalem in the seventh century, Muslims built two sacred monuments of their own on or near the Temple Mount: the Dome of the Rock and Al-Aqsa Mosque.

SEE ALSO: Diaspora; Jerusalem; Judaism

## Ten Commandments

The ten religious laws held to be sacred by both Jews and Christians. They are given or mentioned in the books of Exodus and Deuteronomy in the Hebrew Bible/Old Testament, and were, according to mainstream tradition, revealed by God to the Prophet Moses on Mount Sinai during the historical Exodus.

Jewish scholars dispute the precise origins and meaning of the Ten Commandments. For some, they are the great symbol of God's renewed covenant with the Hebrews, and date back at least to the thirteenth century B.C. Popular tradition holds that Moses received them in the form of stone tablets inscribed by God, and that these were first carried in honor by the Hebrews during their wanderings and then, after the construction of the first Temple in Jerusalem, placed in the Holy of Holies, Judaism's most sacred shrine. Other scholars suggest that the commandments are a summary of Jewish laws that not only date from sometime after the destruction of the first Temple but were intended only for adult Jewish males. Still others see them simply as examples of Jewish prophetic traditions. Christians, meanwhile, might refer to the Ten Commandments as the Decalogue, Greek for "ten utterances." They apparently received little attention by Christian theologians until they were incorporated into manuals of religious instruction in the thirteenth century. The Protestant churches that arose beginning in the sixteenth century place them at the center of their learning and as fundamental sources of moral belief. According to the book of Deuteronomy of the Revised Standard Version of the Bible, the Ten Commandments are:

> You shall have no other gods before me.

> You shall not make for yourself a graven image, or any likeness of anything that is in heaven above, or that is in the earth beneath, or that is in the water under the earth; you shall not bow down to them or serve them; for I the Lord your God am a jealous God, visiting the iniquity of the fathers upon the children to the third and the fourth generation of those

who hate me, but showing steadfast love to thousands of those who love me and keep my commandments.

You shall not take the name of the Lord your God in vain, for the Lord will not hold him guiltless who takes his name in vain.

Remember the sabbath day, to keep it holy. Six days you shall labor, and do all your work; but the seventh day is a sabbath to the Lord your God; on it you shall not do any work, you, or your son, or your daughter, your man-servant, or your maidservant, or the sojourner who is within your gates; for in six days the Lord made heaven and earth, the sea, and all that is in them, and rested the seventh day; therefore the Lord blessed the sabbath day and hallowed it.

Honor your father and your mother, that your days may be long in the land which the Lord your God gives you.

You shall not kill.

You shall not commit adultery.

You shall not steal.

You shall not bear false witness against your neighbor.

You shall not covet your neighbor's house; you shall not covet your neighbor's wife, or his manservant, or his maidservant, or his ass, or anything that is your neighbor's.

SEE ALSO: Bible; Moses; Old Testament

## theism

Most simply, belief in a divine being that is separate from and above worldly things. This being is considered to be beyond full human comprehension. Theism might take the form of either monotheism, the belief that only one divine being exists, or poly-theism, the belief that there is more than one such being. It is usually associated, however, with monotheistic traditions such as Judaism, Christianity, and Islam due to the sense of separation between this divine being, or God, and worldly things. Theists generally consider this God to be the Creator of the universe from nothing as well as the preserver of the world and one who is constantly present. Many consider it possible for individuals to communicate with God through such means as prayer, ritual, or even mystic rites.

Many theists, especially in the Christian tradition, have attempted to make their beliefs a branch of rationalist philosophy by devising various philosophical "proofs" of the existence of God. None of these proofs is completely convincing, however, since they all depend on assumptions that can neither be proven nor disproven by rational means. Theism is often contrasted with atheism, the belief in no God; pantheism, the belief that all of nature is divine and inseparable, and deism, the belief that God was the Creator yet is not constantly present.

SEE ALSO: atheism; deism; pantheism

## theology

Discussion, study, and inquiry into the nature of God or the gods. The first theology appeared in ancient Greece, with numerous writers and thinkers writing stories about and speculating on the nature of the gods. The tradition continued in Judaism, Christianity, and Islam, and its role was especially distinct in Christianity, where theology emerged as a branch of scholarship as well as of religious thinking. Some of the most important Christian thinkers, notably Augustine and Thomas Aquinas, are properly considered theologians. Among the main concerns of these and other theologians were the nature of God, the human relationship with God, ethics, salvation, and eschatology (the last days). Hinduism, Buddhism, and other Asian religious traditions cannot be said to have theology as such, since they do not consider philosophical inquiry in any way separate from ritual or other kinds of religious practice or belief. The term is used in all religions, nonetheless, in a very broad sense, to refer to the teachings of religious authorities.

SEE ALSO: Augustine, Saint; philosophy of religion; Thomas Aquinas, Saint

## Theosophism

An eclectic yet influential religious movement that emerged in the eastern United States in the late 1800s. Founded in 1875 in New York City by the Russian mystic Helene Blavatsky and her associate Henry S. Olcott, who started an organization known as the Theosophical Society, modern Theosophism was an attempt to restore mystical elements to modern religious experience. Through such means as intuition or meditation, one was able to grasp a deeper spiritual reality than was accessible to "exoteric," or external experiences. Blavatsky and Olcott taught that all world religions possessed such a deeper reality and that, in that sense, they were similar. This underlying unity, they believed, transcended the exoteric differences among the religions. In this, Blavatsky and Olcott were much influenced by Hinduism and Buddhism, and their work helped introduce these to Eastern religions to the West. They believed, further, that a group of spiritual masters existed, likely in Tibet (which was virtually unknown in their time), and that these masters were guiding the process of human spiritual development. Theosophical practice focuses on meditational techniques and discussion

rather than rites and ceremonies.

The Theosophical Society, for its part, sought transformation on the earthly plane as well as the spiritual one. Their goals included the formation of a circle of believers who supported the brotherhood of humanity, the study of science as well as religion, and an examination of the laws of nature and of human potential. After Blavatsky and Olcott moved the movement to India soon after its founding, and after Blavatsky's death in 1877, it suffered a schism due to disagreements between Olcott and the American William Q. Judge. Judge's successor as leader of the American branch, Katherine Tingley, established the headquarters of the American Theosophical Society in the Point Loma area of San Diego; in the 1950s it was moved to Pasadena, California. The Indian branch, meanwhile, came under the leadership of the charismatic social reformer and feminist Annie Besant after Olcott's death in 1907. Besant helped bring attention to the movement, but suffered a setback when a young Hindu she named as one of the spiritual masters, J. Krishnamurti, rejected the claim. Krishnamurti, however, chose to remain in the West as a writer and teacher on Hinduism and other spiritual topics. Branches of the Theosophical Society continue to exist in over fifty countries.

In a generic sense, theosophism or theosophy refers to the seeking of divine wisdom through intuition or meditation in any philosophical or religious tradition. As such, it has been a concern of numerous thinkers including the Greek Plato, the medieval European mystic Meister Eckhardt, and the nineteenth-century German philosopher Friedrich Schilling. The process is also a fundamental component of Hindu thought.

See Also: Hare Krishna; new religious movements, Western

## Theravada Buddhism

Along with Mahayana Buddhism one of the two main forms of Buddhism. Theravada Buddhism is practiced mostly in Sri Lanka, Myanmar (Burma), Thailand, Laos, and Cambodia.

Theravada is a Pali term meaning "way of the elders," and devotees consider the school to be much closer than Mahayana to the Buddhism taught and practiced by the original Buddha and his first followers, although historically the Theravada was just one school among many. Followers prefer that name to Hinayana, which means "lesser vehicle" and is used in a derogatory fashion by Mahayana ("greater vehicle") Buddhists in reference to the Theravada school. The original centers of the school, dating from the last two centuries B.C., were in southern India (where it later mostly disappeared) and at Anuradhapura in Sri Lanka. From those sites it spread to Southeast Asia over a period of many centuries, taking root in the period from 1000 to 1500.

Characteristics of Theravada Buddhism include a commitment to the Tripitaka, compiled by the first century B.C., as the only authoritative Buddhist texts, as well as a fairly strict emphasis on monastic practice as laid out in those texts. They believe that there is no self, that the world is transitory and an illusion, and that nirvana must be the ultimate goal. Theravadins reject any argument that the original Buddha was in any way divine; he was rather the sole human being who is known to have reached enlightenment (although sometimes they consider Maitreya, the "future" Buddha, as an exemplar as well).

Once the Buddha reached enlightenment he was released from the wheel of birth and death. He is therefore no longer present or active in the world, and the Buddhist form of salvation is the task of the believer alone. Theravadins generally dismiss the Mahayana principle of the presence of bodhisattvas as well as the canon of texts and stories describing them and their works. Although some classical Theravadin thought recognizes the possibility of bodhisattvas, they do not see it as a state suitable or reachable for all devotees. The ultimate goal of Theravadins is to become an arhat, a sort of Buddhist saint and the highest level of enlightenment attainable to human beings.

In practice, Theravada rituals differ between monasteries, which follow prescribed doctrines and procedures and are centers of education and community life as well as worship, and outside monasteries. There, laypeople generally combine Theravada practice with various other beliefs ranging from Hindu influences to faith in the presence of spirits. Since few laypeople place themselves on the path to becoming arhats in this life, they seek instead to "make merit" through such means as giving food or other resources to monasteries or by doing good works. In Theravada countries young men frequently serve temporarily as monks, and with their shaven heads, saffron robes, and begging bowls, are thought to replicate the Buddha's original followers. Much more rarely do people devote their entire lives to serving in monasteries. Those who do recognize that the only way to truly achieve arhat-hood is through solitary meditation.

See Also: arhat; Buddhism; Mahayana Buddhism

## Thomas Aquinas, Saint
## (ca. 1225–1274)

An important Christian philosopher and the most prominent of the scholastic philosophers who helped shape Christian thought during the Middle Ages. Aquinas helped to create a systematic theology for the church of Rome. At the heart of his thinking was the argument that reason and faith could coexist. Unlike most philosophers, such as the ancient Greek Aristotle, whom Aquinas recognized as a major influence but who relied on reason alone, theologians based their reasoning on religious faith and religious authority. Firm in their religious foundations, theologians could then employ reason to examine such matters as good and evil and the nature of God's involvement in the world. Aquinas recognized, however, that not all Christian tenets could be explained through reason and must be accepted on faith. These included the Trinity and the Incarnation of Jesus.

Aquinas argued that God created the world out of nothing, and therefore was the cause of everything aside from himself. His order was by definition perfect. Human beings were granted free will, but ultimately this free will was also created by God. When people were using their rational faculties or their free will, according to Aquinas, they were behaving according to their true natures which, again, were created by God. To diminish those qualities was to diminish God's creative power. These arguments, although they have remained controversial, allowed Christian thinkers the intellectual freedom to try to create a systematized Christian theology, since to do so was to act in accordance with God's creation.

Aquinas was canonized by the church in 1323. In 1567 he was named an official doctor of the church and was further recognized as one of the creators of orthodox Catholic thought during the nineteenth century. Those Christians who have adopted Aquinas's thought are known as Thomists.

See Also: Augustine, Saint; Roman Catholicism; theology

## three refuges

A central tenet of Buddhist thought and practice. Buddhists are encouraged to take refuge in the "three Jewels:" the Buddha, the dharma, and the sangha. By taking refuge in the Buddha, believers can find an example of not only the path to enlightenment but of earthly kindness and good will. By taking refuge in the dharma, Buddhists can be assured that their lives proceed along the proper path and that they live ethically. By taking refuge in the sangha, a term most commonly referring to a monastic order, believers can find comfort in the presence of religious authorities or by serving themselves as monks or nuns. These three refuges, or tisarana as they are known in Pali, are often used as a simple motto signifying Buddhist faith. A variation of this motto runs:

> I take my refuge in the Buddha.
> I take my refuge in the Dharma.
> I take my refuge in the Sangha.

## Tibetan Buddhism

The distinct branch of Buddhism that emerged in the isolated region of Tibet north of the Himalayan mountains. Largely an esoteric version of the "greater vehicle" known as Mahayana Buddhism (although it also contains elements of the Theravadin variation), the Tibetan form of the faith is renowned not only for its distinctness but because of the twentieth-century fate of Tibet and its leaders. The

*Prayer wheels are an important ritual object used by followers of Tibetan Buddhism, and the act of spinning the wheel is considered an act of devotion.* © JEREMY HORNER/CORBIS

nation was incorporated into the People's Republic of China in the 1950s, resulting in widespread suppression of its religion. Tibetan Buddhist leaders, notably the Dalai Lama, went into exile, establishing India as the headquarters of Tibetan Buddhism. The current Dalai Lama, meanwhile, is one of the worlds's most recognizable Buddhists.

Buddhism entered Tibet in two stages. The so-called first diffusion of the dharma took place in the seventh and eighth centuries. Then, Tibetan kings established numerous important monasteries, often with the assistance of Indian Buddhist saints and scholars. One of these was the Tantric saint Padmasambhava, who brought with him such methods as meditation involving a view of the divine contained within the body as well as the use of sacred mantras and mandalas. This 1st diffusion came to an end when resistant Tibetan kings suppressed the faith, preferring their indigenous traditions such as Bon.

The second "diffusion" began in the tenth century, and by the end of the eleventh century the main Tibetan Buddhist sects had appeared. A major figure of this era was Atisa, an important Buddhist reformer from India. Atisa argued that Buddhists should follow the three major schools—Theravada, Mahayana, and Tantra—in succession. All four of the major Tibetan Buddhist sects follow versions of this succession. The four are known as the Kagyupa, Sakyapa, Nyingmapa, and Gelugpa, and although each has its own traditions, philosophies, rituals, and monasteries, they share some common characteristics.

Primary features of Tibetan Buddhism include worship and devotion of Buddhas and bodhisattvas. Unlike in other forms of Buddhism, but somewhat like Hindu worship, these enlightened figures are often worshipped in male-female pairs. Male and female are thought to be complementary, with the male Buddhas and bodhisattvas representing activity and creation while the female ones represent intuition, contemplation, and natural wisdom. All are descended from an original Buddha-essence described as Adi-Buddha. In artwork and mythology Adi-Buddha is depicted as a god ready to throw a magic thunderbolt. In Sanskrit the term for this thunderbolt is vajra, thus leading to the name of vajrayana that is sometimes used for the Tibetan form of Buddhism. It means roughly "thunderbolt vehicle." Among the most powerful and widely worshipped of the vajrayana bodhisattvas is Tara, the consort of Amitabha or his avatar Avatokitesvara. Tara has been thought to be incarnated into the wives of Tibetan kings and, depending on the color in which she is pictured, she might be angry and vengeful or loving and generous.

Individual Tibetan devotees, meanwhile, often develop a personal identification with a particular Buddha or bodhisattva to whom they direct chants, prayers, and other rituals. One form of enlightenment for them is the attainment of spiritual union with the object of their devotion. Among the factors that makes this possible, Tibetan Buddhists believe, is the fact that each human being contains a microcosm of the universe within him or herself. Meditational exercises can awaken a person's spiritual energies until Adi-Dhamma's thunderbolt strikes, or until the moment when enlightenment is experienced.

*Rituals and Ritual Objects* Aside from meditation, Tibetan devotees employ mandalas in worship, which are circular designs representing microcosms of the universe in various forms and which allow the worshipper to "place" the Buddhas and bodhisattvas. The chanting of mantras and giving of offerings might attract these celestial deities, thus establishing the opportunity for "contact" with them. An added benefit of these practices was that they helped to fend off the many demons and evil spirits, whose presence is really as much a relic of pre-Buddhist Tibetan religions as they are of Tantric Buddhism. An important ritual object used by Tibetans, meanwhile, is the prayer wheel. Prayer wheels can be small and hand-carried, or large and fixed inside temples or monasteries. They consist of written prayers and other sacred statements that the user can rotate around a central axis. Keeping the rotation of prayer wheels going is considered an emphatic act of devotion, and devotees often carry them on foot-borne pilgrimages to holy sites, keeping them in rotation all the while.

Tibetan Buddhism underwent a period of reform in the fourteenth century, when the monk Tsong-kha-pa (1367–1419) established the Gelugpa order as the nation's dominant one. Members of the order came to be known as Yellow Hat Buddhists because of the color of their hats and other garments, and they belonged to the so-called Yellow Church (Red Hat Buddhists were ones who resisted these reforms). Among the major legacies of the Yellow Hat school was a much stronger monastic discipline, including the practice of celibacy, and the introduction of principle of the reincarnation of head lamas, or leaders of monasteries. The head of the main Yellow Hat monastery at Lhasa, the Tibetan capital, was held to be a reincarnation of Avalokitesvara. He came to be known as the Dalai Lama, or "oceans of wisdom" lama. The leader of the Tashilunpo monastery, the Panchen Lama, was thought to be a reincarnation of Amitabha. When incumbents died, a complex search began for the new incarnation. Candidates had to be children born forty-nine days after their predecessor's death, be familiar with his possessions, and show various indications of wisdom, knowledge, or divine selection.

The fifth Dalai Lama, Ngawang Lozang Gyamtsho (1617–1682), became the Tibetan head of state as well as its leading cleric, and he unified the nation under the authority of the Yellow Hat sect. He also built the vast Potala Palace in Lhasa. By that era Vajrayana Buddhism was not only the state religion of Tibet, it had spread beyond Tibet's borders to Mongolia and the border areas of Russia, China, and India. Its importance to Tibetan life is reflected by the fact that, by the time of the Chinese takeover, up to one quarter of all Tibetans lived in monasteries and each family, commonly, had at least one son enter monasteries for a lifetime. The Chinese tried to suppress Buddhism, both because of their official atheist stance as Communists and because they wanted to diminish Tibetan culture in order to integrate the country into China. This resulted in the wholesale destruction of hundreds of monasteries and the forced secularization (and sometimes worse) of many monks. In recent years China has lifted a few restrictions on Tibetan Buddhist practice, but heavy state controls remain in place. The fourteenth and current Dalai Lama, Tenzin Gyatso, went into official exile in 1959. The Chinese government has invited him to return, but under conditions that remain unclear. For the time being the main center of Tibetan Buddhism is Dharamsala in northern India.

SEE ALSO: Dalai Lama; Mahayana Buddhism; Tantricism

## Torah

An important term in Judaism that has several related uses, all connected with Jewish teachings. Most literally, the Torah is a collection of texts also known as the Pentateuch, the first five books of the Tanakh, or Hebrew Bible: Genesis, Exodus, Leviticus, Numbers, and Deuteronomy. Many synagogues traditionally maintain scrolls of the Pentateuch, which are known as sefer Torah, or "book of the Torah." In the Rabbinic Jewish tradition this written Torah has been combined with an oral Torah. Both were handed down by God to Moses at Mount Sinai during the historical exodus. But while the book of the Torah was eventually committed to writing, the oral Torah was passed down to an inner circle of elders and teachers until it, too, was eventually written down. The Talmud is the tradition of commentary and interpretation of both the written and oral Torah.

In a wider sense, Torah, which simply means "teaching," is the entire Hebrew Bible, the entire collection of texts including the Hebrew Bible and Talmud, or even all Jewish teachings, history, and lore. Most Jews view exploration of the Torah as an essential part of their faith. It is an ongoing process of continued examination and interpretation, a way for believers to actively take part in an evolving tradition.

In another, different sense, the Torah is an object of devotion with sefer scrolls, again, maintaining prominent place in the synagogues. Jews view the Torah as the sign of the covenant between their people and God, an offering that God made to other peoples but which only the Jews accepted. It is therefore an essential part of their identity as well as their religious and intellectual practice. Torah is also, for most Jews, the guide to their behavior, the source of all laws, although those laws might be interpreted differently by the various Jewish sects. It is also the representation of their hope for eventual salvation.

SEE ALSO: Hebrew Bible; Judaism; Talmud

## torii

The gates of entrance to Shinto shrines. In Shinto thought, the torii are thought to signify the border between earthly space and sacred space, and therefore in order to perform shrine rituals properly, believers should enter through the gates. Because they are of symbolic rather than physical or architectural importance, torii are often stand-alone structures unconnected to other shrine buildings. They generally consist of two horizontal beams supported by two cylindrical posts, and they are often painted red. Some torii stand by themselves and signify the separation between earthly space and the sacred realms of certain mountains, bodies of water, or other natural things and are not part of shrines. A variation on this theme is the so-called floating torii standing in Hiroshima Bay. Rising from the water, it guards the Itsukushima Shrine on Miyajima Island, a renowned pilgrimage site. Devotees must pass through it by boat before visiting the shrine.

SEE ALSO: Ise shrines; Shinto; stupa

## trimurti

A Sanskrit word meaning "triple form" and referring to the "trinity" of Brahma, Shiva, and Vishnu, the main Hindu deities. Use of the term usually connotes worship of the divine as a composite of these three forms, as opposed to the separate worship of one of the three gods, and it does not refer to any overarching trinity comparable to the Trinity of Christianity. Worship of the trimurti, which can be found as early as the fourth century, describes the three gods as each representing one "face" of the divine. Brahma is the creator, Shiva the destroyer, and Vishnu the preserver. Trimurti can also consist of Sarasvati, Lakshmi, and Parvati, three of the female consorts of the male deities and representatives of the female, or Shakti, aspects of the divine. The conception was probably invented by priests seeking to reconcile differences among separate Hindu sects.

SEE ALSO: Shiva; Trinity; Vishnu

## Trinity

A fundamental Christian doctrine claiming that God is "three in one," that a single God reveals Himself using three "persons." These are God the Father, God the Son (Jesus Christ), and God the Holy Spirit. Although the three are separate they still remain a unity, sharing a single "substance." The doctrine was defined by a series of early church councils in the third and fourth centuries, which sought to reaffirm both the separate and unified aspects of the Trinity and to reconcile Christian history and teachings with monotheism. The scriptural basis of the notion appears in such New Testament books as Matthew and Corinthians, where the three are celebrated together. The precise nature of the Trinity is considered different, however, in the Roman Catholic and Eastern Orthodox branches of Christianity. Roman Catholics, and most Protestants, believe that the Holy Spirit "proceeds" from the Father and the Son, and placed that assertion into the Nicene Creed; it is known as the filioque ("and from the Son") clause. Eastern Orthodox Christians believe instead that the Holy Spirit proceeds from the Father through the Son.

SEE ALSO: councils, early Christian Church: Holy Spirit; Nicene Creed

## Tripitaka

The earliest and most authoritative Buddhist texts. The term is a Sanskrit one meaning "triple basket" and in most Buddhist traditions the Tripitaka consists of three "baskets" of wisdom. The *Vinaya Pitaka*, thought to be the oldest, consists of rules for monks and monastic orders. The *Sutta Pitaka*, the largest, contains the teachings attributed to the original Buddha as well as those of some of his followers; it includes the Buddha's first sermons. The *Abhidamma Pitaka* is primarily a further examination of the *Sutta Pitaka*, although various versions of it have appeared.

The Tripitaka was compiled in India in the last few centuries B.C. The authoritative versions of the texts are in Pali, although they appeared originally in Sanskrit as well. The Tripitaka forms the entire textual canon of the Theravada school of Buddhism and provides much of the basis of the school's claim to pure form of Buddhism. In Mahayana and Tibetan Buddhism, the Tripitaka is often extended to include numerous other texts considered authoritative.

SEE ALSO: Buddhism; Dhammapada; sangha

## Twelvers

A familiar name for the main school of Shia Islam. Believers are known as Twelvers because of their devotion to the twelve imams, beginning with Ali, the son-in-law of the prophet Muhammad, followed by Ali's martyred sons Hassan and Hussein. The twelve imams are considered not only caliphs, or leaders of the faith, but also divinely chosen figures guiding the destiny of humankind. Each of the twelve imams has special prayers devoted to him, which are commonly recited weekly. Believers also frequently make pilgrimages to their tombs, notably the tombs of Ali in Najaf, Iraq, and Hussein in Karbala, Iraq. The pilgrimages are thought to bestow special merit on those who make them. Twelver Islam is the official religion of the modern nation of Iran.

SEE ALSO: Islam; Ismailis; Shia Islam

## ulema

The class of learned men in Islam, particularly those well versed in Islamic theology and law. Members of the group generally are educated in Islamic schools known as madrasas, although they might receive secular educations as well. They often work as judges, religious lawyers, or advisers to high officials, and they have generally been the men consulted on matters of religious law and ethical behavior, with their decisions establishing community norms or standards. Since Islam does not have a clergy as such, members of the ulema have also fulfilled pastoral or mosque leadership roles. The ulema have been very influential in Muslim states historically and continue to be so in some conservative countries, although their importance has often waned in recent decades with the rise of secularly educated classes. In a narrower sense found in the histories of some Islamic states, the ulema has been specifically the group of religious advisers consulted by leaders and therefore an element of government bureaucracy.

SEE ALSO: madrasas; sharia

## 'umra

A "minor" pilgrimage to Mecca in Islam that believers can make on its own or in conjunction with the larger and more fundamental pilgrimage known as the hajj. It can be done at any time of the year rather than in the more specific hajj season, and is considered especially meritorious for actual residents of Mecca. Many of the elements of the 'umra are the same as those of the hajj, although not all are required. These include entrance into a state of ritual purity before entering Mecca, circling the Ka'aba shrine seven times, touching the black stone at one corner of the Ka'aba, and running seven times between the hills known as as-Safa and al-Marwah.

SEE ALSO: calendars; hajj; Mecca

## Unitarianism

A religious movement arising from within Christianity but rejecting some of Christianity's basic doctrines, most notably the Trinity and the divine nature of Jesus Christ as well as Christian concepts of sin and salvation. Unitarians believe instead that God only exists in that person and that Jesus was a human. They also emphasize the use of reason in religion as opposed to unquestioning faith.

Although aspects of Unitarian thought can be traced back to early Christianity, and the first Unitarian denomination was founded in central Europe during the Protestant Reformation in the 1500s, Unitarianism became widespread only after the founding of the first English congregation in 1774 and the first American one in 1782. Influenced by the rise of modern science, the Protestant clergy who founded these congregations wanted to emphasize reason as a source for and explanation of ethical behavior as well as religious belief. In England, where Unitarians were influential in government, they supported social reforms as well in the name of a kind of practical Christianity. In the United States, the American Unitarian Association was founded in 1825, with members arguing that truth came out of experience, not prayer or religious teachings. Although it has largely faded in England, there are still more than a thousand Unitarian congregations in the U.S. and Canada, with each governing itself. Their rituals and practices, which are mostly based on Protestant models, vary.

SEE ALSO: ecumenism; Protestantism; Vatican Councils

## Upanishads

An important and varied collection of Hindu texts in both prose and poetry. Chronologically they are considered to have followed and completed the Vedas, and they began to appear in written form around the sixth and fifth centuries B.C., although they may have been part of a much older oral tradition. Since they follow upon and comment on the Vedas, the Upanishads are considered the core of Vedanta, which means the "end of the Vedas." They differ from the Brahmanas, a collection of texts from the same era, in that they focus on mystical and philosophical concerns rather than rituals and early deities, although some overlap exists with the oldest of the Upanishads. Traditionally, scholars accept that there are 108 Upanishads, although a few count up to 200 of them.

The term Upanishad means, roughly, "closeness to a guru," and many of them are thought to be the teachings of individual religious masters. The theme that is most common to these teachings was the nature of reality, and in discussing the notion the Upanishads present ideas that were fundamental to later Hindu thought. Among these were the argument in some

of the texts that the self, or atman, was identical to brahman, the ultimate reality. Atman nonetheless is reincarnated into a succession of living beings in accordance with the laws of karma. The realization of their ultimate sameness or connection, what the gurus simply called "knowledge," was what allowed the believer to achieve moksha, or liberation from reincarnation. It was the earlier Upanishads, such as the Chandogya and Brihadaranyaka, that examined these concerns most directly. Later Upanishads modified their emphasis to include the nature and roles of Hindu deities within the context of this larger philosophical discourse, and are thus a source for the understanding of popular Hinduism. Among these is the Bhagavad Gita, which in this context is a Vaishnava Upanishad, or a text concerned with the god Vishnu, here described in the form of the avatar Krishna.

SEE ALSO: Bhagavad Gita; Puranas; Vedas

## Uthman
### (−656)

The third caliph, or leader of Islam, according to the tradition of Sunni Islam. Uthman followed Abu Bakr and Omar as successors to the Prophet Muhammad. A member of the Ummayad clan, one of the wealthiest and most powerful in Mecca, Uthman became a follower of Muhammad in about 620. His presence helped to give added status and respectability to Muhammad's fledgling religion, and he went on to marry one of the Prophet's daughters.

Uthman was a compromise selection as caliph. His opponents represented diverging viewpoints about the future course of Islam, and Uthman's membership in the Umayyad clan gave him the support he needed to marginalize them. Following his election in 644, Uthman helped to strengthen early Islam's institutional elements: he helped to confirm an official version of the Qur'an and created a centralized administrative system. He also continued the pattern of military conquests begun by his predecessors. When too much of the new Islamic empire's revenue began to be diverted into the hands of Uthman's family members, however, new conflicts arose, especially within the army. He had also offended some religious thinkers; ironically, his "official" Qur'an placed control of religious thought in the hands of the centralized administration rather than with the so-called Qur'an reciters who had exercised it previously. Those opposed to Uthman coalesced around Ali, the Prophet's cousin and son-in-law. Uthman was killed by a group of rebels in 655.

SEE ALSO: Abu Bakr; companions of the Prophet; Islam

## Varanasi

Hinduism's holiest city, also known in English as Benares and in India by its ancient name, Kasi. Varanasi stands on the banks of the Ganga (Ganges) River, Hinduism's holiest river, in Uttar Pradesh state in the north Indian plains. It is one of seven sacred Hindu cities connected by a network of long-standing pilgrimage routes.

Varanasi is one of the world's oldest living cities. It was already an important commercial and religious center when the original Buddha delivered his first sermons nearby in the sixth century B.C., and from that time on numerous travelers noted its importance in India's religious life. Many of its temples were destroyed and reconstructed several times during the centuries when much of northern India was under Muslim control (ca. 1206–1757), and the city continues to maintain a large Muslim presence. After a short period as an independent princely state in the late 1600s and 1700s, Varanasi was added to Britain's Indian possessions in 1794, although the British allowed the local rulers, or maharajahs, to keep their titles.

The chief deity worshipped in Varanasi is Shiva, here revered under the name of Vishnavath, the Lord of the World. Devotees of Shiva consider the city to be a living symbol of Shiva, and it is dotted with numerous temples devoted to Vishnavath. There are numerous other temples too, devoted both to other deities and to great gurus and teachers. Many Hindus hope to make trips to Varanasi once in their life-

times, and a central ritual of the pilgrimage there is to walk a path around the city known as the Pancakosi. It is also believed that to die and be cremated in Varanasi allows for instant moksha, release from the wheel of birth and death. At the center of the city, along the Ganga, are long cremation grounds, or "ghats," to provide for this, while elsewhere along the front are other ghats for ritual bathing. Meanwhile at Sarnath, a few miles to the north, there

*Shiva is the chief deity worshipped in Varanasi, which is considered Hinduism's holiest city.* © EYE UBIQUITOUS/CORBIS

stand monuments to the earliest periods of Buddhism as well as contemporary Buddhist pilgrimage sites. Well over a million pilgrims travel to Varanasi every year.

SEE ALSO: Ganga River; Kumbh Mela; Shiva

# Vatican

The centralized institution of the Roman Catholic Church. Also, the area of some 110 square acres within the Italian capital of Rome where the top church officials reside and house the base of their operations. Although except for some brief interludes these top officials, notably the popes, have always resided in Rome, the Vatican in its current form was not established until 1929. Then, the area was given a degree of self-government by the government of Italy in order that it might remain free from undue influence from that government, which was at the time under the control of the Fascist dictator Benito Mussolini. The Vatican retains this degree of self-government, and remains the home of both the papacy and the curia, the organization in charge of the day-to-day operations of the church.

SEE ALSO: papacy; Roman Catholicism

# Vatican Councils

Two Roman Catholic Church councils that helped to set doctrine for the Church in the modern era. They were 20th and 21st such meetings in the history of the Church in a series dating back to the early centuries of Christianity.

The first Vatican Council took place in 1869 and 1870, called together by Pope Pius IX. It produced two doctrinal "constitutions." The first, Dei Filius, provided a shortened but definitive statement on the Church's view of the relationship between faith and reason. The second, Pastor Aeter-

nus, was concerned with the authority of the popes. It decreed that the pope, as the successor to Saint Peter, had full authority over the entire Church, including its pastoral and teaching functions. The constitution also established the principle of papal infallibility, which stated that the pope's pronouncements are free from error when he speaks on matters concerning faith or morals as they pertain to the entire Church. Pastor Aeternus was very controversial, but it passed despite strong resistance. The council was disbanded when Italian troops occupied Rome in 1870 as part of the process of Italian political unification, although it was never formally closed by church officials.

The Second Vatican Council lasted from 1962 to 1965 It was begun by the reforming Pope John XXIII and, after his death, concluded under Pope Paul VI. It resulted in the most substantial changes to the Church since the Council of Trent in the 1500s, and its observers included leading figures from other Christian denominations.

The Second Council, or Vatican II as it is commonly known, produced five particularly important constitutions refining or reforming central Church functions or attitudes. The Constitution on the Church grounded the organization of the Church in scriptural and theological rather than legalistic terms and gave renewed authority to the bishops. The Constitution on Divine Revelation reaffirmed the importance of holy scripture as the basis for salvation but also noted the importance of Roman Catholic teachings as another source of the divine word. It also further opened both to scholarly examination and criticism. The Constitution on the Church in the Modern World dealt with the

Church's attitudes toward such worldly matters as marriage, war, and economic development, which were considered to be undergoing great and rapid changes at the time and which many believed the Church must adapt to. The Constitution on the Sacred Liturgy dealt with ritual practices, and provided means for greater participation in the Mass and other rituals by laypeople. It also authorized more use of vernacular languages in rites, a matter particularly important in the non-European world. The Decree on Ecumenism was concerned with the Church's attitudes toward other Christians, and it promulgated both a vision of religious freedom among Christians and proposals for reunification, particularly between Roman Catholicism and Eastern Orthodoxy. Aside from these important statements, Vatican II concerned itself with such matters as the education of priests, missionary work, and the attitude of the Church toward non-Christians.

SEE ALSO: councils, early Christian Church; councils, Roman Catholic Church; ecumenism

## vedanta

The philosophical foundation of most modern schools of Hinduism. The term *vedanta* means "culmination of the Vedas," and in its most literal sense refers to a group of texts central to the school: the Upanishads, the Brahma Sutras (which are brief commentaries on the Upanishads), and the Bhagavad Gita. Vedanta arose out of a study of these texts, mostly in the first millennium A.D., although it later branched out to include a number of different schools.

The primary concerns of these schools are those of Hinduism in general, and they differ more in terms of emphasis than general content. They share in common the belief in the reincarnation of the self over many lifetimes and the ultimate goal of release from the "wheel of existence." They also share the belief that Brahman, the ultimate reality, is the ground of all existence and that the individual self, or atman, is subject to karma, or the consequences of action. They differ on such matters as the precise nature of the separation between Brahman and atman; the advaita vedanta of the eighth century, for instance, argued that no such separation, or dualism, exists. The eleventh- and twelfth-century thinker Ramanuja, by contrast, argued that the individual soul is real, but depends completely on Brahman.

SEE ALSO: Bhagavad Gita; Shankara, Vedas

## Vedas

The earliest, foundational Hindu texts. Properly speaking, the Vedas are texts of a pre-Hindu faith in India generally termed the Vedic religion, but there are many clear and identifiable links between them and later Hindu religious thought and practice, and the Vedas continue to be used for ritual and devotional purposes. Scholars generally accept that they were composed or compiled between 1500 and 1000 B.C., the period when Indo-European migrants were settling across India's northern regions. Tradition claims that they were "heard" by religious adepts known as rishis at the beginning of the current world cycle, and are therefore even more ancient than modern scholarship would claim. After having been passed down orally for centuries the Vedas were finally written down, probably between 1000 and 600 B.C., in an early form of Sanskrit, the language of the Indo-European migrants and still Hinduism's sacred tongue. The word *veda* means "knowledge" and is likely derived from the same root word as the English "idea."

There are four Vedas. The oldest is the *Rig Veda*, the "Veda of Hymns." It contains 1,028 ritual chants to be employed by priests and their families. Most of these are devotional in nature, dedicated to such Vedic deities as Agni, the god of fire, Indra, the god of war, and Varuna, the god of the sky and waters.

The *Yajur Veda*, or "Veda of Sacrificial Prayers," is made up of numerous prayers, in both prose and poetry, to be used in ceremonies. As the title indicates, they were often employed in sacrificial rituals, with the person praying asking for blessings or benificence. A fire ceremony, directed to Agni, was perhaps the most basic. It might include, beyond the performance of prayers, animal sacrifice and the use of an intoxicating beverage called soma.

The *Sama Veda*, or "Veda of Chants," is an elaboration on many of the verses contained in the Rig Veda, with the chants modified to be used by specific groups of brahmin priests. It also contains musical notations to aid in the proper performance of some of the chants.

Finally, the *Atharva Veda*, the "Veda of the Atharvans (magician-priests)," is the latest. It contains a wide variety of prayers and other formulas designed for personal and popular devotion as well as for such earthly benefits as health and well-being.

These four texts formed the foundation for much later Hindu writing. Each of the four, for instance, was later appended by the so-called Brahmanas, which further elaborate on the uses of the Vedas in ceremonies and rites. The Aranyakas and Upanishads are also considered elaborations of the ideas and symbolism in the Vedas. These later groups of texts also effectively trace the decline of Vedic religion and the rise of classical Hinduism. Vedic rites, apparently, grew so complex that fewer and fewer brahmin priests were able to carry them out. In reaction to this, Indian religious thought began to grow more philosophical, with a greater focus on meditation as opposed to sacrificial rites. Over time, this gave rise to such conceptions as karma, reincarnation, and moksha, as well as the sense that there was an ultimate reality, brahman, which encompassed all deities.

Vedic influence is still apparent in Hinduism. Some sects continue to practice animal sacrifice on certain ceremonial occasions, and the use of fire is common in worship. The Vedic gods themselves are also still present, although they are granted relatively small roles such as guardians of the directions. India's caste system, as well, reflects the Vedic era, which was when the earliest versions of the caste system appeared; then, religious teachings were restricted to the top three castes and only Brahmins were permitted to perform religious ceremonies. Today, moreover, most Hindus continue to accept the authority of the Vedic chants, which are, again, still commonly used.

SEE ALSO: Brahmanas; Hinduism; smriti

## vipassana

A form of Buddhist meditation found more often in Theravada than in Mahayana Buddhism. The goal of vipassana meditation is direct insight into the true nature of reality, that reality is impermanent and filled with suffering and that no self truly exists. Meditational techniques may involve, first, exercises focused on breathing to achieve perfect calm. A next step is to achieve perfect concentration, or one-pointedness of mind. In this state, one has complete awareness of the so-called four foundations: body, feelings, state of mind, and mental habits. Eventually, the meditator will gain a level of concentration that will allow him or her to fully realize the impermanence and insubstantiality of reality, and to develop increasing levels of detachment from that reality. The meditator must also take care to guard against "stopping" at any of these levels, or becoming prematurely satisfied with his or her level of detachment, since a key to vipassana is to realize that even higher states of consciousness are transitory. Followed fully, this path is thought to lead to full enlightenment. Traditionally vipassana meditation should be carried out only with proper guidance and preparation. The term is a Pali one meaning "see clearly" or "insight."

SEE ALSO: Four Noble Truths; meditation; Theravada Buddhism

## Vishnu

Important Hindu god and, along with Brahma and Shiva, part of the central Hindu trinity of deities. His name is a Sanskrit word meaning "all pervading," and Vishnu is held to be the preserver and protector of the world as well as the defender of the dharma, or moral order. He traditionally is thought of as king, in contrast to Brahma the priest and Shiva the yogi

Vishu first appears in the Vedas, Hinduism's oldest texts, although he plays only minor roles there in connection with the sun. In later texts, notably the Mahabharata, Ramayana, and Puranas, Vishnu is one of Hinduism's main focuses of religious devotion. He is thought to have the ability to take any form necessary in order to preserve life or the moral order, and he is most generally known in the form of one of ten of these so-called avatars

(although there are thousands of others). These ten avatars are, in a sequence thought by some to mirror the process of evolution, a fish, a tortoise, a boar, a half man/half lion, a dwarf, Rama with an ax, the Rama of the Ramayana, Krishna, Siddhartha Gautama (the original Buddha), and Kalki (a final avatar yet to appear). Rama and Krishna are the avatars most commonly worshipped, and they stand at the center of many bhakti, or devotional, cults. Worshippers of Vishnu directly are known as Vaishnavites, and they hold Vishnu to be the supreme deity. In this form he is also known as Isvara, the creator of all things and the refuge and sustainer of life who makes his presence known in various forms.

Vishnu has many wives and consorts, many of whom represent prosperity and good fortune. Most prominent among them is Lakshmi. In South Indian devotional and popular art he is often depicted standing or reclining between Lakshmi (there known as Sri Devi) and Bhumidevi, the goddess of the earth. His skin is blue or another dark shade. His sacred symbols include a conch shell, a lotus or padma, a club, and a flaming wheel or discus, known as a chakra. Other artistic depictions have him in motion, generally upon the sacred bird known as Garuda, or awaiting the start of a new cosmic cycle (which are simply "days" to Vishnu) by reclining on a serpent known as Sesa or Ananta, who sleeps on the endless, cosmic ocean. Vishnu is known by many names, and some devotees seek to recite the "one thousand" names of Vishnu as a form of worship. In addition to Rama and Krishna some of his common names are Hari, Vasudeva, and Narayana.

SEE ALSO: bhakti; Krishna; Shiva

# Wah'habism

A conservative Islamic sect founded in the 1700s by Muhammad ibn 'Abd al-Wahhab and adopted as official by the Saudi clan in Arabia in 1744. The sect is more properly known as the Muwahhidun, or "Unitarians" in Arabic, the name that followers themselves use in their attempt to emphasize the oneness of God. The Muwahhidun insist on a literal interpretation of the Qur'an and Hadith and urge a return to Islam in its earlier forms, without the theology and legal thought that emerged in the religion's later centuries. They also reject all ceremonial or ritual acts whose effect might be to minimize God's oneness. These might include pilgrimages to the tombs of saints or martyrs or ceremonial commemorations of such figures. Strict Wah'habites regard Muslims who perform these acts as heretics and apostates, particularly the Shia. The movement also urges the creation of states based on their strict and puritanical reading of Islamic law.

The Muwahhidun movement achieved great influence thanks to the rise in power of the Saudi clan, which by the end of the 1700s controlled much of inner Arabia and occupied Mecca and Medina. After being briefly subdued by the Turkish Ottoman Empire in the 1800s, the Saudis rose again in the late nineteenth and twentieth centuries. When the modern kingdom of Saudi Arabia was established in 1932, with the Saudis as rulers, Muwahiddunism became the dominant religious form in the country. Leaders enforced a strict moral code using, among other measures, a sort of religious police known as mutawwi'un. This force has the right to enter homes since traditionalist Islam recognizes no difference between public and private devotion or behavior. The movement has been influential in recent decades thanks to the growth of Saudi wealth and influence not only in the Arab world but in Pakistan and Afghanistan as well.

SEE ALSO: Islamism; sharia

# Wailing Wall

The most important pilgrimage site in Judaism. The Wailing Wall is all that remains of the western wall of the second Temple in Jerusalem after its destruction in A.D. 70 by the Romans. After this event many Jews still considered the site of the Temple, known as the Temple Mount, sacred, even after most of the structure itself was reduced to rubble and carted away for construction elsewhere. The custom was for Jerusalem's Jewish leaders to restrict access to the site, for fear that people might step on the spot where the Holy of Holies, Judaism's most sacred shrine, had stood. Because of this, and because it is both a remembrance and symbol of the promise of Israel, the Wailing Wall is Judaism's holiest spot. It is linked to the wall, built later, which surrounds the current Islamic edifices on the Temple Mount, the Dome of the Rock and Al-Aqsa Mosque. After the modern nation of Israel took control of the old city of Jerusalem in 1967 authorities conducted an outer area by the wall where Jews could gather.

SEE ALSO: Diaspora; Temples, Jerusalem; pilgrimage

## wu-wei

An important concept in philosophical Daoism. Wu-wei is a Chinese term that might be translated as "not doing" or "inaction." It describes an attitude toward human existence that allows one to live in accordance with the Dao, to achieve without doing. The concept might be further described as avoiding action that interferes with or interrupts the true "way" of nature. These actions might include excessive ambition or, simply, restless, nervous activity, which Daoists believe inspire one to believe in a way contrary to his or her true nature. On this level, the doctrine of not doing should not be taken too literally. Instead, one should simply "do" in accordance with his or her true nature. From another perspective, wu-wei might also be explained as simply accepting natural processes and change, such as birth, illness, and death. To accept them, Daoists believe, gives one not only greater peace but greater power than one who resists natural processes. As one verse from the Dao De-jing put it, "the farther one travels, the less one knows," so the truly knowledgeable person will be the one who stays put, who does not "do."

SEE ALSO: Chuang-tzu; Dao De Jing; Daoism

## Yahweh

The God of Judaism as revealed to the Prophet Moses on Mount Sinai during the era of the exodus. Yahweh is an elaboration of the four Hebrew language letters YHWH, also known as the Tetragrammaton. The Orthodox Jewish tradition considers the name too holy to be pronounced out loud or even written, as do many individual Jews in other traditions. In writing, it is often depicted as Y**H. In synagogue and other rituals, meanwhile, other names of God are used, such as Elohim, which means simply "god," and Adonai, or "my Lord." The precise meaning of the name is unclear, with many scholars believing that it refers to "He who brings into existence" or even simply "I am." "Jehovah" is a Christian variation of the name.

See Also: Elohim; Exodus; Jehovah

## Yasukuni Shrine

A major Shinto shrine in Tokyo, Japan, and a source of controversy in recent years. Yasukuni Shrine was built in 1869, during Japan's era of State Shinto. It's purpose was to commemorate the war deaths of those who sacrificed themselves for Japan in the years from 1853 to 1945, which are thought to number around 2.5 million and who include many women and children as well as men. The shrine is thought to hold the kami, which might be translated as "spirits" in this context, of all of those people. It also contains records of their names in a Book of Souls. The Yasukuni Shrine, whose name means "peaceful country," has therefore come to be a kind of national shrine to some believers. Among those revered at the shrine are one thousand Japanese soldiers convicted as war criminals after World War II; among them are fourteen "class A" war criminals who were executed for their actions.

Until 1945 and the end of State Shinto, the Yasukuni Shrine was a government-sponsored institution. Since then it has been supported privately. Some 8 million people visit the shrine every year, mostly to pay respects to the ancestors whose souls are still thought capable of intervening in everyday life. In recent years, Japanese prime ministers and other important politicians have made regular visits to the shrine, and some have even tried to restore its official status. This has given rise to controversy, since to many non-Japanese these visits imply a restoration of a "nationalized" form of worship and a rejection of Japan's World War II crimes.

See Also: Ise shrines; *kami*; State Shinto

## yeshiva

In its broadest sense, a Jewish school emphasizing study of the Torah. The yeshivas, or yeshivot in Hebrew, are most commonly associated with Orthodox and other traditionalist forms of Judaism and are ostensibly designed to train and ordain rabbis. Other students tend to receive their Jewish educations in other institutions. Yeshivot were derived from the so-called bet

*The traditional symbol of yin and yang, or Taijitu.* © Royalty Free/Corbis

Midrash ("house of study") of the Talmudic period of the first millennium.

Yeshiva students are all male and range in age from the midteens to the midtwenties. Their study generally takes the form of the examination, in small groups, of a particular Talmudic text. Then the students will hear a rabbi's lecture on that text, followed by further examination and discussion. Although yeshiva methods have been criticized for their narrowness, at the heart of these methods is the encouragement of students to become active participants in the centuries-old Talmudic tradition.

SEE ALSO: madrasas; Orthodox Judaism; Talmud

## yin-yang

A central idea in Chinese thought and religion but which is most common in Dao-ism. Yin-yang represents the balance of opposite but complementary forces. This balance of opposites is thought to be necessary for the preservation of both cosmic and earthly order. Yin is generally thought of as female, or as dark, cold, the earth, or the moon. It is also associated with passivity and acceptance, and its common animal symbol is the tiger. Yang forces are male and active, and are connected to the sun, light, heat, and the skies. Its animal symbol is the dragon. Even though such forces are thought to be in opposition, they are not necessarily the source of tension, as they are commonly thought to be in Western philosophy. Instead they complement one another, and to bring both into balance is necessary for complete wholeness. In the famous symbol of the yin-yang, opposites are represented by a black and a white sylized half circle, both of equal size and placed to form a full circle, a complete whole. But to show that elements of the yin are necessary within yang, and vice versa, each half circle contains a smaller full circle of the opposite color. Much of Chinese religion and thought, particularly in Confucianism and Daoism, is built around the necessity of establishing balances in individual life, in the family, in society and politics, and even in one's relationship with the divine. It also is a common theme of Chinese folklore, for instance in the faith that seven bad years must be followed by seven good ones.

The origins of yin-yang are unclear, but by the time of the Han dynasty (206 B.C.–A.D. 220), the Confucian philosopher Tung Chung Shu (176–104 B.C.) had developed an influential view of the universe based on it. Tung claimed that the natural order operated in a cyclical way, with yin and yang repeating one another in succession. He also argued that a balance needed to be maintained between humanity and nature.

SEE ALSO: Confucianism; Daoism

# yoga

A word commonly associated with practices of meditation in Hinduism, but which actually has several meanings. Derived from a Sanskrit word that might be roughly translated as "spiritual work," yoga is one of the main branches of Hindu philosophy. In this sense, yoga emphasizes the need for the soul to free itself from the material world and its illusions and restraints. More broadly, the term refers to a particular Hindu approach to faith that a person might take. Karma yoga, for instance, is a focus on religious ritual, while bhakti yoga emphasizes devotion, usually to a particular god or goddess. The yoga-

darshana, thirdly, is one of the six classical schools of Hinduism, which date back over two thousand years. It is characterized by developing expertise in the eight steps that are thought to lead the believer to full awareness.

As meditational practice there are three distinct schools of yoga. Hatha yoga is training in certain physical techniques thought to aid in meditation and to lead to "mastery" of the body and of physical processes. Following rites of bodily purification, one engaged in hatha yoga works on the regulation of breathing, on the tensing and flexing of particular muscles, and on perfecting postures such as the cross-legged lotus position. Its purpose is not necessarily to achieve peace of mind or relaxation but to awaken the spiritual forces that lay within the body. Variations of hatha yoga have grown popular in the West. Tantra yoga builds upon the process of hatha yoga. There, meditational techniques allow for the unleashing of the sexual and spiritual forces contained within certain centers of the body known as chakras. Most important among them is the sakti, or female force, which is portrayed as the serpent Kundalini. Once awakened, and with continued meditation, Kundalini moves up along the spinal column until, if the techniques are perfected, it unites with the male force represented by Shiva, which is thought to hover above the head. In *Samadhi* yoga, meanwhile, the purpose of meditation is less on the body than on the reaching of a state where the mind can focus, undisturbed, on the ultimate reality. This is often achieved through meditation on a particular object of perception. Those who perfect *samadhi* meditation are considered to have entered a higher state of consciousness than most people are capable of. The term dhyana yoga is also used to refer to this attempt to achieve a higher state of consciousness as well as, according to some, special mental or physical powers.

SEE ALSO: Hinduism; meditation; Tantricism

## Yom Kippur

The Day of Atonement, one of the most important festival days in the Jewish calendar. It takes place during the tenth month of the Jewish lunar calendar, in the period during September or October known in the United States as the High Holy Days, which also includes Rosh Hashanah. Yom Kippur is fundamentally a day of fasting for the purposes of purification and to show both forgiveness for the sins of others and contrition for one's own sins. The festival commonly begins at sundown with a period of meditation and the reading of a special service of atonement known as the kol nidre. Then, for a twenty-five-hour period devotees abstain from eating, drinking, washing, and sexual activity. Many Orthodox Jews also avoid wearing leather shoes. The wearing of white is encouraged. Yom Kippur services include prayers of repentance and readings from texts such as the Hebrew Bible book of Jonah. Family members and friends may also ritually ask one another for the forgiveness of their sins. The festival commonly ends with prayers and the blowing of the ram's horn, the shofar.

The modern Yom Kippur festival is an echo of a similar ceremony conducted during the period, over two thousand years ago, when the second Jerusalem Temple was the focal point of the Jewish faith. During that ceremony a high priest, wearing white, would enter the Holy of Holies and ask God not only for the forgiveness of his own sins but for those of the nation of Israel. He would also burn incense and offer the blood of a sacrificial goat, the scapegoat. The goat would then be driven away from the Temple, symbolically carrying away the sins of Israel.

SEE ALSO: Exodus; Judaism; Rosh Hashanah

## yoni

A Sanskrit word meaning "source" or "womb." It is used in Hinduism to refer to symbolic representations of the female sexual organs as well as their implied religious significance. The yoni is the sign of the goddess Shakti, representation of the female powers of the universe. In artwork it is depicted as a stylized triangle and is often associated with the linga, the phallic symbol connected with the god Shiva. Together, the two symbols not only connote the link between Shakti and Shiva but more generally the eternal process of creation and rebirth.

SEE ALSO: Shakti; Shiva

## Zen Buddhism

A form of Buddhism centered on techniques that might enable devotees to reach rapid flashes of, or alternatively the calm sense of, enlightenment. The term zen is a Japanese version of the Chinese ch'an, which in turn is derived from the Sanskrit dhyana, which simply means "meditation." Zen Buddhists seek to emulate the meditational experiences of the Buddha, in particular his rapid awakening under the bohdi tree.

The Ch'an school arose in China in the sixth century A.D. and is usually attributed to the monk Bohdidharma, who was thought to have spent nine years in motionless meditation. Ch'an played an important role in the diffusion of Buddhism in China, although many of its specific schools faded by the ninth and tenth cen-

*The Zen temple garden of Ryoan-ji (The Temple of the Peaceful Dragon) in Kyoto, Japan, a place of contemplation and meditation.* © Archivo Iconografico, S.A./Corbis

turies, perhaps because of a resurgence of Daoism, with which Ch'an shares similar practices. It was taken to Japan in the same era, and reached full flower in the twelfth century, becoming one of the most important forms of Buddhism in that country and a major influence on its culture and artistic life.

Zen teaches that the true experience of enlightenment is available to everyone, a fundamental tenet of most other branches of Mahayana Buddhism. The way to achieve this awakening is to gain a realization of the true nature of things, to go beyond traditional assumptions and habits of thought. This realization is commonly known as satori. Japan's different Zen schools emphasize different techniques used in gaining satori. The Rinzai school uses meditation of riddles and paradoxes known as koan, a famous example of which is, "What is the sound of one hand clapping?" Rinzai Zen devotees also understand that meditation and enlightenment can take place at any time, and do not necessarily involve seclusion or monasteries. The Soto sect emulates the Buddha and Bohdidharma, emphasizing long sessions of meditation known as zazen, or simply "sitting meditation." In Rinzai the experience of satori comes in an instant, while in Soto it is slower and steadier.

By the sixteenth century, Zen monks and priests played important roles in Japan's political life as well as its cultural activities. Traditional Japanese gardens, for instance, are largely "zen" environments designed to reflect the calm Soto version of satori, as is the elaborate tea ceremony, which became customary in that era. Zen has also grown popular in the West, imported by such teachers as Dr. D.T. Suzuki (1870–1966).

SEE ALSO: Mahayana Buddhism; satori; Siddhartha Gautama

## Zionism

The modern Jewish movement to first create and then sustain a national homeland. The movement is named for Zion, originally simply a hill in Jerusalem but also a literary reference to the traditional land of Israel.

Diaspora Jews never truly lost the hope that one day they could return to their homeland, the area of the eastern Mediterranean shore commonly referred to as Palestine. By the late nineteenth century, however, many Jews living in the wealthier nations of western Europe or the United States had focused their attentions on assimilation into the cultures of those countries, often with considerable success. Jews who favored a return to Palestine tended to be Russian Jews who lived under much more oppressive conditions than those elsewhere. Meanwhile, the only people then seriously thinking in terms of a Jewish nation-state were racial nationalists who tended to have Christian backgrounds.

That changed rapidly. The modern Zionist movement, sometimes known as political Zionism, was founded by an Austrian Jewish journalist named Theodor Herzl. While covering the trial of Alfred Dreyfus, a French Jewish army officer falsely convicted and then imprisoned for betraying military secrets, Herzl grew convinced that Jews could never be fully assimilated into European nations; they would always be in some ways a people apart. Only with a state of their own could they maintain full self-respect and command an equal voice among the nations. Publicizing his ideas in books and newspapers, Herzl reached a ready audience, particularly among eastern European Jews. The first Zionist Congress met in Basel, Switzerland, in 1897, where members devised a plan to "create for the Jewish people a home in Palestine secured by public law." The Zionist movement spread rapidly, publishing its own newspaper and raising funds in order to establish communities of settlers in Palestine. It also helped to inspire a Jewish cultural rebirth featuring, among other things, the restoration of Hebrew as an everyday spoken language rather than a scholarly language mainly restricted to experts, comparable to Sanskrit in India or Latin and Ancient Greek in Europe.

By the outbreak of World War I in 1914, there were some 90,000 Jewish settlers in Palestine, then under the control of the Islamic Ottoman Empire, which largely welcomed them. In 1917, Zionist leader Chaim Weizmann secured the support of the British, who were shortly to take over Palestine, in setting up a Jewish state. Settlers continued to move there in the 1920s and 1930s, ultimately reaching a population of some 250,000, until the British stopped their migrations in the face of widespread riots among Palestinian Arabs. Following the Holocaust of World War II, many European Jewish refugees displaced from their homes or unwilling to remain in Europe set out for Palestine despite the legal restrictions then in place. The British soon turned the region over to the United Nations. On November 29, 1947, the UN voted to recognize the modern State of Israel, and local Jewish fighters confirmed its establishment in the Arab-Israeli War of 1948 and 1949. Herzl's dream had come to pass. Since 1947 and 1948 the Zionist movement has focused on raising funds to support Israel and encouraging Jews to move there. The Hebrew name for the na-

tion is Eretz Israel, or "Land of Israel," to distinguish it from the people of Israel, who might reside anywhere.

SEE ALSO: Diaspora; Holocaust; Jerusalem

## Zoroaster
## (ca. 628 B.C.–551 B.C.)

The prophet and founder of Zoroastrianism, one of the great religions of the ancient world. He is also called Zarathustra or Zardusht. Little is known of the life of Zoroaster, with much of it derived from stories in the Avesta, the Zoroastrian scripture, as well as other ancient Iranian texts. According to them, the prophet's coming was divinely foretold. After living an early life as a priest, Zoraster at the age of thirty received the first of his many visions of the "Wise Lord" of Zoroastrianism, Ahura Mazda. He came to believe that Ahura Mazda had selected him as a prophet, to preach that Ahura Mazda was the creator of all goodness and the only true god. Human beings seeking to live righteously should worship him alone as well as to spread the word of his goodness. They should also seek to live in harmony with nature, a way of life Zoroaster contrasted with that of the warlike, unstable nomads who threatened the Iran of his day. Zoroaster also taught that human beings had free will; they could choose between devotion to the Wise Lord or to follow, instead, the evil spirit known as Ahriman. This choice would be the basis for a final judgment placed upon human beings after their deaths.

Zoroaster faced a great deal of resistance to his teachings at first. Iranian communities preferred their versions of the Indo-European gods who had also been brought to ancient India, including a version of the Vedic deity Indra. The prophet was disowned by his family and unwelcome wherever he went. Only after he converted the Iranian king Vishtapa was his faith more broadly accepted, and for over 1000 years, until the arrival of Islam in the seventh century, Zoroastrianism was the major religion of various powerful Iranian empires. According to tradition, Zoroaster was killed at the age of seventy-seven by invaders while worshipping at an altar. Modern understandings of him differ among the major Zoroastrian communities. Those remaining in India consider him to be a prophet of god while many of the Parsis of India, the largest remaining Zoroastrian community, think of him as a sort of avatar of God. The Parsis continue to commemorate his birth and death with major festivals.

SEE ALSO: Avesta; Parsis; Zoroastrianism

## Zoroastrianism

One of the major religions of the ancient world, and likely an important influence on Judaism, Christianity, and Islam. Arguably (Judaism is its major competitor in this regard), Zoroastrianism is the oldest prophetic faith, the oldest monotheistic religion, and the first to preach that human beings would face a final judgment after their deaths, when their bodies would be resurrected either in heaven or in hell. Zoroastrianism was the state religion of several successive Iranian (Persian) empires—the Achaemenid (549–331 B.C., the Parthian (ca. 170 B.C.–A.D. 224, and the Sassanid (224–652)—which in various periods dominated an area stretching from Greece in the west to India in the east from the sixth century B.C. to the seventh century A.D. Their possessions often included Mesopotamia, Jerusalem, and other important cultural centers of the ancient Near East.

Zoroastrianism was founded by the prophet Zoroaster (ca. 628–551 B.C.), who appeared in a period of Iranian history when branches of the Indo-European tribes, who migrated to areas as far ranging as Western Europe and India, were establishing permanent communities. At the age of thirty, according to Zoroastrian tradition, the prophet received his first vision of a god whom he called Ahura Mazda, the "Wise Lord." This and later visions were later written down in the form of seventeen gathas, or hymns. These gathas were later to form the core of the Avesta, the main holy scripture of Zoroastrianism. According to the gathas, the divine world contains two opposing forces. Good forces are represented by Ahura Mazda, the creator of life and the source of all light. Evil forces are represented by a "twin spirit" of Ahura Mazda known as Ahriman. Ahriman is the source of non-life, of chaos, and of instability. Zoroastrian thought later built upon this conflict by asserting that Ahura Mazda acted in daily life through seven good spirits known as Amesha Spentas. A key to early Zoroastrianism was the belief that the influence of these spirits was plain in everyday life. Ahura Mazda and the Amesha Spentas were associated with stability, hard work, care for nature and the environment, and with living according to a high moral code. Ahriman's influence, meanwhile, could be seen in the violent, immoral actions of the nomadic tribes that continually threatened early Iran.

Zoroastrianism preaches that good will ultimately triumphs over evil, and some of its later schools envisioned the coming of a savior known as Soysant. But in the meantime, human beings are endowed with free will and can choose whether to follow Ahura Mazda or Ahriman. The choice people make will determine whether, after their deaths, they spend eternity in the Zoroastrian version of heaven or hell. This emphasis on individual free will is probably related to Zoroaster's belief that all people had to claim responsibility for their own religious lives. Those who make the "right" choices will not only live righteously, they will also try to convince others to do the same and to continually fight the forces of evil and instability. Since Zoroastrianism makes no distinction between the matter and the spirit, considering both good by virtue of their having been created by the Wise Lord, human beings must care for the physical world as well.

Zoroastrian worship is known as yasna. Originally, worshippers conducted their rites in the open air, on mountaintops or near rivers, in the effort to remain close to Ahura Mazda's creation. Household worship was also common. But as Zoroastrianism became more institutionalized, temple worship became the norm. There, priests maintain sacred fires, while many ceremonies involve prayers and symbolic offerings to the Amesha Spentas. Initiation into Zoroastrian communities, known as naujote among the Parsis of India, is a very important ritual, and it takes place when initiates are nine or eleven years old. Zoroastrianism is a way of life, however, rather than a collection of rituals and beliefs, and devotees are expected to adhere to community norms in matters like marriage and also to show high morality and personal integrity.

Thanks to the power and importance of the Iranian empires, Zoroastrianism was a major religion across a wide region. Its prophet was respected and even revered among followers of other faiths, while its ideas were likely influential in the mystery cults of the ancient Near East as well as in the evolution of Judaism and Christianity although direct, specific influences are difficult to trace.

Zoroastrianism remained the state religion of Iran until the Sassanid king, Yazdegird, died in 652 and the region was converted to Islam. Thereafter, Zoroastrians in Iran were at times harshly persecuted but at other times were granted official protected status as Peoples of the Book, or dhimmi. In the tenth century, during a period of oppression, communities of believers migrated to India in search of religious freedom there. Indian Zoroastrians are known as Parsis, after a local term for Persians. In Iran, meanwhile, Zoroastrianism entered a brief period of revival in the twentieth century until, after the Islamic revolution of 1979, its small communities were once again marginalized. In the modern world, these small communities make up the second largest Zoroastrian group, with the Parsis the first. Together they include over 100,000 believers. Small communities of Zoroastrians or Parsis have also arisen in Great Britain, the United States, and Canada.

SEE ALSO: Ahura Mazda; Parsis; Zoroaster

# Chronology

## B.C.

**ca. 2800–1800** The Indus Valley Civilization in northwest India, where people worship a divine mother god as well as, perhaps, an early version of the Hindu deity Shiva.

**ca. 2000** The Hebrew prophet Abraham establishes the covenant between his people and their God. His descendants by his wife Sarah practice the Jewish faith. According to Islamic tradition Abraham's descendants by Sarah's servant, Hagar, become leading Arab clans.

**ca. 1766–1050** The Shang dynasty in China, where believers worship a deity known as Shangdi, and practices such as ancestor worship become widespread.

**ca. 1500–800** Indo-Europeans migrate into India, where they settle and integrate with the local population. Among their religious products are the Vedas, Hinduism's oldest texts.

**ca. 1250** According to Judaism and Christianity, the event known as the Exodus, in which the prophet Moses leads the Hebrews out of Egyptian captivity and receives the Ten Commandments from God.

**1000–900** The creation of ancient Israel and the construction of the first Jewish Temple in Jerusalem.

**660 (attributed)** The accession of the first Japanese emperor, Jimmu Tenno, who claims descent from the Shinto goddess Amaterasu.

**ca. 628–551** Life of Zoroaster, founder of Zoroastrianism.

**ca. 600** Life of Lao-tzu, founder of Daoism.

**586** Jerusalem is sacked and the Temple destroyed by Babylon. Many Jews go into exile or slavery. Jewish elders begin to assemble the Hebrew Bible.

**ca. 566–486** Life of Siddhartha Gautama, founder of Buddhism.

**551–479** Life of Confucius, founder of Confucianism.

**549–477** Life of Mahavira, founder of Jainism.

**516** The second Jewish Temple in Jerusalem is dedicated.

**ca. 400 B.C.–A.D. 400** Composition of Hinduism's most popular texts, including the Mahabharata, Ramayana, Bhagavad Gita, and Laws of Manu.

**ca. 370–286** Life of Chuang-tzu, a founding Daoist.

**268–239** The reign of Indian king Ashoka, who helps to expand Buddhism both within his realm and to the island of Sri Lanka.

**206 B.C.–A.D. 220** China's Han dynasty, when Confucianism becomes the empire's ruling ideology and Daoism its major popular religion.

**ca. 4** The birth of Jesus of Nazareth, founder of Christianity.

## A.D.

**ca. 30** Crucifixion of Jesus.

**ca. 40–64** The conversion and preaching of Christian apostle Paul.

**70–100** The New Testament Gospels are written, joining Paul's letters as important early Christian scripture.

**70** The second Jewish Temple is destroyed

by Roman armies. The Jewish Diaspora begins along with the tradition of Rabbinic Judaism.

**ca. 100–200** Buddhism spreads to China.

**ca. 300–400** The Christian New Testament canon is assembled.

**397** The Roman emperor Theodosius declares Christianity to be the official religion of the empire.

**476** Rome is sacked by Germanic tribes. Constantinople remains the headquarters of both the Roman (Byzantine) Empire and the Christian religion.

**ca. 500–600** Buddhism spreads to Japan.

**ca. 500–900** The bhakti, or devotional, movement of Hinduism takes shape, as does the mainstream Vedanta movement.

**ca. 500–1000** Europe's Germanic tribes convert to Christianity, declaring their loyalty to the bishop of Rome, or pope.

**570–632** Life of Muhammad, founder of Islam.

**619–907** China's Tang dynasty, when Buddhism is the most popular religion among elites aside from brief periods of conflict. Buddhism integrates with Confucianism and Daoism in China.

**622** The early Islamic hijra to Medina, where Muhammad founds the first Islamic community.

**ca. 640–665** Islam spreads across the Middle East and North Africa.

**640s** The third Islamic caliph, Uthman, presides over the compilation of a definitive version of the Qur'an.

**656** Muhammad's son-in-law Ali becomes the fourth caliph, or successor to the Prophet. The Shia tradition of Islam considers Ali the first legitimate caliph.

**ca. 700–800** Tantric Buddhism's "first diffusion" to Tibet.

**710–794** Japan's Nara period, when Shinto and Buddhism begin a long period of coexistence.

**712–720** Japanese chroniclers compile the Shinto-related Kojiki and Nihon-Shoki.

**750–1258** The Islamic Abbasid caliphate, a golden age of religion, science, and culture based in the city of Baghdad.

**960–1279** China's Song and Yuan dynasties, when Confucian scholar-officials are educated according to the Confucian Four Books, Five Classics, and other products of Chinese tradition.

**1054** The schism between Eastern Orthodox and Roman Catholic Christianity becomes formal.

**1095** Pope Urban II issues the call to Crusade. European Christian armies set out to conquer Jerusalem and parts of the Middle East.

**1099** The crusaders take Jerusalem from its Islamic rulers, holding it for nearly one hundred years.

**ca. 1100–1200** Buddhism largely disappears from India following Islamic conquests and raids.

**1106** Several centuries of Islamic rule over much of India begin.

**1130–1200** Life of Chu Hsi, leading figure in China's neo-Confucian movement.

**1453** The Islamic Ottoman Empire conquers the city of Constantinople, formerly the capital of the Byzantine Empire and headquarters of Eastern Orthodox Christianity. Ottomans soon seize Mecca, Medina, and Jerusalem, Islam's three holiest cities, as well.

**1469–1539** Life of Guru Nanak, founder of Sikhism.

**1500s–1600s** Christian missionaries take

their faith to Africa, India, East Asia, and the Americas.

**1517** Martin Luther begins the Protestant Reformation, Christianity's second great schism.

**1545–1563** The Roman Catholic Church's Council of Trent inaugurates the Counter-Reformation.

**1617–1682** The life of the fifth Dalai Lama, the head of both Tibetan Buddhism and the Buddhist state. He builds the Potala Palace in his capital, Lhasa.

**1700s–1800s** Western European Jews are emancipated and begin the Conservative and Reform Jewish movements. Western European nations colonize India, Africa, and much of the Middle East, inspiring religious reform movements in those areas.

**1726** The first Great Awakening in America begins, and along with it the beginning of the Protestant evangelical movement.

**1838** The beginning of Tenrikyo, one of Japan's many new religions.

**1830** The founding of Mormonism by Joseph Smith in New England.

**1868–1945** The era of State Shinto in Japan.

**1869–1948** Life of Mohandas K. Gandhi, the Mahatma.

**1878** The founding of the Theosophical movement, a new religious movement that helps introduce Buddhism and Hinduism to the West.

**1910** The Christian ecumenical movement begins with the Edinburgh Missionary Conference.

**1919** The Ottoman Empire is disbanded and many of its territories distributed, as colonial mandates, to Britain and France.

Most of these areas become the independent states of the modern Middle East in the 1920s and 1930s.

**1923** Turkey, the former heartland of the Ottoman Empire, becomes a secular state and abolishes the institution of the Islamic caliphate.

**1941–1945** World War II and the Holocaust, resulting in the wholesale genocide of some 6 million European Jews by Germany's Nazi regime.

**1945** State Shinto ends in Japan, as the emperor renounces any claim to divinity.

**1947** India gains its independence from Britain in the form of two new states: India and Pakistan. The resulting partition riots inspire much communal bloodshed among Hindus, Muslims, and Sikhs.

**1948** The modern State of Israel is established.

**1949** A Communist regime takes power in China, suppressing Confucianism, Daoism, and other religious movements. They continue to flourish in Taiwan as well as in other areas with Chinese populations.

**1950s** Zen Buddhism becomes popular in America and Western Europe.

**1959** Following a 1950 invasion, Communist China begins the suppression of Tibetan Buddhism. The fourteenth and current Dalai Lama goes into exile, eventually in Dharamsala in India.

**1963–1965** The Roman Catholic Church's Second Vatican Council institutes major reforms.

**1965–2006** Many Muslim immigrants move to Western Europe and the United States.

**1967** Israel takes possession of Jerusalem following the Six-Day War against a coalition of Arab states.

**1967** The Beatles and other Western celebrities visit the ashrams of Hindu gurus, helping to popularize Hindu practices in the West.

**1979** The Islamic Revolution in Iran. The Soviet Union invades Islamic Afghanistan. Anti-Soviet rebels, many from outside Afghanistan, form the core of militant Islamic fundamentalist groups later active in terrorist attacks around the world.

**1982** Sikh attempts to carve an independent Sikh state out of northwestern India result in much communal violence.

**1989** The Buddhist Dalai Lama receives the Nobel Peace Prize.

**1990s** The former Soviet Central Asian Republics, most of them Islamic, become independent states.

**1995** The Oslo Accords provide for recognition of an official political entity among Muslim Palestinians in Israel.

**1995** The Aum Shinrikyo, one of Japan's new religions, stages a poison gas attack in Tokyo's subway system.

**2005** The death of John Paul II, Roman Catholic pope since 1979.

# For Further Research

## Books

C.L. Albanese, *America: Religion and Religions*. Belmont, CA: Wadsworth, 1992.

Ahmed Ali, *Al-Qur'an*. Princeton, NJ: Princeton University Press, 1988.

Muhammad Ali, *A Manual of Hadith*. London: Curzon, 1977.

*The Analects of Confucius*. Trans. Arthur Waley. New York: Vintage, 1989.

Karen Armstrong, *Muhammad: A Biography of the Prophet*. San Francisco: Harper, 1992

Michael Ashkenazi, *Matsuri: Festivals of a Japanese Town*. Honolulu: University of Hawaii Press, 1993.

Mahmoud Ayoub, *The Qur'an and Its Interpreters*. Albany: State University of New York Press, 1984.

P. and L. Badham, eds., *Death and Immortality in the Religions of the World*. New York: Paragon House, 1987.

Anne Bancroft, ed., *The Dhammapada*. Rockport, MA: Element, 1997.

E. Barker, *New Religious Movements: A Practical Introduction*. London: HMSO, 1989.

William Theodore de Bary, ed., *The Buddhist Tradition in India, China, and Japan*. New York: Vintage, 1972.

A.L. Basham, ed., *A Cultural History of India*. London: Oxford University Press, 1975.

Judith R. Baskin, ed., *Jewish Women in Historical Perspective*. Detroit: Wayne State University Press, 1991.

Marcus Borg, *Jesus: A New Vision*. San Francisco: Harper and Row, 1988.

John Breen and Mark Teeuwen, eds., *Shinto in History: Ways of the Kami*. Honolulu: University of Hawaii Press, 2000.

Joseph Epes Brown, *The Spiritual Legacy of the American Indian*. New York: Crossroad, 1989.

Mick Brown, *The Spiritual Tourist*. New York: Bloomsbury, 1998.

Peter Brown, *The Rise of Western Christendom: Triumph and Diversity 200–1000 A.D.* Oxford, UK: Blackwell, 1997.

Schuyler Brown, *The Origins of Christianity: A Historical Introduction to the New Testament*. New York: Oxford University Press, 1993.

*Buddhist Teachings*. Selected and trans. Edward Conze. London: Penguin, 1959.

E.A. Burtt, ed., *Teachings of the Compassionate Buddha*. New York: Mentor, 1959.

Michael Carrithers, *The Buddha: A Very Short Introduction*. Oxford, UK: Oxford University Press, 1996.

*Chuang-tzu*. Trans. Burton Watson. New York: Columbia University Press, 1964.

Edward Conze, trans., *Buddhist Scriptures*. London: Penguin, 1982.

Michael D. Coogan, ed., *The Illustrated Guide to World Religions*. Oxford, UK: Oxford University Press, 2003.

Frederick Copleston, *A History of Chris-*

*tian Philosophy in the Middle Ages*. London: Sheed and Ward, 1978.

Barbara Crossette, *So Close to Heaven: The Vanishing Buddhist Kingdoms of the Himalayas*. New York: Knopf, 1995.

The Dalai Lama, *The Joy of Living and Dying in Peace*. San Francisco: HarperSanFrancisco, 1997.

Frederick M. Denny, *An Introduction to Islam*. New York: Macmillan, 1985.

Wendy Doniger with Brian K. Smith, trans., *Laws of Manu*. New York: Penguin, 1991.

H. Byron Earheart, *Japanese Religion: University and Diversity*. Belmont, CA: Wadsworth, 1982.

Diana L. Eck, *A New Religious America: How a "Christian Country" Has Become the World's Most Religiously Diverse Nation*. San Francisco: HarperSanFrancisco, 2001.

Mircea Eliade, *The Sacred and the Profane: The Nature of Religion*. Trans. William Trask. New York: Harcourt Brace, 1959.

W.Y. Evans-Wentz, trans., *The Tibetan Book of the Dead*. 3rd ed. New York: Oxford University Press, 1960.

John Y. Fenton et al., *Religions of Asia*. New York: St. Martin's, 1983.

Elizabeth Fernea, *In Search of Islamic Feminism: One Woman's Global Journey*. New York: Doubleday, 1998.

Gavin Flood, *An Introduction to Hinduism*. Cambridge, UK: Cambridge University Press, 1996.

David Noel Freedman, *The Anchor Bible Dictionary*. New York: Doubleday, 1992.

Richard Eliot Freedman, *Who Wrote the Bible?* New York: Summit, 1987.

Christopher Fuller, *The Camphor Flame: Popular Hinduism and Society in India*. Princeton, NJ: Princeton University Press, 1992.

Mohandas K. Gandhi, *The Gandhi Reader*. Ed. Homer A. Jack. Bloomington: Indiana University Press, 1956.

Gerrie ter Haar and James Bussutil, *Freedom to Do God's Will: Religious Fundamentalism and Social Change*. London: Routledge, 2002.

Helen Hardacre, *Shinto and the State, 1868–1988*. Princeton, NJ: Princeton University Press, 1989.

John Stratton Hawley, *Songs of the Saints of India*. New York: Oxford University Press, 1988.

Jeff Hay, ed., *Buddhism*. Farmington Hills, MI: Greenhaven Press/Thomson Gale, 2005.

———, *Hinduism*. Farmington Hills, MI: Greenhaven Press/Thomson Gale, 2005.

———, *Shinto*. Farmington Hills, MI: Greenhaven Press/Thomson Gale, 2006.

J.R. Hinnells, ed., *Who's Who of World Religions*. London: Macmillan, 1991.

Barry W. Holtz, ed., *Back to the Sources: Reading the Classic Jewish Texts*. New York: Summit, 1984.

*Holy Bible*. Revised Standard Version. New York: American Bible Society, 1942, 1956.

*The Holy Quran*. Trans. Alamah Noorudin. Hockessin, DE: Noor Foundation, 1997.

Hubert Jedin, *The Church in the Modern World*. New York: Crossroad, 1993.

Paul Johnson, *A History of Christianity*. New York: Atheneum, 1976.

Sarah Iles Johnson, ed., *Religions of the Ancient World: A Guide*. Cambridge, MA: Harvard University Press, 2004.

F. Katz, *The Ancient American Civilizations*. New York: Praeger, 1972.

Noel King, *African Cosmos: An Introduction to Religion in Africa*. Belmont, CA: Wadsworth, 1986.

Kim Knott, *Hinduism: A Very Short Introduction*. New York: Oxford University Press, 1998.

James L. Kugel, *The Bible as It Was*. Cambridge, MA: Harvard University Press, 1997.

Lao Tzu, *Tao Te Ching*. Trans. Victor H. Mair. New York: Bantam, 1990.

C.S. Lewis, *Mere Christianity*. New York: Touchstone, 1980.

C. Scott Littleton, *Shinto*. Oxford,UK: Oxford University Press, 2002.

Theodore M. Ludwig, *The Sacred Paths: Understanding the Religions of the World*. Upper Saddle River, NJ: Prentice- Hall, 1996.

Gurinder Singh Mann, Paul David Numrich, and Raymond B. Williams, *Buddhists, Hindus, and Sikhs in America*. New York: Oxford University Press, 2001.

P.J. Marshall, *The British Discovery of Hinduism in the Eighteenth Century*. Cambridge, UK: Cambridge University Press, 1970.

Alister E. McGrath, *Christian Theology: An Introduction*. Oxford, UK: Blackwell, 1996.

John McManners, ed., *The Oxford Illustrated History of Christianity*. Oxford, UK: Oxford University Press, 1992.

Ramesh Menon, *The Ramayana*. New York: North Point, 2003.

Barbara Stoler Miller, trans., *The Bhagavad-Gita: Krishna's Counsel in Time of War*. New York: Columbia University Press, 1986.

———, *The Mahabharata: A Shortened Prose Version of the Indian Epic*. New York: Viking, 1978.

Lui I-Ming, *The Daoist I Ching*. Trans. Thomas Cleary. Boston: Shambhala Classics, 1986.

David S. Noss and John B. Noss, *A History of the World's Religions*. New York: Macmillan, 1990.

Wendy Doniger O'Flaherty, ed., *Textual Sources for the Study of Hinduism*. Manchester, UK: Manchester University Press, 1988.

Daniel L. Overmyer, *Religions of China: The World as a Living System*. San Francisco: HarperSanFrancisco, 1986.

Diana Paul, *Women in Buddhism*. Berkeley, CA: Asian Humanities, 1980.

F.E Peters, ed., *A Reader on Classical Islam*. Princeton, NJ: Princeton University Press, 1994.

Charles S. Prebish, *American Buddhism*. Belmont, CA: Wadsworth, 1979.

Jill Raitt, ed., *Christian Spirituality*. New York: Crossroad, 1989.

T.R. Reid, *Confucius Lives Next Door*. New York: Vintage, 2000.

Francis Robinson, ed., *The Cambridge Illustrated History of the Islamic World*. Cambridge, UK: Cambridge University Press, 1996.

Richard H. Robinson and Willard L. Johnson, *The Buddhist Religion: A His-*

*torical Introduction*. Belmont, CA: Wadsworth, 1982.

Robert M. Seltzer, *Jewish People, Jewish Thought: The Jewish Experience in History*. New York: Macmillan, 1980.

Arvind Sharma, *Hinduism for Our Times*. New York: Oxford University Press, 1996.

Arvind Sharma, ed., *Women in World Religions*. Albany: State University of New York Press, 1987.

Huston Smith, *The World's Religions: Our Great Wisdom Traditions*. San Francisco: HarperCollins, 1991.

N. Solomon, *Judaism and World Religion*. London: Macmillan, 1991.

H.L. Strack and G. Stemberger, *Introduction to the Talmud and Midrash*. Edinburgh: T&T Clark, 1991.

T. Swain and G. Trompf, *The Religions of Oceania*. London: Routledge, 1995.

*Tanakh: A New Translation of the Hebrew Scriptures According to the Traditional Hebrew Text*. Philadelphia: Jewish Publication Society, 1985.

*Tao Te Ching*. Trans. Victor H. Mair. New York: Bantam, 1990.

Laurence G. Thompson, *Chinese Religion: An Introduction*. Belmont, CA: Wadsworth, 1980.

Peter Van der Veer, *Religious Nationalism: Hindus and Muslims in India*. Berkeley and Los Angeles: University of California Press, 1994.

Burton Watson, trans., *The Lotus Sutra*. New York: Columbia University Press, 1993.

Arthur Whaley, trans., *The Analects of Confucius*. 1938. Reprinted, New York: Vintage, 1989.

Linda Woodhead, *Christianity: A Very Short Introduction*. New York: Oxford University Press, 2005.

Michiko Yusa, *Japanese Religious Traditions*. Upper Saddle River, NJ: Prentice-Hall, 2002.

## Web Sites

Adherents.com (www.adherents.com). Offers detailed statistics on various aspects of the world's religions such as membership totals. Also contains lists, charts, and links to other resources.

BBC World Service: Religions (www.bbc.co.uk/religion/religions). The British Broadcasting Company's useful surveys of the histories and beliefs of the world's major religions.

Buddhanet (www.Buddhanet.net). A comprehensive site with many articles, links, multimedia, e-books, and other resources.

Christian Post (www.christianpost.com). An online Christian newspaper with many articles, links, and other resources. It focuses on global Christian issues and ecumenism.

Confucius (wwww.friesian.com/confuci.htm). Emphasizes the philosophical aspects of Confucianism but also solid and thorough summaries of the Confucian viewpoint on various issues. Lots of images and links.

Confucius Publishing Co., Ltd. (www.confucius.org). Offers Confucian texts and stories as well as articles and speeches relating to Confucianism over the centuries.

Fundamental Buddhism Explained (www.fundamentalbuddhism.com). Teachings, articles, links emphasizing a traditionalist view of Buddhism.

Hawaii Korahiru Jinshu. (www.e-shrine.org). The Web site of a Shinto shrine in Hawaii. Provides many links to other Shinto resources.

The Hindu Universe. (www.hindunet.org). Articles on current problems and concerns in Hinduism as well as the history of the faith, customs, and rituals. Many links to other resources.

Hindu Website (www.hinduwebsite.com). A thorough resource designed to reinforce awareness of Hindu traditions and customs among believers today. Many links to articles on gods, scripture, and Hinduism's relations with other faiths.

Internet Christian Library (www.iclnet.org). Numerous articles, versions of Christian texts, discussion forums, and links to other resources on Christianity.

Internet Sacred Text Archive (www.sacred-texts.com/world.htm). A comprehensive collection of texts, held in public domain, from major religious traditions. Also offers scans of original manuscript images.

Islam.com (www.islam.com). A thorough resource on Islam, offering many articles, links (including those to newspapers), discussion forums, and calendars.

Islam Online (www.islamonline.net). Articles and links emphasizing Islam in the modern era, including such concerns as Islam in relation to other major faiths.

Judaism 101 (www.jewfaq.org). A broad introduction to Judaism, organized from the Orthodox viewpoint but with a thorough treatment of other perspectives as well. Easy-to-use links and features.

Religious Tolerance (www.religioustolerance.org). Maintained by the Ontario (Canada) Consultants on Religious Topics. An open-ended collection of essays and other resources on both the major world religions and the attempts to build bridges between them.

The Shinto Online Network Association (www.jinja.org.jp). Provides basic definitions, a historical overview, descriptions of Shinto sects, and historical photographs.

Sikhseek (www.sikhseek.com). Devoted to providing information and other resources on both the Sikh religion and community. Offers links, news, photographs.

Taoism.net (www.taoism.net). A collection of summaries of Daoism, Daoist stories, and other articles. It focuses on both past and present Daoist practices.

Torah.org (www.torah.org). A Jewish educational site focusing on outreach to both Jews and non-Jews. Many articles from reputable sources, and an interesting "features" section. Also useful for Torah scholarship in particular.

# Index

Aaron, 115
al-Abbas, 66
Abbasid dynasty, 65, 66, 153
Abd al-Qadir al-Jilani, 304
'Abd al-Wahhab, Muhammad ibn, 331
Abd ol-Baha, 49
'Abduh, Muhammad, 156
Abhidamma Pitaka, 322
abinza, 18
aboriginal religions, 45–47
Abraham, 15–16, 34, 109, 168, 280
absolution, 115
  see also atonement; confession
Abu Bakr
  as caliph, 24, 65, 155, 212, 288
  as companion of the Prophet, 79
  overview of, 16
  tomb of, 198
Abu Hanifa, 287
Acts of the Apostles, 16, 39, 131
*Acts of the Buddha* (Asvaghosa), 295
Adam, 128, 224–25, 299
Adi-Buddha, 319
Adi Granth, 16–17, 132, 133, 297, 299
Aditi, 284
Adonai, 161, 170, 333
Advaita Vedanta, 286
Advent, 64
*Aeneid* (Virgil), 30
Aesir, 245–46
al-Afghani, Jamal al-Din, 156
Africa, 17–18, 179, 265–66
African Americans, 215–16
Afro-Brazilian religions, 19–20
Afro-Caribbean religions, 20–22, 265–66
afterlife
  in Australian aboriginal religions, 47
  in Buddhism, 61, 138, 202
  in Celtic religions, 244–45
  in China, 138
  in Christianity, 112, 137–38, 138–39
  in Confucianism, 83
  in Germanic religions, 245–46
  in Greek and Roman mythology, 29, 30
  heaven, 137–38
  hell, 138–39
  in Hinduism, 138

in Islam, 112, 137–38, 138–39, 271
in Judaism, 112, 137, 138–39
in Near East religions, ancient, 32–33
in Roman Catholicism, 137
in Zoroastrianism, 139, 340–41
*Against Apion*, 167
Aga Khan, 159, 289
agape, 22
Age of Reason, 241, 268
Aggadah, 310
Agni, 329
agnosticism, 22–23, 43
ahimsa, 23, 126, 188
Ahmad, Muhammad, 191
Ah Puch, 248
Ahriman, 24, 339, 340
Ahura Mazda, 23–24, 339, 340
*The Aims of the Philosophers* (al-Ghazali), 129
A'isha, 212
Aitareya, 57
Akhenaten, 33
Alexander the Great, 30, 48
Ali
  as caliph, 65, 67, 212, 288
  children of, 117–18
  as companion of the Prophet, 79
  as imam, 150, 155, 289
  overview of, 24–25
Alighieri, Dante, 139
'aliyah, 242
Allah, 25, 153
Allah, Ubayd, 191
Amar Das, 297
Amarna, 33
Amaterasu
  birth of, 159
  importance of, 111, 175, 291, 292, 293
  overview of, 25
  in Ryobu Shinto, 276
  shrines for, 152, 293
*amatsu-kami*, 175
American Theosophical Society, 315
American Unitarian Association, 324
Amesha Spentas, 24, 340, 341
Amhitabha, 25–26, 55, 61, 255–57, 320
Amida, 256–57
  see also Amhitabha

Amitayus. See Amhitabha
Amma, 19
Amon. See Re
Amram, 208
amrita, 178
Amritanandamayi, Mata, 43
*Analects*, 26–27, 81, 82, 83, 85, 122
Ananta, 330
ancestors, 17, 18–19, 27, 119
Ancient Order of the Druids, 245
Andes, pre-Columbian, 250–52
Andrew (apostle), 39
Angad, 133, 297, 298
angels
  in Christianity, 35–36, 166, 206, 280
  in Islam, 36, 152, 166, 211, 213, 259
  in Judaism, 35, 166
  overview of, 35–36
Anglican Church
  Apostles' Creed in, 40
  Congregationalism and, 86
  foundation of, 268
  Mass in, 196
  monasticism in, 205
  overview of, 36–37
  saints in, 278
animism, 36
Ansar, 79
Antiochus IV (Antiochus Epiphanes), 136, 312
anti-Semitism, 37–38, 145–46, 169–70
Antony, 204
Anu, 31
Apache tribe, 219
Aphrodite, 28, 34
apocalypse, 36, 38, 201–2, 271–72
Apocrypha
  in Christianity, 39, 129, 131, 138, 227, 283
  in Judaism, 38, 54, 138
  overview of, 38–39
Apollo, 28, 30
apostles, 39, 72, 78
  see also individual apostles
Apostles' Creed, 40
Apu Illapu, 252
al-Aqsa Mosque, 40, 163, 209, 313, 331
al-Arabi, Ibn, 305
Aramaic, 40–41
aramitama, 292

# About the Author

Jeff Hay teaches history at San Diego State University. The history of world religions has always been a secondary interest for him, and his publications include edited volumes on Hinduism, Buddhism, and Shinto in Greenhaven's Religions and Religious Experiences series. He has also published *A History of The Third Reich*, recognized by the American Library Association as an outstanding reference work, as well as numerous other books and anthologies. Dr. Hay received his Ph.D. from the University of California, San Diego in 1994.

# About the Consulting Editor

Linda Holler is professor and former chair of the Department of Religious Studies at San Diego State University, in which she taught World Religions and other courses for 25 years. Presently, she is Associate Dean of the College of Arts and Letters. Her major publication is *Erotic Morality: The Role of Touch in Moral Agency*, published by Rutgers University Press.